Sweet Land of Liberty?

STUDIES IN MODERN HISTORY

General editors: John Morrill and David Cannadine

This series, intended primarily for students, will tackle significant historical issues in concise volumes which are both stimulating and scholarly. The authors combine a broad approach, explaining the current state of our knowledge in the area, with their own research and judgements: and the topics chosen range widely in subject, period and place.

Titles already published

[Titles not currently available, 1998]

Sweet Land of Liberty?

The African-American Struggle for Civil Rights in the Twentieth Century

ROBERT COOK

Longman
London and New York

Addison Wesley Longman Limited
Edinburgh Gate,
Harlow, Essex CM20 2JE,
United Kingdom
and Associated Companies throughout the world

Published in the United States of America
by Addison Wesley Longman Inc., New York

© Addison Wesley Longman Limited 1998

First published 1998

ISBN 0 582 215323 PPR
ISBN 0 582 215315 CSD

British Library Cataloguing in Publication Data
A catalogue record for this book is available from the British Library

Library of Congress Cataloging-in-Publication Data
Cook, Robert, 1958–
Sweet land of liberty? : the Black struggle for civil rights in
twentieth-century America / Robert Cook.
p. cm. — (Studies in modern history)
Includes bibliographical references and index.
ISBN 0–582–21531–5. — ISBN 0–582–21532–3 (pbk.)
1. Afro-Americans—Civil rights—History—20th century. 2. Civil
rights movements—United States—History—20th century. I. Title.
II. Series: Studies in modern history (Longman (Firm))
E185.61.C773 1997
323.1′196073—dc21
97–8579
CIP

Set by 35 in 10/12pt Baskerville
Produced by Longman Singapore Publishers (Pte) Ltd.
Printed in Singapore

To the memory of
George Atkinson
(1905–1988)

and

Lenore Atkinson
(1904–1996)

My Country 'tis of thee,
Sweet land of liberty,
Of thee I sing;
Land where my fathers died;
Land of the pilgrim's pride;
From every mountain side
Let Freedom ring!

Samuel Francis Smith (1808–1895), 'America'

With this faith we will be able to work together, to pray together, to struggle together, to go to jail together, to stand up for freedom together, knowing that we will be free one day. This will be the day when all of God's children will be able to sing with new meaning – 'my country 'tis of thee; sweet land of liberty; of thee I sing; land where my fathers died, land of the pilgrim's pride; from every mountain side, let freedom ring' – and if America is to be a great nation, this must become true.

Martin Luther King Jr., 'I Have A Dream' speech,
28 August 1963

Contents

Note on Terminology

The interchangeable use of the terms *black* and *African American* in this book reflects common usage in the United States today. Readers, however, should be alerted to the fact that earlier in the century blacks and whites alike preferred the terms *Negro* (or *negro*) and *coloured*. When such terms appear in the text quotation marks are employed in order to reflect their current redundancy.

Acknowledgements

I have incurred numerous debts in the course of researching and writing this book. Particular thanks go to Bruce Collins for giving the project his initial support and to those historians who read and commented critically on draft chapters: David Cannadine, Peter Ling, John Morrill, John White and my colleagues at the University of Sheffield, Richard Carwardine and Patrick Renshaw. Several American and British scholars of the civil rights movement provided me with much-needed advice, information and encouragement along the way: not only Peter Ling (whose fine work on the SCLC citizenship schools did much to alter my perception of the movement) but also Tony Badger, Maureen Cressey-Hackett, Adam Fairclough, Rick Halpern, Richard King, John Kirk, Keith Miller, Bruce Nelson, Mark Newman, Jenny Walker, Brian Ward and Clive Webb. I have also benefited from several years of seminar discussions with undergraduate and postgraduate students who participated in my civil rights special subject class at Sheffield. Financial aid, gratefully acknowledged, from my own institution and the British Academy enabled me to deliver conference papers in Newcastle, Chicago and Rome and to make essential research visits to the United States where Joe Glazer enlightened me with his first-hand accounts of labour organising in the 1940s and where I was heavily dependent on the generosity of my long-suffering friends Mary Beveridge, Julianne Borton, Barbara Holmlund, Mary Wright and John Zeller. I should also like to thank my editors at Addison Wesley Longman, Andrew MacLennan and Terka Bagley, as well as Wordwise Edit for assistance with the index and the helpful staff of the King Center in Atlanta, the Library of Congress's Manuscript Division, the Moorland–Spingarn Research Center at Howard University, and the State Historical Society of Wisconsin. My greatest debt, however, is to my mother, Margaret, and my father, John, and to Andrea, Martha, and Daniel for their unwavering love and support. This book could not have been written without them.

List of Abbreviations

AAA	Agricultural Adjustment Administration
ACMHR	Alabama Christian Movement for Human Rights
AFDC	Aid to Families with Dependent Children
AFL	American Federation of Labor
AFSC	American Friends Service Committee
AHR	*American Historical Review*
BBC	British Broadcasting Corporation
BSCP	Brotherhood of Sleeping Car Porters
CAP	Community Action Program
CBS	Columbia Broadcasting System
CCCO	Coordinating Council of Community Organizations
CDGM	Child Development Group of Mississippi
CEP	Citizenship Education Program
CFM	Chicago Freedom Movement
CIA	Central Intelligence Agency
CIC	Commission on Interracial Cooperation
CIG	Civic Interest Group
CIO	Congress of Industrial Organizations
CNAC	Cambridge Nonviolent Action Committee
COFO	Council of Federated Organizations
CORE	Congress of Racial Equality
CPUSA	Communist Party of the United States
CRDP	Civil Rights Documentation Project, Moorland–Spingarn Research Center, Howard University, Washington, DC
CREB	Chicago Real Estate Board
EEOC	Equal Employment Opportunity Commission
ESCRU	Episcopal Society for Cultural and Racial Unity
FBI	Federal Bureau of Investigation
FEPC	Committee on Fair Employment Practice
FOR	Fellowship of Reconciliation
FSA	Farm Security Administration
FTA	Food, Tobacco, Agricultural and Allied Workers Union

HEW	Department of Health, Education and Welfare
ICC	Interstate Commerce Commission
JAH	*Journal of American History*
JAS	*Journal of American Studies*
JSH	*Journal of Southern History*
KC	Martin Luther King, Jr Center for Nonviolent Change, Atlanta, Ga
LC	Library of Congress, Washington, DC
LCCMHR	Lowndes County Christian Movement for Human Rights
LCFO	Lowndes County Freedom Organization
MFDP	Mississippi Freedom Democratic Party
MIA	Montgomery Improvement Association
MOWM	March on Washington Movement
NAACP	National Association for the Advancement of Colored People
NBC	National Broadcasting Company
NCC	National Council of Churches
NCNP	National Convention for a New Politics
NRA	National Recovery Administration
NYA	National Youth Administration
NYT	*The New York Times*
OEO	Office of Economic Opportunity
OFCC	Office of Federal Contract Compliance
PUSH	People United to Save Humanity
PWA	Public Works Administration
SCEF	Southern Conference Education Fund
SCHW	Southern Conference for Human Welfare
SCLC	Southern Christian Leadership Conference
SCU	Sharecroppers Union
SDS	Students for a Democratic Society
SNCC	Student Nonviolent Coordinating Committee
TCA	Tuskegee Civic Association
TVA	Tennessee Valley Authority
UAW	United Auto Workers
UMWA	United Mine Workers of America
UNIA	Universal Negro Improvement Association
USCC	United States Civil War Centennial Commission
VEP	Voter Education Project
WiSH	State Historical Society of Wisconsin
WPA	Works Progress Administration
WPC	Women's Political Council

Introduction

The past intrudes upon the present

Ninety-four years after the demise of the southern Confederacy, the people of the United States paused to mourn the passing of the last surviving veteran of the American Civil War. Walter W. Williams died in Houston, Texas, on 19 December 1959. He claimed to have been born in the cotton kingdom of Mississippi in 1842 and to have enlisted in the Confederate army at the age of 22. President Dwight D. Eisenhower accepted these remarkable assertions and issued a short proclamation to mark the historic event. Having observed thankfully that 'the wounds of the deep and bitter dispute which once divided our nation have long since healed', he went on to contend that 'a united America in a divided world now holds up on a larger canvas the cherished traditions of liberty and justice for all'. With Williams's death, he said, 'the hosts of Blue and Gray who were the chief actors in that great and tragic drama a century ago have all passed from the world stage. No longer are they the Blue and the Gray. All rest together as Americans in honored glory.'[1]

While purporting to look back to a bygone era, the president's carefully crafted words were designed to have maximum relevance for contemporary affairs. By 1959 the United States was embroiled in an ongoing power struggle with the Soviet Union. Proclaiming the Civil War's contribution to the unity of modern America made sound political sense in the context of the battle for global hegemony between the two nations. There was more to Eisenhower's proclamation, however, than its obvious Cold War resonance. Rapid

---

1. *NYT*, 21 December 1959, p. 27; *Public Papers of the Presidents: Dwight D. Eisenhower 1959* (Washington, DC, 1960), pp. 864–5.

1

social and economic change in the United States after 1941 had
begun to erode the sectional harmony between North and South
which Eisenhower was so keen to posit. This was indicated most
clearly by the growth of racial tensions in the wake of the US
Supreme Court's rejection of segregated schools in 1954. Eisenhower himself had been forced to dispatch American marines to
Little Rock, Arkansas, in order to protect black schoolchildren from
a baying white mob. Solemnifying the patriotic endeavours of Walter
Williams and his peers may have made nonsense of the veterans'
motives for fighting (enlisting in the Confederate army was an odd
way to preserve American unity) but the president could hardly be
blamed for seeking to sanitise the past, given the burgeoning problems of the present.

Eisenhower's strenuous efforts to gloss over resurgent sectional
tensions were soon undermined by the approach of the Civil War
centennial.[2] The long series of commemorative events began in
early 1961 with a wreath-laying ceremony at the tomb of Union
commander Ulysses S. Grant in New York City, a week-long celebra-
tion of the founding of the Confederate government in Montgomery,
Alabama, and a spectacular pageant and rocket display in Charleston,
South Carolina, where the first shots of the war had been fired.
Such festivities were intended to contribute towards national unity
(in the same way that Eisenhower's proclamation had attempted to
do) as well as give a boost to the domestic tourist industry. In fact,
while the centennial did attract the crowds, it did little to promote
the sectional harmony that federal officials were determined to
accentuate.

In April 1961 the United States Civil War Centennial Commission (USCC), set up by Congress to oversee the heritage jamboree,
scheduled its annual meeting in Charleston to coincide with a grand
re-enactment of the Confederate bombardment of Fort Sumter.
Sadly for the Commission, anxious to avoid the slightest hint of
controversy, New Jersey's centennial commission chose to send a
black delegate, Madeline Williams, to attend the national convention. When it became clear that municipal segregation laws would
prevent Mrs Williams from being accommodated in the same hotel
as the other delegates, a political storm ensued.

2. For a full account of the centennial and its impact on the civil rights movement
see R. Cook, 'From Shiloh to Selma: The Impact of the Civil War Centennial on the
Black Freedom Struggle in the United States, 1961–65' in *The Making of Martin
Luther King and the Civil Rights Movement*, ed. B. Ward and A.J. Badger (Basingstoke,
1996), pp. 131–46.

Furious at the slight delivered to their delegate, the New Jerseyans announced immediately that they would not attend the Charleston convention. Segregation was a thing of the past in the North, they insisted, and Mrs Williams was an American citizen entitled to equal treatment with the other delegates. Other northern state commissions followed suit and declared that they would be withdrawing from the planned proceedings.

This concerted response was mirrored by America's oldest civil rights organisation, the National Association for the Advancement of Colored People (NAACP), a long-time opponent of racial segregation. On 17 March the organisation's New York office directed its branches across the country to promote a boycott of the Fort Sumter observances. A segregated gathering, it was contended, would constitute 'a betrayal of everything the Civil War was fought for'.[3]

Initially the national Centennial Commission sought to stand its ground, rejecting even a plea from the newly inaugurated president, John F. Kennedy, that all delegates to the Charleston meeting should receive equal treatment. At this point liberal northern state governors like Otto Kerner of Illinois and Richard Hughes of New Jersey denounced the Commission's behaviour as supine and President Kennedy stepped in once again, this time decisively, to insist that a federally funded body like the USCC must find a solution which would accord equal treatment to black delegates under the Constitution. The USCC's elderly chairman, Major General Ulysses S. Grant III, had no alternative but to back down. On 25 March he announced that the Commission would hold its meeting at the desegregated US naval station outside Charleston. The New Jerseyans declared themselves satisfied with this partial victory with even Madeline Williams declaring that it had wrought 'a victory for the democratic process in America'.[4]

The second battle of Fort Sumter was the first of many controversies over race during the Civil War centennial. The problem was that far from concluding an era of bitter sectional tension, as Eisenhower asserted in his proclamation, Walter Williams's death had occurred at a time when the meaning of America's Civil War was being contested by two of the key groups most directly affected by that conflict, namely southern whites and African Americans. The truth was, as the president well knew, that the nation's racial problems remained unsettled, General Lee's surrender at Appomattox

3. H.L. Moon to R. Wilkins, 26 January 1960, General Office File, Box A76, Group 3, NAACP Papers, LC.
4. *NYT*, 26 March 1961, I, p. 72.

Court House in April 1865 notwithstanding. As the southern writer
Robert Penn Warren made plain in his sensitive reflections on the
centennial, the Civil War held 'in suspension so many of the issues
and tragic ironies – somehow essential yet incommensurable – which
we yet live'.[5]

The civil rights movement in context

African Americans have been struggling for freedom in the United
States since the birth of the Republic in the eighteenth century.
Originally brought to North America against their will, they have
consistently put abstract promises of freedom, equality and democracy to the test and frequently found them dismally wanting in practice. Of all the nation's diverse ethnic groups, blacks (in common
with Native Americans) have always been best placed to discern the
gap between the fiction and the reality of the American Dream.

During the course of the twentieth century the black search
for equal citizenship developed into a full-blown social revolution
designed to achieve what Martin Luther King, Jr called 'certain basic
structural changes in the architecture of American society'.[6] This
social revolution was labelled 'the civil rights movement' by contemporaries – a term which is generally accepted by most scholars
of post-1945 American history. The movement provides the central
focus of this study, for it was during the 1950s and 1960s, particularly the latter, that African Americans launched a major challenge
to southern segregation (or 'Jim Crow' in contemporary parlance),
the success of which was dependent on organised protest at every
level of the federal polity. This does not mean that black people
did not contest their subordinate status in the years before the
Montgomery bus boycott of 1955–56 nor does it imply that their
struggle ended with the breakdown of the civil rights coalition in
the late 1960s. What it does mean is that the pace, shape and style
of black protest altered significantly in the middle decades of the
twentieth century. A shift in gear occurred which culminated in
the movement's greatest triumph: the destruction of the southern
caste system.

5. R.P. Warren, *The Legacy of the Civil War: Meditations on the Centennial* (New York,
1964), p. 108.
6. Quoted in D. Garrow, *Bearing the Cross: Martin Luther King, Jr., and the Southern
Christian Leadership Conference* (New York, 1986), p. 323.

For most Americans, black as well as white, the civil rights movement was pre-eminently the work of one man: Martin Luther King. King, assassinated in the spring of 1968, was rapidly apotheosised and has now taken his place in the pantheon of great American heroes. His once controversial career has been sanitised by the myth-makers, his home has become a museum-piece owned by the National Park Service, and his birthday is now a national holiday. By no means all Americans regard him as a saint but few would question his historic role as leader of the civil rights movement.

During the 1960s, however, King's place within the civil rights movement was a hotly contested one. As well as being ridiculed by black nationalist critics such as Malcolm X, he was not regarded as leader by many of those active within the movement. As early as the winter of 1964–65 a white scholar, August Meier, wrote an important essay in which he reflected on '[t]he phenomenon that is Martin Luther King':

> The Nobel Peace Prize winner is accepted by the outside world as *the* leader of the nonviolent direct action movement, but he is criticized by many activists within the movement. He is criticized for what appears, at times, as indecisiveness, and more often denounced for a tendency to accept compromise. Yet in the eyes of most Americans, both black and white, he remains the symbol of militant direct action. So potent is this symbol of direct actionist, that a new myth is arising about his historic role.[7]

Meier's concern with the paradoxical nature of King's career was largely a product of his own grass-roots involvement in the movement.[8] Prior to his appointment as a lecturer at Roosevelt University in Chicago, he had served as an adult adviser to the Civic Interest Group, a student organisation founded on the campus of Morgan State College in Baltimore. The group participated in a number of civil rights campaigns, notably an attempt to bring social and economic justice to the segregated town of Cambridge on Maryland's eastern shore. King, viewed by so many contemporaries as the movement's figure-head, played no role in Baltimore or Cambridge or, indeed, in most southern communities where demonstrations and boycotts were taking place.

Meier's experiences at the local level taught him that the movement was much more than Martin Luther King. His path-breaking

---

7. A. Meier, 'On the Role of Martin Luther King' in Meier, *A White Scholar and the Black Community 1945–1965: Essays and Reflections* (Amherst, 1992), p. 212. The essay first appeared in *New Politics* 4 (1965), 52–9.
8. Meier, *White Scholar*, pp. 24–33.

essay emphasised the role played by organisations other than King's Southern Christian Leadership Conference (SCLC) as well as the complementary nature of their roles and the potential dynamism of inter-organisational competition. Significantly, however, while Meier cast doubt on King's political status within the movement, he did not deny that the SCLC leader exerted a disproportionate amount of influence. He did so, argued Meier, partly through his symbolic appeal to whites but also because of his position at the 'vital center' of the civil rights coalition. King was thus the linchpin of the movement, a 'conservative militant' capable of appealing to vast numbers of people in the United States.[9]

Much of the scholarship on the civil rights movement has, consciously or unconsciously, reflected the duality underpinning Meier's thesis – the gap between the local and national which Meier attempted to bridge with his notion of King as a symbolic leader. In the immediate aftermath of King's death, scholars tended to view the movement as a top-down phenomenon with the Great Man at the centre of the narrative. A welter of books and articles appeared examining King's life and stressing the overriding significance of high-profile SCLC campaigns such as the Montgomery bus boycott, Birmingham and Selma.[10] By no means all of these works were hagiographical in intent, but very few of them countered the prevailing King-centric wisdom in the wider community.

By the mid-1980s, however, a number of memoirs and well-crafted local studies had begun to alter the way historians thought about the movement. Many of the retrospective accounts of the 1960s re-emphasised Meier's point that Martin Luther King played little or no role in the bulk of protest campaigns.[11] Some were openly critical of King, contending that his presence undermined the capacity of ordinary blacks to think and fight for themselves.

9. Meier, *A White Scholar and the Black Community 1945–1965*, pp. 214, 218.

10. See e.g. M.L. Sharma, 'Martin Luther King: Modern America's Greatest Theologian of Social Action', *Journal of Negro History* 53 (1968), 257–63; C.S. King, *My Life With Martin Luther King, Jr* (London, 1970); D. McKee, *Martin Luther King, Jr.* (New York, 1969); L.G. Davis, *I Have a Dream – The Life and Times of Martin Luther King, Jr.* (Westport, Conn., 1969); D.L. Lewis, *King: A Critical Biography* (New York, 1970); K. Slack, *Martin Luther King* (London, 1970); J. Bishop, *The Days of Martin Luther King, Jr.* (New York, 1971); A.F. Westin and B. Mahoney, *The Trial of Martin Luther King* (New York, 1974); B.E. Goodwin, *Dr. Martin Luther King, Jr: God's Messenger of Love, Justice and Hope* (Jersey City, NJ, 1976); C.E. Lincoln, ed., *Martin Luther King, Jr: A Profile* (rev. edn, New York, 1984).

11. See e.g. J. Forman, *The Making of Black Revolutionaries* (New York, 1972); C. Sellers with R. Terrell, *The River of No Return: The Autobiography of a Black Militant and the Life and Death of SNCC* (Jackson and London, 1990); M. King, *Freedom Song: A Personal Story of the 1960s Freedom Movement* (New York, 1987).

Recalling the decision of black leaders in Albany, Georgia, to invite King into town during the winter of 1961–62, James Forman, at that time a prominent activist in the Student Nonviolent Coordinating Committee (SNCC), stated that he had opposed the move as unnecessary:

> A strong people's movement was in progress, the people were feeling their own strength grow. I knew how much harm could be done by interjecting the Messiah complex – people would feel that only a particular individual could save them and would not move on their own to fight racism and exploitation.[12]

Although Forman's attitude to King was not unpredictable in the light of his career as a radical black activist, the new local studies gave added credence to the view that the civil rights movement had drawn most of its strength from local people and community institutions.[13] This was confirmed by the sociologist Aldon Morris who contended forcefully that the freedom struggle was rooted in 'movement centres' such as Nashville, Tennessee, and Birmingham, Alabama.[14] The black church in these cities, suggested Morris, played a vital role in the development of direct action tactics such as sit-ins and street demonstrations. Without its considerable cognitive and material resources, the movement would have lacked the organisational strength which was a necessary precondition for successful protest.[15]

While some of these local studies rejected Morris's stress on the importance of the black church, all of them highlighted the critical role of ordinary African-American men and women in the struggle. Moreover, the common assumption that southern blacks did not begin to resist segregation until the Montgomery bus boycott was found to be untenable in the light of overwhelming evidence of community-level protest dating back at least as far as the Second World War. The new 'history from below' which came into its

12. Forman, *Black Revolutionaries*, p. 255.
13. Among the most important local studies of the civil rights movement are W.H. Chafe, *Civilities and Civil Rights: Greensboro, North Carolina, and the Black Struggle for Freedom* (New York, 1980); D.R. Colburn, *Racial Change and Community Crisis: St. Augustine, Florida, 1877–1980* (New York, 1985); R.J. Norrell, *Reaping the Whirlwind: The Civil Rights Movement in Tuskegee* (New York, 1985); K.L. Rogers, *Righteous Lives: Narratives of the New Orleans Civil Rights Movement* (New York, 1993); C.W. Eagles, *Outside Agitator: Jon Daniels and the Civil Rights Movement in Alabama* (Chapel Hill, 1993).
14. A.D. Morris, *The Origins of the Civil Rights Movement* (New York, 1984), pp. 68–72, 174–7.
15. Ibid., pp. 1–16.

own in the 1970s and 1980s made particularly effective use of oral history as well as the voluminous records of the NAACP.[16] It revealed not only a plethora of grass-roots activism in the first half of the twentieth century, much of it centred around NAACP voter registration campaigns, but also highlighted the hitherto unheralded efforts of countless southern black professionals and labouring people to procure first-class citizenship for themselves and other members of their race. Continuity of protest has thus become a major theme of civil rights scholarship in recent years.[17]

While King-centred orthodoxy and grass-roots revisionism continue to influence our understanding of the movement, Steven F. Lawson noted a growing trend in 1991 towards 'a more interactive model':

> Only by emphasizing the element of struggle – between national institutions and local activists, moderates and radicals, whites and blacks, women and men, predecessors and contemporaries – can we fashion more complete syntheses of the civil rights movement.[18]

The account of the black freedom struggle which follows is written in the context of Lawson's challenge to historians of the movement. I have opted to stress four major themes: (1) the primary role of black civil rights organisations, aided at times by white allies, in developing effective strategies to destroy southern segregation; (2) the concerted attempt by black leaders, of whom Martin Luther King was *primus inter pares*, to secure the intervention of the central

16. Several collections of oral testimony have enriched our understanding of the civil rights movement. These include H. Raines, *My Soul Is Rested: The Story of the Civil Rights Movement in the Deep South* (New York, 1983); H. Hampton and S. Fayer, *Voices of Freedom: An Oral History of the Civil Rights Movement from the 1950s through the 1980s* (New York, 1990); Youth of the Rural Organizing and Cultural Center, *Minds Stayed on Freedom: The Civil Rights Struggle in the Rural South, an Oral History* (Boulder, 1991).

17. See esp. J. Egerton, *Speak Now Against the Day: The Generation Before the Civil Rights Movement in the South* (New York, 1994); J. Dittmer, *Local People: The Struggle for Civil Rights in Mississippi* (Urbana and Chicago, 1994), pp. 1–40; and A. Fairclough, *Race and Democracy: The Civil Rights Struggle in Louisiana, 1915–1972* (Athens, Ga, 1995), pp. xiv–xv, 21–163.

18. S.F. Lawson, 'Freedom Then, Freedom Now: The Historiography of the Civil Rights Movement', *AHR* 96 (1991), 457. Recent works emphasising King's centrality to the movement include Garrow, *Bearing the Cross*; J.A. Colaiaco, *Martin Luther King, Jr: Apostle of Militant Nonviolence* (Basingstoke, 1988); T. Branch, *Parting the Waters: America in the King Years 1954–63* (New York, 1988); J. White, *Martin Luther King, Jr, and the Civil Rights Movement in America* (British Association for American Studies pamphlet, 1991). For a more grass-roots perspective see esp. C.M. Payne, *I've Got the Light of Freedom: The Organizing Tradition and the Mississippi Freedom Struggle* (Berkeley, Los Angeles and London, 1995).

state in southern affairs; (3) the national scope of the movement, its initial concentration on the South notwithstanding; and (4) the persistent struggle of ordinary African Americans to be treated as equals in the most powerful democracy on earth. Shot through with moral fervour, the civil rights movement was a black-led, interracial crusade for freedom, dignity and justice. Its roots were planted firmly in community institutions and heavily reliant on the remarkable courage of individual men and women at the local level. Without the assistance of supra-local organisations, however, grass-roots protests alone would not have destroyed segregation. In their own very different ways, the constituent elements within the civil rights coalition of the 1960s harnessed local energies to national goals and sought, with an array of creative strategies, to counter the power of southern segregationists with the might of the federal government in Washington. Their success may have been a partial one in the sense that racism and poverty continue to blight the lives of many African Americans, but it was total in the light of their initial aim which was to destroy *de jure* segregation in the South.

Chapter one examines the origins and nature of the southern caste system in an attempt to explain its durability and the potential for change. Chapter two constitutes a broad acceptance of Adam Fairclough's contention that the civil rights movement may be thought of as a two act play with the first act based on events before the mid-1950s.[19] The movement possessed what can loosely be termed a pre-history; certainly, no proper understanding of the play's denouement, to persist with the metaphor, can be arrived at without investigating the early tensions between accommodationists, reformers, and black nationalists and the substantial impact of the Great Depression and the New Deal on black life in America. The continuity theme is developed further in Chapter three. The outbreak of the Second World War heralded a discernible quickening in the pace of black protest even if the ensuing Cold War – the *Brown* decision and the Montgomery bus boycott notwithstanding – eventually brought down the curtain on the first act of the drama.

Chapters four, five, six and seven constitute act two of the drama. Chapter four analyses the golden age of the civil rights movement from a national perspective. Although many of the principal players and events here are familiar ones, not least Martin Luther King and the SCLC campaigns in Birmingham and Selma, the central event

19. Fairclough, *Race and Democracy*, p. xii.

in the making of a genuine social movement is deemed to have been the student sit-ins of 1960. These largely, though by no means entirely, spontaneous demonstrations gave black leaders what they had lacked hitherto: mass support. Thousands of highly motivated college and high school students opposed to gradualism provided the shock troops of the civil rights movement. Most of them confined their participation to local campaigns in the early 1960s. A minority abandoned their studies to devote their lives to service in either SNCC or the revitalised Congress of Racial Equality (CORE). Chapter five shifts the focus from the national campaign against segregation to the SNCC-led struggle to foster participatory democracy in rural areas of the South where patterns of deference were most firmly entrenched. The campaign culminated in the Mississippi Freedom Summer of 1964, a formative event not only in the attempt to transform individuals, the South and the nation, but also in the history of the civil rights coalition. Chapter six details the final collapse of the movement as a national force from the failure of the SCLC's Chicago campaign in 1966 to the assassination of Dr King and the fiasco of the Poor People's Campaign in 1968. After Chapter seven, a thematic examination of the civil rights movement, a concluding chapter charts the progress – or lack of it – of black protest in the last third of the twentieth century.

There is still much work to be done on this subject. Topics such as organised labour, the role of women, and the civil rights struggle in the North, as well as the impact of Black Power and the Vietnam War, have been poorly dealt with. Much of the historiography tends to be focused on Mississippi and Alabama. The history of the NAACP in the 1960s remains to be written. Many key individuals within the movement have yet to have their contributions properly assessed by scholars. Inevitably, therefore, this account of the black freedom struggle represents something of an update on the state of play so far as civil rights scholarship is concerned. It is also a predominantly political synthesis which attempts to give ordinary people their due without writing either Martin Luther King or the federal government out of the narrative.

The civil rights movement operated on several different levels and attracted supporters with varying ideas about how social, political, economic and cultural change could best be achieved in the United States. Not surprisingly, those activists who have committed their accounts of the movement to paper have produced memoirs which reflect their own battle-hardened experience of events. Thus lawyers such as Jack Greenberg and Fred Gray have written valuable books stressing the central importance of litigation to the movement.[20] SNCC activists like James Forman and Mary King have written equally significant autobiographies which highlight their own preoccupation with long-term community organising as distinct from the SCLC's reputedly more superficial stress on short-term mobilisation.[21] Historians wielding their own personal biases and political commitments have frequently lined up behind one of the movement's various factions to write SNCC-, NAACP- or SCLC-oriented history. Although the bulk of this work has contributed hugely to our understanding of the movement and some of it represents a perfectly healthy reaction to the orthodox preoccupation with Martin Luther King, historians would do well not to involve themselves in what Americans like to call 'a zero-sum game'. Giving visionary leaders like King a share of the credit does not automatically detract from the innumerable acts of endurance, courage and defiance performed by those whose names may or may not be lost to history. After all, the movement's initial strength lay not in uniformity of approach, but in its diversity, its complexity, its eclecticism and its toleration of alternative strategies.

20. J. Greenberg, *Crusaders in the Courts: How a Dedicated Band of Lawyers Fought for the Civil Rights Revolution* (New York, 1994); F. Gray, *Bus Ride to Justice: Changing the System by the System; the Life and Works of Fred Gray* (Montgomery, 1996).
21. Forman, *Black Revolutionaries*; King, *Freedom Song.*

CHAPTER 1

Change and Continuity in the Jim Crow South

The main target of the civil rights movement between 1955 and 1965 was the system of *de jure* segregation which underpinned the second-class citizenship of African Americans in the southern states. No understanding of the black freedom struggle is possible without an awareness of how the southern caste system developed over time and a recognition that the system was neither monolithic nor entirely immutable.

Reconstruction and the post-Civil War South

The crushing military defeat of the Confederacy in the spring of 1865 settled two outstanding questions. Firstly, it preserved the American Union, President Abraham Lincoln's 'last, best hope of earth' for which so many northern volunteers had fought and died.[1] Although southern whites would continue to regard themselves in a somewhat different light from other Americans, they would never again be in a position to launch a serious bid for nationhood. Secondly, while the war was fought to save the Union and not to free the slaves, it did result in the liberation of four million black bondsmen and women who had provided the bulk of the labour force in the antebellum South's vibrant cotton economy.

What the Civil War failed to do was provide equal citizenship for the so-called freedmen. True, Republican-dominated Congresses took steps in this direction by passing the Fourteenth and Fifteenth Amendments to the Constitution. Supported by moderate and

---

1. A. Lincoln, Annual Message to Congress, 1 December 1862, in *The Collected Works of Abraham Lincoln*, ed. R.P. Basler (9 vols, New Brunswick, 1953–55), vol. v, p. 537.

Radical members of the Republican Party and ratified in 1868 and 1870 respectively, these amendments aimed to give full citizenship rights to African Americans. Such rights included the 'equal protection' of the laws under the federal Constitution and, remarkably in the context of the time, manhood suffrage. Attempts to secure these rights in practice for southern blacks, however, foundered on pervasive interracial factionalism within the southern state Republican organisations, the tenacious resistance of local whites, the salience of new issues, the persistence of systemic racism throughout the nation, the reluctance of moderate Republican leaders to countenance a permanent increase in the powers of the central state, and a growing desire for sectional reconciliation on the part of northern whites. As a consequence, while Reconstruction did advance black rights, many of the resulting gains were quickly eroded after 1877 when the federal government finally abandoned the freedmen to their fate.

For all its failings, Reconstruction anticipated some of the actions necessary to reform the South's repressive caste system in the twentieth century. Particularly significant was the positive role taken, at least initially, by the federal government. Washington not only set up the Freedmen's Bureau in 1865 to oversee the transition from slavery to freedom, but also evinced a readiness to exert military power over southern whites when the latter proved reluctant to accept the consequences of their wartime defeat. In 1867 Congress responded to the South's rejection of the Fourteenth Amendment by dividing the rebel states into five military districts under the command of Union generals. This action demolished the conservative, white-dominated regimes fostered by the excessively lenient Reconstruction policy of President Andrew Johnson, a conservative Tennessee Unionist who had served as Lincoln's vice-president in the final stages of the Civil War, and provided for black participation in southern politics. In states containing large black populations such as South Carolina, Mississippi and Louisiana, the extension of the electoral franchise to blacks combined with the consciousness-raising efforts of black Union Leagues to overturn the existing political order. Scores of African Americans were elected to local and state office as Republicans during the late 1860s and early 1870s and a handful, including US Senator Hiram Revels of Mississippi, were sent to Congress.[2] Without federal intervention southern blacks,

2. E. Foner, *Reconstruction: America's Unfinished Revolution 1863–1877* (New York, 1988), pp. 351–7.

outgunned and outnumbered by their former masters, would never have experienced the heady years of political activism in the 1870s. It was a lesson that did not go unheeded by civil rights campaigners in the twentieth century.

Reconstruction left many legacies for the future. One of them was the bitterness felt by most southern whites at their sufferings during the period of alleged misrule by the three leading elements in the southern Republican coalition: 'carpetbag' adventurers from the North; opportunistic southern white race-traitors whom they dubbed 'scalawags'; and supposedly ignorant blacks perceived as dupes of their white Republican allies. Such sufferings were more imagined than real. There was corruption aplenty in the post-war South, not least in Radical-controlled states like South Carolina and Louisiana.[3] Some former Confederates, moreover, were disfranchised by congressional legislation, civil liberties were adversely affected by military rule, and the tax burden on ordinary southerners, hard hit by the economic consequences of war and defeat, did increase after 1867. Corruption, however, transcended race, party and region in Gilded Age America and was certainly not confined to the carpetbag governments of the 1870s. Leading Confederates quickly regained their political rights; withdrawal of habeas corpus was an infrequent occurrence; and southern tax rates were not especially high relative to other regions of the country. What southern whites really resented about Reconstruction was the fact that they had been forced to surrender power to their northern conquerors and former slaves. In spite of the fact that they had regained political control in all the ex-Confederate states by 1877, southern whites remembered the humiliating years of 'subjugation' long after the last federal troops had been withdrawn to barracks. Reconstruction was seared into the public memory of the white South by historians and movie-makers alike, with predictably damaging results for the cause of social progress below the Mason–Dixon Line.

There were, however, more positive legacies of Reconstruction. Congressional policies enabled African Americans to seize a much greater measure of control over their own lives. Although blacks were far from passive victims of white domination under slavery, efforts to forge a genuinely autonomous culture were inevitably constrained by the dictates of their confinement. During Reconstruction the obstacles to independent activity were reduced, enabling black men and women to test the limits of their newly won freedom. As well

3. Foner, *Reconstruction*, pp. 384–9.

as allowing the liberated slaves to engage in political activities, Reconstruction gave the freedmen the space and tools necessary to build more of their own durable institutions. Churches, schools, small urban businesses, and a plethora of self-help organisations mushroomed after Appomattox, contributing to black self-confidence and the social diversity of the black community.[4] Some of the institutions founded during the Reconstruction era, including colleges of higher education like Howard and Fisk, would provide the kind of race leaders necessary to carry the struggle for civil rights into the next century. Reconstruction may have been less a part of black folk memory than that of the white variant, but as a time of unprecedented social and political opportunity for blacks it had no parallel in African-American history.

One of the principal reasons why southern blacks were unable to thwart the conservative counter-revolution ('Redemption') which occurred in the 1870s was their lack of economic power. Great swathes of the southern states were devastated by the war and cultivation of the South's chief export staple, cotton, had been severely disrupted. Most congressional Republicans believed that a swift return to plantation agriculture offered the best chance of restoring prosperity and order to the late rebel states. In their view, the emancipated slaves (ill-equipped for freedom as most of them were held to be) could be best provided for as wage labourers on southern plantations. Rejecting Radical calls for the destruction of the plantocracy's economic power base and the granting of material aid (encapsulated in the slogan 'forty acres and a mule') to southern blacks, moderates and conservatives hoped that temporary institutions like the Freedmen's Bureau would help to inculcate planters and freedmen alike with the values of 'free-labour' democracy. Bureau officers had orders to enforce binding contracts, and to use their extensive authority to preserve a precarious balance between employers and employees.[5]

Black aspirations were dashed not only by the demise of Reconstruction (including the termination of the Freedmen's Bureau), but also by a multiplicity of economic problems which consistently hindered the South's post-war recovery.[6] The most serious of these was the region's continuing dependence on cotton well into the twentieth century. Prior to 1861 high world demand for southern cotton had helped to augment the fortunes of the region's dominant

4. Ibid., pp. 88–102.   5. Ibid., pp. 164–70.
6. On the postbellum southern economy see esp. G. Wright, *Old South, New South: Revolutions in the Southern Economy Since the Civil War* (New York, 1986), pp. 17–123.

planter class, thereby swelling sectional confidence in the face of the perceived threat from the antislavery Republican Party. A number of respected southern commentators had warned that the South's over-reliance on monoculture was unhealthy but even defeat in the Civil War failed to stem the general enthusiasm for cotton, particularly in the immediate postbellum years when the staple continued to fetch attractive prices on the international market. 'New South' proponents of economic diversification were forced to confront the reality that cotton continued to be far more profitable per acre than any other southern crop. As a consequence thousands of indebted whites who had previously played a marginal role in the region's economy were drawn into the cotton nexus during the late nineteenth century. Their initial intention was to become thriving commercial farmers like their peers in the Midwest. However, when the surge in world demand for American cotton began to slow in the 1870s, many yeoman farmers found themselves mired in the same vicious cycle of debt and poverty which quickly trapped the freedmen on the plantations. Visions of wealth and independence proved to be as great a mirage for most southern whites as did liberty and justice for African Americans.

Southern blacks were unable to escape from the grip of King Cotton for two reasons: they lacked land and credit. The failure of the Republicans to carry out a systematic programme of land reform in the South after the Confederate surrender at Appomattox has long been seen as a fundamental precondition for the rise of Jim Crow. Deprived of the means of achieving economic independence by northern politicians intellectually and politically indisposed to compensate blacks for their years of captivity, African Americans were inevitably handicapped in their search for equal rights in a capitalist republic where landownership had always been viewed as an integral component of citizenship. Equally damaging to black aspirations was the paucity of available credit which the freedmen needed to engage successfully in commercial farming. They lacked access to wealth for obvious reasons: few blacks had received wages under slavery and the federal government showed even less inclination to provide them with hard cash than it did to give them forty acres and a mule. It was not just blacks, however, who were deprived of the means to take full control over their own lives. The entire South was starved of capital, not only because of the war, but also because the nation's economic power lay in the industrialising Northeast. Like their midwestern counterparts, with whom they had much in common, southerners lacked economic muscle in the shape of essential credit institutions and an elastic circulating medium. This had always been the case, even during the antebellum years when regional self-confidence had reached its apogee, but after the war the rapid pace of northern industrialisation combined with the predominance of cotton culture to maintain the South's position as an economic colony within the Union.

These material deficiencies meant the halting growth of a full-blown wage labour economy in the southern states. For all their attachment to the meritocratic values of commercial capitalism, the victorious Republicans made little attempt, beyond setting up the Freedmen's Bureau and pouring substantial amounts of taxpayers' money into shaky railroad schemes, to develop a modern capitalist economy in the South. Strapped of credit and hard currency, southern planters found it difficult to comply with the dictates of a wage economy. The result was the rapid emergence throughout the Deep South of the sharecropping system by which planters furnished their credit-starved tenants with tools, animals and fertilisers in return for a share of the cotton crop at the end of the year.

Although Marxist scholars tend to view sharecropping as a coercive labour system imposed on the freedmen by a reactionary planter class, most historians view the rise of sharecropping as a compromise between planters and their workforce.[7] Planters often lacked the ability to pay regular wages, but needed labourers to cultivate the cotton crop on a year-round basis. While the freed slaves could no longer be forced to work from sun-up to sun-down for virtually nothing beyond their keep, their desire for a greater measure of independence was usually thwarted by their poverty. In this sense both groups gained something from sharecropping: planters secured a cheap and relatively reliable labour force to which they could devolve some of the risks inherent in commercial farming; blacks no longer had to labour under constant supervision and won a degree of material security in an era of unsettling change.

While devotees of classical economics have sought to argue that a relatively free labour market developed in the post-war South, it would be wrong to discount the Marxist interpretation entirely.[8] The relationship between planters and labourers was not an equal

7. H.D. Woodman, 'Sequel to Slavery: The New History Views the Postbellum South', *JSH* 43 (1977), pp. 523–44, and J. Wiener, *Social Origins of the New South: Alabama, 1860–1885* (Baton Rouge and London, 1978), pp. 66–72; Wright, *Old South, New South*, pp. 85–7; Foner, *Reconstruction*, pp. 172–4.

8. See e.g. R. Higgs, *Competition and Coercion: Blacks in the American Economy, 1865–1914* (New York, 1977).

one as was clearly demonstrated by the former's legal right to a first lien on the crop and the latter's inability to break out of the cycle of debt inflicted on them by the furnishing system. Rural croppers and tenants not only rented the means to farm from their employers but also purchased basic foodstuffs and luxuries from the plantation store, owned either by the planter himself or a local merchant with whom the former was often allied. Normally such goods were supplied on credit. As a result, because the yield from the cotton crop was invariably deemed insufficient to pay off their cumulative debt, farm workers found themselves plantation-bound for yet another year. Southern labour mobility did increase after 1865 as the regional economy began to expand and the existence of a farm-ladder of sorts did allow space for some labourers to achieve a measure of economic independence. In general, however, the advent of sharecropping restored a significant degree of coercion to the lives of the former slaves – one that was increased by the growth of a formal caste system at the turn of the century.[9]

The chief beneficiaries of the South's predominantly agricultural, labour-intensive economy were the planters and merchants who possessed the necessary links to outside capital. By no means all of them had been in power before the war, but the survivors of the old slave-holding class quickly combined with *arrivistes* to form a dominant elite in the post-war South. Centred in the cotton regions of the Deep South (the so-called Black Belt) as well as other outposts of plantation agriculture like Virginia's tobacco-growing Southside, this privileged group of largely white males proceeded to impose their political will on society in most of the former Confederate states. They were allowed to do so for a variety of reasons, not least of which was the retention of a decentralised system of government in the United States after the Civil War. A pervasive *laisser-faire* ideology (which did much to undermine Reconstruction) combined with the requirements of a federal constitution to place severe constraints on the capacity of the federal government to influence events in the South after the 1870s. Even if Washington had possessed the will to counteract the power of racist southern elites (which to a large extent it did not), the Supreme Court's cautious interpretation of the post-war constitutional amendments and the reserved powers of the states would have made it difficult for the central government to improve the lot of southern blacks. What the latter needed most in post-Civil War America were local

9. P. Daniel, 'The Metamorphosis of Slavery, 1865–1900', *JAH* 66 (1979), 88–99.

allies. Unfortunately for them, the power of the county-seat elites who dominated southern life in the late nineteenth and early twentieth century was bolstered by a fragmented opposition which proved unable to contend successfully for the rights of ordinary whites, let alone those of the emancipated slaves.

While plantation agriculture (principally cotton, but also tobacco, rice and sugar) provided the fundamental basis for the development of the southern caste system, one should not make the mistake of viewing the post-war South as an unchanging and uniform landscape dotted solely by large commercial farms. The expanding towns and cities of the region, parts of the upper and peripheral South with ties to the dynamic northern economy, and the increasingly market-oriented hill country all contained sources of potential opposition to the regnant planter-merchant elite of the Black Belt. New South industrialists, merchants and publicists, salaried professionals, hard-pressed small farmers and mountain whites drawn into the region's burgeoning textile manufacturing sector – all had very different interests from the kind of men who dominated southern political life. However, as the eclipse of Republicanism in the region during Reconstruction had revealed, their commitment to white supremacy was too great for the creation of a progressive alternative to the conservative Democrats who had redeemed the South from the thraldom of wicked carpetbaggers.

As Armstead Robinson has shown, Reconstruction proved short-lived partly because southern Republicans were unable to harmonise the interests of their logical constituents: elite former Whigs, lower-class whites (who had sometimes challenged the hegemony of slave-holding planters in the antebellum period) and blacks.[10] Assuming black support for the party as axiomatic, white southern Republicans bid aggressively for the support of ex-Whigs on the grounds that such influential voters would favour policies designed to promote economic growth.[11] Generally speaking, the party's southern leaders ignored the possibility that blacks and lower-class whites could be united against the planter elite. They did so partly because they were themselves well-to-do professionals with an aversion to inciting class conflict, partly because they were well aware that respectable southerners were unlikely to appreciate measures designed to improve the lot of the lower orders, and partly because

10. A.L. Robinson, 'Beyond the Realm of Social Consensus: New Meanings of Reconstruction for American History', *JAH* 68 (1981), 276–97.
11. M. Perman, *The Road to Redemption: Southern Politics, 1869–1879* (Chapel Hill and London, 1984), pp. 87–107.

they possessed a realistic awareness of the power of southern racism. Sadly for the Republicans, they were never able to rid themselves of their alien, carpetbag image with the inevitable result that their central policy of state support for railways failed to hold the coalition together in the face of widespread corruption and Democratic violence during the 1870s.

The era of segregation

Although subsequent decades witnessed attempts by various groups in southern society to challenge planter dominance, elite rule was too entrenched to allow the development of a strong progressive opposition. One of the reasons why a New South party failed to gel in the late nineteenth century was the ability of industrialists and planters to make common cause in spite of their divergent interests, most notably their competing demand for labour. This was particularly evident in Alabama, where 'Big Mule' industrialists centred in the boom town of Birmingham carved out a *modus vivendi* with planters in the Black Belt. This alliance was built partly on the development of the convict labour system which enabled coal mining companies to procure a reliable supply of predominantly black workers at the expense of the state.[12] Ultimately tensions between businessmen and planters would prove to be the Achilles' heel of the caste system but it took more than half a century of economic growth and change for divisions between the two dominant groups to become evident. For most of the time between 1880 and 1940, planters, merchants and industrialists seemed united in their support for segregation and a low-wage, labour intensive economy.

Prospects for an alliance between blacks and lower-class whites were brightest during the Populist revolt of the 1890s.[13] The complex modernising trends sweeping across the postbellum United States provoked a strong reaction from southern and western farmers who found their status and material well-being in terminal decline. Many of them sought succour in political action by joining

12. A. Lichtenstein, ' "Through the Rugged Gates of the Penitentiary": Convict Labor and Southern Coal, 1870–1900' in *Race and Class in the American South Since 1890*, ed. M. Stokes and R. Halpern (Oxford and Providence, RI, 1994), pp. 3–42.

13. The following account of the Populist movement is based on a variety of sources. Reliable introductory syntheses include E. Ayers, *The Promise of the New South: Life After Reconstruction* (New York and Oxford, 1992), pp. 249–82, and H.N. Rabinowitz, *The First New South 1865–1920* (Arlington Heights, Ill., 1992) pp. 98–117.

the short-lived People's (or Populist) Party in the 1890s. Populist efforts to mobilise the disparate agricultural community of the South took many forms – among them the advocacy of statist solutions to the farmer's problems, fervent appeals to the evangelical Protestant mores which suffused the region's dominant sub-cultures and, in some areas, genuine efforts to forge links with black tenants and sharecroppers.[14] What might have proved a decisive move forward in the history of southern race relations, however, soon turned into a disastrous leap backwards. Fearful of the revolutionary implications of a Populist victory, some representatives of the planter-merchant elite responded by injecting racial hatred into political debate.[15] Cynical appeals to the white southerner's complex sexual and social fears of the black male not only helped to divide lower-class radicals along racial lines but also contributed to the rash of lynchings which broke out across the South during the 1890s. They also paved the way for the rise of *de jure* segregation in the same decade.

Although Jim Crow was in part a product of the unique political and socio-economic circumstances of the late nineteenth century, it did not represent a major break with the southern past.[16] There had never been a golden era of southern race relations, even though Old South devotees like Susan Dabney Smedes, the daughter of a Mississippi planter, strove desperately to recall warm magnolia-blossom days when loyal slaves laboured contentedly in the fields under the benign gaze of their paternalistic 'massa'.[17] It was not that blacks and whites did not interact on a regular basis in the antebellum South. House servants were in perpetual contact with the planter's family on the plantations, slaves worked under close supervision of their master on the smaller farms, and fraternisation between the lower orders of both races was far from uncommon in the larger towns of the region. Even field workers, often seen by modern historians as the principal carriers of African-American culture because of their relative distance from the planter, cannot be said to have lived entirely separate lives from the whites around them, particularly if their master happened to be a paternalistic

---

14. On the complex relationship between blacks and the Populist Party see G.H. Gaither, *Blacks and the Populist Revolt: Ballots and Bigotry in the 'New South'* (University, Ala, 1977).

15. C.V. Woodward, *The Strange Career of Jim Crow* (rev. edn, New York, 1966), p. 79.

16. H.N. Rabinowitz, 'More than the Woodward Thesis: Assessing the Strange Career of Jim Crow', *JAH* 75 (1988), 842–56.

17. S.D. Smedes, *Memorials of a Southern Planter* (Baltimore, 1887).

individual whose frequent intrusions into the everyday lives of his slaves hampered the development of a separate black community. At no stage in the antebellum South, however, did adult blacks and whites come together as equals. Isolated friendships grounded in mutual respect did occur but for the most part the social order of the peculiar institution rested firmly on the basis of black subordination to white rule. Slaves, therefore, were required to exhibit due deference to their masters at all times. Failure to carry out appointed tasks or attempts to challenge the existing regimen through laziness, sabotage, or flight invariably resulted in punishment. The relatively small number of free blacks in the Old South found their meagre liberties increasingly constrained as the slave system tightened around them after 1830. They too were expected to conform to the region's complex system of racial etiquette and lived under the permanent threat of bondage. Significantly, those free blacks who resided in towns appear to have congregated in informally segregated neighbourhoods.

Emancipation, congressional Reconstruction and the penetration of capitalist labour relations into the South undoubtedly eroded much of the old paternalism, but there is little evidence that they did much to promote genuine racial integration. Indeed, most of the Republican regimes in the South were so concerned about the salience of racial prejudice among whites that they declined to combat the *de facto* segregation of schools, housing and public accommodations which proceeded apace after 1865, particularly in the urban areas. New Orleans public schools were desegregated for a brief period in the 1870s and some states in which blacks became a dominant component of the Republican coalition, notably South Carolina, did enact laws designed to prohibit racial discrimination in public places. Those laws which were passed, however, were seldom enforced and hopes that federal legislation might procure equal treatment evaporated with the Supreme Court's invalidation of the largely ineffective 1875 US Civil Rights Act.[18]

The rise of *de jure* segregation in the 1890s was underpinned by the ideological hegemony of scientific racism which posited a global hierarchy of races in which blacks and persons of mixed race were defined as biologically inferior to Caucasians. Its emergence gave official sanction to existing patterns of *de facto* segregation which were, only in part, an inevitable consequence of a general desire on the part of blacks and whites to live in their own communities. As

18. Foner, *Reconstruction*, pp. 368–72.

was the case with contemporaneous racial segregation in South Africa, Jim Crow had many sources and assumed various guises in different regions.[19] In South Africa, the formal separation of whites and blacks served the economic ends, firstly, of employers who wished to guarantee a constant supply of labour to the mines and fields and, secondly, of ordinary whites who wished to guarantee their own privileges and status in an ethnically diverse society. In the United States, lawmakers who enacted segregation ordinances were well aware that their white constituents generally assented to measures which institutionalised a formal separation of the races as the processes of urbanisation and industrialisation gathered pace. Segregation underpinned a two-tier system in which white workers, particularly skilled workers, were guaranteed substantial material and psychological benefits because blacks were normally confined to the most arduous, poorly paid jobs and increasingly defined as second-class citizens.[20] Although segregation did not always make economic sense to southern capitalists whose main concerns were productivity and cheap labour, businessmen usually shared the racial mores of the community in which they lived and did little, beyond the sporadic employment of black strike-breakers, to undermine Jim Crow.

At the heart of the southern caste system, a hierarchically organised society based on inequalities of race as well as class, lay a bewildering array of state and local laws, passed between 1881 and 1915, mandating racial segregation in all walks of life. Such statutes banned blacks and whites from travelling in the same railway carriages, tram-cars and steamboats; provided for the separation of races in most other public places including theatres, cinemas, parks, churches, schools and even cemeteries; and zoned off urban blacks from their white counterparts. Although the majority of southern blacks doubtless preferred the company of their own people, the more wealthy among them resented the loss of power and dignity occasioned by the hardening of Jim Crow practices. Their efforts to stem the tide of legal segregation continued throughout the period

19. W. Beinart and S. Dubow, eds, *Segregation and Apartheid in Twentieth-Century South Africa* (London and New York, 1995) provides a useful introduction to the ongoing scholarly debate over the sources of racial separation in South Africa. Important comparative works on the development of segregation in the two societies include G.M. Fredrickson, *White Supremacy: A Comparative Study in American and South African History* (New York, 1981) and J.W. Cell, *The Highest Stage of White Supremacy: The Origins of Segregation in South Africa and the American South* (Cambridge, 1982).

20. H.M. McKiven, Jr, *Iron and Steel: Class, Race, and Community in Birmingham, Alabama, 1875–1920* (Chapel Hill, 1995), pp. 29–30.

in the form of legal challenges and boycotts, but the prospects of success were dimmed by the decision of the US Supreme Court in the seminal case of *Plessy v. Ferguson* in 1896. Homer Plessy, a well-to-do Louisiana mulatto, had brought suit in state court claiming that a local law mandating segregated railway cars was void under the Constitution. The nation's highest court rejected his claims on the grounds that 'separate but equal' railway accommodation was constitutionally permissible and chided Plessy for being overly sensitive to the stigma he attached to segregation.[21] This decision, followed as it was by further Supreme Court rulings extending the doctrine of 'separate but equal' to other public spaces, legitimised the activities of southern states and municipalities and gave the green light for yet more legislation. By the time the United States entered the First World War, the gains of Reconstruction had been almost totally undermined by the welter of Jim Crow statutes.

'Separate but equal' was one of the basest fictions ever peddled by the American legal system. Southern governments had no intention of spending taxpayers' money to protect Fourteenth Amendment rights as was confirmed by their underfunding of black schools and health care, and their blatant refusal to provide decent public facilities for their black populations. Conservative regimes were notoriously penurious in their provision of services, for whites as well as blacks, but the disparities in public spending on the races were evident for all to see. Black education was particularly hard hit. After 1890, for example, Mississippi invested most of its school money in white tuition with the result that by the turn of the century blacks received 19 per cent of the total education budget in spite of constituting 60 per cent of the state's school-age population.[22] Schooling was worst in rural areas where child labour was important to planters and black farmers alike. Buildings were usually wooden huts, teachers lacked proper qualifications, illiteracy rates were high, resources were at a premium, and few black children could hope to continue beyond the fifth grade. While urban blacks generally received higher quality education, all of them suffered from the discriminatory policies of local school boards. Some southern states, such as North Carolina, did attempt a modicum of reform during the Progressive era of the early twentieth century, and rural blacks across the region benefited from the uplift

21. R. Kluger, *Simple Justice: The History of* Brown v. Board of Education *and Black America's Struggle for Equality* (London, 1977), pp. 73–83.
22. N.R. McMillen, *Dark Journey: Black Mississippians in the Age of Jim Crow* (Urbana and Chicago, 1989), pp. 72–3.

programmes of northern philanthropic foundations like the Rocke-
feller and Rosenwald Funds.[23] For the most part, however, while
literacy rates for southern blacks did show a steady increase, the
standards of black education lagged well behind those of whites
throughout the first half of the century. As late as the Second World
War, Mississippi blacks (by then 57 per cent of the local school-age
population) were still receiving only 13 per cent of the state's education budget.[24]

Central to the stability of the southern caste system was the rapid
disfranchisement of blacks in the late nineteenth and early twentieth century. To some extent this development was an inevitable
consequence of the anti-black rage of the 1890s and the defeat of
the Populist crusade. Almost as significant, however, were white
middle-class attempts to clean up state and municipal politics. Progressive reformers like Alexander J. McKelway and Edgar Gardner
Murphy regarded ordinary blacks as immature human beings whose
ignorance and irrationality made them prey to the baser instincts
and liable to manipulation by corrupt politicians.[25] Black disfranchisement was thus seen as a necessary tool of political reform,
alongside the direct election of United States senators, the referendum and recall, and the replacement of inefficient municipal
governments by new city commissions. Black Belt elites had done
their fair share of manipulating the black vote in the past, but as
long as southern legislatures remained apportioned to their advantage, most planters were only too happy to see blacks deprived of
the vote. Their enthusiasm for reform was increased by the fact that
many lower-class whites were also affected by the techniques used
to disfranchise blacks. The established order had been shaken by
the Populist revolt and its leaders welcomed the opportunity to
minimise the possibility of future earthquakes.

As the Fifteenth Amendment prohibited interference with a citizen's right to vote on the grounds of race, southern state governments and constitutional conventions, unusually creative in matters
designed to undermine the rights of their black populations, formulated a wide range of new provisions designed to complete a
process that had begun during Redemption. Payment of poll taxes
(often on a cumulative basis) became a mandatory precondition for
registration. So too did literacy and other residency and citizenship
tests, the most famous of which were the ubiquitous grandfather

23. W.A. Link, *The Paradox of Southern Progressivism, 1880–1930* (Chapel Hill and
London, 1992), pp. 125–42.
24. McMillen, *Dark Journey*, p. 73.   25. Link, *Paradox*, pp. 68–9.

clauses by which even the most illiterate whites were allowed to register if they possessed an immediate relative who had voted in the period prior to Congressional Reconstruction. Although ordinary whites were adversely affected by some of these measures, it was blacks who suffered most, principally because the various tests were administered in a discriminatory manner by white employees of the state. In the Mississippi Delta, where thousands of poorly educated sharecroppers laboured on the sprawling cotton plantations, only a handful of favoured blacks were permitted to vote while illiterate whites were registered without compunction by local registrars. Although disfranchisement of blacks was greatest in the rural areas of the Deep South where the 'coloured' population was most concentrated (and to whites the most threatening), the vast majority of the race had lost its principal badge of citizenship by the advent of the First World War.

The chief political vehicle by which segregation and disfranchisement were accomplished was the same one that had engineered secession and rescued the South from the ignominy of carpetbag rule. The Democratic Party had been the party of white supremacy and state rights for most of the nineteenth century, so it was hardly surprising that most southern whites gravitated towards it at election time. Blacks played virtually no role in the organisation, not only due to the various discriminatory suffrage provisions but also because of the white primary – a racially exclusive contest to decide party nominees prior to general elections – which was introduced in most southern states during the early years of Jim Crow. As Democratic strength in the region made nomination tantamount to election, 'reform' laws allowing the ruling party to dictate its own membership criteria provided one more way of depriving blacks of their political voice. While the Republican Party maintained a following among mountain whites and the few blacks allowed to vote, its loyalists lacked the means to challenge the Democratic nominees at all levels of the federal system. Almost the only influence possessed by the Republicans in the lower South derived from their organisation's domination of the presidency between 1877 and 1932. Control of the federal spoils, however, was a poor substitute for voter support, particularly when the party's national leaders remained divided over the racial implications of patronage policy.

The Democrats' domination of southern politics made the South the major player within the national Democratic organisation until the 1936 presidential contest but resulted in frequent intra-party factionalism below the Mason–Dixon Line. While each of the southern states had its own distinctive political culture, Richard Scher has identified three separate groupings: stable unifactional states such as Virginia and Tennessee (dominated respectively by the machines of the patrician Harry F. Byrd and Memphis boss, Edward Crump); bifactional systems in which two wings of the Democratic Party contended regularly for power on the basis either of personality (as in Louisiana and Georgia) or socio-economic fault-lines (as in Alabama); and multifactional states such as North Carolina, Arkansas and particularly Texas (whose heterogeneous social and economic base made for the richest in-fighting of all).[26] Scher's categorisation indicates that politics in the 'Solid South' were less uniform than many historians have suggested. Occasionally Democratic factions did appeal to those urban blacks who could vote, sometimes with positive consequences for the supply of public services. This was especially true of states and localities where the Democratic organisation was controlled by populist factions (dependent partly for support on whites outside the Black Belt) or growth-oriented city machines which had always been prepared to trade votes for services. With few exceptions, however, southern Democratic politicians during the first half of the twentieth century remained wedded to the basic structures and values of Jim Crow. The region's politics were far from monolithic, but they left African Americans with little opportunity to exert what remained of their political clout.

Life for most southern blacks would have been hard enough had Jim Crow been solely a matter of law. Tragically, its extra-legal supports added another more frightening dimension to everyday life for most members of the race. The perpetual threat of white violence hung over the region like a summer storm cloud. Its oppressive presence created a stifling climate of fear in many black communities and thereby reinforced obstacles to free expression under the caste system. Lynching was the most high-profile form of violence meted out to African Americans in the Jim Crow South. Tuskegee Institute statistics record that 3,446 blacks were lynched in the United States between 1882 and 1968, 88 per cent of them in the 11 states of the old Confederacy.[27] Although this horrific practice reached its peak in the 1890s when political and social turmoil galvanised the popular myth of the black rapist, a majority

26. R.K. Scher, *Politics in the New South: Republicanism, Race, and Leadership in the Twentieth Century* (New York, 1992), pp. 75–80.
27. Figures cited in R.L. Zangrando, *The NAACP Crusade Against Lynching, 1909–1950* (Philadelphia, 1980), pp. 5–7.

of blacks lynched were accused of murder rather than rape. Vigil-
ante terror, therefore, was the ultimate sanction for caste discipline, not simply an expression of the deeply ingrained sexual fears
harboured by white men and women. The fact that those responsible for the killings were never convicted for their crimes indicated
not only the degree of public sanction for lynching which existed
at the turn of the century, but also re-emphasised the powerlessness
of southern blacks under the law. Other forms of coercion existed
to keep blacks in their place. Some of these, including the discriminatory use of capital punishment against blacks and the infamous
convict-lease system, received legal sanction from the state; others
such as the 'riot' (a euphemism for the mass slaughter of blacks),
physical violence short of death, and economic intimidation constituted informal modes of keeping 'coloured' people in their place.

   Although it would be wrong to exaggerate the deleterious psychological consequences for the African-American community, fear
of physical intimidation was a constant for most blacks. This was
particularly true for those living in the plantation districts where
memories of the lash were still alive. Croppers and tenant farmers
in areas like the Mississippi Delta and the Alabama Black Belt that
would one day become the focus for civil rights activity had little
choice but to conform, at least outwardly, to white expectations if
they wanted to survive and perhaps even prosper. The threat and
reality of white violence, therefore, re-enforced existing patterns of
deference in the region. Most blacks at least feigned respect and
submission to the whites with whom they came into contact in the
fields, lanes and country towns of the Deep South. They had little
choice for, as all black children knew from their parents, a cross
word to a farm manager or a careless glance at a white woman
could have the direst consequences.

   Privately, the vast majority of blacks did not worship the ground
upon which white people trod. Servile Uncle Toms did exist, but
the bulk of their race retained a strong suspicion of whites and
harboured deep (if often inchoate) resentment about the conditions under which they lived. The problem was that while these
emotions were proof that many blacks were able to preserve their
self-respect under the caste system, such feelings necessarily remained hidden from whites. Most members of the dominant race,
confronted daily by an outwardly contented domestic servant or
plantation worker, had few grounds for supposing that there was
anything wrong with southern race relations. Deluded self-interest

and racist preconceptions about black goals and capabilities prevented most white southerners from realising the need for reform. Black grievances persisted, but deeply-felt emotions were as often channelled into self-destructive rage or apathy, as into creative protest against the caste system itself.[28]

Instruments of change

The greatest challenge to the existing order in the American South during the first three decades of the twentieth century came not from any civil rights movement but from the decision of thousands of blacks to abandon the plantation districts. In 1910 89 per cent of all black people in the United States resided in the South. By 1970 that proportion had been reduced to 53 per cent.[29] What occurred in the interim is known to historians as the 'Great Migration', a steady outward movement of roughly 6.5 million blacks from the rural South to the urban North.[30] Although this demographic trend had its roots in the postbellum era and grew in pace after 1941, it began in earnest between 1916 and 1920 when nearly half a million blacks left the Southland. Push and pull factors, varying over time, influenced the thousands of individual decisions to go north. Negative stimuli included the ravages of the boll weevil, the high incidence of white violence, and the limited prospects which existed for black advancement in the South. Equally significant, however, was the positive attraction of a better life in the industrial North where stalled European immigration and the demands of wartime production had begun to open up jobs to blacks in cities like Chicago, Detroit, Cleveland, Philadelphia and New York. Southern legislatures responded with a rash of laws to prevent the shrinkage of their labour pool but the sheer scale of the exodus revealed their ineffectiveness.

As well as moving northwards, southern blacks headed for the expanding towns of their own region where they generally sought work as unskilled labourers and, in the case of women, domestics

28. See R. Wright, *Black Boy* (New York, 1945), for a searing personal account of the psychological impact of Jim Crow on southern blacks.
29. C.R. Wilson and W. Ferris, eds, *Encyclopedia of Southern Culture* (Chapel Hill and London, 1989), p. 177.
30. N. Lemann, *The Great Black Migration and How It Changed America* (London, 1991), p. 6.

for the new white middle class. Rural planters, therefore, found themselves confronted by a worrying trend. Black labour mobility threatened not only their reservoir of cheap agricultural labour, thereby undermining the chief economic basis of the caste system, but also contributed significantly to the growth of the very population centres which posed the greatest internal threat to the existing social order. As Black Belt elites were only too aware, the anonymity of urban life and the complexity of its social arrangements were far from conducive to the well-being of a rigid caste system. Patterns of authority were harder to maintain in cities, civic elites were not necessarily as committed to Jim Crow customs as rural whites, and urban blacks were likely to be better paid, better educated, and quite possibly more militant than their more isolated peers in the countryside.

The county-seat elite's best hopes of maintaining power at home lay in preserving the South's dominant influence within the national Democratic Party. Their efforts appeared to bear fruit during the early twentieth century. Indeed, after Woodrow Wilson, a Virginia-born Democrat, was elected president in November 1912, it seemed for a brief moment that the Southern Way might become the American Way. Bowing to the demands of powerful Democrats within his party, Wilson initially allowed several of his Cabinet members to announce plans to introduce segregated facilities into their departments. Although opposition from the NAACP and liberal politicans like Robert La Follette of Wisconsin resulted in the plans being shelved, Wilson revealed his dislike of black assertiveness by rudely dismissing an African-American protest delegation from the White House.[31]

Any hopes, however, that southerners might have had of using the Democratic Party to maintain the caste system were undermined by the rapid transformation of that political institution from a bastion of white supremacy into the nation's most powerful vehicle for progressive liberalism. This development had its roots in the Democrats' longstanding commitment to ethnic and religious pluralism which made it the obvious political home for the millions of Catholic and Jewish immigrants who migrated to the United States between 1880 and the mid-1920s. The bulk of these new voters dwelt in the industrial cities of the North. While their relative poverty and lack of resources tended to make them supporters

    31. J.M. Cooper, *Pivotal Decades: The United States, 1900–1920* (New York and London, 1990), pp. 207–8.

of measures designed to improve municipal services, the immigrants' cultural concerns rendered them hostile to the growing movement for governmental prohibition of liquor sales. Northern Democratic leaders had few problems accommodating themselves to these preferences with the result that the urban wing of the Democratic Party, heavily influenced by city bosses dependent on immigrant votes, rapidly emerged as a powerful counterweight to the Solid South which was politically and intellectually hostile to statist policies in the economic realm, but somewhat more sympathetic on cultural grounds to prohibition.

Of equal concern to southern Democrats was the growing influence of black voters within the national party. When increasing numbers of African Americans moved north in search of a better life, they gained not only jobs but also the right to vote. Finding the twentieth-century Republican Party dominated by big business and rather less supportive of their interests than its nineteenth-century precursor, they were generally attracted by the liberal, statist policies of the city machines. This was particularly true during the depressed 1930s when federal welfare monies were distributed to blacks via municipal governments dominated mainly by Democratic bosses like Ed Flynn in the Bronx district of New York. The political significance for blacks of President Franklin Roosevelt's interventionist response to the Great Depression – the 'New Deal' – was revealed for the first time in the 1934 congressional elections when thousands of African Americans switched allegiance from the Republicans to the Democrats. The trend continued two years later when an estimated 76 per cent of northern blacks voted for Roosevelt in the presidential election of 1936.[32]

The entry of northern blacks into the national Democratic coalition bolstered the forces of liberalism within the party and increased concerns among southern political leaders that their own power was on the wane. Such fears were well founded. At the 1936 Democratic national convention the northern wing of the party flexed its muscles by abolishing the two-thirds rule for nomination which had provided the South with a veto over presidential candidates. Convinced that New Deal policies were corrosive of the established order below the Mason–Dixon Line, conservative southern Democrats publicly lambasted the administration for its meddlesome activities. The demagogic Georgia Democrat, Herbert

---

32. H. Sitkoff, *A New Deal for Blacks – The Emergence of Civil Rights as a National Issue: Vol. I, The Depression Decade* (New York, 1978), pp. 84–101.

Talmadge, for example, denounced the New Deal as 'a combination of wet-nursin', frenzied finance, downright communism, and plain damn-foolishness'.[33]

Given the erosion of their power within the Democratic coalition, white southerners' best hope of retaining Jim Crow intact lay in two directions. Firstly, their dominance of local politics and strict seniority rules gave them a grip on US Senate committees from which vantage point they could, in combination with the filibuster (an organised prolongation of debate designed to prevent obnoxious bills coming to a vote) and shifting alliances with conservative Republicans, block what they regarded as anti-southern legislation. A second source of hope was careful protection of the nation's federal system of government which had been altered but not destroyed by the Civil War. The persistence of a multi-layered polity in which power was divided between political institutions and geographic interests had enabled Black Belt elites to recover and then perpetuate their rule after Appomattox. As a consequence, there was no national police force to protect blacks from the discriminatory effects of southern state law – murder was not a federal crime and only individuals acting in their capacity as state officials were deemed subject to federal laws and amendments passed during the Reconstruction era.

Although white southerners fought with some success to retain their power base in the Senate, the balance within the federal polity between local and central government came under increasing threat as the twentieth century wore on. The reasons for this are numerous but chief among them was the inability of the decentralised post-Civil War system to cope with the demands of a modern, industrial society. This became evident first during the depression of the 1890s when radical Populists looked to government to solve the farmers' ills and then later during the Progressive era when urban reformers advocated the expansion of the federal bureaucracy as an organisational counterweight to the rapid rise of giant industrial corporations and as a cure-all for some of the worst effects of industrialism. Southern Progressives were more suspicious of federal power than their northern counterparts, but even they endorsed state-level reforms in the fields of health care, education and the family which served to erode, though not to destroy completely, traditions of localism in the South.[34] The First World War accentuated the

---

33. H. Talmadge quoted in D.E. Grantham, *The Life and Death of the Solid South: A Political History* (Lexington, Ky, 1988), p. 107.

34. Link, *Paradox*, pp. 124–247.

trend towards governmental activism, fuelling the growth of state and federal bureaucracies. Some of these, like the War Industries Board, proved to be temporary expedients. Other, more established, governmental agencies like the Department of Agriculture emerged from the war with their authority greatly enhanced. The end result was a much greater intrusion of the central state into the lives of ordinary Americans – a process made irreversible by the New Deal response to the Great Depression and, most importantly of all, by the United States' entry into the Second World War in December 1941. The growth of federal power after 1917 may not have made the demise of the southern caste system inevitable, but it signalled to all white southerners that the days of conservative rule by local elites were numbered.

By no means all of the threats to Jim Crow were political. The Great Migration continued during the 1920s and 1930s, altering the face of urban and rural communities alike and depleting still further the cheap labour pool on which southern planters had depended for so long. One of the main factors behind this ongoing demographic movement was the disastrous decline in cotton prices, caused principally by overproduction and stagnant demand, which took place after a temporary upswing during the First World War. The situation grew even worse after the Wall Street Crash. Between 1929 and 1932 the value of cotton sales decreased dramatically from $1.5 billion to $45 million.[35] This precipitous fall resulted in further drops in southern farm wages which helped to impel yet more croppers and tenant farmers of both races to abandon the soil for city life. The interwar depression in the cotton sector also undermined the southern textile industry from which blacks had traditionally been excluded. Further shaken by drought and the devastating Mississippi flood of 1927, the regional economy was poorly placed to withstand the onset of the Great Depression.

Given the enormous hardships confronting southern farmers and industrial workers in the early 1930s it is hardly surprising that so many of them placed their faith in the statist policies of the Roosevelt administration. New Deal welfare, labour and economic reforms brought hope, dignity and material aid to many southerners mired in despair through the loss of their livelihoods. However, while there is no denying the basic popularity of the New Deal among ordinary southerners, the damaging effects of many federal policies belied the overtly populist propaganda of government agencies.

35. R. Biles, *The South and the New Deal* (Lexington, Ky, 1994), p. 18.

This was particularly true of the Agricultural Adjustment Administration (AAA) which successfully boosted the price of southern
staples by curbing overproduction but helped to force thousands
of local farm families off the land by fostering the growth of agribusiness along midwestern lines.[36] The gainers from this process were
the politically powerful cotton and tobacco planters who received
substantial financial incentives from the AAA to withdraw land from
cultivation; the losers were the ordinary farm families of both races
who received the smallest proportion of federal money and who
were impelled to leave the land either because their labour was
no longer required by the local planter or because their own farm
fell victim to the process of land consolidation. Other New Deal
agencies had a similarly disruptive effect on the lives of rural folk
in the southern states. The Tennessee Valley Authority (TVA), for
example, provided cheap electricity for individuals across a broad
swathe of the South, but also contributed significantly to the urban
drift by promoting the ends of industry and agribusiness rather
than those of the small farmer.

Although some historians have justly criticised the New Deal's
impact upon the South, it would be wrong to see the 1930s as an
unmitigated disaster for ordinary southerners. The decade *was*
a watershed in the history of the region, but its importance lies
primarily in the modernising trends which it helped to accelerate.
Some of these trends had beneficial consequences for ordinary
southerners. Leaving the land for the city could mean a break with
rural poverty and a more comfortable life in one of the region's
growing towns. New Deal labour legislation combined with grass-
roots union activity to boost industrial wages, eroding the South's
isolation (or competitive edge, depending on one's point of view)
as a low-wage economy. The US Department of Agriculture's aggressively developmental strategy certainly helped to end the world of
the sharecropper, but it would be wrong to romanticise that existence, hard, back-breaking work as cotton cultivation undoubtedly
was.[37] What is clear is that New Deal agencies such as the TVA
and the AAA brought the South closer to the American mainstream by undermining its distinctiveness and opening up its people
to the uneven benefits and harsh realities of modern industrial
capitalism.

36. P. Daniel, *Standing at the Crossroads: Southern Life Since 1900* (New York, 1986),
p. 121.
37. M. Crawford, 'The Legal System and Sharecropping: An Opposing View' in
Race and Class, ed. Stokes and Halpern, p. 109.

The anti-Roosevelt reaction of the late 1930s failed to stem the pace of change. Indeed, America's entry into the Second World War merely intensified the pressures on the old order. As Pete Daniel has rightly indicated, for many southerners the war was their New Deal.[38] Massive federal defence spending contributed significantly to the processes of urbanisation and industrialisation. The shift to wartime production eventually doubled the region's industrial plant over its 1939 level and led to the dramatic growth of many cities. The metropolitan area of Alabama's premier Gulf port, Mobile, nearly doubled in size to 200,000 owing to the expansion of naval facilities, and numerous smaller towns saw their populations grow as army bases proliferated.[39] Roughly 25 per cent of the South's farm population left the land during the war, not only because of job opportunities in the cities but also because higher wage costs and federal subsidies led many planters to replace their labourers with machines.[40]

The South, in short, was dragged into the modern era by a variety of factors beyond the control of those political elites most committed to the retention of Jim Crow. Yet Jim Crow itself appeared remarkably resilient in the face of unparalleled change. Violence against blacks, including sporadic lynchings, continued during the 1930s and 1940s. Public transport remained rigidly segregated. So too did southern theatres, cinemas, churches, parks, beaches and schools. Black career prospects were still heavily circumscribed and services for African-American communities showed minimal signs of improvement. Why, after all this social turmoil, did the ideological superstructure of the old plantation system remain intact as late as 1950? Why, to rephrase the question, was a fully-fledged civil rights movement necessary when the main economic rationale for segregation – the demand for a reliable pool of cheap labour – had been destroyed by the forces of historical change?

The answers to these questions are numerous. One of the most obvious is that southern segregation rested on much more than just a need for cheap labour. As the persistent popular antipathy towards miscegenation revealed, there was a powerful psychological and sexual dimension to southern racism which no amount of economic change could have dispelled. Lower-class whites, moreover, had always had a large stake in the maintenance of the caste system – one which arguably became stronger during times of

38. Daniel, *Standing*, p. 136.
39. N.V. Bartley, *The New South 1945–1980* (Baton Rouge, 1995), p. 10.
40. Ibid., p. 11.

social stress. Possession of a white skin gave individuals a distinct status advantage over blacks enabling members of the Herrenvolk to transcend some of the barriers imposed by class.[41] There were, of course, very real material benefits for ordinary whites to be derived from the maintenance of the caste system. Segregation in the work-place proved particularly resistant to change, even during the late 1930s and 1940s when industrial unions were most active in the fight for racial justice on the shop-floor. Unless pressured by unions or federal agencies, company managers made little attempt to alter a system which reserved the most salubrious and skilled occupations for whites. To do otherwise, they reasoned (not entirely without justice), would be to stir up racial antagonism among white workers whose material privileges depended on maintenance of the colour line. Cracks did begin to appear in the caste system as the twen-tieth century wore on, most notably in the upper South where the burden of racial discrimination had always been less onerous. In general, however, blacks moving from the countryside to the towns found Jim Crow to be rather more adaptable to economic change than many contemporary commentators believed. It would take more than an agricultural revolution to bring about racial justice in the South.

Strong cultural and historical forces also inclined a large pro-portion of southern whites to maintain the racial status quo. Many whites clung to the old stereotypes of blacks as lazy, childlike, licen-tious, criminal and ignorant. This did not mean that they were unable to forge workable relations with the individual blacks they met in their daily life. Some of these relations – for example, those between white women and black domestics – could be genuinely close and empathetic.[42] On the whole, however, whites remained suspicious and not a little fearful of blacks *en masse*. Aside from a minority of humanitarian radicals they were wedded to the notion that white culture was superior to its black counterpart which they regarded as having contributed little of value to the life and mind of the South. They were wrong, of course, for 'coloured' folk were an integral part of the cultural fabric of the southern states. As home-grown civil rights leaders were well aware, southern blacks

41. On the use of the term 'Herrenvolk' in an American context see K.P. Vickery, ' "Herrenvolk" Democracy and Egalitarianism in South Africa and the US South', *Comparative Studies in Society and History* 16 (1974), 309–28, and Fredrickson, *White Supremacy*, pp. xi–xii and *passim*.
42. S. Tucker, 'A Complex Bond: Southern Black Domestic Workers and their White Employers', *Frontiers* 9 (1987), 6–13.

and whites had much in common – an intertwined history, a culture shaped by evangelical Protestantism and, though this would not become entirely apparent until the late 1960s, a shared understanding that southern life had significant advantages over that of the North. That this realisation was not grasped by most whites in 1950 was due firstly to their own ingrained prejudices and secondly, and less obviously, to their acute awareness that white 'civilisation' – the one which their ancestors had fought so valiantly to preserve during the Civil War – was under threat from powerful historical forces.

Southern intellectuals were the first to react to the encroachment of corporate capitalism and statism. The liberals among them, white as well as black, tended to welcome the changes wrought by industrialisation, urbanisation and the New Deal. Aware that the South lagged culturally and economically behind the northern states, they insisted that the region would have to shed its devotion to the past, to the existing social and political order, if it were to prosper in the modern age. Those of a more conservative disposition rejected criticism of the South and feared that the alienation of ordinary southerners from the soil would destroy the gains they had derived from a predominantly rural, close-knit and organic society. Some, like the poet, Allen Tate, found a degree of refuge in the agrarian past which liberals chose to excoriate – the putative opposition of the South's antebellum political hero, John C. Calhoun, to industrial capitalism and the patriotic deeds of Confederate warriors like Robert E. Lee.[43] Others, notably the influential Chapel Hill sociologist, Howard Odum, sought a middle way between centralism and sectionalism by elevating the concept of regionalism to new heights during the interwar period. Odum's progressive emphasis on data collection and evaluation made him aware of the South's shortcomings in the realm of wealth creation and race relations, but his sensitivity to the distinctiveness of southern life led him to endorse a regional planning organisation as the solution to local problems. Federal intervention in local affairs or radical protest against the caste system, he believed, would be counter-productive because they jarred with the essential rhythms of southern history and society.[44]

Ordinary southern whites, the folk in whom academics like Odum and Tate placed so much faith, were poorly placed to rationalise

43. M. O'Brien, *The Idea of the American South 1920–1941* (Baltimore and London, 1979), pp. 141–3.
44. Ibid., pp. 51–93.

the trends which were changing their lives so quickly during the 1930s and 1940s. They knew, however, that their lives *were* being transformed and that the old ways, the old certainties, were no longer secure. Their inclination was not to understand the hidden processes of change in clinical academic terms but rather to identify the visible threats to the existing social order. Unsurprisingly, given the lead provided by politicians and the press as well as their own strong sense of history and unshaken commitment to the values of American conservatism, southern whites discovered two overriding threats to their way of life. The first of these was the mushrooming power of the federal government; the second, the meddlesome activities of northern civil rights organisations. And the event which contributed most to this discovery and crystallised white opposition to racial justice after the Second World War was the decision of the US Supreme Court to declare segregated schools unconstitutional in May 1954. Chief Justice Earl Warren's landmark ruling in *Brown v. Board of Education* set in train a long series of events that culminated, via 'massive resistance' and the direct action phase of the modern civil rights movement, in the destruction of the southern caste system during the 1960s. But *Brown* itself was the product of a lengthy and concerted campaign against Jim Crow spearheaded by the NAACP. To the first phase of the struggle for black freedom we now turn.

CHAPTER 2

A Pre-history of the
Civil Rights Movement

In 1956 the recently appointed head of the NAACP, Roy Wilkins, rejected a claim by Dr Martin Luther King that the ongoing bus boycott in Montgomery, Alabama, revealed the emergence of 'the New Negro'. Insisted Wilkins, 'The Negro of 1956 who stands on his own two feet is not a new Negro; he is the grandson or the great grandson of the men who hated slavery. By his own hands, through his own struggles, in his own organised groups – of churches, fraternal societies, the NAACP and others – he has fought his way to the place where he now stands.'[1]

Wilkins had several reasons for making this statement. He was suspicious of King's sudden rise to national fame and had grave doubts concerning the utility of the southern preacher's principal strategy of nonviolent direct action. Moreover, he was understandably keen to highlight the central role that his own organisation had played in the battle for freedom, a role that had done much to produce the Supreme Court's invalidation of segregated schools in the case of *Brown v. Board of Education* and would eventually bring the Montgomery bus boycott itself to a successful conclusion. Notwithstanding the existence of personal and political motives, however, few modern historians would reject Wilkins's contention that the embryonic civil rights movement was built on a myriad of past struggles. The mobilisation of an entire community in Montgomery did suggest that the scale and pace of protest activity was beginning to change, but the bus boycott was not the first indication that ordinary black people were ready to fight for their rights. During the first 40 years of the twentieth century black Americans,

---

1. R. Wilkins quoted in D.L. Watson, 'Assessing the Role of the NAACP in the Civil Rights Movement', *The Historian* 55 (1993), 462–3.

in the rural South as well as the urban North, developed a multiplicity of strategies intended to bring them a greater measure of justice, dignity and equality. Each of these strategies relied for success
partly on organisational development (which in turn was heavily
dependent on existing institutions and networks in the black community) and partly on the working of impersonal historical forces.
Pre-eminent among the latter was the economic collapse of the
1930s which shook American capitalism to the core and tested the
nation's faith in liberal democracy to the limits. The Roosevelt
administration's interventionist response to the profound social and
economic problems caused by the Depression produced a political
atmosphere conducive not only to the NAACP's increasingly coherent strategy of undermining Jim Crow through the courts but also
to the class struggle of the Communist Party and the mainstream
labour movement. Large numbers of ordinary black folk throughout
the country were politicised and radicalised by these developments,
all of which contributed to the evolution of a fully-fledged civil
rights movement.

Community building and political struggle before 1933

It is one of the many ironies of American history that the modern
civil rights movement was in large measure a product of the black
communities created by *de jure* and *de facto* segregation. There was,
of course, no such thing as an entirely healthy, homogeneous and
united black community anywhere in the United States during the
early twentieth century. One of the chief goals of the civil rights
movement was actually to forge a degree of black unity in places
where, historically, it had not existed. Black communities throughout
the expanding Republic were riven, like white ones, by differences
of class, culture, colour and gender which were often accentuated
by the pressures induced by racism and segregation. Cities like
Detroit, New York and Chicago were home to small but relatively
affluent elites made up principally of black businessmen who catered
to the material needs of ordinary African Americans. Setting up
banks, insurance companies, stores and newspapers in the ghetto,
they clearly had a stake in the maintenance of the existing system,
for segregation provided them with a ready (if far from captive)
market for their products. Predictably their political instincts were

often conservative, even though many of them sought to utilise their ties to white political and business leaders to improve the lot of blacks less fortunate than themselves. Such elites existed on a smaller scale in most southern towns, although larger cities like Atlanta were able to support thriving upper-class communities of their own. Further down the urban social ladder was a growing black middle class of preachers, lawyers, clerical workers, teachers and editors who provided some of the impetus for the first phase of the civil rights struggle. Although, to some extent, they too were beneficiaries of segregation (black schools, for example, usually required black teachers), middle-class blacks had weaker ties to the white power structure and, because of their relatively high level of educational attainment, held positive expectations of what they could achieve in the United States, particularly in the North where there had been no counter-revolution after Reconstruction.

The vast majority of black people belonged to neither of these privileged socio-economic categories. Those with jobs in the urban North tended to work as unskilled labourers in the nation's manufacturing and service industries. Those who could obtain an assembly-line job with a firm like Ford in Detroit were fortunate. Henry Ford had something of the old-style paternalist's attitude towards blacks and recognised that a workforce segmented along racial lines was likely to prove more pliable than an ethnically homogeneous one.[2] Consequently he offered competitive wages to black workers thereby making Detroit one of the most attractive destinations for migrant southerners after 1915. Most lower-class blacks in the North, however, toiled for long hours and poor pay in unsanitary and often unsafe conditions. Their daily work experience in the ubiquitous factories and stockyards of industrialising America resembled that of European-stock migrants, but the prospects for promotion were severely reduced by discriminatory rates of pay, occluded seniority lines and shop-floor racism. While black women were employed in northern industry, particularly during wartime, the bulk of them found employment as domestic service workers as did their peers in the urban South.

The black community of Kansas City typified those to be found in large metropolitan centres across America. When the young Roy Wilkins arrived there to take up a newspaper job in 1923 he found local blacks deeply divided among themselves. At the foot of the

2. A. Meier and E. Rudwick, *Black Detroit and the Rise of the UAW* (New York and Oxford, 1979), pp. 5–14.

social pile, he observed, 'was a floating world of hustlers, torpedoes, fly-by-night artists, and easy women. The center was held by solid workingmen, railroad porters, hod carriers, and truck drivers . . . At the top was a prosperous upper-middle class of doctors, lawyers, dentists, pharmacists, teachers, school principals, and a scattering of businessmen.' What passed for black society in this segregated town was 'a tight little circle' dominated by members of the all-male Ivanhoe Club whose family residences stood on the Paseo overlooking the industrial sprawl below.[3]

The tensions apparent in black communities across America were not entirely a product of economic disparities between social classes. Upper- and middle-class blacks differed from the mass of their peers not only in terms of their wealth and education, but also because of their colour – many of them were light-skinned mulattoes whose closer proximity to 'whiteness' gave them a greater measure of status in a society taught to regard blackness as a badge of inferiority. It was no accident that many of the early twentieth-century civil rights leaders were light-skinned blacks, including the controversial Walter White, executive secretary of the NAACP between 1930 and 1955, who was able to 'pass' as a member of the dominant race on investigative trips to the Deep South. Lower-class blacks, many of whom had recently migrated from the countryside to the city, were also derided for cultural attachments (to types of food, clothing, music and religion) arising out of their rural past. Indeed, one of the chief functions of the National Urban League, a northern-based equal rights organisation founded in 1910 to pro-mote better job and housing conditions for blacks, was to socialise displaced southerners into the more modern, and supposedly more sophisticated, world of the urban North.

Although internal divisions posed an obstacle to black unity in the United States, they did not constitute an insuperable barrier to the development of viable protest movements. For while lower-class blacks led a less comfortable existence than the kind of men who dominated the elite dining clubs of the larger cities, all members of the race had one thing in common: each of them was stigmat-ised as inferior by whites because they possessed a black skin. Even Walter White discovered that his light features and father's respect-able position as a mail carrier did not protect him from the spectre of white violence when a riot engulfed his Atlanta neighbourhood

3. R. Wilkins with T. Mathews, *Standing Fast: The Autobiography of Roy Wilkins* (New York, 1982), pp. 76–7.

in 1906.[4] Members of the Ivanhoe Club in Kansas City were forced to dine in private homes because they were not allowed into downtown restaurants.[5] Widespread racial prejudice, therefore, meant that blacks of every hue, sex and social class possessed a common enemy – a fact which highlighted the potential for mutual struggle against segregation even if it could hardly be said to have indicated the existence of racial solidarity.

It is something of a commonplace in recent studies of the African-American experience in the twentieth century to assert that segregation empowered blacks by fostering strong community institutions in which successful civil rights activity was grounded.[6] This view is not without merit, for blacks were able to create durable grass-roots institutions in the Jim Crow South and the urban North. However, references to 'empowerment' and 'community building' overstate the ability of blacks to control their own lives in an age in which racism and capitalist development were twin barriers to black advancement on a community front. The reality was that American blacks were not empowered by segregation any more than black South Africans were empowered by apartheid. Institutions like the family, the church, schools, civic clubs, Masonic lodges and black businesses imparted a fair degree of dignity and autonomy to blacks in the United States, but none of them alone offered a concrete threat to the existing socio-economic order on which white dominance was based. Many of the institutions lauded by modern historians were far from stable. This was true, for example, of most black businesses which were typically undercapitalised and therefore especially vulnerable to the devastating shocks which periodically hit the American economy. Others, including the black family and underfunded public schools, were under constant strain, particularly in the most overcrowded neighbourhoods of the ghetto and poverty-stricken areas of the Deep South. The reality for African Americans in the first half of the twentieth century was not power, but lack of it.

This said, the existence of strong community-based institutions was an essential precondition for the development of a viable civil rights movement which could appeal to black people across classes

4. W. White, *A Man Called White: The Autobiography of Walter White* (London, 1949), p. 12.
5. Wilkins, *Standing Fast*, p. 76.
6. See e.g. A. Morris, *The Origins of the Civil Rights Movement: Black Communities Organizing for Change* (New York, 1984), pp. 1–16, and E. Lewis, *In Their Own Interests: Race, Class and Power in Twentieth-Century Norfolk, Virginia* (Berkeley, 1991), p. 47.

and geographical space. In this respect, kinfolk and educators played a critical role in inculcating a sense of racial pride into generations of black children, an achievement of inestimable value given the potentially demoralising impact of white racism on morale. Widely read black newspapers such as the *Chicago Defender*, the *Pittsburgh Courier*, and the *Baltimore Afro-American* served a similar purpose, although by no means all black editors were fearless opponents of racial discrimination, particularly in the southern states where there were obvious constraints on crusading zeal.[7] A variety of fraternal organisations and civic clubs run largely but not exclusively by middle-class blacks provided important forums for community activism throughout the nation's urban centres. Many of these local groups were spawned by the Progressive era's confidence in organisation as a tool for effective social and political reform. Black women often took the lead in forming such groups, most of which sought improvements in individual moral conduct as well as municipal services such as housing, transportation, schools, recreational facilities and street-lighting.[8] Arguably the most significant black institution of all, however, was the church; for religion, specifically the African-American variants of evangelical Protestantism, lay at the heart of popular culture and daily life.

While the bulk of black Christians worshipped in one of the churches of the black Baptist and Methodist establishment, a significant minority belonged to the increasingly popular holiness churches or the mainstream white denominations (which possessed separate black wings of their own). Catering as they did for all manner of occupational groups and creeds, the black churches did not contribute as much to the unity of the race as one might have expected. All of them, however, constituted a focal point for black social life throughout the working year. Not only did they act as a physical and emotional refuge from the strains of everyday life – public spaces where black men and women (particularly women) could worship and socialise together beyond the gaze of white employers – but they also provided a structured arena for surrogate political activity and furnished essential resources for community building.[9] Many of the civic clubs alluded to above could not have

---

7. N. McMillen, *Dark Journey: Black Mississippians in the Age of Jim Crow* (Urbana and Chicago, 1989), p. 175.

8. G. Lerner, 'Early Community Work of Black Club Women', *Journal of Negro History* 59 (1974), 158–67.

9. E.F. Frazier, *The Negro Church in America* (pbk edn, New York, 1974), pp. 35–51.

existed without the funds, buildings and leadership capabilities furnished by the black church. Indeed, many of them grew directly out of prominent religious establishments like the Abyssinian Baptist Church in Harlem and the Bethel African Methodist Episcopal Church in Detroit.

A pronounced commitment to distinctively emotional and demonstrative forms of evangelical Protestantism, of course, was not necessarily a threat to the racial status quo. For many blacks, particularly those belonging to quietistic denominations, worship was essentially a sacred and otherwordly experience which did not feed into civil rights activity. In many cases local preachers were too reliant on the white power structure for approval or funding and therefore reluctant to embrace any cause that smacked of social radicalism. At the very least, however, the vast majority of black ministers and congregations helped to promote the spirit of self-help which was so visible a feature of the African-American experience in the early twentieth century. In some cases this did result in efforts to reform the wider society – to make the soaring promises of the Republic's civil religion a reality for blacks. In others, particularly northern storefront churches remote from the black and white Protestant establishments, the impetus to rely on one's own resources led individuals and whole congregations to espouse the tenets of radical black nationalism.

The growth and evolution of remarkably sturdy institutions within the segregated world of black America furthered the development of a vibrant African-American culture in the United States evidenced in the day-to-day interactions of countless individuals and, more specifically, in distinctive forms of music, kinship patterns, dialect, recreation, food preferences and spirituality. While many of these cultural manifestations, not least the lower class's preference for drinking dens and soul food, were distasteful to elite blacks who often shared the mores of white America, they nevertheless imparted meaning to the lives of ordinary blacks and underlined the reality of African-American distinctiveness. And while culture could and did accentuate class divisions at times, it is important to point out that it was just as often a unifying factor. One did not, for example, have to be a factory worker in Detroit to appreciate Joe Louis's stunning first-round victory over the German heavyweight, Max Schmeling, at Yankee Stadium in 1938. 'I think that must have been the shortest, sweetest minute of the entire thirties', remembered Roy Wilkins who had left Kansas City for New York to take up a permanent position with the NAACP.[10] Millions of black Americans, poor and middle-class, shared his pride in the exploits of the 'Brown Bomber'.

Yet cultural resources, no matter how firmly grounded in community institutions, were flimsy weapons with which to confront Jim Crow, let alone the virulent racism which pervaded the entire country. The reality was that blacks lacked political and economic power and did so in large measure because they constituted a demographic minority, roughly a tenth, of the population of the United States.

Inevitably, perhaps, given the extent of intraracial friction and the different constraints which existed on protest activity in the northern and southern states, no common strategy for progress emerged during the first half of the twentieth century. Historians have tended to analyse black protest activity in this period in terms of three broad and largely discrete strategies: accommodationism, integrationism and separatism (black nationalism). While this categorisation possesses validity, it not only tends to obscure the fact that race leaders of all stripes had a number of similar goals, but also disguises the debates over tactics and allies which took place between advocates of the same strategy, and ignores some of the common cultural and institutional foundations on which many of these high-profile figures built their respective organisations.

Mainstream black protest in the first three decades of the twentieth century was primarily the work of middle-class leaders committed to the task of racial uplift.[11] They believed that if blacks could prove their worth by adopting the much-touted values of the civilised (i.e. white) world then they would finally be accepted as equals in American society. Heavily infused with the values of turn-of-the-century bourgeois morality, the ideology of racial uplift encapsulated the black leadership's longing for white approbation. Although it is tempting to dismiss their calls for hard work, thrift, sobriety, cleanliness, and education on the part of the black masses as entirely selfish, their credo was rooted in concepts of service to the group even if it frequently encapsulated a rather ambivalent attitude towards the 'Negro' race as a whole. On the one hand the masses, often romanticised as 'the folk', represented the future of the black race in the New World; on the other, they were considered disreputable and unruly because of their lack of bourgeois discipline.

10. Wilkins, *Standing Fast*, p. 164.
11. K.K. Gaines, *Uplifting the Race: Black Leadership, Politics, and Culture in the Twentieth Century* (Chapel Hill and London, 1996), pp. 1–46.

The duality inherent within the credo was made more pronounced by its mix of assimilationism and black nationalism. This was most clearly evident in the elite's stress on self-help as a strategy designed not only to persuade whites that black people were capable of progress, but also to promote a greater sense of racial pride.

The foremost exponent of racial uplift in the United States in the early twentieth century was Booker T. Washington, a former slave who rose to become, in the eyes of most whites and many blacks, the Moses of his race. From his power-base at the all-black Tuskegee Institute in Alabama, Washington exhorted blacks to soft-pedal on their Civil War-era struggle for the suffrage and shift their focus to education.[12] In part, Washington's reasoning was pragmatic. Influenced by the upsurge in lynching during the 1890s, he contended that a primary emphasis on self-help in the form of industrial training would quell white suspicions of black struggle. However, while Washington's variant of racial uplift, an ambiguous combination of accommodationism and separatism, clearly made a good deal of common sense in the context of the time, it did not go unchallenged within the black community.

One of Washington's principal opponents was a northern-born academic, W.E.B. Du Bois. Although Du Bois ended his long life as a Stalinist in exile, he was, during his early career, an unrepentant elitist who believed that middle-class blacks like himself – the so-called 'talented tenth' – had to bear the burden of uplifting the race. Initially a strong supporter of Washington, his intellectual training as a social scientist eventually combined with the press of events (in particular a murderous, anti-black race riot in Springfield, Illinois, in 1908) to make him an advocate of more confrontational strategies. In 1909 he opted to join sympathetic whites, some of whom possessed direct links to the old abolitionist movement, in forming the NAACP.[13] During the first two decades of the NAACP's existence Du Bois served as editor of its official newspaper, *The Crisis*, while the organisation itself attempted to promote racial change through the courts and by publicising the horrors of lynching. Notwithstanding the limited nature of its initial successes, the NAACP proved attractive to many working-class and middle-class blacks in the 1910s and 1920s. The formation of branches in some of the South's leading commercial centres was a clear indication

12. G.M. Fredrickson, *Black Liberation: A Comparative History of Black Ideologies in the United States and South Africa* (New York and Oxford, 1995), pp. 35–6.
13. D.L. Lewis, *W.E.B. Du Bois: Biography of a Race 1868–1919* (New York, 1993), pp. 386–407, and Fredrickson, *Black Liberation*, pp. 104–14.

that a distinct political consciousness existed among blacks in that region, Booker T. Washington's enormous popularity (even after his death in 1915) notwithstanding.

Although black socialists like A. Philip Randolph, the Florida-born founder of the all-black trade union, the Brotherhood of Sleeping Car Porters (BSCP), urged African Americans to concentrate on cooperation with the nation's emerging labour movement, the fiercest competition to the reformism of the NAACP and the putatively apolitical strategy of Washington and his disciples was provided in the 1920s by a Jamaican immigrant, Marcus Garvey. Expertly blending self-help with spell-binding appeals to race pride and a compelling (some said ludicrous) use of ritual pageantry, Garvey won the support of large numbers of urban blacks frustrated by the lack of racial progress in the aftermath of the First World War.[14] By 1925 his Universal Negro Improvement Association (UNIA) claimed half a million members, a substantial grass-roots following which dwarfed that of the NAACP. This fact alone made Garvey a grievous threat to the mainstream black establishment. The African Methodist Episcopal bishop of Michigan, Charles S. Smith, denounced Garvey to the Justice Department in Washington as a Bolshevik 'who should either be required to discontinue his present vicious propaganda and fake practices or be deported as an undesirable'.[15] The federal government needed no convincing that Garvey was a menace to good order in the United States. In 1923 he was found guilty of mail fraud, jailed, and finally, in December 1927, deported.

There was little love lost between the West Indian and his African-American civil rights opponents who favoured interracial cooperation and who were embarrassed by his fondness for pomp and ceremony. Du Bois, never one to mince his words, called Garvey 'a little, fat black man' who was 'the most dangerous enemy of the Negro race in America and the world', while Randolph's *Messenger* labelled him 'the supreme Negro Jamaican Jackass', a 'monumental monkey', and 'an unquestioned fool and ignoramus'.[16] Such ungenerous criticisms (to which Garvey did not hesitate to respond in kind) foreshadowed the ferocious slanging matches which would scar the relationship between Garvey's nationalist heir, Malcolm X,

---

14. Fredrickson, *Black Liberation*, pp. 152–61.
15. Quoted in R.W. Thomas, *Life for Us Is What We Make It: Building Black Community in Detroit, 1915–1945* (Bloomington and Indianapolis, 1992), p. 195.
16. All quotations from L.W. Levine, 'Marcus Garvey and the Politics of Revitalization' in *Black Leaders of the Twentieth Century*, ed. J.H. Franklin and A. Meier (Urbana and Chicago, 1982), pp. 133–4.

and leaders of the civil rights movement in the early 1960s. However, they should not be allowed to obscure significant points of agreement between Garvey and his opponents, above all their mutual insistence that self-help must be an integral component of racial uplift and that people of colour everywhere should not have to apologise for being black. Garvey's strident calls for the internationalisation of the racial struggle, moreover, a product of his British imperial background, were echoed by Du Bois, himself an influential figure in the interwar Pan-African Congress movement. Nor did one have to be a member of the dispossessed or the black working class to find his message appealing. Representatives of the petite bourgeoisie occupied the majority of leadership positions in local branches of the UNIA. Charles Hamilton Houston, an elite Washington lawyer was not one of them – indeed, he would soon commit himself to the NAACP's legal campaign against segregation – but he too was inspired by Garvey's powerful appeals to race pride.[17] Rhetorically, the gap between Garvey and his critics was substantial; ideologically, it was often narrower than many contemporaries supposed.

On the eve of the Great Depression in 1929 black protest had achieved only minor successes. Garvey had helped to raise the consciousness of many African Americans, but he had failed to make significant inroads into the culture of fear and deference which obstructed racial progress below the Mason–Dixon Line. The National Urban League contributed to the stability of rapidly expanding urban communities but did little to alleviate the poverty which stifled so many black lives in the cities. A. Philip Randolph continued to lambast the economic system which underlay many of the injustices of American life but struggled to find a voice in the labour movement (dominated by the conservative American Federation of Labor), let alone in the country at large. The NAACP managed to win a handful of legal victories against the grandfather clause, the white primary and mob violence, but discrimination remained rife throughout the nation and the southern caste system was largely untouched by its activities. Its campaign against lynching had generated interest and there were signs that the practice was dying out. This latter fact, however, was a consequence not only of the NAACP's struggle for a federal anti-lynching act (which failed to overcome the potent obstacle of southern political power in the Senate) but

17. G.R. McNeil, *Groundwork: Charles Hamilton Houston and the Struggle for Civil Rights* (Philadelphia, 1983), pp. 99–100.

also of the activities of home-grown white reformers, principally those associated with the Commission on Interracial Cooperation (CIC).[18] Founded in Atlanta in 1919 to combat the racial violence which flared after the First World War, the Commission tried to persuade southern whites that lynching ran counter to their own interests by bringing the region into disrepute, by stalling modernisation and by undermining social order. Led by prominent lay Methodists and Presbyterians, and spawning the Association of Southern Women for the Prevention of Lynching led by Jessie Daniel Ames, it had helped to reduce the number of blacks lynched annually to single figures by 1932.[19] For all their successes, however, most southern white liberals remained creatures of their section. This is to say, firstly, that they rejected the NAACP's call for a federal anti-lynching law on the grounds that such a measure would inflame white opinion and endanger southern liberties under the Constitution; and secondly, that their struggle against mob violence took place within the confines of the southern caste system. Not until the late 1930s would some southern liberals (perhaps 'radicals' is a more accurate description in this context) like Will Alexander, head of the CIC, begin to conclude that lasting social progress in their region was dependent on the destruction of *de jure* segregation.

  Most blacks, it should be emphasised, did not take part in overt reform activities in the first three decades of the twentieth century. Generally speaking, southern croppers and tenant farmers were preoccupied with scratching out a living. Lacking both resources and political consciousness, their protests were confined largely to the realm of what Robin D.G. Kelley has termed 'infrapolitics' – the consolidation of an alternative African-American culture largely hidden from the view of whites in the segregated world of the rural and small-town South, sporadic acts of sabotage in the workplace, and generally unpremeditated contraventions of southern racial etiquette.[20] The black middle class in the rural and urban areas of the region tended to adhere to a distinctly Washingtonian view of life. While a minority such as the Atlantans, Walter White and Martin Luther King's maternal grandfather, the Rev. A.D. Williams, opted to organise a branch of the NAACP, others sought advancement through involvement in mainstream politics (often in the

  18. R.L. Zangrando, *The NAACP Crusade Against Lynching, 1909–1950* (Philadelphia, 1980), pp. 51–97.
  19. M. Sosna, *In Search of the Silent South: Southern Liberals and the Race Issue* (New York, 1977), pp. 20–41.
  20. R.D.G. Kelley, ' "We Are Not What We Seem": Rethinking Black Working-Class Opposition in the Jim Crow South', *JAH* 80 (1993), 75–112.

Republicans' rotten boroughs of the Deep South); in community organisations like the Young Men's Christian Association, the Young Women's Christian Association and the church which brought them into contact with liberal whites; or in business ventures dependent on the existence of a segregated body of black consumers. As Ralph Abernathy, the scion of an independent black landowning family in rural Alabama, recalled, African Americans brought up in the Jim Crow South knew that the system was wrong, but 'felt too intimidated by the pervasiveness of it and by the fact that it seemed so old and so ingrained, a part of the landscape, like the slant of a hillside or the hang of a massive oak tree'.[21] He might have added that southern blacks were only too aware that, potentially, opposition to the status quo was punishable by death.

Reform activity was a more viable option outside the South. Northern blacks could vote, participate more freely in civic affairs and had a better chance of attaining wealth and status. In spite of experiencing police harassment, resurgent Klan activity and high rates of crime, they did not dwell in a society built largely on the threat of violence. Their chief concern during the 1920s was the attainment of a higher quality of life than that experienced by most southern blacks. This objective led a small number of mainly middle-class professionals into the NAACP or the National Urban League, but most upwardly mobile blacks focused their energies on personal advancement in the workplace and/or the establishment of stable communities through their membership of the churches, Ys, fraternal lodges, political clubs and black business organisations. Working-class blacks were also involved in institution building, seeking advancement through membership of company unions, churches and the UNIA. Their fragile economic base and preoccupation with poor social conditions, however, left them with fewer opportunities to engage in civil rights activities than their middle-class counterparts. Those who sought to promote their cause by participating in politics often found that their efforts were derailed by professional politicians of their own race who, as in parts of the South, channelled black votes to white political leaders in return for minor patronage rewards rather than community development. By 1930, then, protest activity had failed to undermine significantly the nationwide system of segregation and discrimination which confined most blacks to the bottom of the pile. A new phase of civil rights protest, however, was about to dawn and the economic depression of the 1930s was its harbinger.

---

21. R.D. Abernathy, *And the Walls Came Tumbling Down* (New York, 1990), p. 33.

The New Deal era

One might suppose that the Great Depression had a relatively light impact on African Americans because they had less to lose than whites from the Wall Street Crash and the general economic collapse which followed in its wake. Nothing could be further from the truth. On the whole whites did have further to fall than blacks – more of them had prospered during the 1920s and there can be no denying the traumatic effect that the loss of wealth and jobs had on the country's once buoyant middle and upper classes. Whites, however, had greater resources on which to fall back than the bulk of black people: land, kinship networks, residual investments and even, if necessary, menial jobs previously occupied by African Americans or other minority groups. Blacks were less equipped to ride out the storm and middle-class and lower-class communities alike were devastated as a consequence. Two million black farmers were forced off the land in the South by the collapse of staple prices and the federal government's policy of favouring planters over tenants and croppers. Many of them swelled the ranks of the jobless in the region's urban centres. Black unemployment in some cities reached at least 30 per cent – up to 75 per cent in Atlanta's poorest neighbourhoods.[22] Initially, municipal and state authorities were unprepared to meet their needs. Hunger, disease and squalor brought many to the verge of despair. Roy Wilkins's statement that the 1930s were 'a terrible time for Negroes' was something of an understatement.[23]

Black efforts to resist the appalling impact of the Depression took many forms but can be divided into three permeable categories: leftist activism, mainstream reformism within the New Deal coalition, and the development of a coherent strategy of litigation on the part of the NAACP. Although the third of these protest forms culminated in the *Brown* decision of 1954, it was arguably the first two which offered blacks the most immediate hope of equal justice.

From early 1933 onwards the Democratic administration of Franklin D. Roosevelt intervened decisively to shore up the ramparts of the nation's economic system and protect ordinary Americans from the worst effects of the Depression. Encouraged by the 1935 National Labor Relations Act which aimed to enhance the bargaining power of workers, industrial labour leaders launched a series of

22. R. Biles, *The South and the New Deal* (Lexington, Ky, 1994), p. 19.
23. Wilkins, *Standing Fast*, p. 146.

grass-roots organising campaigns intended to promote the growth of trade unions in what had hitherto been poorly organised sectors of the economy such as coal, steel, textiles, and meat packing. The prevalence of African-American workers in the bulk of these industries forced ambitious union leaders to begin the difficult task of forging a biracial movement strong enough to withstand the twin threats of white racism and conservative hostility to labour radicalism.

Because the historical relationship between blacks and organised labour was at best an ambivalent one, it was hardly surprising that when the Depression unleashed a wave of labour unrest upon the country, blacks tended to remain wary of organised labour's attempts to improve the condition of ordinary working-people. To some extent, however, their suspicions were eroded by the rapid growth of industrial unionism spearheaded by John L. Lewis of the United Mine Workers of America (UMWA) and other trade union leaders in the mass production sectors of the economy. The founding of the Congress of Industrial Organizations (CIO) in November 1935 posed an immediate threat to the AFL's conservative grip on American labour – a threat which became evident within months as CIO organisers began to mobilise groups of workers hitherto ignored by the trade union movement.[24] Significantly, many of these organisers recognised that if industrial workers were to be unionised effectively they had to operate on an interracial basis. Failure to extend their activities to workers belonging to minority racial groups, particularly those occupying strategically vital positions in the production process (for example, the kill floors of midwestern meat-packing plants), would merely allow employers to utilise blacks as strike-breakers as they had done in the past.[25] Some of them, moreover, were ideologically predisposed to interracial organising. In theory neither socialism nor Communism distinguished between white and black proletarians.

The consequence of this dramatic upsurge in union activity, encouraged as it appeared to be by New Deal labour legislation, was that increasing numbers of blacks began to join CIO unions. This is not to say that all industrial workers embraced interracial cooperation although there was evidence in certain areas that the severity of the Depression helped to promote class solidarity across

24. CIO stood for Committee for Industrial Organization until November 1938.
25. R. Halpern, 'Organized Labor, Black Workers, and the Twentieth Century South: The Emerging Revision' in *Race and Class in the American South Since 1890*, ed. M. Stokes and R. Halpern (Oxford and Providence, 1994), pp. 63–4.

the colour line. In the port city of Seattle, for example, black and white maritime workers struck together in 1934, whereas during the previous decade African Americans had been happy to act as strike-breakers in a dispute involving the Pacific shipping companies and their white employees.[26] White working-class racism, however, was a major obstacle to interracial unionism. So too was the understandable suspicion felt by many black workers and community leaders towards trades unionism and their loyalty to paternalistic corporations like Ford in Detroit. Yet, while labour organisers often trod warily on the race question, the key unions behind the legendary organising campaigns of the 1930s sometimes made strenuous efforts not only to promote interracial solidarity, but also to ensure that blacks enjoyed equal rights in the workplace.[27] It was, after all, unlikely that black workers would flock to join the new CIO unions unless they saw concrete evidence that union practices were beginning to change for the better.

From the outset mainstream CIO unions like the UMWA, its offshoot, the Steel Workers Organizing Committee, and the United Auto Workers (UAW) evinced a relatively strong commitment to equal rights. They took on black organisers, emphasised interracial solidarity on the shop-floor, and accepted the right of blacks to participate equally in union affairs and occupy leadership positions in union locals (i.e. branches). The pattern was not a uniform one. In the South, where organising was particularly hazardous owing to the entrenched, often violent, resistance of state authorities and company police, CIO unions found white working-class racism a major barrier to interracial unionism. In Birmingham, Alabama, Steelworkers' locals cut a deal with the powerful Tennessee Coal and Iron Company which preserved white interests by augmenting the seniority rights of white workers.[28] Because efforts to unionise blacks in many southern cities threatened to drive whites into rival AFL-affiliated locals, some CIO leaders concluded that it might be necessary to delay organising blacks for the foreseeable future.[29] Mobilising southern workers proved somewhat easier during the Second World War, principally because the federal bureaucracy

26. Q. Taylor, *The Forging of a Black Community: Seattle's Central District from 1870 through the Civil Rights Era* (Seattle and London, 1994), pp. 68–70.

27. Halpern, 'Organized Labor', pp. 43–76.

28. R.J. Norrell, 'Caste in Steel: Jim Crow Careers in Birmingham, Alabama', *JAH* 73 (1986), 677.

29. Ibid., p. 674; M. Honey, 'Industrial Unionism and Racial Justice in Memphis' in *Organized Labor in the Twentieth-Century South*, ed. R.H. Zieger (Knoxville, 1991) pp. 139–40.

displayed a greater willingness to enforce collective bargaining rights and the closed shop. Nevertheless, the CIO's southern leadership remained decidedly reluctant to launch a frontal assault on Jim Crow. Indeed, some of their number, like Memphis labour boss, William Copeland, showed every sign of wanting to retain the essential bulwarks of the caste system which so many white workers regarded as crucial to their economic well-being.[30]

American trade unions during the 1930s and early 1940s indulged in a wide range of racial practices. Generally speaking those on the left of the political spectrum, particularly unions led by or containing significant numbers of communists and those in which black workers played a major role, proved to be the most radical supporters of equal rights.[31] Thus, the communist-led Food, Tobacco, Agricultural and Allied Workers Union (FTA) successfully organised low-paid black workers, many of them women, at the R.J. Reynolds Tobacco Company in Winston-Salem, North Carolina. The FTA's Local 22 inaugurated citizenship classes, voter registration campaigns and mass meetings, all of these initiatives designed to promote civil rights at the grass-roots.[32] Nationally around 50 per cent of the union's members were women and 75–80 per cent of its adherents black. Other left-led and black-dominated unions such as the International Union of Mine, Mill and Smelter Workers of America and the United Packinghouse Workers of America also contributed to the growth of protest activity at the local level.

Although black pressure appears to have led the Sixth Communist International to sanction the notion of a separate state for African Americans in 1928, communists and blacks did not, on the face of things, have a great deal in common.[33] Black evangelical Christianity, its openness to the Social Gospel notwithstanding, was hardly compatible with the secular materialism peddled by white radicals, most of whom, it was widely believed, were interested in what blacks could do for them, not what the Party could do to advance the cause of racial equality. This apparent stumbling block did not prevent the Communist Party of the United States (CPUSA)

30. Honey, 'Industrial Unionism', p. 145.

31. M. Goldfield, 'Race and the CIO: The Possibilities for Racial Egalitarianism During the 1930s and 1940s', *International Labor and Working-Class History* 44 (1993), pp. 1–32.

32. R. Korstad and N. Lichtenstein, 'Opportunities Found and Lost: Labor, Radicals, and the Early Civil Rights Movement', *JAH* 75 (1988), 791–3.

33. Fredrickson, *Black Liberation*, pp. 189–202; S. Campbell, ' "Black Bolsheviks" and Recognition of African-America's Right to Self-Determination by the Communist Party USA', *Science and Society* 58 (1994–95), 440–70.

from appealing directly to black nationalist aspirations, nor from seeking to mobilise the black masses against the forces of capitalism during the early 1930s. Significantly, their efforts were directed not only at the minority of blacks engaged in manufacturing industry, but also at the bulk of black farm workers untouched by the organising campaigns of the CIO. Particularly important in the mobilisation effort was the Party's decision to furnish legal help for the Scottsboro boys, nine black youths accused of raping two white women on a freight train in Alabama in March 1931. The case received national media coverage, enabling the communists to pose as stauncher defenders of black civil rights than more mainstream groups like the NAACP.[34]

Communists were not the only radicals who attempted to strike at the heart of the caste system during the Great Depression. Small numbers of southern whites, motivated by Christian compassion, socialist ideology, and the very visible suffering around them, took steps to politicise downtrodden southerners of both races in the early 1930s. In 1932 Myles Horton, a graduate of Union Theological Seminary in New York City, co-founded the Highlander Folk School in Monteagle, Tennessee, as an educational centre for the spread of labour organising techniques and the principles of grassroots, interracial democracy.[35] His efforts would bear fruit in two generations of labour and civil rights workers. Two years later a white socialist, Henry L. Mitchell, the owner of a dry-cleaning business in Tyronza, Arkansas, organised the Southern Tenant Farmers Union in an attempt to improve pay and conditions in the Delta region.[36] Other radicals similarly immersed in liberal Protestantism, socialism and pacifism joined in the struggle not only for working-class unity across the colour line, but also as part of an embryonic campaign to end segregation and discrimination. Although some, like the Christian Socialist Howard Kester, initially suspected communists of entryism and cynical manipulation of working-class folk, many of them, Kester included, went on to cooperate with CPUSA members in the fight for social justice.[37]

Whatever the communists' motives in seeking to organise tenant farmers and sharecroppers in the Deep South, it is clear that many ordinary workers were only too happy to secure outside assistance

34. D.T. Carter, *Scottsboro: A Tragedy of the American South* (rev. edn, Baton Rouge and London, 1979), pp. 51–103.

35. A.P. Dunbar, *Against the Grain: Southern Radicals and Prophets 1929–1959* (Charlottesville, 1981), pp. 41–4.

36. Ibid., pp. 83–9.   37. Ibid., pp. 33, 49–52.

no matter what its source. In 1931, with the existing economic system close to collapse, two black tenant farmers named Ralph and Tommy Gray set up the Croppers' and Farm Workers' Union in rural Tallapoosa County, Alabama.[38] As communist activists in Birmingham had already called on local black farmers to organise themselves, the Grays, kin to a grandfather who had sat in the state legislature during Reconstruction, followed up their move by requesting that a CPUSA organiser be sent to the area. The efforts of Mack Coad, an illiterate Birmingham steelworker, resulted in a total union membership of 800 by July. Further growth was impeded temporarily by the planters' violent response (Coad himself was forced to flee for his life and other leading figures were either killed or arrested), but in August the union was reconstituted successfully as the Sharecroppers Union (SCU). Operating in secret, the union undertook a number of strikes during the 1930s, one of them in Lowndes County, a focal point for radical civil rights activity three decades later. Confronted by more killings and arrests, the SCU failed to prevent the wholesale eviction of tenants and farmworkers. Nonetheless, its members' tenacious determination to protect their livelihoods indicated that southern blacks were not the loyal, docile peasantry that some observers had supposed them to be.

By no means all blacks who embraced Communism or accepted help from communists during the 1930s and early 1940s endorsed the fundamental tenets of orthodox Marxism-Leninism. One of the reasons why Communism was a significant force in pockets of the Deep South was the ability of its defenders to mix secular politics with black Christianity. In Winston-Salem, for example, the local Communist Party (which had recruited approximately 150 blacks by the end of the Second World War) met regularly in a black church and opened its gatherings with a hymn and prayer.[39] In Alabama nearly all CPUSA members attended church on a regular basis, party propaganda never attacked religion, and popular spirituals were transformed into labour songs.[40] There was certainly a wide gulf between atheism and Christianity, but communists enjoyed a modicum of success in bridging the gap and forging a political culture energised by the prophetic qualities of African-American Protestantism.

38. On the SCU see esp. R.D.G. Kelley, *Hammer and Hoe: Alabama Communists During the Great Depression* (Chapel Hill and London, 1990), pp. 34–56, 159–75.

39. Korstad and Lichtenstein, 'Opportunities Found', p. 792.

40. Kelley, *Hammer and Hoe*, p. 108.

While only a tiny minority of blacks actually joined the CPUSA in the early 1930s, there can be no denying the attractiveness of left-wing causes to significant numbers of African Americans during this troubled period. As well as the mainstream CIO unions (in which communists often played a major role) other leftist organisations such as the Workers Defense League attempted to mobilise the urban unemployed. Many of those politicised by these campaigns were black women. Among them was Ella Baker, one of the most prominent organisers in the modern civil rights movement. Reared by proud, independent-thinking parents in North Carolina, Baker moved to New York City after graduating from Raleigh's Shaw University in 1927.[41] There she was introduced to Communism by a young Russian immigrant and subsequently emboldened to help found the Young Negroes Cooperative League in the winter of 1930. Designed as a vehicle for the attainment of economic power through consumer action, the League functioned for several years as a decentralised body emphasising the kind of qualities which Baker, cognisant of the fact that 'there were certain social forces over which the individual has no control', would later seek to instil into the civil rights movement: 'the inclusion of women, the importance of grass-roots involvement, and rank-and-file decision making'.[42] One of the chief links between the labour-oriented radicalism of the 1930s and the 1960s concept of participatory democracy, Baker opted to eschew involvement in CPUSA affairs in favour of active service with the Workers Education Project of the federal government's Works Progress Administration (WPA). In 1941 she embarked on her formal career in the incipient civil rights movement as an assistant field secretary for the NAACP: she spent several months each year in this capacity establishing personal links with black community leaders in the South, a fact of no little importance in the evolution of a coordinated struggle against the caste system.

Baker's decision to accept a post with the WPA helps to explain how the New Deal undercut political radicalism in the 1930s. Without evidence that the United States government was prepared to give material help to African Americans, it is likely that many more blacks would have been alienated from the mainstream. True, the New Deal did not go out of its way to aid blacks in the 1930s.

41. On Baker's early career see B. Ransby, 'Ella Josephine Baker' in *The American Radical*, ed. M.J. Buhle *et al.* (New York and London, 1974), pp. 288–92, and C. Payne, 'Ella Baker and Models of Social Change', *Signs* 14 (1984), 886–9.
42. E. Baker Interview (1968), CRDP.

Overtly pro-black policies would have drained Roosevelt of southern support for recovery measures. Moreover, the president himself, in contrast to his wife, had little interest in specifically black affairs. However, while New Deal programmes were seldom targeted to help blacks (and some were positively harmful to them), the very fact that African Americans were among the chief beneficiaries of government welfare policies meant that they were attracted to the ruling Democratic Party whose positive response to the Depression contrasted markedly with the *laisser-faire* stance of the Republicans. Notwithstanding the existence of racial discrimination in job allocation procedures, the WPA alone provided basic earnings for one million black families in 1939, rivalling agriculture and domestic service as the chief source of black income.[43] Consequently, blacks who possessed the vote – primarily those in the urban North – proved increasingly willing to use their limited power to support the Democrats. As indicated above, they rapidly became an integral bloc within the emerging New Deal coalition, their political influence greatly enhanced as a result.

Although the Roosevelt administration's reliance on southern votes in Congress placed obvious constraints on federal action on behalf of civil rights, growing black political influence ensured that Washington could no longer discount African Americans. The main civil rights organisations in the United States were slow to react to the rapidly changing circumstances brought on by the New Deal, but by September 1933 the NAACP and the National Urban League had combined with the National Industrial League, newly formed by two Washington-based black professionals, Robert Weaver and John Preston Davis, to create the Joint Committee on Economic Recovery as a vehicle for ensuring that blacks received equal treatment from the burgeoning roster of New Deal agencies. The Joint Committee helped to ensure that the National Recovery Administration (NRA) did not formulate discriminatory wage and hour standards for black workers. Even though NRA codes were not properly enforced in the southern states, the Committee functioned effectively as a clearing-house for data on code violations.[44] In late 1933 Weaver's efforts as the Committee's director of research bore fruit when he was asked to become an aide to Clark Foreman, Special Adviser on the Economic Status of Negroes to the WPA

43. A.J. Badger, *The New Deal: The Depression Years, 1933–1940* (Basingstoke, 1989), p. 254.

44. P. Sullivan, *Days of Hope: Race and Democracy in the New Deal Era* (Chapel Hill and London, 1996), pp. 46–50.

overlord, Harold Ickes. His subsequent efforts to ensure that blacks were given a voice in federal policy-making were greatly aided not only by the activities of sympathetic New Dealers like Ickes himself and Eleanor Roosevelt, but also by a significant increase in the numbers of blacks in the secondary ranks of the federal bureaucracy. By the middle of 1935 around 45 African Americans had been appointed to posts in various cabinet and government departments. The following year they designated themselves the Federal Council on Negro Affairs (the so-called 'Black Cabinet' or 'Black Brains Trust'). Meeting regularly at the Washington home of Mary McLeod Bethune, the highest ranking African American in Washington, they attempted to ensure that the administration did not lose sight of civil rights issues in its search for economic recovery.[45]

In view of the federal government's lack of interest in blacks before 1933, their efforts were remarkably successful. Blacks occupied at least a third of all public housing units constructed by the Public Works Administration (PWA) and received nearly the same proportion of the PWA's total wage budget in 1936 though, as Harvard Sitkoff notes, local practices varied considerably across the United States.[46] The National Youth Administration (NYA) not only provided direct aid for roughly half a million black youths but also made strenuous efforts to include African Americans in its skilled manpower training programmes. The Farm Security Administration (FSA) was seriously underfunded but it provided critical aid to many hard-pressed sharecroppers, in some cases enabling them to set up as independent farmers. In the late 1930s, for example, the FSA established a series of model farming and industrial communities, 13 of which were reserved for blacks. Among them was the Mississippi Delta town of Mileston where over a hundred black families were settled. Although the land was initially worked on a cooperative basis it was eventually divided into family farms – viable economic units which provided a strong basis for later civil rights activism.[47] By no means all New Deal agencies were as sympathetic to blacks as the FSA, but the very existence of a black voice in Washington ensured that African Americans were not forgotten during the Depression.

45. H. Sitkoff, *A New Deal for Blacks* (New York, 1978), pp. 78–9.
46. Ibid., pp. 67–8.
47. C. Payne, *I've Got the Light of Freedom: The Organizing Tradition and the Mississippi Freedom Struggle* (Berkeley, 1995), p. 281; Youth of the Rural Organizing and Cultural Center, *Minds Stayed on Freedom: The Civil Rights Struggle in the Rural South, an Oral History* (Boulder, 1991), p. 10.

Apart from the growing influence of the northern black vote and the employment of blacks in the federal bureaucracy, one of the main reasons for the racially progressive policies of the PWA, the NYA and the FSA was the prominent part played in these agencies by sympathetic southern New Dealers such as Clark Foreman, Aubrey Williams, and the former head of the CIC, Will Alexander. Convinced that the caste system was to blame for the South's economic backwardness and political sterility, they provided African Americans with important allies in the corridors of power. Each of them, moreover, believed that the central state offered the best hope of a more just and prosperous society below the Mason–Dixon Line. Foreman, a well-to-do Georgian heavily influenced by the utopian socialism of H.G. Wells, developed close links with a number of leading black intellectuals in the 1920s and had already rejected the CIC as overly conservative by the time he visited the Soviet Union in 1932–33. There he was impressed by the government's efforts to promote not only full employment but also the rights of minorities and women.[48] Williams, an Alabaman who headed the NYA after 1935, had refined his notions about the ability of the state to alleviate social distress while working as executive secretary of the Wisconsin Conference of Social Work.[49] Alexander, always a more advanced liberal than many of those who belonged to the CIC, was an immediate convert to the idea that the New Deal would promote southern betterment and proceeded to put his views into practice as head of both the FSA and its predecessor, the Resettlement Administration.

During the second half of the 1930s opportunities for cooperation between southern New Deal radicals, blacks and communists increased as a result of the Soviet Union's decision to fight fascism with the adoption of a united front strategy in May 1934. As a consequence of this policy communists everywhere were urged to promote alliances with progressive bourgeois democrats. In the United States this resulted in the formation of two new civil rights groups: the National Negro Congress and the Southern Conference for Human Welfare (SCHW).

The former, an umbrella organisation rapidly dominated by communists, sought to promote equal civil and economic rights for black Americans along social democratic lines. Its apparent moderation attracted a number of prominent mainstream leaders, including

---

48. Sullivan, *Days of Hope*, pp. 25–40.
49. J. Salmond, *A Southern Rebel, The Life and Times of Aubrey Willis Williams 1890–1965* (Chapel Hill, 1983), pp. 26–42.

A. Philip Randolph who was elected its first president. The Council sponsored a number of protest actions such as economic boycotts of urban stores which refused to appoint blacks, but it never won the wholehearted support of the black church or the NAACP.[50]

The biracial SCHW was less radical (and less communist-influenced) but its founding in Birmingham, Alabama, in November 1938 represented an advance on the gradualist work of the CIC.[51] Whereas most progressive whites in the South had previously balked at launching a direct challenge to the caste system, the heightened consciousness produced by the struggles of the 1930s forced the SCHW delegates to confront the issue of segregation. An attempt to hold an integrated meeting was thwarted by the intervention of Birmingham's racist police chief, Eugene 'Bull' Connor but, in a famously symbolic gesture, Eleanor Roosevelt insisted on sitting in the central aisle between the delegates of both races. Ultimately and perhaps predictably, given the wide range of opinion represented in the hall, the Conference eschewed an outright condemnation of Jim Crow in favour of a more moderate set of resolutions including support for equal rights under the law, the abolition of the poll tax (to boost black and poor white voter registration) and funding for graduate school programmes in state-supported black educational establishments. Notwithstanding its initial caution, however, the SCHW acted as a halfway house for some southern liberals on the verge of abandoning gradualism for good. By the end of the Second World War influential members like Clark Foreman and Virginia Durr were ready to accept federal intervention to undermine the caste system.

The NAACP campaign for racial justice

Both the Depression and the New Deal had a radicalising impact on the country's most important civil rights organisation, the fervently anti-communist NAACP. During the 1930s the Association overcame potentially damaging policy disputes and internal rivalries to develop a serious challenge to the existing racial order in the United States. This challenge took two forms. Firstly, the NAACP leadership sought to broaden and strengthen the incipient political

---

50. R.G. Wolters, *Negroes and the Great Depression: The Problem of Economic Recovery* (Westport, 1970), pp. 353–82.
51. Sosna, *Silent South*, pp. 88–104; Sullivan, *Days of Hope*, pp. 98–100.

coalition which had begun to develop around specific civil rights issues. Secondly, it streamlined its legal campaign to focus primarily, though by no means exclusively, on the problems occasioned by segregated education.

Although both of these strategies illustrated the NAACP's continuing faith in the country's existing political and legal institutions, their integrationist objectives proved far from controversial within the organisation. The critical internal debate took place in the mid-1930s.[52] W.E.B. Du Bois, cerebral, aloof and increasingly at odds with the suave new executive secretary, Walter White, presented the nationalist alternative in a controversial *Crisis* article in 1934. Frustrated by his own waning power and the general lack of concern for the desperate plight of ordinary blacks during the early stages of the Great Depression, Du Bois argued that black people should abandon what he saw as the fruitless struggle for interracial working-class solidarity and concentrate primarily on the development of their own cooperative economy. His support for what he called 'voluntary segregation' gave White the opportunity he needed to terminate Du Bois's influence in the NAACP. In a public response backed by the board of directors, he lambasted his rival's separatist stance as defeatist, contending that only integrationist policies could solve the black race's problems in the United States. Few key figures in the Association saw Du Bois's position as anything other than abject surrender. Devoid of support, the *Crisis* editor was left with little choice but to resign from the organisation.

Du Bois's defeat allowed White to press on with his evolving strategy of forging a united civil rights coalition in cooperation with organised labour, church groups and progressive liberals. The policy had begun to bear fruit earlier in the decade when the NAACP launched a successful campaign to prevent the confirmation of John Parker as a supreme court judge. Parker, a North Carolina Republican was President Herbert Hoover's choice to succeed Justice Edward T. Sanford who died on 8 March 1930. Hoover was hoping to appeal to southern white voters in preparation for the 1932 presidential election and saw Parker as the kind of southern leader who could help the Republicans make inroads into the Solid South. Information that Parker was an opponent of black voting rights, however, induced Walter White, at that time the NAACP's acting secretary, to initiate a nationwide campaign to prevent senatorial

52. See Wolters, *Negroes*, pp. 230–301, for an account of the split between Du Bois and White.

confirmation of the new Supreme Court nominee. As well as tele-
graphing all NAACP branches to lobby their senators to oppose
Parker's appointment, White urged branch members to enlist the
help of all available institutions in the black community. The campaign won enormous support from the 250,000-strong National
Association of Colored Women, the black press, churches, and fraternal organisations. Significantly, Parker's appointment was also
opposed by organised labour which resented his judicial support of
yellow-dog contracts, widely used in the 1920s to prevent the union-
isation of mineworkers. Although no formal alliance between the
NAACP and the AFL occurred at this time, the fact that Parker was
opposed on two fronts contributed greatly to his defeat in the Senate
in May 1930. As Kenneth W. Goings has contended, the Parker
fight not only enhanced the appeal of the NAACP within the black
community, but in some senses it was also 'a precursor to the New
Deal coalition'.[53]

Cognisant of the growing threat to the NAACP's appeal represented by the communists, White stepped up the search for mainstream allies in the mid-1930s by mobilising impressive support for
a federal anti-lynching law inside and outside Congress.[54] Sustained
pressure from the NAACP and its liberal Protestant, Catholic and
Jewish allies resulted in the passage of anti-lynching bills by the
House of Representatives in 1937 and 1940. While the Senate proceeded to block the legislation, the forging of a nascent inter-
organisational civil rights coalition was itself a positive step forwards
in the fight for racial equality.

By no means all of the NAACP's political activities in the 1930s
were undertaken at the national level. Charles H. Houston, one of
the organisation's leading figures in the Depression years, was a
keen exponent of the view that the Association should make greater
efforts to mobilise southern blacks. As a result of his grass-roots litigation strategy (see below) and the influx of unionised blacks into
the NAACP, several of the organisation's southern branches were
revitalised. Although the growth of NAACP activism in the South
during the 1930s was limited largely to urban areas, it is clear that
significant numbers of black NAACP members below the Mason–
Dixon Line were prepared to challenge the existing caste system
politically by supporting activities such as voter registration and
abolition of the poll tax. Inevitably, this development increased the

53. K.W. Goings, *'The NAACP Comes of Age': The Defeat of Judge John J. Parker*
(Bloomington and Indianapolis, 1990), p. 53.
54. Zangrando, *Crusade*, pp. 98–165.

amount of common ground between African Americans and white radicals who saw the liberalisation of the franchise as a vital precondition for the modernisation of the South. In 1941 the NAACP joined groups such as the AFL, the CIO, and the National Negro Congress as a co-sponsor of the National Committee to Abolish the Poll Tax – yet another indication that a potentially powerful civil rights coalition was in the process of being forged on the eve of the entry of the United States into the Second World War.[55]

A second, and related, prong of NAACP policy was the Association's concerted legal campaign against segregated education. During the 1920s the organisation's mainly white lawyers had targeted a wide range of civil rights abuses without singling out any one of them for particular attention. In 1930 a prominent New York Jewish lawyer, Nathan Margold, was appointed by the board of directors to coordinate and plan a major attack on the various legal handicaps confronting black people. The campaign was to be financed by a substantial $100,000 grant from the left-wing Garland Fund. Margold produced his preliminary report in May 1931. In it he outlined the case for making a finely tuned, direct attack on segregated schools one of the organisation's top priorities. Whereas the NAACP–Garland Fund Joint Committee had suggested a series of taxpayers' suits to equalise state spending on black and white schools, Margold argued that this type of litigation would be complex and laborious. Much better, he contended, to seek higher court rulings that unequal expenditures were unconstitutional under the Fourteenth Amendment. Southern states would then have the option either of desegregating their schools or furnishing additional money to bring black educational facilities up to the same standards as those enjoyed by whites.[56]

Two developments intervened to prevent this strategy from being put into operation in the 1930s. Firstly, the onset of the Depression dramatically reduced the Garland Fund grant to $10,000, thereby mandating a scaling down of the anticipated campaign against racial discrimination. Secondly, Margold announced soon after completing his report that he would not be available to head the campaign himself. Rebuffed by its second choice, Karl Llewellyn of the Columbia University Law School, the NAACP appointed Charles H. Houston to direct the organisation's revamped litigation strategy. It could not have made a better choice.

55. Sullivan, *Days of Hope*, p. 115.
56. M.V. Tushnet, *The NAACP's Legal Strategy against Segregated Education, 1925–1950* (Chapel Hill, 1987), pp. 25–8.

Houston's appointment in 1934 represented a major shift in the NAACP's appointing policy. Vice-dean of the Howard University Law School, Houston had long advocated the view that more black lawyers should be utilised in the Association's litigation campaign. At Howard he had done much to augment the race's tiny pool of legal expertise by training a cadre of black lawyers who, he believed, were morally obliged to promote equal justice through the American judicial system.[57] Under Houston, the first black NAACP lawyer to argue a case before the US Supreme Court, and Walter White, the Association employed increasing numbers of blacks not only to fight its cases at the local level, but also to help direct the national litigation campaign. Foremost among these new appointments was Thurgood Marshall, arguably the most able graduate of the legal programme at Howard. Described by Roy Wilkins as 'lean, hard, and Hollywood handsome, a black Ronald Coleman', Marshall was hired as a full-time NAACP lawyer in 1936.[58] Three years later he was given the job of heading the Legal Defense and Education Fund (generally known as the 'Inc Fund') set up as an offshoot of the NAACP to take advantage of new federal tax laws.[59] Together, Houston and Marshall directed the fight against segregated education in the 1930s and 1940s.

Crucial to any understanding of Houston's strategy is an awareness of his grounding in what were, during the New Deal era, the increasingly fashionable principles of Legal Realism.[60] Like Karl Llewellyn, one of the leading exponents of the doctrine in the United States, Houston believed that both the law and the judges who made it were products of the contemporary social environment. As a consequence he also regarded the law as an instrument of social change – a powerful tool which could be used to improve conditions for black people in all walks of American life. Significantly, Houston's status as a race man and a strong proponent of social democracy made him more aware than most that a successful litigation strategy was dependent upon winning community support. Recommending that Margold's plan be converted into a targeted assault on unequal education facilities (even within the context of segregation) he insisted that the main aims of any legal campaign should be '(1) to arouse and strengthen the will of the local communities

57. McNeil, *Groundwork*, pp. 63–75.   58. Wilkins, *Standing Fast*, p. 161.

59. R. Kluger, *Simple Justice: The History of* Brown v. Board of Education *and Black America's Struggle for Racial Equality* (London, 1975), p. 221. The Inc Fund was formally separated from the NAACP in 1957.

60. On Legal Realism see Tushnet, *NAACP's Legal Strategy*, pp. 117–19.

to demand and fight for their rights; [and] (2) to work out model procedures through actual tests in court which can be used by local communities in similar cases brought by them on their own initiatives and resources.'[61] For Houston, fully aware of the ongoing competition between the NAACP and leftists for popular backing, the law offered an effective means of mobilising blacks to fight for their rights under the Constitution. The NAACP could assist their efforts, but it should not, and would not, seek to fight for civil rights without the cooperation of ordinary African Americans.

Although the Houston plan was not as coordinated as he and Marshall might have hoped, it had two chief elements, both of which were designed to undermine the existing system of discriminatory education in the United States by securing judicial enforcement of the separate-but-equal verdict handed down in *Plessy*. The first of these was a series of salary equalisation cases, overseen by Marshall, in the upper South states of Maryland and Virginia. As teachers were an influential segment of the region's black middle class and demonstrably worse off than their white counterparts, Houston regarded a sustained attempt to equalise their salaries as an effective means of winning popular support for the overall campaign. Although conservatism, vested interests and fear of dismissal resulted in a good deal of opposition to the strategy among black teachers, enough of them came forward to secure precedent-setting victories in both Maryland and Virginia between 1935 and 1940.[62]

The primary mode of attack also focused on the need to gain precedents, but led more directly to an open assault on segregated schools. Recognising, firstly, that victories were essential to establish and maintain the campaign's momentum and, secondly, that public school segregation was likely to prove a hard nut to crack, Houston opted to focus initially on discrimination at the graduate school level. Positive rulings following the logic in *Plessy* were likely to promote desegregation through the back door by imposing too onerous a financial burden on states wishing to maintain separate educational institutions for blacks. Failing that, blacks would at least begin to achieve parity with whites in terms of teachers' pay and quality of resources. The result was a series of landmark judgments by the US Supreme Court, significantly liberalised by new appointments during the later stages of the New Deal. Beginning with the decision in *Gaines ex rel. Canada v. Missouri* in 1938 and culminating

61. Quoted in McNeil, *Groundwork*, p. 116.
62. Tushnet, *NAACP's Legal Strategy*, pp. 58–65, 78–80.

in *Sipuel v. Oklahoma, McLaurin v. Oklahoma* and *Sweatt v. Painter* after
the war, the nation's highest legal tribunal upheld the right of
blacks to receive the same quality of graduate education as whites.[63]
This meant that southern blacks barred from attending white-only
establishments could no longer be given bursaries to attend law
schools in other states and that segregated graduate facilities had
in all respects to be equal to those provided for whites (which, in
effect, meant that blacks would have to be admitted to the same
institutions as those attended by whites). Although the graduate
school cases affected a small minority of individuals, they had serious repercussions for the welfare of the caste system. Indeed, the
stage was set for an all-out legal challenge to Jim Crow which would
culminate in the US Supreme Court's epochal decision in *Brown v.
Board of Education* in 1954.

Although hindsight suggests that many of the foundations for a
successful civil rights movement in the 1950s and 1960s were laid
during the New Deal era, Jim Crow was still very much intact when
the Japanese attacked the United States Pacific fleet at Pearl Harbor
in December 1941. Greater federal intervention in American life
as a response to the profound economic problems of the decade certainly encouraged blacks to see the national government as an ally
in the developing struggle against racial oppression. Intellectual
currents, moreover, appeared to be running on the side of progress.
The ongoing work of social anthropologists like Franz Boas, for
example, which stressed cultural relativism and the overriding
importance of environmental factors in individual human development, undermined the primacy of scientific racism, even though the
latter continued to have credence in the southern states and the
American courts.[64] Jim Crow, however, survived the 1930s in large
measure because the liberal attack on the small-town elites who
dominated southern life failed to generate sufficient momentum.
In 1938 President Roosevelt attempted to purge conservative southern Democrats who opposed the New Deal. Backed by liberals of
both races (including those who joined the SCHW) the attempt
foundered on the entrenched state-level power of segregationist
politicians like Harry Flood Byrd of Virginia who had come to view
the enhanced activity of the federal government as a direct threat

63. For a full account of the graduate school cases see Kluger, *Simple Justice*,
pp. 202–3, 256–84.
64. Sitkoff, *New Deal*, pp. 190–93; P. Pascoe, 'Miscegenation Law, Court Cases,
and Ideologies of "Race" in Twentieth-Century America', *JAH* 83 (1996), 44–69.

to their own interests.[65] By the time the United States entered the Second World War a conservative coalition composed of congressional Republicans and anti-New Deal southern Democrats constituted a major obstacle to the passage of fundamental reforms. After Pearl Harbor the president's overriding need for congressional support for the war effort left conservatives well placed to launch a counter-offensive against racially progressive New Deal agencies like the FSA and the NYA.

Given the severity of the Great Depression, what is most remarkable about the 1930s is not perhaps the extent of radicalism in the United States but the persistence of American conservatism.[66] While the vast majority of whites retained their faith in the existing social and economic system and often remained suspicious of federal intervention in local affairs, most African Americans were too preoccupied with the task of day-to-day survival to countenance protest activity inside or outside the system. Liberalism did grow in strength during the 1930s but in the South it was a delicate plant, particularly in the hands of governors like Olin Johnson of South Carolina and Paul Johnson of Mississippi who understood well the racial proclivities of their constituents. Even the SCHW, the sturdiest manifestation of biracial cooperation along New Deal lines, failed to secure mass support. Further progress on race in America awaited greater systemic shocks to the southern caste system and the strengthening of the incipient civil rights coalition.

65. A. Cash Koeniger, 'The New Deal and the States: Roosevelt versus the Byrd Organization', *JAH* 68 (1982), 876–96.
66. On the strength of American conservatism in the 1930s see A.J. Badger, 'The New Deal and the Localities' in R. Jeffrey-Jones and B. Collins, *The Growth of Federal Power in American History* (Edinburgh, 1983), pp. 102–15.

CHAPTER 3

A Movement Stirs 1940–60

Although historians continue to debate the origins of the modern black freedom struggle, few would now accept the once prevalent view that the latter began with Mrs Rosa Parks's refusal to give up her seat on a Montgomery, Alabama, bus to a white man. The celebrated bus boycott which ensued was certainly a seminal event in the history of African-American protest in the United States, not least because it launched the career of the movement's most visible leader, Dr Martin Luther King. Mrs Parks's defiant act, however, did not come out of the blue. It must be seen in the context of a distinct shift in the pace of social change in America brought about initially by the country's embroilment in the Second World War – an event which not only accelerated the process of southern modernisation but also prompted black leaders and organisations to build on the protest strategies developed in the early twentieth century. Although the US Supreme Court's decision in the case of *Brown v. Board of Education* appeared to vindicate the litigation strategy of the NAACP, other civil rights groups began to experiment with more radical forms of protest including the use of nonviolent direct action tactics such as sit-ins and mass demonstrations. Initially, the onset of the Cold War in the mid-1940s gave black leaders a degree of leverage in their struggle for basic constitutional rights but ultimately the pressure for national unity in the face of the perceived communist threat played into the hands of conservatives who regarded any attempt to change the status quo as treacherous. The Montgomery bus boycott signalled southern blacks' ability to launch a sustained challenge against Jim Crow but it did not result immediately in the development of a mass-based, national civil rights movement.

The Second World War

The Second World War stands as a defining event in twentieth-century history. Its acceleration of a plethora of modernising forces including technological change, bureaucratic statism, and urbanisation had inevitable social consequences for African Americans, 80 per cent of whom were still resident in the South in 1940. The mushrooming of defence industries pulled yet more black families into the cities from the countryside, at the same time as agribusiness and the mechanisation of southern farming were pushing more of them off the land. An estimated four million people, many of them black sharecroppers and tenant farmers left southern farms during the war years. Some found employment in the region's urban economy which diversified rapidly with the growth of local defence plants and military installations. Others left the Southland for good. By the end of the decade roughly 1.6 million African Americans had migrated northwards and westwards. Chicago, for example, was home to nearly half a million blacks in 1950 compared to roughly 277,000 in 1940.[1]

The domestic consequences of these rapid demographic changes were not unpredictable although national, state and local authorities were unprepared to deal with them. Housing shortages were acute in most major towns and cities throughout the United States during the early part of the war and living conditions for large numbers of urban dwellers were squalid: crowded, unsafe and unsanitary. City governments were generally unsympathetic to the plight of transplanted black southerners and devoted most of their energies to improving housing conditions for whites. The burdens of wartime fell particularly hard on the established black community of Washington, DC. A massive expansion of the federal bureaucracy prompted widespread annexation and demolition of black neighbourhoods in the city. One government report noted that black homes were bulldozed to make way for 'government buildings, highways, schools and recreational facilities; and no compensating housing has been built'.[2] Across the Potomac 200 black families were removed to make way for the War Department's vast new Pentagon building. Several hundred more lost their homes as a consequence of the expansion of Arlington national cemetery.[3]

1. P. Kleppner, *Chicago Divided: The Making of a Black Mayor* (DeKalb, 1985), p. 17.
2. D. Brinkley, *Washington Goes to War* (pbk edn, New York, 1989), p. 236.
3. Ibid., p. 236.

Urban growth placed major strains on race relations as blacks and whites were thrown together in a variety of workplaces and public spaces. Tensions resulted across the country but were worst in the South where *de jure* segregation had previously ensured a large measure of physical separation between the races. Several job-related riots occurred, the most serious of these on 25 May 1943 when male and female white workers at the Alabama Dry Dock Company in Mobile indiscriminately attacked black co-workers with a motley assortment of weapons including bricks and metal tools. Miraculously no-one was killed, but federal investigators estimated the number of injured at no fewer than 50. While contemporary reports on the rioters' motives varied, the most recent historian of the event suggests that white workers may have been influenced not only by a desire to preserve skilled jobs for themselves but also by an instinctive horror at the idea of black men working alongside white women.[4]

Military bases in the region, usually located on the edge of towns, were major flashpoints because they subjected large numbers of black servicemen, many of them northerners, to the rigours of a segregated military establishment. Mistreatment of black soldiers by white Military Policemen was rife, interracial sexual friction was heightened, and black officers resented the way their lack of privileges undermined their authority in the ranks. Simmering frustration led to several camp-related riots. One of the worst of these occurred in downtown Alexandria, Louisiana, on 10 January 1942 when the arrest of a drunken soldier sparked off two hours of mayhem involving black troops, white MPs, state troopers and local police and civilians. By the time the trouble was over 13 blacks had been shot. Five other southern camps experienced significant outbreaks of unrest during the following summer.[5]

As Robin Kelley has noted interracial tensions were particularly evident on city buses where white drivers and passengers struggled to maintain the colour line in the face of overcrowding and what was perceived to be growing black dissidence.[6] Nine months prior to the dockyard riot in Mobile, a white bus driver in the same city shot dead a black soldier who had asked merely to be transported to his

4. B. Nelson, 'Organized Labor and the Struggle for Black Equality in Mobile During World War II', *JAH* 80 (1993), 979–81.

5. A. Fairclough, *Race and Democracy: The Civil Rights Struggle in Louisiana, 1915–1972* (Athens, Ga, 1995), pp. 74–5, 78.

6. R.D.G. Kelley, '"We Are Not What We Seem": Rethinking Black Working-Class Opposition in the Jim Crow South', *JAH* 80 (1993), 103–9.

base on time.[7] In September 1943 a New Orleans driver ordered a black serviceman to vacate the front seat of his bus. Serious violence was avoided on this occasion, but all 24 black passengers were arrested by city police.[8]

Although the Second World War placed intense pressure on Jim Crow practices, evidence of organised, collective black resistance was most evident in the North where African Americans enjoyed a freer political climate. Here the majority of mainstream black leaders endorsed the thinking behind the *Pittsburgh Courier*'s 'Double V' campaign which, recalling the race's failure to benefit from wartime service in 1917–18, urged the masses to fight for victory abroad and justice at home. The campaign was aided by the Allies' lofty rhetoric encapsulated in the Atlantic Charter. Meeting in Placentia Bay, Newfoundland, in August 1941, Roosevelt and Churchill announced their support for 'the right of all peoples to choose the form of government under which they will live'. They also expressed a wish to see 'sovereign rights and self-government restored to those who have been forcibly deprived of them' and a desire 'to see established a peace which will afford . . . assurance that all men in all the lands may live out their lives in freedom from fear and want'.[9] Although neither premier was thinking primarily of dispossessed racial groups under their own charge, coloured elites throughout the United States and the British Empire took them at their word and made their loyalty to the Allied cause conditional on substantial progress being made towards racial equality.

While the Allied war effort against Japan was shot through with virulent racism, official propaganda contrasting liberal democratic freedoms with fascist gangsterism was bound to play into the hands of black leaders in the United States.[10] Veteran crusaders like A. Philip Randolph, however, were far too canny to suppose that the war gave blacks enough leverage to eliminate racism and segregation at home. It was Randolph, no friend of the petit bourgeois *Pittsburgh Courier*, who initiated the era's most daring experiment in direct action by threatening to immobilise the nation's capital in pursuit of two aims: the integration of America's armed forces and a fair share of defence jobs for his race.

Having failed to seek re-election as president of the National Negro Congress in 1940 because of communist infiltration of the

7. Nelson, 'Organized Labor', 966–7.   8. Fairclough, *Race and Democracy*, p. 83.
9. I.S. McDonald, ed., *Anglo-American Relations Since the Second World War* (Newton Abbot, 1974), p. 18.
10. J.W. Dower, *War Without Mercy: Race and Power in the Pacific War* (New York, 1986).

organisation, the BSCP leader, still a committed socialist, cast around for alternative ways to mobilise the black masses. With frustration building in black communities across the country even before the Japanese attacked Pearl Harbor, Randolph decided to use the threat of a mass march on Washington as a device to pressure Roosevelt into making the desired concessions on jobs and military integration. Although comparisons were made between Randolph and Gandhi, the former's principal model in the early months of 1940 was the radical labour activism of the New Deal period.

Having gained the support of the NAACP's national secretary, Walter White (who hitherto had shied away from support of civil disobedience but was growing impatient with Roosevelt's failure to deliver an anti-lynching law), Randolph did enough to convince the president that the threat of mass civil unrest in the capital was a real one. After a meeting with black leaders on 18 June, Roosevelt agreed to set up an executive agency to promote equal treatment of blacks in defence-related industries but stalled on the issue of integrating the armed forces because of opposition from his military advisers.[11] While the wartime demand for labour had more impact on black employment than the new Committee on Fair Employment Practice (FEPC), the decision to create such an agency represented a major victory for the civil rights forces, indicating as it did that the threat of direct action could produce significant gains for black Americans. The lesson was not lost on Randolph who attempted to capitalise on his triumph by transforming a partly paper threat into a powerful grass-roots organisation. His March on Washington Movement (MOWM) explicitly excluded whites, for Randolph feared communist entryism and believed that an appeal to nationalist tendencies among northern blacks would promote greater mobilisation. Although he met with a modicum of success (staging an impressive rally at Madison Square Garden in New York in 1942), the NAACP withheld its backing, fearing that Randolph was aiming to create a rival organisation and suspicious of his insistence on racial exclusivity.[12] Too heavily reliant on the limited resources of the BSCP and hardly helped by its name (which suggested limited goals), the MOWM had begun to founder by the beginning of 1943 and Randolph was impelled to channel his activities in other directions.

11. H. Garfinkel, *When Negroes March: The March on Washington Movement in the Organizational Movement for FEPC* (New York, 1969), pp. 37–61.
12. J.H. Bracey and A. Meier, 'Allies or Adversaries? The NAACP, A. Philip Randolph and the 1941 March on Washington', *Georgia Historical Quarterly* 75 (1991), 17.

The demise of the MOWM did not mean the end of direct action experiments in wartime. Committed bands of students deployed a variant of the union sit-down (or 'sit-in') tactic to challenge the existence of segregated facilities in the urban North. Among them was a small interracial group of students in Chicago who met during the winter of 1941–42 to discuss the application of Gandhian tactics to the race question in the United States. Mohandas K. Gandhi, the most prominent of India's contemporary resistance leaders, had pioneered the use of confrontational, yet nonviolent, protest against the country's British rulers during the 1920s and 1930s and his successes had not gone unnoticed by black intellectuals, political leaders and students in the United States.[13] The admirers of so-called 'passive resistance' included anti-war Christian Socialists like James Farmer, a black Methodist divinity student who had worked as an undergraduate at Howard University with Howard Thurman, one of black America's principal exponents of Gandhianism. On 19 February 1942 Farmer sent a memorandum entitled 'Provisional Plans for Brotherhood Mobilization' to A.J. Muste, head of the pacifist Fellowship of Reconciliation (FOR) to which Farmer belonged. In it he asked FOR to back the development of 'a semi-autonomous' project designed to pave the way for a general campaign of 'relentless noncooperation, economic boycott, civil disobedience, etcetera'. This was vital, contended Farmer, because race had become America's number one problem, the war having rendered the 'industrial' question a secondary concern. 'Several contemporary approaches to the problem,' he noted,

> such as the NAACP and the Urban League, have proved their value from specialized angles, and must therefore be encouraged and supported.
> But they have also demonstrated their inadequacy in dealing effectively with the total aspects of a problem as comprehensive as that of race in America. Hence, the need for a virile and comprehensive program such as our study and experimentation in nonviolence should logically lead into.

The project, continued Farmer, should have pacifists at its core, but embrace all those wanting an end to racial discrimination in America and willing to accept the discipline of nonviolence. It should be grounded in religious values and not based on 'an uncritical

13. S. Kapur, *Raising Up a Prophet: The African-American Encounter with Gandhi* (Boston, 1992), pp. 10–100.

duplication' of Gandhian strategy. 'The American race problem', he observed pointedly, 'is in many ways distinctive, and must to that extent be dealt with in a distinctive manner.'[14]

The immediate outcome of Farmer's memorandum was a meeting of FOR's national council in Columbus, Ohio, at which the organisation's predominantly white officers expressed concern that the proposed project failed to emphasise pacifist goals and appeared overly confrontational. Farmer, however, was convinced that it was necessary to exert pressure in order to eradicate racial discrimination and went ahead with the foundation of the Congress of Racial Equality (CORE).[15] The group launched its first sit-in in May 1942 at Jack Spratt's segregated restaurant in Chicago and managed to retain loose ties with FOR throughout the war years as well as to secure the support of Randolph, interested, as ever, in forging links with the black masses.

Isolated instances of nonviolent tactics occurred elsewhere in the United States in the early 1940s providing yet more evidence of the extent to which the war was raising black consciousness. In 1941, for example, the Rev. Adam Clayton Powell, Jr, the pastor of Abyssinian Baptist Church in Harlem, led a popular (and ultimately successful) bus boycott to increase the number of black workers employed by one of the local transportation companies.[16] In February 1943 three female students at Howard University sat down at a segregated soda fountain in a Washington, DC store and ordered drinks. Refusing to pay excess charges for the service, they were hauled off by police and jailed. Larger student-organised demonstrations occurred elsewhere in the capital during the course of the year.[17] For all their historic significance, however (sit-ins would become one of the primary weapons of the modern civil rights movement), it would be a mistake to exaggerate their contemporary importance. In a telling comment, the Chicago labour and community activist, Saul Alinsky, recalled that 'everybody in town who was involved in a mass power basis' looked on the first CORE members as 'sort of Quaker-like kookies'.[18]

14. J. Farmer, *Lay Bare the Heart: An Autobiography of the Civil Rights Movement* (New York and Scarborough, Ont., 1985), pp. 355–60.

15. On the foundation of CORE see A. Meier and E. Rudwick, *CORE: A Study in the Civil Rights Movement 1942–1968* (New York, 1973), pp. 3–39.

16. C.L. Greenberg, *'Or Does It Explode?': Black Harlem in the Great Depression* (New York and Oxford, 1991), pp. 204–5.

17. Brinkley, *Washington Goes to War*, pp. 251–2.

18. Saul Alinsky Interview (1967), CRDP.

The vast majority of American blacks were not involved in direct action demonstrations during the Second World War. Those belonging to the middle class tended to be wary of confrontation, not only because they regarded themselves as patriotic Americans, but also because they feared that calls for direct action and mass demonstrations might result in social unrest. This was particularly true after violent race riots erupted in Detroit and Harlem in the summer of 1943. Such events convinced many African Americans that Randolph and other radical leaders were irresponsible. Predictably, they combined with war-born prosperity to dampen black activism in the later stages of the war.[19]

If the global fight against fascism occasioned the first stirrings of militant nonviolent direct action on the part of equal rights crusaders, it did not make a national civil rights movement. The chief obstacle to the formation of a coordinated campaign along the lines of that envisaged by James Farmer was the persistence of the southern caste system. Jim Crow's stranglehold on political and social institutions below the Mason–Dixon Line militated against the development of interregional ties between African-American leaders and the forging of grass-roots radicalism in the Black Belt. This is not to say, however, that southern blacks were unaffected by the growing radicalism of their northern counterparts.

Elite southern black leaders were visibly active during the war, strengthening their ties to white liberals in an attempt to force the pace of reform in the region. Although their efforts were hampered by the growth of racial tensions brought on by wartime change, a group of them including the respected educators, Charles S. Johnson, Benjamin F. Mays and Horace Mann Bond, convened in Durham, North Carolina, in October 1942 to discuss strategy. For tactical reasons they stopped short of demanding an immediate end to Jim Crow, but they nonetheless made clear their opposition to 'the principle and practice of compulsory segregation in American society' and called for specific reforms such as a federal anti-lynching law and the abolition of the poll tax and the white primary.[20] Less than a year later the Durham group met with liberal whites in Richmond, Virginia, to draw up a common statement that blacks were 'entitled to and should have every guarantee of equal

19. H. Sitkoff, 'Racial Militancy and Interracial Violence in the Second World War', *JAH* 58 (1970), 679.

20. B.F. Mays, *Born to Rebel: An Autobiography* (Athens, Ga, and London, 1987), p. 217.

opportunity that every other citizen of the United States has within the framework of the American democratic system of government'.[21]

These deliberations can hardly be said to have shaken Jim Crow to its foundations, but they betokened continued cooperation between elite black and liberal white leaders which found institutional form in February 1944 with the formation of the Southern Regional Council. Such biracial ties, however, should not be seen as proof that the two groups were in agreement on all points. Most white reformers remained convinced that it would be folly to move too far in advance of public opinion and looked askance at the idea that federal intervention was the key to racial progress. Their view was that instead of becoming impatient and demanding the kind of radical action urged by Randolph in the North, southern blacks should promote gradual reform in order to prevent the region from descending into racial chaos. The influential Richmond editor, Virginius Dabney, endorsed the Durham statement but proved a harsh critic of northern black militancy.[22] For the most part moderate southern black leaders accepted the cautionary advice of their liberal allies and as a result contacts between northern and southern civil rights reformers remained relatively limited during the Second World War. In 1944 the black Harvard academic, Rayford Logan, deplored the lack of contact between the nation's two black communities and called for a wartime conference to bridge the gap. His hope was that coordinating committees could be set up to discuss strategy, funding and research on civil rights, and that a central inter-organisational planning body might be installed in Washington.[23] Nothing came of Logan's suggestions, not least because southern black leaders remained wary of alienating local white liberals by aligning themselves too publicly with putatively militant northern blacks.[24]

One of the main reasons for the relatively cautious approach adopted by southern blacks to civil rights in the early 1940s was the failure of limited federal intervention to undermine the caste system. The newly created FEPC accomplished enough to suggest the importance of federal help but limited resources rendered it something of a blunt instrument. Two-thirds of the 8,000 job-discrimination

21. Quoted in M. Sosna, *In Search of the Silent South: Southern Liberals and the Race Issue* (New York, 1977), p. 119.

22. Ibid., pp. 131–3.

23. R.W. Logan, 'The Negro Wants First-Class Citizenship' in *What The Negro Wants*, ed. Logan (Chapel Hill, 1944), pp. 18–20.

24. According to Benjamin Mays, the organisers of the Durham Conference rejected inviting northern representatives on the grounds that 'the white South would have used that as an excuse to decline cooperation'. Mays, *Born to Rebel*, p. 216.

complaints to the Committee were dismissed; only a fifth of those originating in the South were resolved successfully.[25] Even this record was too much for southern Congressmen who, as part of their gathering assault on liberal New Deal agencies, fought successfully to deprive the FEPC of funding after the latter was granted enhanced powers in 1943. Thereafter the increasingly desperate fight against employment discrimination was undertaken at the national level by A. Philip Randolph's National Council for a Permanent FEPC and, later, by the NAACP- and CIO-dominated Leadership Conference on Civil Rights. It would be another two decades before their efforts finally bore fruit.[26]

Other elements of the federal bureaucracy made their presence felt during the war years – not least the National Labor Relations Board, which proved a useful ally for southern union organisers during the Second World War, and the US Justice Department which grew markedly more sympathetic to civil rights under the stewardship of Attorney General Francis Biddle, a liberal Pennsylvania Democrat who supported the efforts of his new Civil Rights Section to suppress lynching and curb the brutality of some southern police officials.[27] But while these manifestations of federal power proffered the hope of greater assistance in the future, they did little to alter the quality of life for most southern blacks. More significant in this respect was probably the experience of military service itself which subjected thousands of black farm folk to a host of modernising experiences (for example, army discipline, commercialism, and wider human contacts) which helped to erode the traditional values of the sharecropper.[28] Wartime service in the segregated armed forces of the United States could often be a debilitating experience, but large numbers of southern black war veterans returned home with a determination either to seek a better life outside the restrictive

25. J.M. Blum, *V Was for Victory: Politics and American Culture During World War II* (New York and London, 1976), p. 214.

26. Several northern states and municipalities set up their own versions of the FEPC in the second half of the 1940s and 1950s, some of them, e.g. New York (1945) and New Jersey (1945), equipped with real enforcement powers modelled on those possessed by the National Labor Relations Board. Their achievements were slender but the very existence of such bodies indicated the growth of government backing for civil rights outside the South. See H.D. Graham, *The Civil Rights Era: Origins and Development of National Policy 1960–1992* (New York and Oxford, 1990), pp. 19–22.

27. For evidence of increased Justice Department involvement in civil rights below the Mason–Dixon Line, see D.J. Capeci, Jr, 'The Lynching of Cleo Wright: Federal Protection of Constitutional Rights during World War II', *JAH* 72 (1986), 859–87.

28. J. Modell, M. Goulden and S. Magnusson, 'World War II in the Lives of Black Americans: Some Findings and an Interpretation', *JAH* 76 (1989), 838–48.

world of the rural South or to refashion southern society along more democratic lines.

Given the Roosevelt administration's overriding commitment to winning the war (a commitment which required the support of anti-New Deal conservatives in Congress), it was hardly surprising that southern blacks felt unable to adopt a uniformly confrontational approach to civil rights. What they did do during the war years was exhibit their dissatisfaction with the status quo with countless individual acts of defiance (such as those which occurred on segregated buses throughout the region) and by joining the local branch of the NAACP in increasingly large numbers.

Between 1940 and 1945 the NAACP's membership increased nationally from around 50,000 to 450,000. Generated in part by the grass-roots mobilising efforts of Ella Baker, an assistant southern field secretary, the bulk of this impressive growth occurred below the Mason–Dixon Line where many previously moribund chapters were revitalised and scores of new ones were formed. By the war's end over a third of NAACP members were based in the South.[29] Although professional people tended to provide the majority of recruits, closer links to the trade union movement continued to spur activism and reform in many urban areas. In Mobile friendlier relations between the NAACP and the CIO resulted in accelerated voter registration efforts and other local civil rights activity.[30] In New Orleans in 1941, the ruling conservative NAACP clique was ousted by a band of radicals which included several US postal workers in its ranks as well as the impressive black lawyer, A.P. Tureaud, who shared Charles H. Houston's faith in the mobilising capacity of litigation. 'The Group', as the progressives were known, shunned the gradualist mentality of the old leadership and embarked on a more direct challenge to Jim Crow. While Tureaud cooperated closely with Thurgood Marshall on school equalisation, The Group as a whole channelled NAACP energies into a variety of other reform areas, including voting rights.[31]

Wartime efforts to advance the political power of southern blacks were greatly aided by the US Supreme Court's decision in *Smith v. Allwright* delivered on 3 April 1944. *Smith* marked the culmination of the NAACP's Texas-based legal campaign against the white primary. The Court deemed the supposedly private white primary an integral part of the election process in Texas. Thus, the exclusion

29. P. Sullivan, *Days of Hope: Race and Democracy in the New Deal Era* (Chapel Hill and London, 1996), p. 141.
30. Nelson, 'Organized Labor', p. 985.
31. Fairclough, *Race and Democracy*, pp. 57–65.

of blacks from the primary amounted to state action and was held to be unconstitutional under the Fifteenth Amendment. Southern state legislatures responded by trying to expunge all references to primaries on the statute books. Federal judges like J. Waties Waring in South Carolina, however, blocked attempts to evade the *Smith* ruling, inducing segregationists to fall back on extra-legal means to prevent blacks from voting. Their efforts were not entirely successful. Court action and grass-roots voter registration efforts resulted in a sharp rise in the number of blacks registered to vote in many southern states during the 1940s. In Texas, 70,000 blacks were added to the rolls between 1940 and 1947.[32] Overall, during the same period, the number of southern blacks registered to vote increased from 3 to 12 per cent.[33] Gains occurred in the Deep South as well as the region's fringe states. Georgia, for example, registered even more new African-American voters than Texas.

Although one scholar has suggested that *Smith* was 'the watershed in the struggle for black rights', it would be wrong to exaggerate the case's importance, particularly in the case of the lower South.[34] Many of those blacks who were allowed onto the rolls were little more than clients of moderate segregationist politicians like Governor Ellis Arnall in Georgia and Earl Long in Louisiana. Such men allowed blacks to vote in larger numbers because they wanted their support. A full-scale enfranchisement of blacks, however, was not envisaged for centrist white politicians had no intention of destroying the caste system – still less of alienating the bulk of their white supporters. *Smith* gave added impetus to the growing number of voter registration drives in the region, but political power in the Black Belt itself remained in the hands of white supremacists.

Notwithstanding the limited nature of civil rights gains during the early 1940s, the Second World War did more than any other previous event to drag the South into the twentieth century. It also allowed the Swedish sociologist Gunnar Myrdal to conclude in his influential work, *An American Dilemma* (1944), that: 'More progress has been made, in this five-year period, toward a realistic understanding of the issues involved in what we still call "the race problem" than in the entire period from the Civil War to 1940.'[35] Unfortunately the optimistic notion propounded by Myrdal – that whites had only

32. D.C. Hine, *Black Victory: The Rise and Fall of the White Primary in Texas* (Millwood, NY, 1979), p. 238.

33. S. Lawson, *Running for Freedom: Civil Rights and Black Politics in America Since 1941* (New York, 1991), p. 17.

34. Hine, *Black Victory*, p. 233.

35. Quoted in N.V. Bartley, *The New South 1945–1980* (Baton Rouge, 1995), p. 35.

to live up to their democratic creed to ensure justice for blacks –
was about to be sorely tested as the United States prepared to join
battle once again: this time with its wartime ally, the Soviet Union.

The Cold War, Brown, *and massive resistance*

As the Cold War brewed during late 1945 and 1946, southern blacks
pressed ahead with the struggle for voter registration. Especially
visible were returning military personnel, most of them eligible for
a range of federal benefits under the 1944 GI bill. In Mississippi,
where a majority of the state's veterans were black, a 21-year-old
ex-serviceman named Medgar Evers led a group of soldiers to the
Decatur County court house in July 1946 in an effort to vote in the
local Democratic primary. Although the veterans were subjected to
various forms of intimidation, they subsequently participated in a
concerted attempt to contest the election of the bigoted US senator, Theodore 'The Man' Bilbo. A Senate investigating committee
held hearings in Jackson in December 1946 attended by nearly 200
blacks, a majority of whom had fought for democracy during the
war. Although a conservative filibuster prevented the full Senate
from passing judgment on the case before Bilbo's death in August
1947, the very fact that Mississippi blacks were now prepared to
challenge their state's most powerful white racist indicated the extent
to which some of them had been emboldened by their wartime
experiences.[36]

Similar evidence of growing black militancy existed in other
southern states in the second half of the 1940s as revitalised NAACP
branches joined civic groups and the CIO's Political Action Committee in the fight against the caste system. The bulk of their efforts
took place in southern cities, all of which were hoping to participate fully in the new prosperity by presenting themselves as dynamic
commercial and industrial centres ripe for outside investment.
Southern blacks seeking better services, an end to petty apartheid
and a greater measure of political power found white civic elites
and populist politicians more sympathetic to their objectives than
ever before. Yet while the number of southern black voters continued to increase in the late 1940s, progress was limited by the
discernible white backlash which developed as a reaction to the

36. J. Dittmer, *Local People: The Struggle for Civil Rights in Mississippi* (Urbana and
Chicago, 1994), pp. 1–9.

new mood of assertiveness displayed by African Americans. Black veterans were targeted specifically as threats to the old order. A few were subjected to horrific assaults after the defeat of Japan. Isaac Woodward, still in uniform, was blinded after being beaten *en route* home through South Carolina. John C. Jones, a black officer who had fought in the Battle of the Bulge, was lynched in Minden, Louisiana, for reasons that remain obscure.[37] With Black Belt areas continuing to enjoy a disproportionate degree of political power in southern state legislatures, it seemed clear to most African-American leaders that the best hope for a swift change in black fortunes remained with the federal government in Washington.

Even though Franklin Roosevelt had evinced a much greater sympathy for civil rights than any previous president, his chief priority had not been to end racial discrimination in America. His successor, Harry Truman, a Missourian, was equally disinclined to give top priority to racial equality, but he recognised the significance of black votes to the Democratic Party and appears to have been genuinely appalled by the brutal treatment meted out to some of the returning black veterans.[38] The result was his decision to set up his own President's Committee on Civil Rights which held hearings during the spring and summer of 1947 and produced a path-breaking report, *To Secure These Rights*, in the following October.

Packed with progressive-thinking northerners and southerners, the Committee represented the apogee of war-born liberalism. Its report supported the elimination of segregation from American life and called for a much greater application of federal power in the struggle against racial injustice, particularly in the form of congressional legislation to protect and enhance basic citizenship rights and executive action to strengthen federal enforcement mechanisms.[39] Acknowledging constitutional restraints, the Committee recognised that state and local governments (as well as private organisations and individual citizens) had an important role to play in the development of a more just society in the United States. However, its members needed little convincing that the primary lead had to be

37. On the Minden lynching and its aftermath see Fairclough, *Race and Democracy*, pp. 113–18.

38. The following analysis of Truman's civil rights policy owes much to B.J. Bernstein, 'The Ambiguous Legacy: The Truman Administration and Civil Rights' in *Politics and Policies of the Truman Administration*, ed. Bernstein (Chicago, 1970), pp. 269–314, and H. Sitkoff, 'Harry Truman and the Election of 1948: The Coming of Age of Civil Rights in American Politics', *JSH* 37 (1971), 597–616.

39. President's Committee on Civil Rights, *To Secure These Rights* (Washington, DC, 1947), esp. pp. 139–73.

taken by the central state whose influence over American life had been greatly increased by the recent domestic and global crises and whose power was in the process of being further augmented by the nascent Cold War. Significantly, the Committee justified the need for greater federal intervention in the sphere of civil rights in conservative terms. The United States, it contended, could not call itself a true democracy (let alone the leader of the free world) until it began to live up to its high ideals. What the Committee called 'an aristocracy of talent and achievement' – an equality of opportunity for all – was laid down as the principal objective of national policy.[40] It would remain one of the chief goals of progressive liberals for the rest of the century.

To a large extent Harry Truman shared the objective of a genuinely meritocratic society which would embrace blacks as well as whites. A self-made man in the Lincoln tradition, he was arguably more capable of empathising with African Americans than the patrician Roosevelt. Unfortunately for black leaders like Roy Wilkins, who contrasted Truman's open, direct style with the 'slick', 'slippery' operations of his illustrious predecessor, the president was forced to confront the reality of southern power in Congress.[41] With a coherent response to Soviet expansionism as his overriding concern, Truman knew he could not afford to alienate racist Democrats who had already begun to flex their muscles against New Deal statism. Consequently, while he welcomed the report of the President's Committee and incorporated many of its proposals into his historic civil rights message to Congress in February 1948, he made little attempt to secure the passage of substantive legislation. Crudely put, he was not prepared to endanger the Democratic coalition (or his own chances of election in November) by seeking to advance what, in stark political terms, was a lost cause. Blacks, he assumed, would continue to support the Democratic Party in large numbers as long as it was perceived to be a more effective vehicle for civil rights than its Republican rival. Largely symbolic gestures, such as the decision to set up the President's Committee and Truman's speech to Harlem blacks during the 1948 presidential campaign, certainly contributed to this perception. So too did the decision of some southern Democrats to reject the liberal civil rights pledges adopted at the party's Philadelphia convention and campaign as independent 'Dixiecrats' in the general election. Developments such

40. President's Committee on Civil Rights, *To Secure These Rights*, p. 4.
41. R. Wilkins with T. Mathews, *Standing Fast: The Autobiography of Roy Wilkins* (New York, 1982), p. 198.

as these helped Truman ward off the danger from the renegade progressive Democrat, Henry Wallace, who appealed openly for black votes but whose own presidential ambitions foundered on his calls for a less confrontational foreign policy at a time of mounting Cold War hysteria.[42] However, the more assertive stance of African Americans made it clear that growing numbers of them were no longer prepared to accept symbolic gestures. Even before his surprise election victory in the autumn, therefore, Truman responded positively to persistent black pressure for integration of the armed forces and sanctioned the Justice Department's mounting assault on *de jure* segregation in transportation and education. The Fahy committee, set up by Executive Order 8981 in July 1948 (partly in response to threats from Randolph to encourage black resistance to a segregated military), paved the way for integration in the armed services – an objective finally accomplished by the military imperatives of the Korean War which began in June 1950. The Justice Department, meanwhile, prepared pro-desegregation briefs in several important Supreme Court cases culminating in *Brown v. Board of Education.*

The US Supreme Court's decision in May 1954 to declare segregated public schooling unconstitutional provided the clearest signal yet that the federal government was prepared to throw its weight against segregation. In the late 1940s southern state governments desperately sought to stave off a Supreme Court decision on public schools by increasing spending on black educational facilities. But having assumed leadership of the NAACP's litigation campaign in 1939 Thurgood Marshall was in no mood to let the states off the hook. In the Inc Fund's 1949 brief in *Sweatt v. Painter*, a graduate school case, the NAACP lawyers argued strongly for the first time that *Plessy* itself should be overturned. The Court sidestepped the issue, but a supporting brief from the US attorney general's office appeared to confirm Marshall's growing confidence in the federal judicial system. His optimism, buoyed by the persistence of New Deal liberalism into the early years of the Cold War, was shared by the Association's national board which in 1950 declared school desegregation to be one of its paramount objectives.

Pursuing his campaign in cooperation with black lawyers like Spottswood Robinson and Oliver Hill in Richmond, Virginia, and Howard Boulware in Columbia, South Carolina, Marshall and his

---

42. For a sympathetic assessment of the Wallace campaign, see Sullivan, *Days of Hope*, pp. 249–73.

team identified plaintiffs and cases which would allow them to take
the issue to the Supreme Court. In many instances they were able
to take advantage of growing civil rights militancy in local black
communities. Hill and Robinson, for example, took charge of a
desegregation case in Virginia's Southside which arose from a pupil
strike against inferior school facilities in the Farmville area.[43] Charles
H. Houston worked closely with mobilised working-class blacks in
Washington, DC. Initially Gardner Bishop, a black barber in the
northeastern section of the capital, had been impatient with middle-
class litigation strategy. As a result he had successfully circumvented
the power of the elite-run Parent Teachers' Association by founding
his own neighbourhood's Consolidated Parent Group which in
December 1947 withdrew children from schools to protest against
the inadequate standards of local black education. Notwithstanding Bishop's suspicion of the NAACP, Houston's receptivity to
community-based action made him a natural ally for the radical
parent group until his death in 1951. At that stage Bishop turned
to another Howard University law professor, James Nabrit, who
played a key role in pursuing the District's desegregation test case,
Bolling v. Sharpe, through the federal courts during the early 1950s.[44]

The NAACP's litigation campaign against segregated education finally bore fruit on 17 May 1954 when the US Supreme Court
ruled in the organisation's favour in a group of cases consolidated
under the heading of *Brown v. Board of Education of Topeka, Kansas*.[45]
Brown was selected to head the docket because it was the only non-
southern case before the Court. As the justices well knew, their
ruling was bound to prove controversial below the Mason–Dixon
Line – hence the decision not only to place the spotlight on a
midwestern city, but also, on the part of the new chief justice, Earl
Warren, to procure a unanimous verdict from the Court.

The decision was short, non-technical in character and solidly
grounded in Cold War liberalism. In spite of rejecting the NAACP's
contention that the original intent of the framers of the Fourteenth
Amendment had been to prohibit segregated schools, Warren firmly
endorsed the increasingly fashionable view (supported as it was
by a growing body of contemporary social science research) that
separate education was psychologically harmful to black children

---

43. R. Kluger, *Simple Justice: The History of* Brown v. Board of Education *and Black
America's Struggle for Equality* (London, 1977), pp. 451–507.
44. The role played by Bishop and Houston in *Bolling* is detailed in ibid., pp. 508–40.
45. On the *Brown* decision and the subsequent implementation decree, see ibid.,
pp. 700–47.

and that as a consequence their treatment was unequal and unconstitutional. Particularly revealing was his assertion, following hard on the ending of the Korean War, that the fiction of 'separate but equal' education had no place in a meritocratic, capitalist democracy:

> Compulsory school attendance laws and the great expenditures for education both demonstrate our recognition of the importance of education to our democratic society. It is required in the performance of our most basic public responsibilities, even service in the armed forces. It is the very foundation of good citizenship. Today it is a principal instrument in awakening the child to cultural values, in preparing him for later professional training, and in helping him to adjust normally to his environment. In these days, it is doubtful that any child may reasonably be expected to succeed in life if he is denied the opportunity of an education. Such an opportunity, where the state has undertaken to provide it, is a right which must be made available to all on equal terms.[46]

Warren's message to the South, then, was clear and in total conformity with the view of George F. Kennan, one of the chief architects of American containment policy after the Second World War, that to avoid destruction 'the United States need only measure up to its own best traditions and prove itself worthy of preservation as a great nation'.[47] Segregation represented a negation of modern American democracy as defined not only by the NAACP, but also by substantial elements of northern public opinion and certain arms of the federal government. On the face of things, *Brown* was thus a substantial vindication of the Association's persistent and often controversial claim that the Republic's institutions, values and historic-cultural symbols could be made to work for blacks. However, while the optimism espoused by Thurgood Marshall and his colleagues in the wake of the decision was understandable, the scepticism of some observers was equally merited. Over the next six years, African Americans would discover that the barriers to racial advancement in the 1950s were much greater than the *Brown* decision seemed to imply.

Although *Brown* neither resulted in the immediate demise of the caste system in the Deep South nor prompted a major grass-roots revolt against Jim Crow, it did crystallise the hitherto inchoate white

---

46. Quoted in A.P. Blaustein and R.L. Zangrando, eds, *Civil Rights and the American Negro* (New York, 1968), p. 436.
47. 'X' [G.F. Kennan], 'The Sources of Soviet Conduct', *Foreign Affairs* 25 (1947), 582.

opposition to the profound changes under way in southern society.[48]
Public opinion in parts of the region was polarised dramatically,
forcing moderate whites to abandon thought of gradual reform
and causing blacks to reassess their tactics and strategy. As white
intransigence grew, it became increasingly obvious to African Americans living in the Deep South that neither the federal courts nor
the traditional reformist strategy of negotiating with civic elites was
in itself likely to promote the kind of rapid social change that the
Second World War had led them to expect. The way was left open
for more militant action by blacks on both sides of the Mason–
Dixon Line.

In evaluating the impact of the *Brown* decision on southern white
opinion, it is important to distinguish between the Deep South,
particularly the main centres of plantation agriculture, and the peripheral and urban South outside the Black Belt. The Court's initial
decision was received with resignation by many white southerners,
especially by those living in parts of the region which had been most
affected by the modernising trends of the immediate past. School
desegregation began swiftly in places such as suburban Maryland
and Virginia, Washington, DC and various municipalities in Texas,
Arkansas, North Carolina, Tennessee and Florida. Few whites in
these areas welcomed the idea of integrated schools, but they preferred to accept the law of the land rather than countenance open
resistance to the national government. The most adverse reaction
came from the core states of the old Confederacy – Georgia, South
Carolina, Alabama, Mississippi and Louisiana – states where regional
distinctions were most highly prized and white supremacy was most
firmly entrenched. Although moderate urban voices such as Ralph
McGill, editor of the *Atlanta Constitution*, counselled acceptance of
the decision, major political leaders in the Deep South lost no time
in publicising their opposition to the ruling and linking it to Cold
War fears. Senator James O. Eastland, the owner of vast tracts of
cotton land in the Mississippi Delta, contended that the Court had
been 'indoctrinated and brainwashed by Left-wing pressure groups'.[49]
Most of his white constituents agreed. In the summer of 1954,
shortly after a local judge had called on patriotic Mississippians to
form 'law-abiding' resistance groups to combat school desegregation, the first White Citizens' Council was formed at Indianola, the

48. M.J. Klarman, 'How *Brown* Changed Race Relations: The Backlash Thesis',
JAH 81 (1994), 81–118.
49. Quoted in N.V. Bartley, *The Rise of Massive Resistance: Race and Politics in the
South during the 1950's* (Baton Rouge, 1969), p. 67.

governmental seat of Eastland's Sunflower County fiefdom.[50] Elsewhere, other influential southern senators began to speak the language of defiance. The name of John C. Calhoun, the nineteenth-century defender of southern rights, was frequently on the lips of Georgia's Richard Russell and Virginia's Harry F. Byrd. Not surprisingly, perhaps, *Brown* was an important election issue in a number of southern state elections in the second half of 1954. Two arch-critics of school desegregation, George Bell Timmerman and Marvin Griffin, were elected governor of South Carolina and Georgia respectively – an indication that white voters in those states were not yet resigned to the demise of Jim Crow. In other state elections that year, however, *Brown* was less of an issue. Moderate governors were elected in North Carolina and Florida, and Alabama's populist (not to say, bibulous) champion, James Folsom, won another term in the executive office in Montgomery.

With parts of the South poised to accommodate themselves to the decision and others on the verge of open defiance, the Court rendered its implementation decree in the *Brown* case in May 1955. The most significant portion of the verdict was the concluding section giving federal district courts the task of supervising the transition from segregated to integrated public schools. That task, contended Chief Justice Warren in the most famous oxymoron in American history, should be carried out 'with all deliberate speed'.[51]

The Court's cautious implementation decision (*Brown II*) represented something of a retreat from the confident tenor of the original ruling. Concern that southern whites would react violently to a desegregation decree had always been a factor in the justices' minds, but the adverse response of some powerful southern politicians during 1954 undoubtedly added to the Court's reluctance to impose rigid deadlines for integration. More critical, however, was the reluctance of President Eisenhower to give the Court his unqualified backing. Preoccupied with Communism abroad and the economy at home, Ike had limited empathy for African Americans. He did appoint a number of liberal southern Republicans to the federal bench – men like John Minor Wisdom of Louisiana – but did so on the basis of their partisan allegiance not their stance on civil rights.[52] Moreover, while he gave his backing to the desegregation

50. N.R. McMillen, *The Citizens' Council: Organized Resistance to the Second Reconstruction, 1954–64* (Urbana, Chicago, and London, 1971), pp. 17–19.

51. Quoted in Blaustein and Zangrando, eds, *Civil Rights*, p. 446.

52. J.R. Young, 'Eisenhower's Federal Judges and Civil Rights Policy: A Republican "Southern Strategy" for the 1950s', *Georgia Historical Quarterly* 77 (1994), 551–2.

of public facilities in Washington, DC and allowed Attorney General Herbert Brownell to pursue a relatively activist civil rights policy, the president's natural inclination was to adopt a gradualist stance on the explosive issue of school desegregation. His view, compounded by close friendships with prominent southerners like James Byrnes of South Carolina, was that the government should recognise the legitimacy of white fears on the subject and proceed with due restraint. *Brown II* thus reflected his own belief, privately expressed in October 1954, that the Court's duty was 'to write its orders of procedure in such a fashion as to take into consideration these great emotional strains and the practical problems, and try to devise a way where under some form of decentralised process we can bring this [i.e. school desegregation] about'.[53]

If Eisenhower's moderate stance indicated (to conservatives) a refreshing commitment to the values of American federalism, it evinced little understanding of black frustrations. His refusal to give the Court's decision anything remotely like the presidential seal of approval, moreover, helped to legitimise the resistance of southern politicians and promoted the kind of conditions in which racist demagogues could thrive. For, notwithstanding the relative caution of both president and judiciary, many southern whites found little succour in the expressed moderation of either branch of the federal government. For them the *Brown* decision and its accompanying implementation decree were positive proof that hypocritical northerners were intent on foisting their values on a proud people whose only crime, if crime it was, was to protect their way of life against the intrusive designs of an increasingly bureaucratised central state.

Initially, many black civil rights leaders failed to see *Brown II* as a retrograde step. The Inc Fund's Thurgood Marshall and Robert Carter, general counsel of the NAACP, contended that the 'mild and temperate tone' was deceiving, 'for beneath the velvet there is steel. It concedes nothing to the segregationists but an opportunity to abide by the law without loss of face.'[54] The national NAACP's response was to direct its southern branches to file petitions with local school boards on the assumption that this move would either force the school boards to act or, if action were not forthcoming, prompt intervention by the federal courts. What the Association's

53. Quoted in R.F. Burk, *The Eisenhower Administration and Black Civil Rights* (Knoxville, 1984), p. 148.

54. R.L. Carter and T. Marshall, 'The Meaning and Significance of the Supreme Court Decree', *Journal of Negro Education* 24 (1955), 399.

lawyers underestimated was the extent to which southern whites would be outraged by the idea of local blacks, hitherto assumed to be happy with their lot, acting under the auspices of an 'outside' organisation to promote race-mixing in schools. Equally naive was the NAACP's belief that the federal government would enforce the law regardless of the extent of the white reaction.

The efforts of black parents to promote school desegregation in the wake of *Brown II* played an important role in the Deep South's decision to meet school desegregation with so-called 'massive resistance'. Although signs of organised opposition had been evident before the implementation decision was announced, the NAACP's attempts to secure enforcement of the law energised the pro-segregation Citizens' Council movement throughout the Deep South. In Alabama only five councils had been formed prior to *Brown II*. By November 1955 black petition campaigns had stimulated the formation of five more.[55] There was similar evidence of a second wave of Council organizing in Mississippi, this time in areas outside the original core area of the Delta. The Jackson Citizens' Council, for example, boasted more than 300 members by mid-July 1955.[56] Largely the preserve of avowedly respectable and law-abiding middle-class whites, the Citizens' Councils used a variety of intimidatory methods to deter blacks from pursuing their legal campaign against segregated schools. In many instances parents attempting to petition school boards were threatened with the loss of their jobs or subjected to physical abuse. Private action to combat integrated schools was paralleled by a range of public laws designed to obstruct the court-supervised desegregation process and disrupt the activities of civil rights campaigners. The preferred means of resisting *Brown* were so-called 'pupil placement laws' (which allowed school boards to maintain segregated facilities by using assignment criteria other than race), state tuition grants to parents wishing to withdraw their children from mixed schools, and legislation requiring state governors to shut down schools threatened with integration. A creative array of laws combined with cruder forms of harassment to obstruct NAACP litigation and voter registration activities in the South for the foreseeable future. In two of the three states where the Association was banned completely, Alabama and Louisiana, the number of registered black voters declined precipitously during the late 1950s.

Virginia took the lead in fashioning an ideology for massive resistance. Controlled since the 1920s by a Democratic machine led

55. McMillen, *Citizens' Council*, p. 43.   56. Ibid., pp. 28–9.

by US Senator Harry F. Byrd, the state incorporated elements of the Old and the New South. The rapid expansion of the federal bureaucracy during the Second World War had made Northern Virginia a prosperous dormitory area for Washington, DC. Compliance with the law here, however, was more than counterbalanced by dogged resistance from the tobacco-growing southeast – Southside Virginia – from which the Byrd organisation drew much of its support and where more than 40 per cent of the population was black. (It was here that the strength of Virginia's genteel equivalent of the Citizens' Council, the Defenders of State Sovereignty, was concentrated.) Whites in the swing central areas of the state generally disavowed violent opposition to the law but had little enthusiasm for school integration. The majority of them, therefore, supported the Byrd organisation's decision to resist *Brown* on the grounds that the latter constituted an unwarranted attack on states' rights by the federal government. The nineteenth-century doctrine of interposition, which contended that states had the power to nullify congressional legislation they deemed unconstitutional, was successfully disinterred by the influential Richmond editor, James J. Kilpatrick, and soon became the rallying cry for Virginia segregationists. On 1 February 1956 the general assembly in Richmond resolved formally to resist *Brown* as an 'illegal encroachment upon our sovereign powers'.[57]

The attempt to shift the debate over school integration from racial prejudice to high political principle involved a good deal of cynicism. By helping to legitimise a shabby-looking cause, it enabled many supposedly law-abiding southern whites to endorse (if not actually to participate in) open resistance to the highest court in the land. Voicing concern for constitutional verities, however, was not just a conveniently respectable way of expressing antipathy for integration. Since the middle decades of the nineteenth century southerners had tended to evince a greater attachment to their locality than most northerners. In the context of the era's profound socioeconomic and intellectual developments, federal support for black rights was seen as genuinely threatening – corrosive of traditional community mores and more redolent of atheistic Communism than Christian, capitalist democracy.

This said, few southerners were ignorant of the fact that massive resistance was as much about defence of racial privilege as states

---

57. J.T. Ely, Jr, *The Crisis of Conservative Virginia: The Byrd Organization and the Politics of Massive Resistance* (Knoxville, 1976), p. 40.

rights. In the short term its advent helped to promote a degree of white unity over civil rights which had not been evident hitherto. During the late 1940s and early 1950s race had been only one of many factors in southern politics. Election contests had found local whites divided over a range of issues – not only civil rights, but also those involving labour unions, economic growth, taxation and the Cold War. Although some of these issues clearly intersected with race (trade unions, for example, were attacked not only for eroding the South's competitive labour market but also for challenging the colour line), many politicians were able to secure election below the Mason–Dixon Line without resorting to racial demagoguery. Some, like 'Big Jim' Folsom of Alabama and Earl Long of Louisiana went so far as to exhibit sympathy for African-American concerns and garnered substantial black support as a result. The onset of massive resistance, however, changed all of this. By making race the cornerstone of southern political life, it undermined attempts of populists like Folsom and Long to create class-based coalitions which transcended race and entirely isolated radical dissenters like Folsom's fellow Alabamans, Aubrey Williams and Virginia and Clifford Durr.[58] The climate was ripe for racial demagogues at all levels to play on the fears of their prospective constituents. Most liberals who refused to adapt their political careers to the new imperatives were clinically isolated by devices such as the Southern Manifesto. The latter, a stinging attack on *Brown* designed not only to promote southern unity but also to rouse ordinary voters from what conservative politicians regarded as slumber, was signed in March 1956 by all but three southern senators and a handful of southern congressmen. Those senators who did not sign – Lyndon Johnson of Texas, and Estes Kefauver and Albert Gore of Tennessee – harboured national ambitions and could ill afford to be seen as sectionalists. Although none of these men suffered politically for their action, two North Carolina congressmen who rejected the Manifesto failed to secure re-election in 1956, in part because of their alleged apostasy. Outside of the peripheral South, therefore, the Manifesto proved a remarkably successful device for rallying whites behind the standard of massive resistance.

Of course, 1956 was not 1861. Most intelligent southerners were well aware that if a power struggle broke out between state and national governments in the middle of the twentieth century, Washington would win hands down. As Governor Folsom put it,

58. Bartley, *New South*, pp. 206–12.

what could segregationists do 'now that the Feds have the nuclear bomb'?[59] The principal hope of most southern politicians was that a jurisdictional clash could be avoided by a combination of limited southern defiance and federal inaction. President Eisenhower's refusal to intervene when Democratic Governor Alan Shivers used state troopers to prevent school integration in Mansfield, Texas, in August 1956 certainly fuelled that hope. Eisenhower, no doubt conscious that Shivers was an important political ally, issued a statement indicating that the federal government had no legal justification to intervene in state affairs as long as order was maintained. He also criticised 'extremists on both sides' for encouraging the mob violence which had prompted Shivers to send in the Texas Rangers. Thurgood Marshall's response – that the president had given comfort to segregationists seeking 'to confuse the issue by trying to divide responsibility for such situations' between lawless mobs and law-abiding civil rights campaigners – fell on deaf ears.[60]

Eisenhower's overriding concern for national unity during a period of frequent foreign-policy crises contributed to his reluctance to rock the southern boat. As long as civil rights problems could be managed peacefully (and therefore prevented from becoming a propaganda asset to the communists) he could claim to be the head of a confident, unified democracy engaged in a global battle of wills with Soviet and Chinese totalitarianism. For this reason, then, once the Cold War had become institutionalised and militarised after 1950, it ceased to have a positive impact on the struggle for civil rights. Initially, the friends of racial justice had won some success by contending that Jim Crow undermined the United States' claims to be leader of the free world. Thurgood Marshall had emphasised this point before Truman's Civil Rights Committee in April 1947 as had Hubert Humphrey, a young Minnesota Democrat, in a speech before the 1948 Democratic convention.[61] Arguing in favour of a liberal civil rights plank (the adoption of which prompted disaffected southern delegates to walk out of the hall), Humphrey insisted that the free world was 'being challenged by the world of slavery. For us to play our part effectively we must be in a morally

---

59. Quoted in T. Badger, 'Fatalism, Not Gradualism: The Crisis of Southern Liberalism, 1945–65' in *The Making of Martin Luther King and the Civil Rights Movement*, ed. B. Ward and T. Badger (Basingstoke, 1996), p. 86.

60. Burk, *Eisenhower Administration*, p. 168.

61. Records of the President's Committee on Civil Rights, Proceedings of the Committee, 17 April 1947 (UPA microfilm, reel 6), pp. 100–1.

sound position.'[62] As noted above, such sentiments found an echo in the *Brown* decision and, indeed, they would continue to exert some influence on the nation's foreign policymakers throughout the 1950s and 1960s.

In the final analysis, however, the Cold War must be adjudged to have been at best a double-edged sword for civil rights campaigners. Although it could be turned to good use by black leaders, its over-riding impact was to stifle political dissent in the United States. Wars, cold or hot, could only be won by unity and it was easy for conservatives to complain that persons attempting to undermine the existing social order were acting unpatriotically. The same red-scare tactics which enabled Senator Joseph McCarthy of Wisconsin to rise to public prominence in the early 1950s enabled southern segregationists to deem virtually all civil rights activity subversive. And because the contemporary political climate was so highly charged, their efforts proved extremely effective.

The red-baiting campaign (which pre-dated massive resistance) affected individuals and organisations alike. Those, such as the black entertainer and activist, Paul Robeson, who made no attempt to disguise the Marxist roots of their civil rights activism, were easily marginalised. So too were white radicals whose advocacy of racial justice had led them into united-front activities during the 1930s. James Eastland's Senate Committee on Internal Security hounded whites belonging to the Southern Conference Education Fund (SCEF), an offshoot of the defunct Southern Conference for Human Welfare. While SCEF and CORE virtually ceased to operate during the mid-1950s, the communist-dominated Civil Rights Congress (of which Robeson was a member) was wrecked completely. The NAACP survived but only because its national leaders took great pains to establish their own patriotic credentials by severing all connections to tainted bodies like SCEF. Even this action did not prevent it from being rendered temporarily inoperative in the southern states by massive resistance legislation. Mainstream black politicians in the North took similar steps in spite of having bene-fited from the kind of 1940s liberalism which produced a rash of local civil rights legislation after the Second World War. Shortly after his election to the Washington state legislature in 1950, for example, Charles Stokes of Seattle introduced a resolution

---

62. Quoted in L. Ianello, ed., *Milestones Along the March: Twelve Historic Civil Rights Documents – From World War II to Selma* (London, 1965), p. 32.

condemning Paul Robeson for claiming that blacks would not serve in a military conflict against the Soviet Union.[63]

The Cold War also had a devastating effect on left-wing labour unions. Under intense pressure to abandon industrial militancy at a time when national unity seemed essential, American labour leaders became increasingly open to the idea of a *rapprochement* with corporate capitalism. With labour a prominent player in the Democrats' New Deal coalition and prosperity returning to the economy as a result of the Second World War, it was hardly surprising that most American workers eventually acquiesced in the decision to scale down confrontational tactics in return for higher wages and improved benefits. As a result of this accommodation with capitalism and the rapid growth of popular anti-Communism in the late 1940s, communists and fellow-travellers who had played an important role in mobilising industrial workers in the 1930s became increasingly isolated within the labour movement, their loyalties suspect because of their sympathies for the Soviet Union. In 1949–50 the CIO leadership demonstrated its patriotic credentials by expelling 11 unions alleged to be dominated by communists. These left-led unions, notably the Food, Tobacco and Agricultural Workers Union and the National Union of Maritime Cooks and Stewards, embraced some of the most downtrodden American workers, many of whom were black.[64] The expulsions therefore deprived thousands of previously powerless workers of a voice in the labour movement and contributed to the growing fear that radicals – or even moderates who could be tarred with the brush of radicalism – were fair game for all red-blooded patriots.

In 1953 the CIO finally wound up Operation Dixie, an attempt to organise large numbers of southern workers after the war. Because the most vociferous opponents of southern labour unions were often the most entrenched defenders of white supremacy, the drive had initially opened up prospects for a full-scale assault on Jim Crow. Very quickly, however, it fell foul of internal expulsions and red-baiting by conservatives.[65] The demise of radicalism brought about by these events ensured that the chances of a civil rights

63. Q. Taylor, *The Forging of a Black Community: Seattle's Central District from 1870 through the Civil Rights Era* (Seattle and London, 1994), pp. 182–3.

64. M. Goldfield, 'Race and the CIO: The Possibilities for Racial Egalitarianism During the 1930s and 1940s', *International Labor and Working-Class History* 44 (1993), 1–32, and S. Rosswurm, ed., *The CIO's Left-Led Unions* (New Brunswick, 1992), pp. 1–17.

65. M. Honey, 'Operation Dixie: Labor and Civil Rights in the Postwar South', *Mississippi Quarterly* 45 (1992), 448–52.

movement grounded in labour activism were heavily reduced. The CIO (merged with the AFL in 1955) did take steps to promote racial equality by creating an internal civil rights committee in 1942 and eight years later joined the NAACP and other organisations in forming the Leadership Conference on Civil Rights, a Washington-based lobbying forum which would later play a significant role in the passage of congressional civil rights legislation. For the most part, though, the CIO's efforts to stamp out shop-floor racism among white workers were patchy and discrimination remained rife every-where. If blacks wanted a weapon with which to attack American racism, it was clear by the mid-1950s that the nation's heavily bur-eaucratised and largely quiescent labour movement would not fit the bill.

By the beginning of 1956 Cold War conformity had left southern white radicals to confront their fate alone. One of the saddest of these isolated dissenters was Aubrey Williams, former head of the National Youth Administration who had sought to promote black rights during the New Deal.[66] Having had his department wound up by conservatives in Congress, he joined SCEF to fight for desegreg-ated education and was one of that organisation's leaders red-baited by the Eastland committee in 1954. Two years later, Williams, his influence confined to writing editorials for a Montgomery news-paper, wrote imploringly to A. Philip Randolph in New York. Respond-ing to a recent call from Randolph for black and white workers to unite, he launched into a scathing attack on northern liberals for abandoning like-minded southern whites. 'What we need if I may say so', he wrote bitterly,

> is the courage to welcome all men of goodwill to our side and not let the enemy tell us whom to include and whom to exclude. Their plan is to destroy every really decent man in the South one by one, and given the help they have had from some of the higher-ups of such organizations as the CIO and the NAACP they have and will continue to succeed beyond, I suspect, their fondest expectations.[67]

Williams' unstinting criticism of northern expediency was under-standable, but it is doubtful whether southern progressives like himself could have accomplished much – even with labour help – in the reactionary climate of the mid-1950s. White radicals were effectively marginalised by massive resistance to the *Brown* decision.

66. J. Salmond, *A Southern Rebel: The Life and Times of Aubrey Williams 1890–1965* (Chapel Hill, 1983), pp. 43–178.
67. A. Williams to A.P. Randolph, 10 July 1956, A. Philip Randolph Papers, LC.

What the cause of black progress needed at this juncture in United States history was a clear signal that African Americans themselves were prepared to mobilise in large numbers against Jim Crow. As it happened, the evidence for just such a mobilisation was available on Aubrey Williams's doorstep.

The Montgomery bus boycott

The Montgomery bus boycott was a remarkable event. Even though a good case can be made for arguing that the 381-day protest did not result directly in the desegregation of local buses, the boycott constituted the first real indication that southern blacks could organise effectively on a community-wide basis to defeat Jim Crow. Montgomery City Lines were eventually forced to integrate their buses because of a court case, *Browder v. Gayle*, which was funded partly by the NAACP and which finally found its way to the US Supreme Court in November 1956. The application of nonviolent direct action – perhaps 'indirect action' is a more accurate description – to the situation in Montgomery, however, enabled local blacks to transcend the barriers imposed by class and caste, providing civil rights campaigners throughout the United States with a potent lesson for the future. The boycott not only spurred grass-roots activity but also promoted inter-organisational cooperation between northern and southern reformers, spawned the Southern Christian Leadership Conference (SCLC) in February 1957, and inaugurated the civil rights career of a charismatic young preacher, Dr Martin Luther King, Jr. In a very real sense the birth of an organised, southern-oriented civil rights struggle dates from the afternoon of 1 December 1955 when 'a medium-sized, cultured mulatto woman', Mrs Rosa Parks, decided that she had had enough of petty apartheid and refused, when requested to do so by the bus driver, to surrender her seat to a white man as she took her usual journey home from work.[68]

Mrs Parks's action may have resulted in one of twentieth-century America's most famous protests but, as we have seen, she was not the first black southerner to register her personal frustration with the burdens of *de jure* segregation. Her arrest for disorderly conduct, however, triggered a vigorous response on the part of local black leaders who had spent the first half of the 1950s trying to procure

---

68. J.A. Gibson Robinson, *The Montgomery Bus Boycott and the Women Who Started It: The Memoir of Jo Ann Gibson Robinson*, ed. D. Garrow (Knoxville, 1987), p. 43.

a better deal for their race in negotiations with Montgomery's white civic leadership.

The first capital of the Confederacy, Montgomery was one of Alabama's largest cities. Less industrialised than either Birmingham or Mobile, it was dependent largely on servicing the surrounding agricultural hinterland but, like other urban areas in the South, it had recently experienced significant population expansion. Two US airforce bases had been constructed on the outskirts of town and businessmen were keen to encourage greater outside investment in local commerce. Demographic and economic growth had produced a rapidly changing community in which a number of groups, not just blacks, were becoming visibly dissatisfied with the city's ruling conservative machine. In 1955, 37 per cent of Montgomery's 120,000 inhabitants were black. Although African Americans constituted less than 8 per cent of the city's registered voters, there were signs during the post-war years that they might be able to use their limited political muscle to alleviate some of the worst effects of Jim Crow.[69] Particularly encouraging was the rise to power of populist politicians who campaigned on the basis of class rather than race. Their emergence meant that local blacks had the potential to hold the balance of power between competing white factions. In 1953 an anti-machine demagogue, Dave Birmingham, was elected to the governing three-man city commission. Birmingham won overwhelming support from blue-collar and lower-middle-class whites resentful of the way their interests were ignored by the city's wealthy elites. The relative liberality of Birmingham's racial views – evinced by the new appointee's support for the addition of four African Americans to the city police force – encouraged black leaders to engage in constructive dialogue with the commission during late 1953 and early 1954.

Their chief concern was the treatment meted out to blacks on local buses. Particularly resented were, firstly, a municipal ordinance requiring the first ten rows of seats to be reserved for whites no matter how crowded a bus might be and, secondly, the lack of courtesy shown to black passengers by some bus drivers. While negotiations did result in buses making more stops in black neighbourhoods, the commission failed to move significantly on the main demands. Prospects of further gains dimmed when Birmingham lost his bid for re-election as police commissioner in early 1955. His

---

69. On the political background to the boycott see J. Mills Thornton III, 'Challenge and Response in the Montgomery Bus Boycott of 1955–1956', *Alabama Review* 33 (1980), 163–235.

opponent, Clyde Sellers, took advantage of the growth in racial tensions after the *Brown* decision to depict himself as a tougher defender of the colour line than Birmingham. Sellers's blatant use of racial prejudice to counter class divisions in the white community enabled him to capture the lower-middle-class white vote which had proved so crucial to Birmingham's victory two years earlier. By the time Rosa Parks made her historic sit-down protest, biracial negotiations over the bus issue were deadlocked and the obvious alternative, litigation, was stymied owing to the lack of an ideal test case.

Rosa Parks was rather more than an ordinary black woman. Born in Tuskegee in 1913 she had been reared in small-town Alabama by her mother and grandparents after her father's death. At the age of 11 she had been sent to Montgomery to live with her aunt, a service worker at the city's Jewish country club. She received a solid education at a local dame-school, learned to sew and make quilts, and in 1932 married Raymond Parks, a college-educated barber heavily interested in the fate of the Scottsboro boys. Like many lower-middle-class southern black women she immersed herself in black civic affairs, not only those of the Methodist church but also, around 1943, the local branch of the NAACP. She rapidly became secretary of the latter although, as she later confessed, at that time 'we were not doing that much'.[70]

While her politically conscious husband, church activities and involvement with the NAACP no doubt stimulated Rosa Parks's engagement with civil rights, she later credited her initial dissatisfaction with the existing social order to her strong-minded mother who, like many black parents in the Jim Crow South, refused to bend to the dictates of the caste system. '[I]f there was anything that came up of a racial nature', recalled Mrs Parks, 'she never impressed upon me, that even with segregation and going through a schoolhouse that was just a little shack . . . that it was the way it was supposed to be.'[71]

The mid-1950s found Rosa Parks sharing the local black community's sense that negotiations with the white elite were unlikely to bring major gains once massive resistance had begun to erode the bases of populist support in Alabama. A visit to the Highlander Folk School (engineered by one of Montgomery's marginalised white dissenters, Virginia Durr), her own limited horizons (sewing for the likes of Mrs Durr was one of her principal mainstays), and the

70. Rosa Parks Interview in *The Black Women's Oral History Project*, ed. R.E. Hill (10 vols, Westport and London, 1991), vol. VIII, p. 253.
71. Ibid., p. 249.

steady decline of her alcoholic husband appear only to have fed her activism.[72] During the mid-1950s she served as the NAACP's youth secretary and refused on several occasions to yield to the humiliating demands of overbearing bus drivers. Her refusal to stand when requested to do so on 1 December 1955 was thus fully comprehensible given her own circumstances and the broader political context in which she acted. 'I felt just resigned', she said later, 'to give what I could to protest against the way I was being treated, and felt that all of our meetings, trying to negotiate, bring about petitions before the authorities . . . really hadn't done any good at all.'[73]

Rosa Parks's brave action and subsequent arrest set in train a sequence of events which resulted in the successful boycott.[74] Two local black organisers played a critical role. The first was Jo Ann Robinson, a teacher who headed the main chapter of the Women's Political Council (WPC), a middle-class civic group which had featured heavily in the recent negotiations with the city commission. Outraged by the news that such a solid member of the black community had been hauled off to jail, the WPC decided to put into operation existing, if rather unfocused, plans for a one-day protest boycott of the city's buses. The idea found favour with another stalwart member of Montgomery's black leadership, Edgar D. Nixon.

Unlike Jo Ann Robinson and the other women of the WPC, E.D. Nixon was a member of Montgomery's working-class black elite. A committed member of Randolph's BSCP, he had first met Rosa Parks in his capacity as a past president of the local NAACP. On hearing of Mrs Parks's arrest he immediately conferred with the city's two most outspoken white radicals, Virginia and Clifford Durr, who enjoyed close relations with many leading figures in the black community not only because of their involvement in the SCHW and SCEF, but also their well-publicised appearances before the Eastland committee in 1954. Nixon, the Durrs and Jo Ann Robinson all agreed that the arrest of such a respectable black woman offered the prospect of a successful test case against Alabama's bus segregation laws. Robinson's suggestion concerning a boycott also found favour as an additional means of exerting pressure on the authorities. She accepted the responsibility of publicising the one-day protest while Nixon sought to procure the support of local black ministers.

---

72. Virginia Durr Interview (1968), CRDP.   73. Parks Interview, p. 253.

74. The following account of the bus boycott relies primarily on D. Garrow, *Bearing the Cross: Martin Luther King, Jr., and the Southern Christian Leadership Conference* (New York, 1986), pp. 11–82, and T. Branch, *Parting the Waters: America in the King Years 1954–63* (pbk edn, New York, 1989), pp. 143–205.

The decision to enlist the help of the clergy was an understandable one, for the black church offered the community's political leadership the best hope of ensuring a united response to the call for a bus boycott on Monday, 5 December, the day of Mrs Parks's trial. Their support was essential because of the church's power to influence blacks across the social spectrum. Lower-class black support for the boycott was not only a crucial precondition for success but also a potentially dangerous resource if things got out of hand. In the words of Jo Ann Robinson, clerical backing was necessary 'to give Christian guidance to a rebellious people, and to keep the masses under control. Had the ministers not assumed leadership, disorganised, irresponsible persons might have resorted to shameful violation or individual retaliation upon certain bus drivers.'[75] Fears of black violence would haunt the determinedly respectable civil rights movement throughout its existence and were clearly very much in evidence at the genesis of the Montgomery bus boycott.

To Nixon's relief the ministers' response was a broadly positive one. At a meeting at the Dexter Avenue Church on 2 December the clergy, pushed into an uncomfortable corner by the community's secular leaders, accepted the *fait accompli* set before them and began to help with plans to publicise the boycott.

Once it became clear that the bus boycott enjoyed virtually unanimous support in the black community, secular and church leaders resolved to maintain the pressure on the city commissioners by extending the protest indefinitely. To coordinate the boycott they formed the Montgomery Improvement Association (MIA) – an umbrella organisation which was enthusiastically welcomed by the first of the southern civil rights movement's great mass meetings held at the Holt Street Baptist Church on the first night of the protest. Of that meeting, the MIA's young black lawyer, Fred Gray, later recalled:

> There was an electricity in the air. Such a feeling of unity, success and enthusiasm had never been before in the city of Montgomery, certainly never demonstrated by African Americans. The people were together. They were singing. They were praying. They were happy that Mrs. Parks had refused to give up her seat . . . They clapped and shouted 'Amen' as the boycott leaders entered the auditorium.[76]

75. Robinson, *Bus Boycott*, p. 64.
76. F. Gray, *Bus Ride to Justice: Changing the System by the System; the Life and Works of Fred Gray* (Montgomery, 1996), p. 58.

The whole event, thought Gray, himself a trained preacher, reminded him of the account of the day of Pentecost in Acts II: 1–2: '[T]hey were all with one accord in one place. And suddenly there came a sound from heaven as of a rushing mighty wind, and it filled all the house where they were sitting.'[77]

The main speaker at this emotional gathering was the new president of the MIA, a 26-year-old, Atlanta-born Baptist preacher named Dr Martin Luther King, Jr who had accepted the pastorship of the elite Dexter Avenue Church in 1953. Largely unconnected to existing factions within the black community, well educated, and a remarkably charismatic speaker, King was an obvious choice for president of the MIA and he accepted the position as a civic, racial and religious duty. By the time the boycott ended he was the most important black southerner in the United States.

Under King's leadership the MIA played a vital role in making the bus boycott a success. Crucial here was its organisation of a car pool, modelled on a short-lived enterprise in Baton Rouge in 1953, to enable local blacks to get to work without using the buses.[78] The MIA procured funding and voluntary drivers for what was, in the eyes of the white authorities, an illicit taxi service. Equally importantly, it helped to sustain community morale by sponsoring regular mass meetings held in local churches. Clerical participation was clearly a vital ingredient in the organisation's success. While the church's enormous prestige helped to legitimise the boycott, its multifaceted resources furnished the MIA with many of the tools necessary to sustain it: money, buildings, leaders and moral direction. Without this backing it is unlikely that Montgomery blacks would have responded to the leadership's call in the unified fashion that so surprised (and so cheered) those who took part in the boycott.

The relatively conservative nature of the MIA's original demands supports J. Mills Thornton's view that the boycott was initially conceived as an extension of the stalled negotiations with the city commission.[79] No demand was made for an end to segregation on the buses – merely a request for more courteous service, the employment of black bus drivers, and a back-to-front seating policy which would have prevented blacks from being forced to stand over empty seats. So rooted in the gradualist tradition of southern reform were

77. Ibid., p. 59.
78. For an account of the Baton Rouge boycott see Fairclough, *Race and Democracy*, pp. 156–62.
79. Thornton, 'Challenge and Response', p. 231.

these negotiating stances that the national NAACP, determined to destroy the caste system completely, rejected the MIA's first invitation to aid the litigation campaign in January 1956. What altered matters was the refusal of the ruling commission to negotiate with blacks on an equal basis and a rapid escalation of white intimidation early in the New Year. The entrenchment of massive resistance in Montgomery, evidenced by Police Commissioner Clyde Sellers' decision to join the burgeoning ranks of the Citizens' Council, the arrest of Dr King on a trumped-up charge of speeding in January, and the subsequent bombing of King's home at the end of the month, marginalised moderate white sympathy for the boycott and forced MIA leaders to raise the stakes.

The events in Montgomery quickly attracted the attention of northerners interested in civil rights, not least radical pacifists who sensed that the boycott presented an ideal opportunity to test their ideas about nonviolent direct action. Among them was James Farmer, one of the wartime founders of CORE, whose wife, Lula, told him on hearing of the boycott that it was 'precisely the spark that you've been working and hoping for, for years'.[80] Struck by the same realisation was Bayard Rustin, a one-time member of FOR and CORE who was keen to convince northern black leaders that he should be allowed to go south and furnish advice to the MIA.

Although Rustin was to become one of the most important strategists of the civil rights movement, there were good reasons why Rustin's allies in New York might not have acceded to his request. Born and brought up in Pennsylvania, Rustin had belonged to the Young Communist League during his days as a Harlem intellectual in the 1930s. Equally seriously, given the hysterical climate of 1955, he had been jailed for draft resistance during the Second World War and subsequently arrested on a vice charge in Los Angeles. A black, homosexual, ex-communist who belonged to a minor pacifist group, the War Resisters League, Rustin looked like a liability to any civil rights crusade in the southern states.[81]

So impressive were Rustin's organising skills, however, that he was eventually permitted to venture south with the blessing of both Randolph and Farmer. Arriving in Montgomery on 21 February 1956, he quickly sought out leading figures in the MIA. Some of them, particularly E.D. Nixon, were concerned that his notoriety might destroy the boycott. Others, including Martin Luther King, listened carefully to what Rustin and FOR representative Glenn

80. Farmer, *Lay Bare*, p. 186.   81. Garrow, *Bearing the Cross*, pp. 66–7.

Smiley, a southern white Methodist, had to say about Gandhi. King confessed that he had only a superficial knowledge of the Mahatma's work and seems to have had his existing faith in Christian love deepened by his conversations with the two radical pacifists. However, the outsiders' impact upon both himself and the boycott was limited – not only by the fact that Rustin was forced to leave Montgomery by stealth at an early stage in the boycott but also because the MIA leaders were more capable of organising a non-violent campaign than many northern activists had suspected. While none of the boycott leaders, King included, adhered to radical pacifism or strict Gandhian standards of morality, they all understood that a resort to violence would have divided local blacks and greatly increased the force of the white backlash in Montgomery. King's commitment to nonviolent direct action would grow as a result of his contacts with people like Rustin and Smiley, but his own antagonism to violence pre-dated his first meeting with the radicals and was a product not of Gandhianism but his own religious upbringing in a relatively well-to-do black suburb of Atlanta. This upbringing rendered him receptive to American Gandhians but made it unlikely that he would ever become their pawn. Indeed, as David Garrow has argued, the bus boycott itself proved to be a more formative experience for King than anything northern pacifists were able to teach him.[82]

While A. Philip Randolph and his allies provided useful intellectual and financial support for the MIA, the most important backing came from the NAACP. Crucial here was its role in the litigation campaign which eventually brought the boycott to a successful conclusion in the courts.[83] Fearing that an appeal against Parks's conviction for violating state segregation laws might become snarled up in the state courts, NAACP attorney Robert Carter suggested that a new suit should be inaugurated in federal court – one which contended that Alabama's bus segregation laws were unconstitutional in the light of the *Brown* decision. The MIA's legal counsel, Fred Gray, endorsed this view and continued to work closely with Carter and Thurgood Marshall while the MIA's new case, *Browder v. Gayle*, made its way through the federal court system. The NAACP had good reason to be confident. In July 1955 its lawyers had secured a ruling from the US Fourth Circuit Court that the *Brown* decision

82. Ibid., pp. 11–82, esp. p. 58.
83. On the legal aspects of the Montgomery bus boycott see R.J. Glennon, 'The Role of Law in the Civil Rights Movement: The Montgomery Bus Boycott, 1955–1957', *Law and History Review* 9 (1991), 59–112.

was probably designed to apply to segregated transportation as well as public schools. The Supreme Court nodded its assent to this verdict the following April.

Harassed persistently by the Montgomery city authorities who sought to bring the full force of state law to bear on both the MIA and the NAACP, the boycott leaders chose to complement *Browder* with a continuation of the grass-roots campaign. To have given up the boycott would have been seen as a sign of surrender by the city commission and they had come too far to give up. *Browder* eventually brought them victory. On 5 June 1956 a three-man federal panel struck down state and municipal bus segregation statutes citing recent Supreme Court decisions impairing the old separate-but-equal rule. Five months later, the Supreme Court itself upheld the lower court's decision – a mandate which finally arrived in Montgomery on 20 December. The following day Glenn Smiley joined King and other bus boycott leaders in riding the first City Lines bus to be desegregated.

The underlying importance of *Browder* should not be allowed to conceal the significance of the grass-roots action campaign. Even though the NAACP hierarchy used the case to defend its conviction that litigation was a more effective tool for social reform than mass action, the example provided by the boycott was an important one. The MIA's successful attempt to sustain morale and commitment over time and across a black community riven by the usual divisions of class, gender, colour, partisanship and personality revealed to watching observers that southern blacks were capable of launching an all-out assault on Jim Crow. African Americans in Tallahassee and Rock Hill, South Carolina, emphasised the fact by learning from the Montgomery example and initiating their own bus boycotts. Several other cities including Birmingham and Chattanooga witnessed less concerted protests. Even though most of these campaigns were not as successful as the MIA's venture, King's inspirational leadership and the dignified resistance of ordinary Montgomery blacks seemed to indicate that nonviolent action did, indeed, possess relevance to the race question in the United States.

Significantly, the MIA's boycott provided the first major example of interregional cooperation between northern civil rights activists and southern blacks. Further evidence of this came early in 1957 when, following suggestions from Rustin and two New York leftists, Ella Baker and a white Jewish lawyer, Stanley Levison, the church-based Southern Christian Leadership Conference was formed in

Atlanta.[84] The northerners believed that it was essential not only to maintain the momentum provided by the success of the Montgomery bus boycott but also to use Martin Luther King's talents and prestige to stimulate direct action on a southwide basis. With the NAACP's southern activities stalled by legal and extra-legal resistance on the part of southern segregationists, the SCLC, King at the helm, began to assume leadership of the struggle for black equality below the Mason–Dixon Line.

Treading water

Although the sociologist, Aldon Morris, has rightly depicted the late 1950s as a period of organisational development for civil rights, it is essential not to use too much hindsight when evaluating the years 1957–59.[85] Discernible 'movement centres' such as Nashville (where the Methodist minister and committed exponent of Gandhian methods, James Lawson, was particularly active), Birmingham, and Atlanta did evolve following the success of the Montgomery bus boycott, but there is much evidence to suggest that the movement trod a good deal of water in the final years of the Eisenhower presidency. Limited organisational goals and relative federal inactivity in the face of massive resistance constituted the main problems.

The SCLC's emergence from the shadow of the NAACP took time. King and his fellow ministers were conscious that the more established civil rights organisation was jealous of its leadership role. Building up the SCLC at a juncture when its potential rival was being harassed by southern state authorities could only have undermined the relationship between the two groups at a time when cooperation between them was essential. This was the reason that the SCLC declined to structure itself along the same lines as the NAACP with a system of local branches, each of them made up of dues-paying members and capable of acting autonomously within the broad policy framework established by national headquarters.[86] Instead the Atlanta-based SCLC remained an autocratic

---

84. The word 'Christian' was actually added to the organisation's title in August 1957 at King's behest in order to alleviate the danger of red-baiting.

85. A.D. Morris, *The Origins of the Civil Rights Movement: Black Communities Organizing for Change* (New York and London, 1984), pp. 174–94.

86. Bartley, *New South*, p. 185.

organisation dominated at the top by King (who moved back to Atlanta in early 1960), and at the local level by black ministers who ran SCLC affiliates in major urban centres like Nashville, Birmingham, and Savannah.

Another reason for the SCLC's failure to mount a more open challenge to the NAACP was King's reluctance to mount a campaign of massive civil disobedience throughout the South in the wake of his triumph in Montgomery. Of course, planning for such an exercise required time and money, but at first King struggled to put his evolving ideas about nonviolence into practice. His central belief in the late 1950s, aided by a visit to India sponsored by some of his Gandhian advisers, was that the white oppressor could be shamed into abandoning Jim Crow by the use of nonviolent resistance. This resistance, he believed, had to be disciplined and dignified – African Americans had to take the moral high ground in order to promote social change. More than that, they had to love their oppressor in the most unsentimental sense of the word. Only then would southern whites see the error of their ways and embrace black people, if not as brothers then certainly as fellow citizens. A nonviolent campaign, insisted King at the beginning of 1957, was essential:

> In struggling for human dignity the oppressed people of the world must not allow themselves to become bitter or indulge in hate campaigns. To retaliate with hate and bitterness would do nothing but intensify the hate in the world. Along the way of life, someone must have sense enough and morality enough to cut off the chain of hate.[87]

Although King was clearly anticipating a shift to nonviolent direct action during this early phase of his civil rights career, he allowed himself to be diverted into a more mainstream voter registration project grandiosely entitled the Crusade for Citizenship. He did so for at least two reasons. Firstly, he was well aware that Roy Wilkins regarded civil disobedience as ineffective and potentially destructive of his own organisation's litigation strategy. Secondly, it was not yet clear that mass action would work in the South. Although the events in Montgomery inspired a number of protests, none of them achieved the same degree of success. The failure of litigation was a key factor in Birmingham (where federal judge Harlan Grooms proved disappointingly obstructive) and Tallahassee (whose MIA

---

87. M.L. King, 'Nonviolence and Racial Justice' in *A Testament of Hope: The Essential Writings and Speeches of Martin Luther King, Jr,* ed. J.M. Washington (San Francisco, 1991), p. 8.

equivalent, the Inter-Civic Council, was unable to develop an effective test case along the lines of *Browder*). Mass action petered out in Rock Hill after it resulted in the collapse of the local bus company.[88] Urban centres in the upper and peripheral South evinced a readiness to end Jim Crow transportation, but most civic authorities in the Deep South remained wedded to traditional racial practices.

Attempting to boost black voter registration made some sense in the stolid climate of the late 1950s, particularly when the Republicans and Democrats were bidding for black support. Unfortunately for King, the two major parties were just as keen to hold on to or increase their share of southern white votes with the result that both declined to endorse radical action on civil rights in the late 1950s. Congressional legislation was limited to two civil rights acts (1957 and 1960), both of them bipartisan compromises which had relatively little impact on the extent of black voter registration in the Deep South. Had the SCLC possessed genuine grass-roots strength, its own voting rights campaign might have proved a positive supplement to the two new federal statutes. Its lack of mass support and early administrative problems, however, rendered the Crusade for Citizenship a damp squib. Voting rights for many southern blacks would remain a chimera until the movement was able to make contact with the disfranchised rural masses and the federal government was pressed to enforce basic citizenship rights at the expense of state authority.

Only one event during the Eisenhower presidency suggested that Washington might have the will to back up the *Brown* decision with federal power.[89] In the autumn of 1957 the moderate Arkansas governor, Orval Faubus, convinced that the administration was unwilling to take responsibility for school desegregation, decided to challenge a US district court ruling that Central High School in Little Rock had to be integrated forthwith. He did so on 4 September by dispatching Arkansas National Guardsmen to the school in order to prevent the admission of nine black children. Negotiations between Faubus and the Justice Department then ensued with the governor asserting his constitutional authority to maintain domestic order (his grounds for obstructing integration) and Attorney-General Herbert Brownell pressing for enforcement of the district judge's

---

88. C. Barnes, *Journey from Jim Crow: The Desegregation of Southern Transit* (New York, 1983), pp. 125, 127.

89. On the Little Rock crisis see Burk, *Eisenhower Administration*, pp. 174–203, and S.E. Ambrose, *Eisenhower: The President 1952–1969* (London and Sydney, 1984), pp. 414–23.

edict. Brownell, a liberal New York Republican steeped in the party's early history as a vehicle for racial equality, had already sought to increase his own statutory power to promote civil rights in line with the *Brown* decision.[90] Eisenhower's caution and southern power in Congress, however, had already drawn the sting from his draft civil rights bill which passed, greatly amended, shortly before the Little Rock crisis came to a head. Faubus would have secured a similar compromise had he accepted the need for some form of token integration at Central High. His refusal to obey a final mandate to allow the black students into the school strengthened the attorney-general's case for intervention.

The Arkansas governor not only declined to obey federal law but also led Eisenhower to believe that he had been double-crossed. At a summit meeting in Newport, Rhode Island, on 14 September the president understood Faubus to say that he would cease to obstruct the court order. He therefore failed completely to understand Faubus's strategy which was to exploit racist and localist fears among the electorate in order to secure his re-election in 1958. By posing as a staunch defender of states' rights, Faubus gambled that his reputation as an Arkansas hero would be guaranteed regardless of the federal reaction. On 20 September he announced that the militia would be withdrawn from Central High and shortly afterwards left to attend a southern governors' meeting on the Georgia coast.

The result was predictable. On 23 September a mob of over 500 whites descended on the high school in order to prevent the first cohort of black students from entering the building. Local police made little attempt to maintain order and Eisenhower was forced to dispatch federal paratroopers to enforce the law. Faubus duly denounced the 'military occupation' upon his return and watched as Eisenhower sought to extricate himself from a situation partly of his own making.

In truth, although civil rights leaders welcomed the dramatic intervention of federal troops in Little Rock, the president had little enthusiasm for such ventures. He remained a reluctant advocate of civil rights, generally wary of undermining the existing polity until pushed into a corner by a southern politician who did not, significantly, belong to his circle of political backers. While Little Rock offered the civil rights movement a model of what could

90. For Brownell's own account of his civil rights policy see H. Brownell with J. Burke, *Advising Ike: The Memoirs of Attorney General Herbert Brownell* (Lawrence, 1993), esp. pp. 202–29.

happen if the federal authorities were stung into action, it did not reflect the general tenor of federal policy in the 1950s. Its very atypicality meant that Little Rock bore some resemblance to the Montgomery bus boycott, a more significant event in the annals of civil rights history, but one which also constituted something of an aberration in the overall context of the black freedom struggle in the late 1950s. For the most part, national civil rights leaders eschewed mass action in favour of a more cautious focus on congressional lobbying and voter registration.

Although federal intervention in Little Rock appears to have convinced increasing numbers of southern whites that desegregation was inevitable, there were fewer outward signs of the impending civil rights revolution at the end of the Eisenhower years than there had been in the 1940s.[91] The beginning of the Cold War marked the interval between Adam Fairclough's two-act play: the first act characterised by new experiments in direct action and growing radicalism on the part of the NAACP and other groups; the second by a concerted grass-roots assault on the caste system which began in 1960.[92] Although there *were* indications that massive resistance had begun to run its course by the end of the 1950s (witness, for example, white parental opposition to public school closures in the South), it requires a good deal of hindsight to see the curtain rising for the second half of the performance.[93] For the most part, the federal courts' readiness to accept token integration meant that in the Deep South the *Brown* decision remained unimplemented throughout Eisenhower's second term. Petty apartheid, racist violence and widespread disfranchisement of southern blacks continued unabated. Without a sterner test, it seemed that Jim Crow might survive the political and social changes of the post-war era – if not intact, then certainly in better health than many segregationists had feared in 1954.

91. Bartley, *New South*, pp. 234–5.   92. Fairclough, *Race and Democracy*, p. xii.
93. P. Ling, 'Dusk and Dawn: Black Protest in the Fifties and Forties' in *Cracking the Ike Age: Aspects of Fifties America*, ed. D. Carter (Aarhus, 1992), p. 76.

CHAPTER 4

The Destruction of Jim Crow 1960–65

Martin Luther King may have been one of the most visible black leaders in the United States by the beginning of 1960 but few whites at this time understood the intellectual basis for his evolving philosophy of nonviolence – this in spite of the fact that King set down his largely derivative ideas in several journal articles in the late 1950s as well as in his partly ghost-written account of the Montgomery bus boycott, *Stride Toward Freedom.* Still less did most observers comprehend the growing impatience felt by most African Americans at a time when decolonisation was proceeding apace outside the United States. Only a handful of Americans, moreover, could have predicted that the early 1960s would one day be labelled 'the King years' or, indeed, that the same period would witness the genesis and rapid maturation of a mass-based campaign designed to secure equal rights for African Americans.[1] The rash of student sit-ins which occurred in the spring of 1960, however, transformed the cautious civil rights coalition of the late 1950s into a genuine social movement. King himself had nothing to do with the original sit-in staged in Greensboro, but through a process of trial and error, he and his organisation – the SCLC – harnessed the new grass-roots energy behind a broad-based struggle to procure federal intervention against southern segregation. Although this process was frequently frustrating and should not be allowed to define the civil rights movement in its entirety, it culminated in the final collapse of the caste system via the passage of the Civil Rights Act of 1964 and the Voting Rights Act of 1965. The victory was certainly not King's alone but it owed much to the Atlanta minister's remarkable appeal among whites as well as blacks and to the SCLC's dramatic

---

1. T. Branch, *Parting the Waters: America in the King Years 1954–63* (New York, 1988).

use of nonviolent direct action in the Alabama cities of Birmingham and Selma.

The student sit-ins of 1960

The grass-roots struggle against Jim Crow began in earnest on 1 February 1960 when four black college students launched their personal assault on the southern caste system. Frustrated with the slow pace of reform in their home town, Franklin McCain and Joseph McNeil walked into the F.W. Woolworth store in downtown Greensboro, North Carolina, and, after purchasing some school supplies, made their way over to the segregated lunch counter where they ordered coffee and doughnuts.[2] When an embarrassed waitress declined to serve them, they politely refused to move on the grounds that having bought goods in the store they were as entitled to eat at the lunch counter as any white customer. Joined at the counter by their friends, Ezell Blair and David Richmond, the students made their point once again to the store's equally uncomfortable and predictably patronising manager. McCain remembered the mixed reaction of onlookers. Two elderly white women approached the students and wished them well. 'Ah', said one of them, 'you should have done it ten years ago.' Other spectators were more hostile and told the 'dirty niggers' to go downstairs to the stand-up hot-dog counter reserved for blacks. A bemused white police officer who had come in off the street stood by knocking his club into his hand 'just looking mean and red and a little bit upset and a little bit disgusted'. The students drew psychological sustenance from his evident discomfort and the good wishes of the elderly white women. Less supportive was a middle-aged black woman washing dishes behind the counter. Fearful of the consequences of the students' action, she called the youths reckless 'rabble-rousers' and 'troublemakers'. 'This counter is reserved for white people,' she said, 'it always has been, and you are well aware of that.'[3]

The students' decision to confront Jim Crow dispelled the strong sense of guilt which many young southern blacks felt about their relative quiescence under a system designed to undermine their basic self-image. In the words of Franklin McCain:

2. W.H. Chafe notes that minimal school desegregation had taken place in Greensboro prior to the first sit-in. Chafe, *Civilities and Civil Rights: Greensboro, North Carolina, and the Black Struggle for Freedom* (New York, 1980), p. 100.

3. H. Raines, *My Soul Is Rested: Movement Days in the Deep South Remembered* (New York, 1983), pp. 76–8.

If it's possible to know what it means to have your soul cleansed – I felt pretty clean at that time. I probably felt better on that day than I've ever felt in my life. Seems like a lot of feelings of guilt or what-have-you suddenly left me, and I felt as though I had gained my manhood, so to speak, and not only gained it, but had developed quite a lot of respect for it. Not Franklin McCain only as an individual, but I felt as though the manhood of a number of other black persons had been restored and had gotten some respect from just that one day.[4]

If, as some southern white liberals believed (even in the wake of the Montgomery bus boycott), outward black conformity was partly to blame for the persistence of the caste system, this perception was no longer tenable after the Greensboro sit-in.[5] A powerful sense of confidence and self-esteem surged through the four participants as they overcame their innermost fears to make a public stand against segregation. They could not know it, but their action was to strike a chord with thousands of their peers across the South. Better educated than their parents and frustrated by the slow pace of change after *Brown*, black students throughout the region saw the events in North Carolina as a reveille for revolt.

When the store closed McCain and his friends returned to the campus of the North Carolina Agricultural and Technical College where they were fêted as heroes. The next morning they embarked on a second sit-in. This time they were joined by over 20 fellow students. As the local press began to get hold of the story, the protest mushroomed. By Friday, 5 February, hundreds of students, some of them white, were crowding into downtown stores to protest against segregated facilities. Woolworth and Kress closed their doors on the 6th and negotiations involving the students, local black leaders, and Greensboro's white elite were soon underway. News of the protests spread rapidly, sparking off copy-cat demonstrations first in the adjacent cities of Winston-Salem, Raleigh and Durham, and then in urban areas further afield. Nashville students began their sit-ins on 13 February; their counterparts in Atlanta just over a month later. By April the peace of 78 southern communities had been disturbed by sit-ins and 2,000 people had been arrested. The student demonstrations were a watershed in the history of black protest in the United States. In effect they kick-started the civil rights movement into action by revealing the extent of grass-roots

4. Raines, *My Soul is Rested*, p. 78.
5. See e.g. J.M. Dabbs, 'The South's Man Across the Table', *New South* 12 (1957), 6.

dissatisfaction with segregation and by providing the existing protest organisations with a mass constituency in the South.

The four Greensboro students had no idea that they were initiating a new phase of the freedom struggle. Although two of them possessed institutional links to the local NAACP youth chapter and Ezell Blair's father was a prominent NAACP member, the freshmen's action was largely spontaneous, their objectives decidedly limited, and their preparations essentially private and devoid of long-term strategy. It did not take long, however, for the established civil rights organisations to intervene in the proceedings. If the momentum generated by the sit-ins were to be sustained, the national leadership's cognitive and practical aid had to be put to good use at once.

As noted above direct action tactics were not a complete novelty in 1960. Members of CORE had been experimenting with the sit-in sporadically throughout the late 1940s and 1950s. Martin Luther King's close associate, the Rev. James Lawson, had been preparing the ground for civil disobedience in Nashville since 1958.[6] His workshops for the Nashville Christian Leadership Conference produced trial sit-ins at city stores in late 1959. These demonstrations involved highly motivated Christians from several local colleges including Fisk and the American Baptist Theological Seminary. Embracing students like John Lewis, Diane Nash, and Marion Barry, the group went on not only to initiate more sustained protests in February 1960, but also to constitute one of the most disciplined cadres of young southern blacks in the civil rights movement.

Certain chapters of the NAACP youth council had also used the sit-in prior to what Taylor Branch has called 'the quickening'.[7] On 2 August 1958, for example, an NAACP youth group occupied all 33 seats at the segregated lunch counter at Dockums drug store in Wichita, Kansas – an act which brought about the abolition of discriminatory practices within two weeks.[8] So impressed was the organisation's national youth director, Herbert Wright, that he hailed the action 'as an outstanding example of what young people can do to help remove discrimination from American life'.[9]

Notwithstanding these early instances of direct action, the Greensboro sit-ins caught all the main civil rights organisations by surprise.

6. A.D. Morris, *The Origins of the Civil Rights Movement: Black Communities Organizing for Change* (New York and London, 1984), pp. 174–7.

7. Branch, *Parting*, pp. 272–311.

8. C.I. Lewis to H. Wright, 12 August 1958, NAACP Youth File, Geographical File, Wichita, K., Box E4, Group 3, NAACP Papers, LC.

9. H. Wright to H.L. Moon, Memorandum, 20 August 1958, NAACP Youth File, Geographical File, Wichita, K., Box E6, Group 3, NAACP Papers, LC.

Their first reaction was to attempt to direct the students' energies into constructive channels which, in effect, meant exercising some control over the southern demonstrations. The black Baptist preacher, Fred Shuttlesworth, leader of the SCLC affiliate in Birmingham, was preaching in North Carolina when the first sit-ins began. 'You must tell Martin that we must get with this', he urged the SCLC's executive director, Ella Baker, convinced as he was that the ongoing events might 'shake up the world'.[10] Although the SCLC was not without influence in subsequent weeks (particularly through its affiliate in Nashville) the leading role was taken initially by the NAACP and CORE.

Shortly after the Greensboro sit-ins began, the students appealed to Dr George Simkins, head of the local branch of the NAACP. Simkins volunteered his own chapter's support for their activities but, on finding that the national office was reluctant to guarantee aid to a protest it knew little about, he contacted CORE headquarters in New York for assistance.[11] Recognising the sit-ins as an opportunity not only to implement Gandhian tactics in the United States but also to boost public awareness of a hitherto marginal civil rights organisation, CORE immediately dispatched its two white field workers to the South. Gordon Carey and James McCain furnished valuable assistance to students in several communities, including Durham, North Carolina, and Rock Hill, South Carolina. The New York office also instigated demonstrations in several northern cities to show support for the direct action protests taking place in the southern states. While such efforts did bring the organisation significant publicity and made a positive contribution to the limited desegregation which took place as a consequence of the first wave of sit-ins, CORE was initially most effective in the handful of areas where it was an established force. In the long run, however, the sit-ins initiated the process which transformed CORE from a cadre of predominantly white pacifists into one of the country's most effective black civil rights organisations.

Yet in terms of members CORE could not hope to compete with the NAACP which, notwithstanding southern state obstruction of its activities in the late 1950s, was better placed than any other civil rights organisation to take advantage of recent events. National Youth Director Herbert Wright was quick to realise that the sit-ins provided the Association with a chance to galvanise its efforts below the Mason–Dixon Line. Arriving in Greensboro on 12 February, he embarked on a tour of North Carolina, speaking with branch heads

10. Quoted in Branch, *Parting*, p. 273.   11. Chafe, *Civilities*, p. 117n.

and student leaders. In Winston-Salem he joined Fred Shuttlesworth in helping students from the local black teachers' college draft a petition to downtown store managers and plan an orderly picket of segregated businesses. In Durham he conferred with the SCLC's Douglas Moore and Gordon Carey of CORE. After attending an inter-organisational gathering on 16 February and meeting with state NAACP youth leaders, Wright helped local students form the Statewide Student Protest Coordinating Body to bring a semblance of order to the largely spontaneous demonstrations taking place in North Carolina. Although Wright was clearly prepared to cooperate with other organisations in the pursuit of racial justice, his overriding commitment was to the NAACP. On 3 March he wrote to Roy Wilkins requesting authorisation to sponsor a one-day national emergency conference to be held in Washington, DC later in the month. The main goals of the conference, he suggested, would be to plan 'a mammoth nationwide sit-down campaign against discrimination in all places of public accommodation in the United States – north and south!'; to educate student leaders in effective direct action techniques; to enable the NAACP to gather information about the southern protests; and '[t]o project the NAACP, and enable it to assume the major coordinating role in the protests'. If the Association failed to act immediately on this subject, noted Wright, 'I am afraid that we might be out-maneuvered by some other organization.'[12]

Although there is evidence to suggest that the youth secretary spoke for a substantial segment of opinion within the NAACP, Wright's superiors ignored his advice that the nation's largest and hitherto most effective civil rights organisation should engage positively with the student activists. The national office did issue a statement endorsing the direct action protests in March and did not seek to prevent many local branches from taking a leading role in the student demonstrations. On the whole, however, Roy Wilkins declined to commit himself to the bold strategy outlined by Wright. Personally sceptical of the view that civil disobedience could secure lasting gains for southern blacks and suspicious of those he regarded as irresponsible radicals, Wilkins was temperamentally unprepared to lead the NAACP into uncharted waters.[13] He recognised, too, that large numbers of middle-class NAACP supporters, particularly

12. H. Wright to R. Wilkins, Memorandum, 3 March 1960, NAACP Youth File, General Department File, Wright Memoranda and Reports 1958–62, Box E53, Group 3, NAACP Papers.
13. R. Wilkins with T. Mathews, *Standing Fast: The Autobiography of Roy Wilkins* (New York, 1982), p. 237.

those resident in areas where the caste system was most entrenched, would balk at the notion of street demonstrations. As a consequence, while the national NAACP took care not to criticise the students and offered them vital legal and financial aid, it failed to embrace wholeheartedly the concept of nonviolent direct action at a critical moment in the history of the black freedom struggle. The result was, as Herbert Wright predicted, that the NAACP began to surrender leadership of the struggle to organisations which were prepared to take the movement onto the streets.

The formation of 'Snick' – the Student Nonviolent Coordinating Committee – in the spring of 1960 signalled the shape of things to come.[14] At the behest of the SCLC's Ella Baker, 120 black and a dozen white students from across the South gathered between 16 and 18 April at Shaw University in Raleigh to hear Martin Luther King urge them to prepare for a southwide campaign to secure federal intervention in the struggle against Jim Crow. Baker, disillusioned with King's autocratic leadership style and his failure to develop a genuinely grass-roots movement, played an important role by suggesting, firstly, that the students should organise separately from the adult civil rights groups; secondly, that they should seek to broaden their objectives beyond the desegregation of lunch counters; and, thirdly, that the experienced Nashville organiser, James Lawson, should preside over the conference.

Lawson's influence on the students was evident from the start. In a powerful address, he urged the audience to begin its deliberations by debating the fundamental moral principles of the incipient organisation. Notwithstanding murmurs of dissent from those who wanted to discuss tactics rather than philosophy, he secured adoption of an explicitly religious-based statement of purpose:

> We affirm the philosophical or religious ideal of nonviolence as the foundation of our purpose, the presupposition of our faith, and the manner of our action. Nonviolence as it grows from Judaic-Christian traditions seeks a social order of justice permeated by love.
>
> Through nonviolence, courage replaces fear; love transforms hate. Acceptance dissipates prejudice; hope ends despair. Peace dominates war; faith reconciles doubt. Mutual regard cancels emnity. Justice for all overthrows injustice. The redemptive community supersedes systems of gross social immorality.[15]

14. On the formation of SNCC see C. Carson, *In Struggle: SNCC and the Black Awakening of the 1960s* (Cambridge, Mass., 1981), pp. 19–30, and Ella Baker Interview (1968), CRDP.
15. Quoted in Carson, *In Struggle*, p. 23.

Lawson also caused a minor furore by criticising the NAACP for its preoccupation with 'fund-raising and court action rather than developing our greatest resource, a people no longer the victims of racial evil who can act in a disciplined manner to implement the constitution'.[16] He was also reported to have attacked the Association's magazine, *The Crisis*, as an organ of the black bourgeoisie. Stung by these criticisms from a representative of the SCLC, John Brooks, director of the NAACP's voter registration project in Richmond, Virginia, suggested that the national office threaten to withdraw legal aid from 'opportunists' who sought to exploit 'the foundation built by the NAACP'.[17] Although Roy Wilkins declined the suggestion (preferring instead to articulate his concern privately to Martin Luther King), the incident revealed the NAACP's acute sensitivity to criticism and highlighted the ambiguous relationship which existed between ostensibly allied organisations competing for valuable publicity and funding.[18] Much to Wilkins's relief, one suspects, SNCC had little impact on events during the early months of its existence. Students arrested for taking part in sit-ins generally accepted bail, thereby reducing pressure on southern officials and contributing to a general diminution of the protests' effectiveness.[19] However, when a permanent organisational structure was put in place at another conference in Atlanta in October 1960, the students' ability to redirect the civil rights movement along a more activist path was greatly enhanced.

While the birth of SNCC in the spring of 1960 heralded a dramatic shift in movement philosophy and culture, the arrival of the new student organisation was easily overshadowed by the year's presidential contest between Richard M. Nixon and John F. Kennedy. Concerns over foreign policy and the domestic economy provided the principal focuses for debate, but both candidates campaigned on platforms broadly supportive of civil rights reform. The Republicans took credit for the recent civil rights acts, expressed support for school desegregation and peaceful sit-ins, and pledged 'the full use of the power, resources and leadership of the federal government' to end racial discrimination.[20] The growing strength of

---

16. Quoted in ibid., p. 23.

17. J.M. Brooks to R. Wilkins, Memorandum, 20 April 1960, SCLC File 1959–62, Box A213, Group 3, NAACP Papers, LC.

18. R. Wilkins to M.L. King, 27 April 1960, King File 1956–65, Box A177, Group 3, NAACP Papers, LC.

19. Carson, *In Struggle*, p. 28.

20. D.B. Johnson and K.H. Porter, *National Party Platforms 1840–1972* (Urbana, Chicago, and London, 1975), p. 620.

the liberal northern wing of the Democratic Party produced an even bolder civil rights plank which was largely the work of King's Gandhian adviser, Harris Wofford, and the Kennedy ally, Chester Bowles. In addition to averring support for *Brown* and the sit-ins, the Democrats called for tougher legislation to protect black voting rights and federal action to curb inner-city blight.[21]

Liberal though these pledges were, neither rival for the presidency sought to publicise them during the election campaign. Nixon had built up a relatively positive reputation as a friend of civil rights during his two terms as Eisenhower's vice-president, but he regarded the issue as a secondary priority and was keen to appeal to white voters in the South. Kennedy's civil rights record was at best a mixed one.[22] As well as voting to limit the impact of the 1957 civil rights bill, he was sympathetic to the southern white interpretation of Reconstruction and received significant backing for his presidential bid from moderate segregationists like Governor J. Lindsay Almond of Virginia. His selection of the powerful Texan, Lyndon Johnson, as his running mate was a blatant bid for southern support. Soon to become the first black national director of CORE, James Farmer called the appointment 'most unfortunate, probably . . . a disaster'.[23] Roy Wilkins, more attuned to the harsh realities of American politics than Farmer, proved less critical of Kennedy in 1960, but the fact remains that the ambitious Massachusetts Democrat paid little attention to equal rights until his need for urban black votes caused him to make a now celebrated phone call to Coretta Scott King in October. Mrs King, six months pregnant, was known to be deeply concerned about the welfare of her husband who had been sentenced to four months' hard labour in Georgia for violating a probation order. Kennedy's aides convinced him that a sympathetic word from the Democratic candidate might boost his appeal among African Americans and induced him to telephone Coretta, much to the dismay of Robert Kennedy, the president's younger brother and campaign manager, who feared that the move would alienate southern white voters. Mrs King certainly appreciated Kennedy's support. However, she knew nothing of the fierce political debate which had taken place over the phone call within

21. I. Bernstein, *Promises Kept: John F. Kennedy's New Frontier* (New York and Oxford, 1991), pp. 28–30.

22. C. Brauer, *John F. Kennedy and the Second Reconstruction* (New York, 1977), pp. 13–29.

23. Quoted in M. Stern, *Calculating Visions: Kennedy, Johnson and Civil Rights* (New Brunswick, NJ, 1992), p. 29.

the Kennedy camp, though her suspicions may have been raised by the Democrats' efforts to publicise the candidate's action in black communities across the country.[24] Nixon's late decision to bid openly for southern white votes prevented him from making a similar gesture – a failure which may have contributed towards his narrow defeat in the November election.

Kennedy and King at centre stage

A central strategy of all the mainstream civil rights organisations during the early 1960s was to encourage, cajole and ultimately coerce the federal government into taking action to guarantee black citizenship rights under the Constitution. SNCC and CORE, the most radical of the major civil rights organisations, did not dissent from this policy even though they possessed very different ideas about how to develop an effective civil rights movement, were as preoccupied with means as with ends, and would become disillusioned with Washington more quickly than the other groups.

The notion that the federal government held the key to dismantling the caste system was a perfectly understandable one. Union troops, to whom some of the Greensboro students compared themselves in early 1960, and a sympathetic president and Congress had played a major role in destroying slavery during the previous century.[25] A century on from the American Civil War, utilisation of federal power – vastly augmented since 1941 – appeared to offer the civil rights movement the surest road to success, for even the sit-ins failed to make significant inroads into Jim Crow outside the peripheral South where hard-pressed civic elites evinced a willingness to negotiate an end to public segregation.

Movement leaders were not unaware of the constraints on Kennedy but they expected him to deliver on some of the pledges in the Democratic platform, both by pressurising Congress into passing tougher civil rights legislation and by bringing the full force of his executive powers to bear on Jim Crow. Recalling a vague suggestion made by Kennedy during the election campaign, Martin Luther King told readers of the *Nation* that 'It is no exaggeration to say that the President could give segregation its death blow through a stroke of the pen.'[26]

24. Brauer, *Kennedy*, pp. 49–50.   25. Chafe, *Civilities*, pp. 118–19.
26. Quoted in Stern, *Calculating Visions*, p. 43.

The White House was unconvinced. Kennedy had two priorities on assuming power: fight the Cold War successfully abroad and promote a healthy economy at home. To do both he required the backing of powerful southern politicians who continued to dominate the most important congressional committees. His initial instinct, therefore, was to abandon any thought of action in the legislative arena and to delegate responsibility for civil rights to Robert Kennedy's Justice Department in the hope that initiatives from this source would depoliticise an issue capable of fracturing the national Democratic Party. He also accepted the advice of his civil rights adviser, Harris Wofford, that the Justice Department should focus on voting rights as a less emotive target than school desegregation and that the White House should place much of the burden for racial reform on the southern vice-president.[27] In March 1961 Lyndon Johnson was placed astutely at the head of a new Committee on Equal Employment Opportunity which took some steps to outlaw discriminatory hiring practices on the part of corporations and labour unions involved in work for the federal government. The following spring the administration secured charitable funding for a large-scale Voter Education Project (VEP) to be carried out by civil rights organisations under the aegis of the Southern Regional Council.

Kennedy supplemented his piecemeal and largely voluntarist approach to the massive problems confronting black Americans with an array of symbolic gestures. As early as March 1961, he ordered the US Civil War Centennial Commission to hold its annual meeting at desegregated military facilities rather than in a Jim Crow hotel in Charleston. The following year, pressured by black leaders, he recorded a speech to be played at a mass rally in Washington to commemorate the centennial of Lincoln's preliminary emancipation proclamation.[28] While such efforts signalled a greater degree of executive concern for racial equality than that evinced by Eisenhower, they did little to dispel a growing sense that the president's civil rights policy had more to do with style than substance. Kennedy's chief ambitions in this area were to neutralise race as a political

27. In a confidential memorandum submitted to Kennedy in December 1960 Wofford described voting rights (guaranteed by the Fifteenth Amendment) as 'the point of which there would be the greatest area of agreement and the greatest progress could be made'. Bernstein, *Promises Kept*, p. 68.

28. R. Cook, 'From Shiloh to Selma: The Impact of the Civil War Centennial on the Black Freedom Struggle in the United States, 1961–65' in *Martin Luther King and the Making of the Civil Rights Movement*, ed. B. Ward and T. Badger (Basingstoke, 1996), pp. 138, 142–3.

issue, keep the movement off the streets (civil rights outbursts were an embarrassment in the ongoing struggle against Communism), and retain the Democratic coalition intact. Unhappily for the new incumbent in the White House, African Americans were no longer prepared to accept gradualism as an adequate response to their demands for greater federal intervention in southern affairs. They wanted freedom and, increasingly, they wanted it without delay.

CORE was the first civil rights organisation to coerce the administration into enforcing constitutional rights in the Deep South. In late April 1961 thirteen volunteers (seven of them black) gathered in Washington to undergo intensive training in nonviolence for the organisation's projected 'Freedom Ride' through the southern states.[29] The aim of the project (modelled on an unheralded 1947 venture into the upper South) was to test the recent decision of the US Supreme Court in *Boynton v. Virginia* that segregated interstate bus facilities were unlawful under the Constitution. Although John Lewis, a black theology student whose civil rights consciousness had first been raised by the Montgomery bus boycott, was attacked by white youths in Rock Hill, the first half of the journey remained largely trouble free.[30] In fact the efforts of the Georgia authorities to preserve order prompted the veteran white CORE activist, Jim Peck, to comment later that his experiences in the Peach state furnished 'clear proof of how desegregation can come peacefully in a deep South state, providing there is no deliberate incitement to hatred and violence by local or state political leaders'.[31]

Matters were different once the activists, travelling in two groups, crossed the Alabama state line. At Anniston riders on a Greyhound bus narrowly escaped being attacked by a waiting mob. The bus drove off before being disabled, but slashed tyres forced it onto the roadside on Highway 78. There it was torched by pipe-wielding whites who might have killed the passengers had an Alabama state investigator not held their attackers at bay with a revolver. A dramatic photograph of the blazing vehicle gave the riders immediate national and international publicity.

Less fortunate was the second group of CORE volunteers. When their Trailways bus pulled into the Anniston depot an hour behind the Greyhound, they were savagely beaten by angry whites. Most badly injured was Walter Bergman, a retired professor at the University

29. For accounts of the Freedom Rides see Branch, *Parting*, pp. 390, 412–91, and A. Meier and E. Rudwick, *CORE: A Study in the Civil Rights Movement 1942–1968* (New York, 1973), pp. 135–58.
30. Raines, *My Soul*, p. 73.   31. J. Peck, *Freedom Ride* (New York, 1962), p. 124.

of Michigan who later suffered a brain haemorrhage as a direct consequence of his attack. The riders limped on to Birmingham where Bull Connor's police allowed segregationists to administer further violence. Jim Peck was hospitalised after being clubbed with a lead pipe (he needed 53 stitches for a gaping head wound) and Bergman received another beating. Physically unable to continue the CORE volunteers were flown to New Orleans, leaving SNCC students from Nashville to complete the Freedom Ride. In spite of growing concern from federal officials (who saw the violence as a propaganda disaster for the United States), the SNCC group found the going as tough as their predecessors. On arriving at the bus terminal in Montgomery they were immediately assailed by yet more white racists. Two black students, John Lewis and William Barbee, were badly beaten in the ensuing mêlée, and Jim Zwerg, a white northerner, had his spinal cord damaged in a particularly vicious attack. Remarkably, Zwerg survived to vow that the Ride would continue. This decision on the part of the SNCC students forced Attorney-General Robert Kennedy to demand tighter security from the Alabama governor, John Patterson. When Ralph Abernathy's First Baptist Church in Montgomery was besieged in the midst of a rally to honour the freedom riders, Kennedy finally (and reluctantly) ordered federal marshals to help disperse the angry crowd outside.

The dispatch of US marshals to Montgomery revealed the extent to which the Kennedys had been embarrassed by media coverage of the Freedom Ride. When the Nashville students expressed their determination to continue the journey into the segregationist stronghold of Mississippi, the administration made strenuous efforts to prevent further violence. The Justice Department's insistence that its enforcement powers were limited by the Constitution necessitated a series of telephone calls between Robert Kennedy and Mississippi Senator James Eastland. As a result of these negotiations the state governor, Ross Barnett, agreed to use his extensive police powers to prevent the riders from being attacked, on condition that Kennedy would permit the civil rights activists to be arrested for breaking state and local segregation ordinances.[32]

Beginning in June 1961, freedom riders began to pour into the Mississippi state capital, Jackson, in a campaign promoted by the Freedom Rides Coordinating Committee of which the SCLC, SNCC, the Nashville Christian Leadership Conference and CORE were all

32. Branch, *Parting*, pp. 469–70.

participating members. By the end of the summer 328 freedom riders had been arrested in Jackson, two-thirds of them students, a quarter of them female, and nearly half of them white. Although the city's conservative black leadership viewed the influx of 'outside agitators' with a fair amount of suspicion, some local blacks did volunteer their support. A church-based civic group entitled Woman Power Unlimited procured essential supplies for the jailed freedom riders and co-sponsored SNCC rallies addressed by the new CORE leader, James Farmer, and Martin Luther King.[33] For the most part, however, community support for the students in Jackson remained limited partly because patterns of deference and gradualism were more entrenched in Mississippi than anywhere else, but also because the state capital was an NAACP stronghold.

While the Kennedy administration's preoccupation with law and order was a recurring feature of federal civil rights policy in the early 1960s, persistent movement pressure in a sphere (interstate commerce) in which the federal government's legal powers were extensive meant that the Justice Department could not sweep the problem under the carpet. On 29 May, a week after he had been forced to send federal marshals to Montgomery, Robert Kennedy petitioned the Interstate Commerce Commission (ICC) to issue regulations barring Jim Crow in interstate bus terminals. The order, expedited by the events in Jackson, was issued on 22 September 1961. Effective from 1 November, it mandated an end to segregation on all interstate buses and barred motor companies from using Jim Crow facilities. The effects were quickly apparent in the Deep South. CORE test groups discovered that outside certain parts of the Black Belt the ICC regulations were being obeyed across the region by the end of the year. Although many African Americans continued to observe Jim Crow customs a combination of movement pressure and federal response had done much to bring about the complete collapse of segregated public transportation (intra- as well as interstate) before the 1964 Civil Rights Act rendered it completely extinct.[34]

The success of the Freedom Rides in prompting effective action by the federal government further energised the southern student movement and was thrown into sharp relief by the failure of the SCLC's first great southern campaign in 1962. The previous October

33. J. Dittmer, *Local People: The Struggle for Civil Rights in Mississippi* (Urbana and Chicago, 1994), p. 98.

34. C. Barnes, *Journey from Jim Crow: The Desegregation of Southern Transit* (New York, 1983), pp. 176–92.

two SNCC freedom riders, Charles Sherrod and Cordell Reagon, had journeyed to Albany, a medium-sized farming town in south-west Georgia, 160 miles south of their organisation's headquarters in Atlanta.[35] Their objective was to mobilise community-wide support for a durable and radical civil rights movement – one which would be capable of dismantling Jim Crow in the heart of Georgia's plantation country. Initially their work among high-school and college students met with success and found favour with a group of young middle-class professionals impatient at the conservative strategies supported by the city's NAACP leadership. In November 1961, shortly after the arrest of several student demonstrators, SNCC field workers helped to organise the Albany Movement, a coalition of civic groups committed to waging a campaign of nonviolent direct action against segregated transportation facilities, discriminatory employment practices by local businesses, and police brutality. Only the NAACP, suspicious of any movement which it did not control, remained aloof.

Although a well-attended mass meeting at Mount Zion Baptist Church on 17 November heralded the beginning of the campaign, it was the arrest of SNCC freedom riders at the local railway station on 10 December which brought Albany blacks onto the streets in large numbers and impelled movement leaders to announce a boycott of downtown stores. A week of mass rallies and protest meetings ensued, resulting in the arrest of hundreds of demonstrators by the local police. At this point Martin Luther King accepted the invitation of Dr William Anderson, a black osteopath who headed the Albany Movement, to assist the campaign. Anderson and some of his fellow professionals believed that the presence of a high-profile figure like King would bring Albany to the forefront of the national news and force the city government to negotiate. SNCC staffers disagreed. They insisted that over-reliance on outside leaders undermined the chances of creating a strong community-based movement which would be able not only to secure concessions from local whites but also to ensure that any agreement reached was put into practice. The views of the adult organisers prevailed. King and his lieutenant, Ralph Abernathy, addressed emotion-laden rallies

35. This account of the Albany campaign is based primarily on D.J. Garrow, *Bearing the Cross: Martin Luther King, Jr., and the Southern Christian Leadership Conference* (New York, 1986), pp. 173–230; A. Fairclough, *To Redeem the Soul of America: The Southern Christian Leadership Conference and Martin Luther King, Jr.* (Athens, Ga, 1987), pp. 85–109; Branch, *Parting*, pp. 524–61; D. Chappell, *Inside Agitators: White Southerners in the Civil Rights Movement* (Baltimore, 1994), pp. 122–43.

at two churches on 15 December. Both of the rallies were notable for the fervour of those in attendance and the centrality of song to the occasion. Next day the SCLC leaders led a protest march to City Hall where they were duly arrested.

Under pressure from federal officials behind the scenes, the city government agreed to reach an accommodation with the movement. Arrested demonstrators would be released without payment of cash bonds. If there were no further public protests over the next 30 days the city would set up a biracial committee to discuss reform measures. In spite of some internal dissension the black leadership agreed to the terms. King and Abernathy left town to deal with other matters.

With King gone, the city quickly reneged on the agreement. The Albany Movement then announced a boycott of city buses and stores and SNCC did its utmost to promote a continuation of the street demonstrations. Events in southwestern Georgia received little media attention, however, until King returned in July to be sentenced for his earlier conviction. Recognising that the Atlantan's arrival might reactivate the civil rights crusade in Albany, Chief of Police Laurie Pritchett directed his efforts towards ensuring that King did not become a martyr to the cause. On one occasion he even arranged for the payment of bond to stymie King's efforts to remain in jail. Although the SCLC leader's reappearance in town did spark off a new round of mass protests, Pritchett's consciously civil treatment of his opponents (and intolerance of white supremacist violence) meant that Albany did not become a byword for southern backwardness in the summer of 1962. As a consequence there was little external pressure on the city government to negotiate with movement leaders. Internal pressure was similarly unforthcoming. Although some white businessmen did urge Mayor Asa Kelley to make concessions, it was the black community which exhibited greater signs of strain. Support for the movement's campaign fell away as it became clear that King's second visit was not going to bring the city commissioners to the negotiating table, let alone secure federal intervention. In this atmosphere accommodationist sentiment began to reassert itself and younger blacks grew frustrated. On 24 July an outbreak of rioting forced Martin Luther King and SNCC's Charles Jones to tour pool halls and drinking dens pleading for calm. It was the ultimate irony. What David Chappell has called Chief Pritchett's 'posture of watchful restraint' over the previous eight months made him appear the guardian of nonviolence and social order, while blacks could be denigrated as destructive, irresponsible lawbreakers.[36] King withdrew from Albany in August knowing that he had suffered the first major defeat of his career as a civil rights leader.

Setback though it undoubtedly was, Albany furnished the movement with several useful lessons. Firstly, it helped to emphasise that inter-organisational rivalry, while unavoidable, had to be kept within bounds if it were not to destroy the national civil rights coalition before it accomplished its objectives. The NAACP, SNCC and the SCLC all bore some of the responsibility for the failure of cooperation in Albany: the NAACP because it seemed keener to protect its turf than promote movement goals; SNCC because its representatives were openly unsympathetic to King's leadership role; and the SCLC because it made little attempt to combine with an essentially community-driven movement. A second – and interrelated – lesson of the campaign was that better strategic planning and stronger ties to the local community were essential preconditions for future success. Unlike SNCC, the SCLC had no support base of its own in southwest Georgia and, as a consequence, King's troubleshooting approach was found desperately wanting.

Set against the success of the early Freedom Ride, Laurie Pritchett's canny reluctance to play into the hands of the movement highlighted the third and most important point to emerge from the Albany campaign: the latter failed because it did not provoke federal intervention by publicising the evils of southern segregation to the nation. As Bayard Rustin put it: 'protest becomes an effective tactic to the degree that it elicits brutality and oppression from the power structure.'[37] By burning a bus and pummelling nonviolent freedom riders Alabama racists helped to condemn both themselves and their caste system in the eyes of the world. By closely studying King's tactics and philosophy set out in *Stride Toward Freedom*, Sheriff Pritchett avoided making the same mistake. In effect he beat King at his own game. Because of the relative paucity of violence in Albany the federal authorities did not feel compelled to act. More than that, they were actually impressed with the effectiveness of police tactics: Robert Kennedy went so far as to congratulate Mayor Asa Kelley for preserving law and order in the face of intense pressure from black and white agitators. Such actions frustrated Martin Luther King but he remained convinced that radical change was impossible without assistance from Washington.

---

36. Chappell, *Inside Agitators*, p. 129.
37. Quoted in Fairclough, *To Redeem*, p. 108.

'The key to everything is federal commitment', he said shortly before the SCLC embarked on its next major campaign in Birmingham, Alabama.[38]

By the beginning of 1963 civil rights activists and leaders had succeeded in bringing their objectives to the forefront of national attention. President Kennedy signalled as much on 28 February when he took a leaf out of Harry Truman's book and delivered a special message on civil rights to Congress. In it he accepted the movement's longstanding contention that the nation had failed to live up to the promises of the Civil War era. Noting that racial discrimination was a damaging issue in the propaganda war against the Soviet Union, he emphasised that his administration was committed to its removal from American life primarily 'because it is right'.[39] He went on to recommend the passage of voting rights legislation designed to bolster African-American efforts to promote the enfranchisement of southern blacks under the VEP, ongoing since the spring of 1962. Missing, however, was any call for a comprehensive civil rights bill which would wipe out *de jure* segregation completely from the South. Indeed, although Kennedy's rhetoric went far beyond anything that Eisenhower had uttered on this subject, there was much of the old emphasis on voluntarism incorporated into the message. If Washington were going to act decisively in the field of civil rights, it was clear that even greater pressure would be necessary.

On the face of things the SCLC's subsequent decision to focus its attention on Birmingham was a strange one.[40] The hub of Alabama's steel industry was notorious for being a centre of racist violence during the years of massive resistance, much of it inspired by blue-collar workers employed in the declining metal trades. Yet it was precisely because 'Bombingham' was such a tough nut to crack that King and his advisers chose to make it the focus for a major campaign. If Jim Crow could not survive in Birmingham, ran the argument, its days were numbered throughout the region.

There were two other reasons why the SCLC opted to target Birmingham. The first of these was that, in marked contrast to Albany, the organisation had a strong base in the city. In spite of persistent harassment the SCLC-affiliated Alabama Christian Movement for

38. Quoted in Garrow, *Bearing the Cross*, p. 228.

39. J.F. Kennedy, 'Special Message to the Congress on Civil Rights' (28 February 1963), in *Public Papers of the Presidents: John F. Kennedy 1963* (Washington, DC, 1964), p. 222.

40. For reliable accounts of the Birmingham campaign see Fairclough, *To Redeem*, pp. 110–39, and Garrow, *Bearing the Cross*, pp. 231–64.

Human Rights (ACMHR) headed by the indefatigable Fred Shuttlesworth, had been seeking to promote social change in Birmingham
since 1956 and wanted King to intervene. Neither the NAACP nor
SNCC presented themselves as potentially troublesome rivals to
Shuttlesworth's group and the way was left open for the SCLC to
devise, implement, and control a civil disobedience campaign of its
own making.

A second reason for acquiescing in Shuttlesworth's invitation to
intervene in the so-called 'Magic City' was mounting evidence of
cracks in the white community. Unlike their peers in the much
smaller and less heterogeneous town of Albany, Birmingham whites
were demonstrably divided over the centrality of Jim Crow to the
city's future. During the late 1940s and early 1950s liberal white
professionals and their allies in the local business world had evinced
a determination to promote good race relations as part of their
overall strategy to boost Birmingham's image as a dynamic and
forward-looking industrial centre. By the time the *Brown* decision
was handed down, New South proponents had met with some success in their efforts to marginalise extremist sentiment in the community. Bull Connor, the racist commissioner of public safety, had
lost much of his political power as a consequence of a minor sex
scandal, while an interracial committee had achieved modest gains
including the desegregation of elevators in downtown office buildings. Even though massive resistance resurrected Connor's political
career and placed moderates on the defensive, the latter were showing signs of making a comeback by the early 1960s. Concerned at
the detrimental impact that racist violence was having on the city's
economy, service-sector businessmen and lawyers combined to press
for a radical overhaul of the existing commission system of government which, in their view, was an obstacle to economic growth.

In November 1962, shortly after Police Commissioner Bull Connor had curbed the efforts of the ACMHR and moderate whites to
desegregate public rest-rooms and water fountains, Birmingham
voters backed political reform in a municipal referendum. Connor
immediately sought election as mayor but was defeated in a run-
off contest on 2 April 1963 by a moderate segregationist, Albert
Boutwell, who had received the backing of business interests. For
many local blacks, particularly older members of the community
and those with business ties of their own, Boutwell's success presaged a new era in local race relations. They therefore advised can-
cellation of the SCLC's imminent campaign of civil disobedience.

The SCLC leaders (particularly Shuttlesworth) had no reason to
trust the good faith of city merchants. They suspected, however,

that the businessman's desire for profit and economic growth represented a weak point of the caste system – capitalism coexisted quite happily with Jim Crow in the United States (just as it did with apartheid in South Africa) but in the middle of the twentieth century it was not central to the maintenance of either system and could flourish without both. As a consequence they rejected the advice of conservative blacks to abort the campaign, their reasoning being that Boutwell was merely a respectable version of Connor and that only pressure from the movement could force local elites and/or the federal government to bring about radical social change. Demonstrations began the day after the run-off election.

In marked contrast to Albany, the SCLC's Birmingham campaign was carefully planned. Wyatt Walker, the organisation's chief strategist, developed close relations with leading figures in the ACMHR and encouraged the formation of various support groups including food, transport and jail visitation committees. The campaign was targeted on segregated downtown lunch counters (diffuseness of goals had proved a major problem in Albany) and relatively well funded thanks to the efforts of the entertainer, Harry Belafonte, those of King himself, and the creation of the SCLC's new northern-based fund-raising conduit, the Gandhi Society. That the principal objective was to coerce whites into making concessions was made clear by Walker's final code-name for the project, 'Project C' – C for confrontation. Initially the demonstrations received lukewarm support from the black community in Birmingham. Many African Americans were understandably afraid of being arrested by Connor's police and being carted off to jail. Others, particularly members of the city's sizeable black middle class, remained convinced that the decision to begin demonstrations after Boutwell's election was counter-productive. Support for an economic boycott of city stores, however, was forthcoming. Nightly mass meetings (addressed by King and Abernathy; their lieutenants, Andrew Young, James Bevel and Dorothy Cotton; and notables from the ACMHR) served to generate enthusiasm for the cause as did an assault on peaceful demonstrators by Connor's police on Palm Sunday. Bull Connor, in fact, was the movement's best hope of securing the much sought-after confrontation with the authorities. Although his early reaction to the demonstrations belied his brutal reputation, the Palm Sunday incident (milked for all it was worth by Walker) indicated for the first time that his nerves were beginning to fray.

Sensing that a dramatic gesture was necessary to bring federal pressure to bear on the recalcitrant city authorities, King chose to disobey a state court injunction against demonstrations and go to jail in the second week of April. There he wrote his 'Letter from Birmingham City Jail' – a scathing condemnation of white liberals who counselled caution and assailed nonviolent direct action as illegal. 'Actually', wrote King in a passionate defence of his tactics,

> we who engage in nonviolent direct action are not the creators of tension. We merely bring to the surface the hidden tension that is already alive. We bring it out in the open, where it can be seen and dealt with. Like a boil that can never be cured so long as it is covered up but must be opened with all its ugliness to the natural medicines of air and light, injustice must be exposed, with all the tension its exposure creates, to the light of human conscience and the air of national opinion before it can be cured.[41]

The epistle was quickly printed as a pamphlet with the help of the American Friends Service Committee (AFSC), a Quaker-based social action agency belonging to the Leadership Conference on Civil Rights. Even though they appeared too late to influence the campaign in Birmingham, King's words helped to galvanise secular and religious liberals across the country as the movement gathered pace.

King's presence in jail, however, had little impact on Washington beyond eliciting a few sympathetic noises from the attorney-general. As had been the case in Albany, the federal government declined to act positively as long as order was maintained by the local white authorities. With the ranks of willing demonstrators thinning daily and Bull Connor refusing to read his script, the SCLC's carefully planned operation was close to collapse by the end of April. At this point a potentially morale-sapping defeat was turned into one of the movement's greatest successes by James Bevel, a fiery black minister heavily influenced by James Lawson as a student in Nashville. Acting on his own initiative Bevel decided that the only way to keep the campaign going was to organise a children's march.[42] Plans for the demonstration were well under way when King (released from jail after nine days) returned from an SCLC board meeting in Memphis. Although he may have had some ethical concerns about the recruitment of children for political ends, he gave his assent. The result was the kind of dramatic street theatre for which the SCLC had long been praying.

Between 2 and 7 May hundreds of singing, shouting and hand-clapping black youngsters marched from the Sixteenth Street Baptist

41. M.L. King, 'Letter from Birmingham City Jail' in *A Testament of Hope: The Essential Writings and Speeches of Martin Luther King, Jr*, ed. J.M. Washington (pbk edn, San Francisco, 1991), p. 295.
42. Fairclough, *To Redeem*, pp. 124–5.

Church towards city hall and were arrested by police. By the end of the week, when the jails were full to overflowing, Connor had cracked. On 3 May he allowed his men to attack the peaceful demonstrators with German shepherd dogs and high-powered fire hoses. Pictures of the chaotic scenes appeared in the national press and on television, prompting the arrival of Robert Kennedy's deputy, Burke Marshall, in Birmingham. Embarrassed by the publicity and fearful of both a violent black counter-response and a corresponding increase in Klan-instigated terrorism, Marshall pressured city merchants into making concessions to the movement. On 7 May they reached an agreement with SCLC leaders who were themselves concerned that mounting black frustrations might erupt in violence and thereby damage the spectacular public relations victory already won. The deal involved an end to civil disobedience and the economic boycott in return for the formation of a biracial committee to discuss black grievances, the desegregation of in-store eating facilities, and the hiring of black employees by downtown merchants. King called a halt to the campaign leaving Shuttlesworth and the ACMHR to ensure that the terms of the deal were implemented in good faith.

In spite of contemporary and subsequent scholarly criticism of the final agreement which was never fully implemented by local merchants, hindsight reveals King's decision to halt the campaign to have been an astute one. The turbulent, if far from murderous, events in Birmingham convinced the attorney-general that civil rights crises could no longer be solved on an *ad hoc* basis and that general legislation to eradicate segregation was the only long-term solution to the problem. Shortly after the negotiations had ended Kennedy and Burke Marshall drafted the outlines of a comprehensive civil rights bill designed to achieve this end.[43] Other events played their part in the Kennedys' shift from an executive to a legislative strategy, but there can be no denying the fact that the SCLC's *coercive* use of Gandhian tactics had created a climate of public opinion receptive to tougher government action on civil rights. Bull Connor had risen to the bait and provided America with a window into the southern caste system.

Although President Kennedy announced his support for civil rights legislation in a televised address on 11 June, large numbers of southern blacks were reluctant to entrust defence of their rights to a Congress in which southern conservatives continued to play a leading

43. Ibid., p. 134.

role. The summer of 1963 saw an impressive second wave of sit-ins and demonstrations inspired in part by the Birmingham example. Although much of the rural South remained untouched, many cities and small towns in the region were wracked by community-based direct action protests (supported by one or more of the national civil rights organisations) for the first time. These included Danville, Virginia; Plaquemine and Shreveport, Louisiana; Jackson, Mississippi; and Gadsden, Alabama. The scale of the protests was revealed by statistics collated by the Southern Regional Council: 930 public civil rights demonstrations were recorded in 1963 in at least 115 cities. Over 20,000 people were arrested in comparison with less than 4,000 in the mass protests which occurred prior to the autumn of 1961. Ten persons, including the NAACP's Medgar Evers, gunned down outside his Jackson home on the night of Kennedy's TV address, died as a direct result of the various campaigns.[44]

College and high-school students spearheaded the mainly urban protests, usually in conjunction with local middle-class leaders and representatives of SNCC, CORE or the NAACP. Adult blacks were often torn by the chaos – sometimes rallying behind their jailed offspring in favour of an immediate end to Jim Crow or mobilising to dampen down the protests. Results were mixed. In some of the border cities like Louisville, Kentucky, the very threat of demonstrations induced white civic elites to ban public segregation.[45] In a number of urban centres in the Deep South (Jackson, for example) the municipal government stood firm against all pressure for reform.[46] When protest marches did occur, business pressure was often a crucial factor in the decision of white civic elites to negotiate. However, not all towns with ambitious business elites desegregated in the wake of the new wave of protests. In Greensboro, where progress had been slow after the original sit-ins of 1960, CORE-affiliated students from North Carolina A & T initiated large-scale demonstrations against Jim Crow facilities during the early summer.[47] After Jesse Jackson, a charismatic student who had transferred to A & T from his school in Chicago, led a well-publicised march to city hall on 5 June, Mayor David Schenck declared that the unrest was

44. Statistics taken from Carson, *In Struggle*, p. 90.

45. G.C. Wright, 'Desegregation of Public Accommodations in Louisville' in *Southern Businessmen and Desegregation*, ed. E. Jacoway and D.R. Colburn (Baton Rouge and London, 1982), p. 209.

46. C. Sallis and J.Q. Adams, 'Desegregation in Jackson, Mississippi', in ibid., pp. 240–2.

47. For an account of the 1963 sit-ins in Greensboro, see Chafe, *Civilities*, pp. 166–214.

undermining Greensboro's reputation as a progressive business centre and called on all places of public accommodations to 'immediately cease selection of customers purely on the basis of race'.[48] A moratorium on demonstrations followed but the new interracial commission on human relations presided over only moderate change. In contrast to other North Carolina cities where there was genuine progress, political and economic leaders in Greensboro chose short-term order over racial justice as their main objective.

While the protests themselves were generally nonviolent, some of them erupted in angry clashes between police and demonstrators. The worst of these occurred in Cambridge, Maryland, where the SNCC-affiliated Cambridge Nonviolent Action Committee (CNAC) was campaigning for better public housing as well as an end to Jim Crow. Black frustrations boiled over on several occasions during the spring and summer of 1963 resulting in the dispatch of National Guard troops to the town. Pressure on the white city government from state and federal authorities finally produced an agreement hammered out in Washington in Robert Kennedy's office. CNAC officials grudgingly accepted the deal because they believed the Justice Department would ensure its implementation. It was not the last time that movement participants would be disappointed by the national government.[49]

Broken promises constituted one of the central themes of Martin Luther King's 'I Have a Dream' speech at the March on Washington on 17 August. Conceived originally as a march for jobs and freedom but canalised swiftly by President Kennedy into a public show of support for his civil rights bill, the March epitomised the new-found strength of the movement at a critical stage in its development. King spoke directly not only to a vast interracial throng (an estimated 250,000 people, perhaps a quarter of whom were white, lined the reflecting pool in front of the Lincoln Memorial) but also to politicians at the other end of the Mall and a massive television audience in the United States and the wider world.[50] He stood before what he called 'the symbolic shadow' of Daniel Chester French's brooding statue of Abraham Lincoln, the Great Emancipator, on a platform with key members of the national civil rights

48. Ibid., p. 205.   49. Carson, *In Struggle*, p. 90.
50. M.A. Watson, *The Expanding Vista: American Television in the Kennedy Years* (Durham, NC, 1990), p. 108, notes that all three major American TV networks covered the March, though only CBS featured live coverage throughout the afternoon. Two transmissions were beamed to Europe via the new *Telstar* satellite and carried live by six countries.

coalition: not only A. Philip Randolph and the leaders of the other four main protest organisations but also influential whites like Walter Reuther, president of the UAW, and the Rev. Eugene Carson Blake of the National Council of Churches.

King's initial contention in his Dream speech, that 'great folk sermon' as Keith Miller has called it, was that while the movement had made a good deal of progress since 1955 the nation had not yet fulfilled its historic pledges to black Americans.[51] Using the metaphor of a promissory note, the SCLC leader asserted that whites had failed to live up to their fine ideals enshrined in the Declaration of Independence and the federal Constitution. Blacks, he said, had come to Washington to cash a cheque. The Republic could never be at peace until it was cashed. 'There will be neither rest nor tranquility in America', said King, 'until the Negro is granted his citizenship rights. The whirlwinds of revolt will continue to shake the foundations of our nation until the bright day of justice emerges.' Two-thirds of the way through his speech King departed from the text and began to preach extemporaneously. Merging his voice with those of Old Testament prophets in the time-honoured tradition of the black clergy, he articulated his vision of an America at peace with itself. He did so with a rhetorical force and patriotic ardour irresistible to all who claimed to love the Republic's much-prized tenets of justice, democracy and freedom of opportunity. 'I still have a dream', King told his fellow countrymen and women, black and white, 'it is a dream deeply rooted in the American dream that one day this nation will rise up and live out the true meaning of its creed – we hold these truths to be self-evident, that all men are created equal.' He made it clear that the movement's aim was not only to integrate blacks and whites but also to reintegrate the South into the wider nation. 'I have a dream', he intoned,

> that one day on the red hills of Georgia, sons of former slaves and sons of former slave-owners will be able to sit down together at the table of brotherhood.
>
> I have a dream that one day, even the state of Mississippi, a state sweltering with the heat of injustice, sweltering with the heat of oppression, will be transformed into an oasis of freedom and justice . . .

His stirring peroration confirmed his position as the most visible leader of the civil rights movement in America:

51. K. Miller, *Voice of Deliverance: The Language of Martin Luther King, Jr and Its Sources* (New York, 1992), p. 148.

So let freedom ring from the prodigious hilltops of New Hampshire.
Let freedom ring from the heightening Alleghenies of Pennsylvania.
Let freedom ring from the snow-capped Rockies of Colorado.
Let freedom ring from the curvaceous slopes of California.
But not only that.
Let freedom ring from Stone Mountain of Georgia.
Let freedom ring from Lookout Mountain of Tennessee.
Let freedom ring from every hill and molehill of Mississippi, from every mountain side, let freedom ring.

And when we allow freedom to ring, when we let it ring from every village and hamlet, from every state and city, we will be able to speed up that day when all of God's children – black men and white men, Jews and Gentiles, Catholics and Protestants – will be able to join hands and to sing in the words of the old Negro spiritual, 'Free at last, free at last; thank God Almighty we are free at last'.[52]

As thunderous applause broke out around him, King, exhausted by his labours, sank down in a pool of sweat. For one fleeting moment his vision of an integrated, beloved community appeared to be an attainable reality in America.

The March on Washington, expertly organised by Bayard Rustin, was a major triumph for the civil rights movement. True, there were signs of inter-organisational tensions prior to and during the event. On 29 June, for example, the civil rights strategist Lawrence Reddick had called on King and Wilkins to maintain a united front prior to the demonstration. 'We argue with our wives at home', he wrote earthily, 'but don[']t beat them up publicly.'[53] Fears, moreover, had been expressed about Rustin's involvement, the AFSC had expressed disquiet at the original and controversial call for an extension of the federal minimum wage, and John Lewis, chairman of SNCC, had been persuaded to tone down fierce criticism of the Kennedys in his own speech at the Lincoln Memorial.[54] Overall, though, the March elicited a positive response from the American public, confirming the existence of a shaky consensus outside the South on mainstream civil rights goals. Its success, moreover, revealed that the leading civil rights groups could cooperate effectively, even though petty jealousies and important differences over strategy and ideology did exist. The formation in June 1963 of the

52. M.L. King, 'I Have a Dream' in *Testament*, ed. Washington, pp. 217–20.

53. L.D. Reddick to M.L. King and R. Wilkins, 29 June 1963, Box 20, Series I, Martin Luther King Papers, KC.

54. B.W. Moffett to A. Philip Randolph, 2 August 1963, Box 35, Series I, Martin Luther King Papers, KC; F.T. Walker to J. Lewis, 21 August 1963, Box 17, Series 4, Subgroup A, SNCC Papers, KC; Garrow, *Bearing the Cross*, pp. 281–3.

Council of United Civil Rights Leadership contributed something to unity within the movement. Providing a forum for regular discussions among the various elements in the civil rights coalition, the Council served to defuse a number of internal tensions at a critical stage in the movement's history.[55] Such tensions, however, were never far from the surface and they would increase dramatically as the campaign for federal intervention reached its peak.

St Augustine and the 1964 Civil Rights Act

Three weeks after the March on Washington, a vicious bomb attack on the Sixteenth Street Baptist Church in Birmingham killed four black children and injured twenty-one others. It was a sobering event, particularly for the SCLC whose campaign in Birmingham had induced the Kennedys to introduce landmark civil rights legislation into Congress. With the administration apparently ready to delay action on its bill until after the 1964 presidential election, King and his advisers joined other black leaders in casting around for ways to intensify pressure on the federal government. During the winter SNCC formulated plans to make Mississippi the focus of a high-profile campaign designed to prompt federal intervention in the most racist of all the southern states. Lacking a base there, the SCLC considered a number of options for a nonviolent campaign of its own. Although the organisation was active in Atlanta and Danville, Virginia, the most obvious target seemed to be Alabama. Local black opposition ruled out another direct action campaign in Birmingham but James Bevel and his wife, Diane Nash, were convinced that civil disobedience could be used on a massive scale to force racial change in the state, then under the sway of Governor George Wallace, a pro-segregation demagogue who was preparing to launch a challenge for the Democratic presidential nomination.

By late 1963, Martin Luther King was under constant electronic surveillance by the FBI as a consequence of his contacts with leftists like Stanley Levison.[56] Material provided by officially sanctioned wiretaps convinced the powerful FBI chief, J. Edgar Hoover, not only that King was a communist stooge but also that he was morally degenerate. (Lurid tapes of King's extra-marital liaisons were hawked

---

55. N.J. Weiss, 'Creative Tensions in the Leadership of the Civil Rights Movement' in *The Civil Rights Movement in America*, ed. C.W. Eagles (Jackson and London, 1986), pp. 39–55.

56. Garrow, *Bearing the Cross*, pp. 310–14.

around by the FBI throughout this period in an attempt to discredit the SCLC leader in the eyes of federal officials and his liberal allies.) In spite of such harassment, however, King remained committed to the search for federal intervention. Initially, he was attracted by the Bevels' Alabama Project, but on closer inspection a statewide campaign of student unrest seemed beyond the limited resources of the SCLC and perhaps unwise given the lack of enthusiasm for direct action on the part of many black leaders in Birmingham and Montgomery. As a result King and his aides opted in May 1964 to support a carefully targeted campaign in the Florida tourist resort of St Augustine.

In view of the SCLC's lack of involvement in Florida up to this date, the choice seemed an odd one. St Augustine, however, was the centre of an active civil rights movement headed by a black dentist, Dr Robert Hayling.[57] During the summer of 1963 Hayling, an adviser to the local NAACP youth council, had organised a series of nonviolent demonstrations designed to undermine segregation in St Augustine, a town characterised by the same culture of 'civility' and paternalistic racism which confronted the students in Greensboro and many other southern cities. The principal demand of a biracial committee was rejected by the city commission and from September onwards black demonstrators, the bulk of them students from Florida Memorial College and community schools, encountered fierce resistance from militant segregationists led by 'Hoss' Manucy, head of a Klan-like organisation named the Ancient City Gun Club. The town's mayor, Joseph Shelley, and his chief of police, L.O. Davis, regarded Hayling and his fellow activists as communist subversives and made no attempt to hinder Manucy's activities. Several of Davis's deputies, in fact, were committed Klansmen.

Although Hayling survived being physically assaulted at a Klan rally in September, his campaign had produced few significant gains by the end of 1963. Only stores belonging to national chains, most notably Woolworth's, had agreed to desegregate and Mayor Shelley, backed up by local businessmen as well as the militants, showed no signs of loosening his attachment to Jim Crow. Determined to energise the movement in St Augustine, Hayling journeyed to Orlando in March 1964 to secure help from the SCLC. The Rev. C.T. Vivian, one of King's closest aides and a fervent believer in the moral and

57. The most detailed analysis of the St Augustine campaign is provided by D.R. Colburn, *Racial Change and Community Crisis: St. Augustine, Florida, 1877–1980* (pbk edn, Gainesville, 1991). But see also Garrow, *Bearing the Cross*, pp. 287–355, and Fairclough, *To Redeem*, pp. 181–91.

tactical strength of nonviolence, urged King to acquiesce. The result was a brief spring campaign overseen by the Savannah activist, Hosea Williams, a rising star within SCLC whose commitment to nonviolence was rather more pragmatic than that of either Vivian or King. Scores of white SCLC supporters and New England students were recruited to give added strength to the direct action campaign which attracted only limited support from older blacks in the town. Although the marches failed to elicit a positive response from the city commission, the campaign did give King an opportunity to call for direct federal intervention as the long-awaited civil rights bill was proceeding through Congress. The arrest, moreover, of Mrs Malcolm Peabody, the 72-year-old wife of an Episcopal bishop and mother of the governor of Massachusetts, secured precisely the kind of media attention which Hayling and the SCLC had been hoping for. Peabody was arrested while participating in a sit-in at the Monson Motor Lodge. More than 50 reporters flocked to the jail on hearing of her incarceration and, shortly after her release from prison, Mrs Peabody appeared on NBC's 'Today Show' to depict St Augustine as a bastion of racial hatred.[58]

In the wake of the Easter demonstrations in St Augustine SCLC staff debated whether to make the town the focus for a more concerted effort. Strong support for this idea was voiced by the SCLC's assistant project director John L. Gibson. Bevel, still committed to a more ambitious campaign in Alabama, was unenthusiastic but lingering concerns over the practicality of his project resulted in its being shelved. As a tourist centre eager to obtain funds for its historic quadricentennial celebrations in 1965, St Augustine represented an ideal opportunity not only to assist a local movement eager for SCLC intervention but also to furnish the nation with visual evidence of segregationist violence at a time when Congress was debating the most important civil rights legislation of the twentieth century. It would also provide further proof, at a juncture when mounting black radicalism was causing some people to doubt its utility, that nonviolent direct action was an effective tool in the battle for equal rights. In his strategic plan for St Augustine, Wyatt Walker emphasised the need for a disciplined and calibrated campaign which would involve a series of high-profile night-marches culminating in 'stepped up demonstrations', involvement by 'outside names or clergy', and a '*big* push' around 14 June. 'Somehow', wrote Walker, 'we must recapture the moral offensive so that it

58. Colburn, *Racial Change*, p. 70.

cannot be suggested that the nonviolent revolution has become surly, irresponsible, and undisciplined.'[59]

On 18 May King publicly revealed the SCLC's decision to return to St Augustine in strength. He referred to the city as 'a small Birmingham' and, cognisant as ever of the broader national context, went on later in the day to wire Attorney-General Robert Kennedy that the crisis in St Augustine indicated 'the need for the protection of minorities provided by the Civil Rights Bill'. Once again he took the opportunity to call for the deployment of federal forces.[60]

Demonstrations, made up primarily of local youths, students from Florida Memorial and northern colleges, and white sympathisers from all parts of the United States, began on 26 May and lasted until the end of June. As Walker had probably expected the down-town night-marches in the vicinity of the old slave market attracted immediate attention from segregationists, some of whom, like the Atlanta Klan leader, J.B. Stoner, were drawn to St Augustine as a last bulwark of Jim Crow, now under putative attack from outside agitators like King, bleeding-heart liberals like Mrs Peabody, a biased media, and hypocritical politicians in Washington. The violence began on the evening of 28 May when angry whites in the market area attacked cameramen and marchers alike. It persisted for the next four weeks. King's rented beach cottage was hit by gunfire and civil rights demonstrators were repeatedly assaulted. The local police, re-enforced by state highway patrolmen dispatched by Governor Farris Bryant, struggled to maintain control of a situation which, by mid-June, was threatening to spiral out of control. Both sides became increasingly desperate as June wore on. White militants were angered by news that the Senate had passed a substitute civil rights bill on 20 June and by the determination of Federal District Court Judge Bryan Simpson to uphold the First Amendment rights of civil rights activists to demonstrate. The SCLC itself was frustrated by the refusal of Mayor Shelley to agree to the movement's demands – even the most basic one of a biracial committee to discuss reforms. Equally seriously, it was confronted by the prospect of dwindling resources and a distinct lack of support from the town's older black leadership. Thus, although the SCLC appears to have sabotaged a possible peace settlement on 18 June, it was clear by the end of the month that deadlock had been reached.[61] King was eager to end the campaign for his chief

59. Garrow, *Bearing the Cross*, p. 326.   60. Colburn, *Racial Change*, p. 80.
61. Ibid., pp. 100–3.

objective, the passage of a tough new civil rights bill, was in sight. On 30 June Governor Bryant supplied him with a face-saving solution. Under pressure to procure a settlement from the White House and aware of the mounting violence, Bryant announced that a biracial committee had been created in St Augustine. King was aware that no such body had been set up but immediately announced a cessation of demonstrations, much to the annoyance of Dr Hayling who was left to pick up the pieces once the SCLC had departed. As had been the case in Birmingham the previous year, King had opted to compromise the needs of local activists once the broader strategic goal had been secured.

What was the significance of the St Augustine campaign? David Colburn has rightly criticised the SCLC for not promoting the development of an efficient grass-roots movement which could have continued to fight for basic political and economic rights after the main campaign had finished.[62] (Hayling and other activists did attempt to mobilise local blacks after 1964 but, in truth, the most effective obstacle to segregation and resegregation in this deeply conservative community was Judge Simpson.) However, while Colburn also blames the St Augustine campaign for intensifying divisions between moderate and radical blacks in the town, he does suggest that the SCLC's work contributed to the climate of public opinion which helped to expedite passage of the 1964 Civil Rights Act.[63] This contention is difficult to prove, for, in contrast to developments arising out of the Birmingham campaign, there is no evidence to suggest a direct or indirect link between media coverage of the violence in St Augustine and passage of the civil rights bill. The real credit for this historic achievement lies elsewhere.

Passage of the Civil Rights Act was primarily the work of Washington-based politicians and the active civil rights lobby in the capital. A central role was played by John Kennedy's vice-president, Lyndon Johnson, who entered the White House in November 1963 after Kennedy's assassination in Dallas. Ambitious to a fault, though far from unprincipled, the insecure Texan had long sought to transcend his southern roots in an effort to gain the greatest political prize in the land. Once the presidency was in his grasp, he emerged from Kennedy's shadow intent on proving himself the most reforming president since Franklin D. Roosevelt. His legendary political skills and unwavering commitment to modernisation of the South helped to promote a bipartisan consensus in Congress which proved

62. Colburn, *Racial Change*, p. 210.   63. Ibid., pp. 211–12.

too strong for the expected southern filibuster in the Senate.[64] Johnson was particularly adept at handling the Republican minority leader, Everett Dirksen of Minnesota, whose backing was essential for passage. Once debate had been closed in the Senate on 10 June, passage of the bill was a virtual formality the following month. An equally vital role in Washington was played by the well-organised lobbying efforts of the Leadership Conference on Civil Rights. Critical here was the coordinating work of the NAACP's Clarence Mitchell and Joe Rauh, a white, former New Deal liberal who served as general counsel for the UAW. Throughout the second half of 1963 and first half of 1964, Mitchell, Rauh and other leading figures in the Leadership Conference's Washington operation met periodically with influential lawmakers, pressed strongly for toughening amendments to the bill, organised gallery watchers to monitor developments on the floor of both House and Senate, and compiled data on politicians which then served as the basis for mobilising grassroots support for the bill in the constituencies.[65] Religious groups belonging to the Leadership Conference, especially the National Council of Churches, worked tirelessly to generate public pressure on key politicians, especially midwestern Republicans whose support for the legislation was essential.[66] Thus, while direct action by the movement had provided the initial impetus for introduction of the bill and certainly gave Lyndon Johnson a compelling reason to act decisively, the St Augustine campaign itself was not the primary factor in the congressional destruction of segregated public accommodations.

The statute signed into law on 2 July 1964 sounded the death-knell for Jim Crow. At its heart was Title II which used the Fourteenth Amendment and the Constitution's interstate commerce clause to allow the federal government to strike at *de jure* segregation in the southern states. Discrimination on the basis of race was outlawed in all places of public accommodation including restaurants, theatres, motels, sports stadia, cinemas, and concert halls. The US attorney-general was given strong powers to initiate federal court action to secure equal treatment under this section – much to the horror of southern senators who regarded the prospect of enhanced federal intervention as evidence of creeping totalitarianism. The

64. Stern, *Calculating Visions*, pp. 160–85.

65. D.L. Watson, *Lion in the Lobby: Clarence Mitchell, Jr's Struggle for the Passage of Civil Rights Laws* (New York, 1990), pp. 541–625.

66. J.F. Findlay, Jr, *Church People in the Struggle: The National Council of Churches and the Black Freedom Movement, 1950–1970* (New York and Oxford, 1993), pp. 48–75.

act also permitted the withholding of federal funds to promote desegregation, extended the life of the US Commission on Civil Rights and created an Equal Employment Opportunity Commission (an updated version of the old FEPC) with powers to outlaw job discrimination by employers and labour unions on the basis of race, colour, religion, sex, or national origin. Although it contained relatively weak provisions on voting rights enforcement and made no attempt to enhance security for civil rights workers in the field, the act gave the federal government and blacks the legal tools they needed to sweep away *de jure* segregation in the Deep South. Jim Crow did not disappear overnight but, as was revealed by the administration's determination during 1965 to break white supremacist resistance in the Louisiana town of Bogalusa, its days were clearly numbered.[67] Faced with the reality that desegregation had the backing of the nation's lawmakers, white business and civic leaders throughout the South continued with their often grudging efforts to integrate public facilities in their immediate locality. The 1964 Civil Rights Act was not a panacea for the enormous problems confronting African Americans, but, by vastly augmenting the power of the federal government to intervene in southern life, it constituted an enormous blow to the caste system which had blighted so many lives in the twentieth century.

The movement triumphant: Selma and the Voting Rights Act of 1965

If passage of the Civil Rights Act appeared to vindicate the dual strategy of litigation and direct action, it could not conceal signs of growing tension within the movement. Whereas radicals within SNCC and CORE were becoming disillusioned with mainstream politics (see below), conservative and moderate leaders within the national civil rights coalition, principally Wilkins, Young and Rustin, urged continued cooperation with the Johnson administration. The White House had delivered on its promises of support for civil rights, they reasoned. Why sever the close links between the movement and the president at a time when further legislation was necessary to promote equal rights in the political and economic spheres? The

---

67. A. Fairclough, *Race and Democracy: The Civil Rights Struggle in Louisiana, 1915–1972* (Athens, Ga, 1995), pp. 370–4, 378.

burgeoning inter-organisational split was revealed by the radicals' refusal to comply with Roy Wilkins's call for a moratorium on demonstrations prior to the presidential election in November 1964. With Johnson pitted against the right-wing Arizona Republican, Barry Goldwater, Wilkins believed that the movement should do everything in its power not to embarrass its liberal ally. King, reluctant as ever to engage in confrontation with the NAACP leader but keen to maintain links with the radicals, attempted to sit on the fence at a meeting of black leaders on 29 July. The result was a rather vague resolution recommending 'a broad curtailment, if not total moratorium of all mass marches, picketing and demonstrations'.[68]

Notwithstanding the ambivalent legacy of the St Augustine campaign, growing evidence of divisions within the civil rights coalition, and several instances of ghetto unrest in the summer of 1964, the SCLC remained convinced that direct action campaigns could deliver impressive results if targeted correctly. After Johnson's landslide victory over Goldwater in November, liberalism seemed to be in the ascendancy everywhere except the Deep South and working-class ethnic neighbourhoods in the North (where George Wallace's strong showing in a number of Democratic primaries provided disturbing evidence of an embryonic northern white backlash against the civil rights movement). Seeking to take advantage of the existing mood, Martin Luther King, a recent recipient of the Nobel Peace Prize, and his aides decided to make Selma, Alabama, the focus of a major campaign designed to promote federal voting rights legislation which would finally deliver political power into the hands of southern blacks.[69]

Located deep in the heart of Alabama's Black Belt, Selma constituted an excellent target for the SCLC's policy of forcing the federal government to intervene in southern affairs through judicious use of nonviolent direct action. Like other ambitious towns in the old plantation regions of the lower South, Selma had begun to develop significantly after the Second World War. By the early 1960s it could boast an airforce installation and a relatively diversified economy based on cotton, fertilisers, lumber and small-scale manufacturing industry. As had been the case in Birmingham, there were signs of tension within the local white community, a fact noted by the Dallas County Voters League, a moribund voter registration

68. Quoted in Garrow, *Bearing the Cross*, p. 343.
69. The following account of the Selma campaign owes much to D.J. Garrow, *Protest at Selma: Martin Luther King, Jr, and the Voting Rights Act of 1965* (New Haven, 1978), pp. 31–132; and Fairclough, *To Redeem*, pp. 225–51.

organisation revitalised in 1963 by a group of black professionals.[70] Whites opposed to the elite-dominated city machine had secured the election of self-made merchant James Smitherman as mayor in the spring of 1964. Smitherman, backed by the city's 200 registered black voters, was no friend of civil rights, but he understood the need for improved race relations and was aware that adverse publicity could affect the city's economic growth. His chief concern was that County Sheriff James Clark, a notoriously bigoted opponent of the movement, might undermine the new regime's programme for orderly change. As a result he appointed a moderate segregationist, Wilson Baker, as director of public safety. Wilson was ordered to keep Clark in check and to begin implementation of the recent Civil Rights Act.

Selma offered the SCLC the same kind of prospects for success which had generated the organisation's much-heralded triumph in Birmingham two years earlier: potentially exploitable divisions within the white community, a brutal law enforcement officer who could be used to personalise and publicise the iniquities of the caste system, a strong local movement with which SCLC could cooperate, and a relatively low level of SNCC involvement. (SNCC workers had contributed to voter registration efforts in Selma but by the end of 1964 no more than two per cent of adult blacks in Dallas County were registered to vote.) Convinced that its goal of a voting rights act was in sight, the SCLC prepared to engineer the final crisis of the southern caste system.

After a month of well-publicised street demonstrations in which a black youth named Jimmie Lee Jackson was killed in a police riot in neighbouring Marion County and hundreds of peaceful black protesters, including King, were arrested and jailed by Clark's men, the Johnson administration redoubled its efforts to secure passage of a voting rights bill as soon as possible. Crisis point was reached on 7 March 1965, 'Bloody Sunday'. Six hundred marchers led by the SCLC's Hosea Williams and John Lewis of SNCC were attacked by state troopers as they attempted to make their way across the Edmund Pettus bridge towards Montgomery. Tear-gassed and clubbed, they retreated in disarray, leaving the national news media to record their shameful treatment at the hands of Alabama police. Determined to increase the pressure on Washington and find a constructive outlet

70. The best introduction to the political situation in Selma on the eve of the SCLC campaign is J.M. Thornton III, 'Municipal Politics and the Course of the Movement' in *New Directions in Civil Rights Studies*, ed. A.L. Robinson and P. Sullivan (Charlottesville and London, 1991), pp. 54–60.

for rising black frustration, King responded by calling for a second march to Montgomery on the following Tuesday. Intense negotiations then took place between the SCLC leader and the federal authorities. The latter urged King to wait, warning him of an impending federal court injunction against the march. King grew desperate, aware of the need to act but reluctant as always to break federal law. The result was a compromise solution hammered out on the day of the march by the former Florida governor, LeRoy Collins, who headed the government's arbitration service set up by the 1964 Civil Rights Act. Collins secured a promise from King that the protesters would turn back before they left town and an agreement from Sheriff Clark and state Public Safety Director Al Lingo that the blacks would not be harmed. On 9 March King led his nonviolent followers across the Edmund Pettus bridge, halted them before the waiting police and then, after a brief period of prayer, ordered a dignified return to movement headquarters at Brown Chapel. SNCC militants (who knew nothing of King's negotiations with Washington) were appalled by what they soon found out to have been a charade. One of them, James Forman, lambasted King's conduct as 'a classic example of trickery against the people'.[71]

Although the dramatic events in Selma exacerbated existing divisions within the civil rights movement, the campaign had the desired effect of galvanising the several branches of the federal government into action. On the evening of 14 March, five days after a white Boston minister, James Reeb, had been beaten to death in Selma, Lyndon Johnson told the nation that he would be sending a comprehensive voting rights bill to Congress. 'The time for waiting is gone', he said. The black cause 'must be our cause too. It is not just Negroes, but it is all of us, who must overcome the crippling legacy of bigotry and injustice. And we shall overcome.'[72] The president's use of the movement's most famous rallying cry appeared to vindicate the long search for federal support. Martin Luther King, watching the address on television, was moved to tears.

On Sunday, 21 March, having been given a green light from Federal District Court Judge Frank Johnson, King finally led a group of civil rights supporters out of Selma and onto the road to Montgomery. Protected by federalised units of the Alabama militia they reached their goal four days later. Fittingly, it was King who capped the campaign with a bravura speech delivered before the

71. Quoted in Garrow, *Bearing the Cross*, p. 405.
72. Quoted in Stern, *Calculating Visions*, p. 226.

state capitol building in the city which had given birth to his own
career as a civil rights leader. Black people, he told the predominantly black crowd before him, were on the move 'to the land of
freedom'. The causes for which they fought – integration, voting
rights and (here was a relatively new emphasis) an end to poverty
– were irresistible ones. Further sufferings inevitably lay ahead, he
admitted, but the only way was forwards. How long would it be, he
asked, before the race was truly free? 'Not long', he answered,
'because no lie can live forever.'[73]

As spring turned to summer the administration's voting rights
bill made its way relentlessly through Congress. Southern Democrats made a desultory attempt to delay passage in the Senate, but
they knew the *Zeitgeist* was against them. The bill as finally amended
passed both chambers of Congress in the first week of August. It
embraced several core provisions. Section four contained a trigger
formula which abolished literacy tests for a five-year period in states
or sub-divisions of states which had used such devices as a fundamental voting requirement on 1 November 1964 or in which fewer
than 50 per cent of voting-age residents had gone to the polls in
the 1964 election. Section five required federal judicial preclearance
for all new voting statutes. Sections six and seven empowered the
US attorney-general to dispatch federal voter registrars to areas
covered by the legislation. Designed to ensure that the so-called Second Reconstruction did not meet the fate of the first, the Voting
Rights Act was a truly 'dynamic statute'.[74] It ended the piecemeal
approach to voting rights which had done little to empower southern blacks and proved to be the final hammer blow to Jim Crow, for
within a year of passage black voter registration in the Deep South
had begun to increase dramatically. It remained to be seen whether
political power brought nearer all the goals outlined by King at
Montgomery, but there was no doubt that in the late summer of
1965, the civil rights movement stood as the most successful social
movement in the history of twentieth-century America.

By no means all blacks, however, were ready to hail Dr King as a
liberator. For those SNCC and CORE field workers who had spent
the early 1960s attempting to mobilise southern blacks in the most
dangerous part of the South, the rural Black Belt, the battle for federal legislation had often been a remote one and the organisational

---

73. M.L. King, 'Our God Is Marching On' in *Testament,* ed. Washington, p. 230.
74. C. Davidson and B. Grofman, eds, *Quiet Revolution in the South: The Impact of
the Voting Rights Act, 1965–1990* (Princeton, 1994), pp. 378, 387.

task an embittering, if sometimes inspiring, experience. To understand why this was the case we must shift our focus from the familiar Montgomery-to-Selma narrative to the less high-profile work of student organisers and local black leaders in Mississippi. Only then is it possible to explain why the civil rights coalition began to unravel in 1966.

CHAPTER 5

Grass-roots Organising and the Mississippi Freedom Summer

If the high-profile civil rights campaigns of the SCLC attracted the bulk of American media attention in the early 1960s, much of the routine organising of southern blacks during this period was undertaken outside the media spotlight by field workers belonging to other civil rights groups. Whereas from 1962 onwards Martin Luther King was chiefly preoccupied with the use of nonviolent direct action to provoke federal intervention in southern affairs, SNCC and CORE were increasingly drawn to the difficult task of mobilising blacks in rural areas of the South where Jim Crow practices were most entrenched and white resistance to civil rights activity was particularly ferocious. Equipped with a significantly different attitude to the movement's objectives from that of the NAACP, the National Urban League and, to a lesser extent, the SCLC, field workers belonging to SNCC and CORE attempted to undo the damage wrought by decades of fear-induced deference. Their goal was the development of strong-minded, politicised individuals capable of sustaining the movement at the local level without the aid of external forces. Grass-roots organisers in states like Mississippi, Arkansas, Georgia and Louisiana, building on the efforts of an earlier generation of civil rights activists, met with some success in the critical task of developing local black leaders but frequently found their efforts stymied by the intensity of white supremacist violence and the failure of federal authorities to protect the lives of endangered field workers. Frustrated with the slow pace of progress in Mississippi, the SNCC-dominated Council of Federated Organizations (COFO) drew up plans for a major political education campaign involving hundreds of white, middle-class students whose presence was designed to focus the attention of the national media and the federal government on conditions in the rural South. The

150

resulting Mississippi Freedom Summer of 1964 highlighted many of
the great strengths of the civil rights movement but, conjoined with
events at that year's Democratic national convention in Atlantic
City, it also contributed to the growth of internal tensions within
the movement's increasingly ramshackle coalition.

Participatory democracy and the organising tradition

The civil rights movement's emphasis on working with and nurturing ordinary black people in the rural South had diverse roots. One
of the most important of these, however, was the form of radical
participatory democracy practised by the Highlander Folk School
in Monteagle, Tennessee, during the 1930s, 1940s and 1950s. Func-
tioning initially as a training school for those involved in the industrial labour movement, Highlander grew increasingly concerned
with black civil rights which were manifestly interconnected with
the development of strong unions and the building of a more just
society. As the American labour movement became more conservative after the Second World War, Highlander's Myles Horton and
his wife, Zilphia, were drawn into a loose alliance with the embryonic civil rights movement, many of whose key figures were deeply
affected by their experiences at the school.

Highlander's major contribution to the movement was its commitment to an ideal of social action grounded in the belief that
responses to oppression had to be formulated from the experiences
of the oppressed. The school therefore rejected established teaching
and training methods which relied almost entirely on the imparting
of knowledge from teacher to pupil. Prospective labour and civil
rights organisers attending one of the school's numerous workshops
were taught to respect and utilise indigenous cultures, to promote
consciousness via an emphasis on ordinary life experiences, and to
nurture existing talents rather than simply forge leadership skills
where previously they had not existed. Because this developmental
approach tolerated diversity and critical thought, Highlander was
seen by many committed liberals and leftists as a bastion against
Cold War conformity during the 1950s. The school was therefore
relatively well funded by foundation grants and individual donations
in spite of its abandonment by the conservative AFL–CIO after the
Second World War. Between 1953 and 1961 Highlander possessed

the resources not only to continue with its series of training work-shops but also to develop an important Citizenship Education Program (CEP) centred on the Sea Islands of South Carolina, an area heavily populated by African Americans since the days of slavery.[1] In 1955 Septima Clark, a middle-aged black woman sacked from her Charleston teaching job because of her work for the NAACP, was appointed director of workshops at Highlander. Clark, well acquainted with the people of the Sea Islands, developed an effective citizenship school programme with the aid of her cousin, Bernice Robinson, a former beautician who had returned to Charleston from New York in 1947. Their objective was to promote the growth of literacy among the poor, rural blacks who inhabited the islands, thereby enabling African Americans to enter the political system and, beyond that, to act as responsible citizens capable of taking control of their own lives. Although Clark and Robinson recognised the need to cooperate closely with existing Sea Island leaders like Esau Jenkins (who first attended a Highlander workshop in 1954), their primary goal was to promote a durable group-centred leadership rather than rely unduly on dominant individuals. This objective may have been reformist in the sense that blacks were being asked to work actively within the existing polity rather than outside it, but clearly it had the potential to revolutionise the lives of ordinary individuals. Refining the radical teaching techniques pioneered by Highlander, the two black women presided over a rapid expansion of the citizenship schools on the Sea Islands. With it went the development of civic clubs and an increase in the number of blacks registering to vote.

So successful was the CEP that when the Tennessee authorities shut down Highlander in 1960 on the grounds that it was a nest of communists, the SCLC agreed to take over the programme. From her new base at the Dorchester Center in Georgia, Septima Clark continued to oversee an impressive series of workshops which provided training for large numbers of established civil rights activists and prospective local leaders. Even though she rightly suspected that the SCLC's clerical hierarchy regarded the CEP as a secondary concern (the latters' stress on grass-roots organising and rejection of orthodox teaching methods hardly gelled with the ministers' fondness for nonviolent direct action and authoritarian leadership), her efforts spawned hundreds of citizenship schools across the Deep

1. P. Ling, 'Local Leadership in the Early Civil Rights Movement: The South Carolina Citizenship Education Program of the Highlander Folk School', *JAS* 29 (1995), 399–422.

South during the 1960s. Their contribution to the growth of a new generation of civil rights activists was incalculable.

One woman who shared the Highlander/Clark preference for grass-roots organising over spectacular street protests was Ella Baker. 'Miss Baker', as she was known respectfully within the movement, had resigned from her post with the national NAACP in May 1946 partly because she chafed at the organisation's top-down leadership style.[2] Heavily influenced by her own family background in North Carolina and her experiences of organising Harlem blacks during the Great Depression, Baker's conviction that civil rights organisations could only make progress by engaging in the unromantic business of local organising led her to continue working with the NAACP in New York during the 1950s. There she came into contact with fellow leftists Bayard Rustin and Stanley Levison. Together they helped to found a group called In Friendship, a fund-raising vehicle for those southern blacks who were suffering for their political activism in the era of massive resistance. This work not only led to her involvement in the foundation of the SCLC but also brought her into direct contact with some of the bravest indigenous social and political activists in the rural South. These included figures like Amzie Moore, a black Mississippian who, after serving in the US armed forces during the Second World War, set up a service station and restaurant business in Cleveland, a small town in the heart of the Delta region.[3] Convinced like so many veterans that it was high time Mississippi blacks demanded their citizenship rights, Moore soon became involved in a variety of reform efforts including the creation of a local voters league and participation in the state NAACP. Because Baker saw grass-roots activists like Moore as critical players in the development of a mass-based civil rights movement, she urged the Mississippian to stay despite attempts by local whites to drive him (and others like him) out of the state. Aided by the support furnished by In Friendship and tolerably well armed (most black families in rural Mississippi possessed guns for hunting purposes), Moore remained at his post to continue the struggle for civil rights during a period – the mid-1950s – when the state's legal assault on the NAACP was at its height and, as the well-publicised slaying of an out-of-state black youth, Emmett Till, revealed, violence against dissident blacks was particularly intense.

2. C.M. Payne, *I've Got the Light of Freedom: The Organizing Tradition and the Mississippi Freedom Struggle* (Berkeley, Los Angeles and London, 1995), p. 90.
3. Ibid., pp. 29–47.

By the spring of 1960 Miss Baker was becoming increasingly frustrated with her position as executive director of the SCLC, partly because she disliked the condescension exhibited by the male preachers who dominated the organisation and partly because she was wary of a group so heavily dependent on the charismatic leadership of one man. For Baker, Martin Luther King represented the antithesis of everything that she stood for, particularly her belief that strong people did not need strong leaders.[4] The student sit-ins which broke out across the South during early 1960 gave her the opportunity to present her ideas to a new and vibrant arm of the civil rights movement. At SNCC's inaugural gathering in Raleigh, North Carolina, she was an influential presence. One of her chief contributions to the meeting was a speech in which she urged the students to cast their net wider than the desegregation of lunch counters. Baker also supported the students' reluctance to become an appendage of one of the existing civil rights organisations. Shortly after the Raleigh meeting she praised the delegates' intolerance of 'anything that smacked of manipulation or domination', adding (with one eye clearly on King) that:

> This inclination toward group-centred leadership rather than toward a leader-centered group pattern of organization, was refreshing indeed to those of the older group who bear the scars of the battle, the frustrations and the disillusionment that come when the prophetic leader turns out to have heavy feet of clay.[5]

Respected by the students for her welter of experience and undogmatic approach, Baker immediately became an adult adviser to SNCC, continuing to influence organisational policy throughout its early years. Hindsight suggests that one of her most significant actions during this period was to foster the commitment to civil rights of a soft-spoken, black New Yorker named Robert Parris Moses.

Like Baker herself, Bob Moses was a central player in the development of the southern civil rights movement. An intense and highly intelligent young man who had been forced to abandon graduate study at Harvard for family reasons, Moses was initially attracted to the movement by the student sit-ins. He visited the South for the first time in the spring of 1960 and participated in a demonstration in Newport News, Virginia. There he heard the Rev. Wyatt Walker

4. Payne, *I've Got the Light of Freedom*, p. 93; D.J. Garrow, *Bearing the Cross: Martin Luther King, Jr., and the Southern Christian Leadership Conference* (New York, 1986), p. 141.

5. E.J. Baker, 'Bigger than a Hamburger', *Southern Patriot* (June 1960) reprinted in *The Eyes on the Prize Civil Rights Reader*, ed. C. Carson *et al.*(New York, 1991), p. 121.

eulogise Martin Luther King as the saviour of the race – a verdict which elicited Moses's telling response, 'Don't you think we need a lot of leaders?'[6] Although these words could have been uttered by Septima Clark or Ella Baker, the chief intellectual influence on the young Bob Moses was the French existential philosopher, Albert Camus. Moses had absorbed Camus while a student at elite Hamilton College in the 1950s and been impressed with the Frenchman's credo which blended a concern for the individual with the need for active and humane involvement in the struggle for social progress. Camus's famous dictum that human beings should avoid being executioners while ceasing to be victims appears to have had a major impact on the young New Yorker's activities as a civil rights activist.[7]

Making contact with Bayard Rustin's circle on his return from the South, Moses was immediately identified as a willing and very gifted civil rights recruit. At Rustin's suggestion he journeyed south again to the SCLC's Atlanta headquarters, on this occasion equipped with a letter of recommendation from Ella Baker. In Atlanta the New Yorker immediately made contact with SNCC workers, then based in an office in the SCLC building, and joined in the picketing of segregated facilities by local black students who, fervently anti-communist in the early days of the movement, were initially wary of the newcomer. 'We thought he was a Communist because he was from New York and wore glasses and was smarter than we were', recalled SNCC's Julian Bond.[8] Soon after his arrival Moses was given the task of drumming up support for the SCLC in states hitherto underrepresented in the organisation. It was in this connection that Ella Baker put him in touch with her friend Amzie Moore – an action which launched a new phase of the black freedom struggle in the rural South.

Bob Moses arrived in Cleveland in the summer of 1960 to find Amzie Moore frustrated by the lack of progress on the civil rights front and, more specifically, by the NAACP's reluctance to move beyond its apparently glacial strategy of litigation. Moses was especially impressed by the Mississippian's strongly held belief that the only effective way for local blacks to secure their constitutional rights was to win a greater measure of political power. (A combination of intimidation, discriminatory electoral legislation, racist voter

---

6. Quoted in E. Burner, *And Gently Shall He Lead Them: Robert Parris Moses and Civil Rights in Mississippi* (New York and London, 1994), p. 19.

7. C. Carson, *In Struggle: SNCC and the Black Awakening of the 1960s* (Cambridge, Mass., and London, 1981), p. 46.

8. Quoted in Burner, *And Gently*, p. 24.

registrars, and voter apathy meant that only 5.2 per cent of adult blacks were registered to vote in Mississippi in 1960 – by far the lowest figure for any southern state.)[9] Although Moore invited SNCC to begin political mobilisation in the autumn of 1960, Moses did not return to Cleveland until July 1961. In the interim SNCC was preoccupied with a heated debate between the proponents of non-violent direct action and those students who wished to give top priority to voter registration. The debate was given added relevance by the Kennedys' decision to support the privately-funded Voter Education Project in the wake of the embarrassing Freedom Rides. Many SNCC members believed, with good reason, that the federal government was attempting to draw the sting of the movement and secure its concentration on what was, in constitutional terms, the less controversial business of voting rights. The lure of significant amounts of money from philanthropic bodies like the Taconic Foundation, the Field Foundation, and the Edgar Stern Family Fund, however, was a powerful counterweight to the fear of co-optation by the establishment; so too was the prospect of mobilising large numbers of ordinary black people as yet untouched by the movement. The internal dispute over this issue was finally ended by Ella Baker. At a SNCC meeting at Highlander in August 1961 Baker persuaded SNCC to form two wings: one focusing on street protest, the other concentrating on the laborious task of political mobilisation. She later recalled this important intervention as 'about the only time I made any special effort to influence'.[10]

Although federal officials and mainstream civil rights leaders like King and Wilkins wanted VEP efforts concentrated in the urban South (generally regarded as a softer target than the unreconstructed plantation districts), SNCC and CORE opted to open up a second front in rural counties of states like Mississippi, Louisiana, Arkansas, and Georgia.[11] This decision was a product of several factors – not only the waning of direct action in 1962 and the desire to mobilise African Americans previously overlooked by the NAACP and the SCLC, but also a growing sense in both organisations that the various sit-ins, marches and boycotts of 1960–61 had delivered little beyond the desegregation of public facilities in the border South. Those civil rights field workers who embarked upon the task of organising rural southern blacks in the second half of 1961 believed,

9. D.J. Garrow, *Protest at Selma: Martin Luther King, Jr, and the Voting Rights Act of 1965* (New Haven, 1978), p. 11.

10. Carson, *In Struggle*, p. 41.   11. Payne, *I've Got the Light*, p. 109.

after several heated meetings with US Justice Department officials over the summer, that they would receive adequate federal protection in the course of their endeavours. As Bob Moses and his peers were about to discover, they were labouring under what proved to be a disastrous misconception. For, as Charles Payne has indicated, the Justice Department had a very different idea about the lengths it could go to protect civil rights workers in the belly of the beast.[12]

Mobilising Mississippi blacks, 1961–63

When Bob Moses returned to Cleveland in July 1961 Mississippi had a well-earned reputation for being the most bigoted state in the country. One contemporary observer famously described it as 'the closed society' because of its stifling commitment to the racial status quo.[13] Economic change – particularly mechanisation – had begun to transform the Delta region in the northwestern part of the state in the late 1940s and 1950s, throwing increasing numbers of black farm folk off the land. This ongoing process did not undermine local whites' entrenched devotion to Jim Crow and the few white liberals in the region such as the Greenville newspaper editor, Hodding Carter, were effectively marginalised by the rapid growth of massive resistance in the mid-1950s.[14] Politically active blacks like Amzie Moore in Cleveland and Aaron Henry in Clarksdale lived in fear of their lives during this period and many local branches of the state NAACP were effectively neutralised. At the end of the decade Medgar Evers, a former army veteran passionately committed to the freedom struggle, had begun the difficult task of re-energising the NAACP from his base in Jackson. With some notable exceptions, however, Mississippi's adult and predominantly middle-class black leadership remained wary of the kind of direct-action tactics supported by Evers and students from all-black Tougaloo College in the early 1960s. They believed that sit-ins and boycotts worsened interracial relations and merely provoked yet more white supremacist violence.

12. Ibid., pp. 109–10. Payne's suggestion (p. 110) that different things were said at different meetings and that both sides placed their own interpretation on ambiguous Justice Department statements does much to explain a misconception which had contributed greatly to SNCC's antipathy towards the federal government by mid-1963.

13. J. Silver, *The Closed Society* (London, 1964).

14. T. Badger, 'Fatalism, Not Gradualism: The Crisis of Southern Liberalism, 1945–65' in *Martin Luther King and the Making of the Civil Rights Movement*, ed. B. Ward and T. Badger (Basingstoke, 1996), pp. 67–74.

Voter registration, however, was generally regarded by the state's African-American leaders as a more acceptable form of civic action and when C.C. Bryant, a railway worker in McComb, asked SNCC to initiate a mobilisation campaign in the state's southern hill country, Bob Moses, with the blessing of Amzie Moore, agreed to help. The McComb campaign (which took place during the second half of 1961) proved to be a baptism of fire for Moses and his organisation.[15] At the outset of the campaign Bryant, head of the Pike County branch of the NAACP, introduced the young SNCC worker to other black activists in the vicinity – men like E.W. Steptoe, a landowning farmer in rural Amite County. Aided greatly by such contacts and sensitive to the wishes of his hosts, Moses proceeded cautiously, opening up a voter registration school on Steptoe's farm with the aid of some local high-school students and receiving invitations to speak from a number of black ministers in the community. His incremental, inter-class strategy, however, was blown apart by the arrival in McComb of a group of SNCC workers, released from jail after their participation in the Jackson Freedom Ride. Several of this group, including Marion Barry, were enthusiastic supporters of direct action and had little patience with the slow business of organising. They immediately embarked upon a sit-in at the Woolworth store in McComb and founded the Pike County Nonviolent Movement to instigate further demonstrations. Moses, aware that civil disobedience was unpopular with most members of the town's black middle class, responded coolly to the new turn of events for they threatened to undermine his credibility in the community.

The rapid expansion of civil rights activity in the area, aided and abetted by those perceived as 'outside agitators', brought a swift response from local whites. Initially, the repression was disorganised but by September it had escalated to such an extent that the Pike County movement was in danger of collapse. Although SNCC workers were harassed, arrested and occasionally beaten by the local authorities, the worst atrocity occurred on 25 September when Herbert Lee, a black farmer who had continued to support SNCC's campaign after the arrival of the freedom riders, was shot dead outside a cotton gin by E.H. Hurst, a state legislator who had threatened the lives of several black activists in the days leading up to the killing. A number of blacks witnessed the event but the pervasive climate

15. For detailed accounts of the McComb campaign see J. Dittmer, *Local People: The Struggle for Civil Rights in Mississippi* (Urbana and Chicago, 1994), pp. 99–115; Payne, *I've Got the Light*, pp. 111–31; T. Branch, *Parting the Waters: America in the King Years 1954–1963* (New York, 1988), pp. 492–500, 503–4, 507–16, 518–23.

of fear stymied Justice Department attempts to bring a case against Hurst who was predictably acquitted by a coroner's jury.

Although Washington's inability or reluctance to protect the movement in McComb contributed to a sense of betrayal among SNCC workers, the killing of Herbert Lee did not stall civil rights activism completely. Voter registration efforts came to a halt but local high-school students energised the grass-roots campaign by marching to city hall to protest against Lee's murder and the failure of their institution to reinstate their peer, Brenda Travis, who had been jailed for participating in a sit-in demonstration. The march, which attracted SNCC organisers as well as students, was the final straw for many whites in the McComb area. An angry mob took particular exception to the involvement of Bob Zellner, a southern-born white SNCC worker. Singling out Zellner as a traitor to his race, several members of the crowd set upon the Alabama preacher's son. Bob Moses and Chuck McDew were soundly beaten by police as they tried to protect their colleague who narrowly escaped being blinded by a man attempting to gouge out his eye-socket. Students and SNCC activists alike were finally arrested for breach of the peace.

Although the movement persisted with a full-scale pupil strike and the creation of 'Nonviolent High' as an alternative source of education, further arrests and persistent intimidation forced SNCC to abandon the project in December 1961. Many of the local leaders who had initially welcomed Bob Moses's arrival – C.C. Bryant included – were happy to see the back of an organisation which had stirred up so much trouble for so little obvious reward. SNCC, however, had learned much from its experience in the McComb area. It had discovered, for example, that cooperation with at least a portion of the indigenous black leadership was a vital precondition for success; that protection would not be provided by the federal government; and that youngsters were the most likely group in a southern black community to respond positively to the arrival of the movement.[16] In no small measure the McComb campaign paved the way for a much stronger attack on Jim Crow in Mississippi the following year.

In February 1962 the major civil rights groups active in the state combined to revive a moribund body entitled the Council of Federated Organizations. COFO was formed not only as a conduit for VEP funds but also as a coordinating body to ensure that internal

16. Dittmer, *Local People*, pp. 114–15; Payne, *I've Got the Light*, pp. 127–8.

tensions within the movement did not result in wasted energies and
resources. Although the state NAACP gave its tentative backing to
COFO and the SCLC contributed to the ensuing voter registration
drive through its citizenship programme, the main task of organising
in Mississippi was undertaken by SNCC and, to a lesser extent, CORE.

The process by which civil rights workers forged a viable grass-
roots social movement in large portions of rural Mississippi in 1962–
63 was a complex one. Charles Payne's illuminating study of events
in Greenwood, the Delta town which became SNCC's main headquarters in the state, draws on a concept first used by Jo Freeman to
suggest that successful organising was heavily dependent on existing
'co-optable networks' developed by local blacks.[17] The leading organiser in Greenwood during the initial stages of the project was a 23-
year-old Cleveland man, Sam Block, who had been talent-spotted for
the movement by his fellow townsman, Amzie Moore. After helping
with SCLC citizenship classes and attending a voter registration workshop at Highlander, Block entered Greenwood as a salaried SNCC
worker during the summer of 1962. Using the techniques pioneered
by the likes of Baker, Clark and Robinson, he established a beach-
head in the town by winning the trust of a handful of prominent
blacks including Ed Cochrane and W.J. Bishop, both members of
the Elks Club, and the Rev. Aaron Johnson who was the only black
minister in this conservative community to support the movement
in its early days. Like Bob Moses in McComb, Block also undertook
vigorous canvassing among young blacks, securing valuable support
from Greenwood's small NAACP youth council. Robert Burns, a black
postal worker and former military veteran, proved to be another
important ally by providing Block with a place to stay in July 1962.
Payne recounts that Burns was attracted to Block because he saw
him as an educated version of himself and as someone who might
actually make a difference to the situation in staunchly segregationist Greenwood.[18]

Aided by these early contacts and help from other SNCC workers
like Bob Moses, Lawrence Guyot, Luvaughn Brown and Willie Pea-
cock, Block managed to build up a small team of local canvassers
committed to the goal of boosting black voter registration. Several
of those given a direct responsibility for mobilising people in their
immediate neighbourhood were black women, drawn into the movement by the activities of their teenage children. Some, including

17. Payne, *I've Got the Light*, pp. 63, 78, 141, 176, 271–2, 274–5.
18. Ibid., pp. 181–5.

Lou Emma Allen, the wife of a Baptist minister, viewed the civil rights workers as family – a fact which may help to explain the movement's attraction to disproportionate numbers of older black women.[19] All the canvassers found the business of encouraging people to register a difficult one, for the perils of political activism in the Delta were well known. In case anyone was unsure of the dangers, whites rammed home the message by repeated harassment of SNCC volunteers. Sam Block received a beating on 13 August when taking a group of prospective voters to register at the county courthouse and the downtown SNCC office was raided shortly afterwards.

Although white repression and discriminatory voter registrars limited the movement's achievements in Greenwood, SNCC received a major boost in November 1962 when the Leflore County Board of Supervisors confirmed an earlier decision not to participate in a federal food surplus programme. This action, a spiteful response to the sudden upsurge in civil rights activism, was a heavy blow to the many poor blacks who lived in the area. SNCC, however, responded quickly by organising a relief effort of its own. The action greatly enhanced the organisation's profile and popularity among local blacks, prompting renewed popular interest in voter registration. After the near-fatal shooting of Jimmy Travis, a black Mississippi-born SNCC worker, in February 1963, Greenwood became the focus of intense COFO activity with at least 50 trained organisers in the county by the beginning of spring.

The movement's arrival in force not only stiffened the resistance of segregationists but also brought the town greater attention from federal officials who feared that a vicious race war could break out in Mississippi. On 30 March the Justice Department instigated a wide-ranging suit intended to force city officials to cease their blatant obstruction of black voter registration. This move was immediately countered by Mississippi Democrats James Eastland and John Stennis who denounced the Justice Department on the floor of the United States Senate. With the Kennedys reluctant to alienate powerful southern members of the party, the Department dropped the case after the city of Greenwood agreed to release a group of jailed SNCC workers. Once again movement people in the Deep South had been dealt a dispiriting lesson in *realpolitik* by officials in Washington.

Although there were signs by the summer of 1963 that the organising drive in the state had begun to stall in the face of federal

19. Ibid., pp. 193–4.

inaction, state obstructionism and racist violence, it had clearly succeeded in mobilising significant numbers of rural Mississippi blacks. Several Delta counties were touched directly by the movement. These included Senator Eastland's Sunflower County, which was the target of a SNCC-led organising drive in the summer of 1962. Among the inhabitants of Sunflower brought into the movement was Mrs Fannie Lou Hamer, a charismatic sharecropper whose remarkable eloquence, mastery of song, and deep humanity were rooted in her unshakable Baptist faith.[20] In common with many of the native blacks who participated actively in the freedom struggle, Mrs Hamer's first contact with civil rights workers postdated her initial entry into civic life. During the 1950s she appears to have been in contact with the NAACP and the Regional Council of Negro Leadership (a Mississippi-based equal rights organisation) and may even have been a name on Amzie Moore's contact list. In August 1962 Mrs Hamer, already in her mid-forties, agreed to attend a voter registration gathering at the behest of a friend. The mass meeting at the local Baptist chapel, an early attempt by movement organisers to mobilise the area around Ruleville, was a typical mix of the sacred and the secular. The Rev. James Bevel of the SCLC took a text from the Bible and related it to the urgent need for blacks to go to the polls. SNCC's James Forman explained how the acquisition of political power would enable local people to rid themselves of racist police officers. Mrs Hamer was among the first group of Ruleville blacks to attempt to register to vote in the county seat of Indianola at the end of the month. Evicted from her plantation for her pains, she rapidly emerged as a dominant figure in the ongoing voter registration drive and, following a characteristically powerful speech at a SNCC rally in Nashville, as one of the great folk heroes of the civil rights movement. In June 1963, she was severely beaten in jail in Winona, Mississippi, along with other movement workers returning from a leadership training programme in Charleston, South Carolina. This humiliating experience merely intensified her determination to rid the country of the scourge of racial oppression.

Organising proved to be most effective in areas in which SNCC and CORE field workers were able to link up with established or

---

20. On Mrs Hamer's entry into the movement see K. Mills, *This Little Light of Mine: The Life of Fannie Lou Hamer* (New York, 1993), pp. 23–42; Payne, *I've Got the Light*, pp. 154–5.

informal local black leaders. Holmes County on the margins of the Delta proved to be an important centre for movement activity after several landowning black farmers from the area began attending mass meetings in Greenwood in the spring of 1963. They urged SNCC to send a field secretary to promote voter registration in Holmes – a request which resulted in the immediate dispatch of John Ball. Aided by Hollis Watkins and Sam Block, Ball, a black Mississippian, began teaching citizenship classes in the Rev. J.J. Russell's Baptist church in Mileston. A product in part of its relatively unique history as a model New Deal township, the solidarity displayed by Holmes County's predominantly black male leadership was a source of some amazement to Ball who contrasted it favourably with the more divided community in Greenwood.[21]

Elsewhere, indigenous black women, many of them deeply enmeshed in church and family networks, tended to play a rather more conspicuous role in COFO's organising drive. SNCC's entry into Hattiesburg, for example, launched the political career of Victoria Gray, a college graduate and small businesswoman in the town who had kept her distance from the cautious, middle-class blacks who dominated the local NAACP. CORE's project in Canton brought to the fore the impressive diplomatic skills of Mrs Annie Devine.

The massive effort to promote voter registration in Mississippi during 1962–63 had a major impact on the organisers and the organised. The campaign nurtured a new breed of radical grassroots leaders well equipped to sustain the civil rights movement on the ground. Aided by the intellectual and material resources provided by COFO, their efforts did much to break down historic patterns of deference which had underpinned the caste system for decades. That rural Mississippi blacks were determined to defend themselves against racist violence was revealed by the volley of shots which Hartman Turnbow, an independent farmer in Holmes County, fired against two white men who attacked his home in the spring of 1963. (Turnbow had been one of the first local blacks to attempt to register at the county courthouse in Lexington.) Although the movement's leadership remained defiantly nonviolent at this juncture, the growing assertiveness of rural blacks began to corrode the attachment of many civil rights workers to Gandhian methods. Placed under enormous strain by the ever-present threat

21. Payne, *I've Got the Light*, p. 280.

of death and the failure of the federal government to respond
adequately to their demands for protection, significant numbers
of SNCC and CORE workers had begun to sanction armed self-
defence by the close of 1963.

Somewhat more representative than the Turnbow incident of
the effect which COFO's campaign had on existing mores was the
extent of the support given by Mississippi blacks to the Freedom
Vote campaign of 1963.[22] The Freedom Vote was the brainchild of
Allard Lowenstein, an accomplished student organiser and 'political troubador' on the left-wing of the national Democratic Party,
who had first gone to Mississippi in the wake of Medgar Evers's
death.[23] Possessing first-hand experience of apartheid in southern
Africa, Lowenstein suggested that black Mississippians declare a
day of voting to publicise their determination to take part in civic
affairs. Lowenstein found Bob Moses and the local NAACP chief,
Charles Evers, supportive and, with their sanction, mobilised nearly
a hundred white students from Stanford and Yale to help with
the planned campaign. The students' presence, though controversial because of their alleged tendency to dominate meetings and
patronise black SNCC staffers, helped to focus national attention
on what rapidly became a mock vote designed to coincide with the
regular 1963 gubernatorial election (from which most blacks, of
course, were excluded). COFO organisers hoped that the Freedom
Vote would not only increase the pace of voter registration, but also
promote the chances for federal intervention. Although this latter
objective was not entirely consistent with the underlying premise
of the organising tradition that means – i.e. personal and group
development – were as important as ends, it had always been a feature of COFO's broad strategic thinking. Still unwilling to alienate
southern conservatives before the 1964 presidential election, the
Kennedy administration did its best to ignore the fact that roughly
83,000 blacks cast unofficial ballots for the interracial COFO ticket
of Aaron Henry and Ed King between 2 and 4 November. A small
but significant growth in media interest in Mississippi affairs, however, was enough to persuade SNCC and CORE leaders that the
experiment was worth trying again on a larger scale.

22. On the Freedom Vote see Dittmer, *Local People*, pp. 200–6, and J.A. Sinsheimer,
'The Freedom Vote of 1963: New Strategies of Racial Protest in Mississippi', *JSH* 55
(1989), 217–44.

23. W.H. Chafe, *Never Stop Running: Allard Lowenstein and the Struggle to Save American
Liberalism* (New York, 1993), pp. 180–6.

Freedom Summer

Anger at the government's inadequate response to white terrorism and pent-up frustration with the slow pace of change were prevalent throughout SNCC ranks by the end of the year. In late December Bob Moses told a civil rights gathering in Washington that the South would not change until it had been 'annealed' – heated to melting point like metal and then moulded in the process of cooling down. What this meant in effect was that the federal government would not intervene positively in Mississippi unless (as had been the case in Birmingham) it was confronted with a major crisis. The Deep South, he said bluntly, would not change unless the central state made it change. SNCC's overriding objective therefore was:

> to bring about a situation in which the fed[eral] gov[ernmen]t must and will act and can act to bring troops, if necessary, or certainly to bring federal marshals, and certainly to bring a federal presence to the degree that local officials must capitulate and must give some substantive change in the situation in the South.[24]

The fact that Bob Moses, one of the movement's most inventive thinkers, was describing federal intervention as the solution to racial progress as late as December 1963 revealed a measure of consensus on strategy among the Big Five organisations at this stage in the movement's development. True, the NAACP and Urban League had greater faith in the national government and were correspondingly less inclined to manufacture crisis situations, but rhetorically and philosophically their leaders were no less committed to the view that Washington must act if Jim Crow were to be eradicated completely.

At a COFO staff meeting in January 1964, only weeks after nervous philanthropic foundations had cut off funding because of the organisation's flirtation with party politics in the Freedom Vote, Moses convinced a majority of those present that Mississippi should be the target of a major voter registration campaign in the summer. There were three main goals. The first of these was to secure direct federal intervention by focusing valuable media attention on the desperate situation in Mississippi – primarily by deploying well-to-do northern white students in even greater numbers than in 1963.

---

24. R. Moses, Speech at SNCC Conference on Food and Jobs, 30 December 1963, Staughton Lynd Papers, WisHS.

Concerns had been voiced throughout the winter that the projected influx of wealthy middle-class whites would undermine morale among black SNCC staff members and undercut attempts to foster indigenous leadership. Such fears were overridden by tactical imperatives and Moses's insistence that a biracial project would promote the movement's long-term goal of racial integration. Clearly an element of cynicism was involved in the decision to invite more white students to Mississippi, for any harm inflicted on a white person was bound to attract a disproportionate amount of media (and hence federal) attention.

The second major objective was to use black political power to promote institutional reform. The prospect of large numbers of African-American voters entering the political system offered a real chance not only to undermine the power of Mississippi's lily-white establishment, but also to turn the national Democratic Party into an effective vehicle for social progress in America. By overseeing the formation of the Mississippi Freedom Democratic Party (MFDP) in April 1964, COFO hoped to pose an immediate threat to Mississippi's regular Democrats at the forthcoming state elections and the national Democratic convention due to be held in Atlantic City, New Jersey, in August. Once blacks were admitted to the party in large numbers they would, it was assumed, liberalise it by pressing for civil rights and economic justice. For some SNCC staffers, therefore, the political goals of the Freedom Summer were essentially reformist. As Charles Cobb, a minister's son and former Howard University student, put it at a staff meeting in early June: 'We are trying to gain control or leverage within the structure; to get the structure to accomodate [*sic*] Negroes. . . .'[25] Others, including James Forman, regarded 'parallel structures' like the MFDP as a means of procuring a more radical reorientation of American society – one which, in the final analysis, would undermine the prevailing bourgeois hegemony in the United States.[26]

The third objective of the Freedom Summer was the promotion of initiative and self-respect among a people deprived of all the normal badges of citizenship.[27] Fostering a liberating sense of self-determination through its encouragement of political participation,

25. SNCC Staff Meeting Minutes, 9 June 1964, SNCC Papers, KC.

26. SNCC Staff Meeting Minutes, 9 June 1964, SNCC Papers, KC. On parallel structures see R.H. King, *Civil Rights and the Idea of Freedom* (New York and Oxford, 1992), p. 147.

27. On the freedom schools, see esp. D. Perlstein, 'Teaching Freedom: SNCC and the Creation of the Mississippi Freedom Schools', *History of Education Quarterly* 30 (1990), 297–324.

COFO undertook to provide separate schools (more 'parallel structures') during the summer campaign in order to give Mississippi blacks an alternative to the poor quality and deeply racist education peddled by white authorities. Several freedom school projects had been set up in the early years of the civil rights movement. 'Nonviolent High', an outgrowth of the McComb campaign in 1961, was one of the earliest examples. So too was the attempt during the summer of 1963 to provide alternative schooling for black children in Prince Edward County, Virginia, where local authorities had closed all public schools in order to prevent desegregation. During the late 1950s and early 1960s, moreover, African Americans in the urban North had begun to mobilise widely against the substandard quality of public education in the inner cities. In Boston on 26 February 1964 roughly a fifth of black students boycotted their neighbourhood schools. Some attended freedom schools to be taught with the aid of curricula written by Noel Day, a community activist who previously had been an innovative junior high school teacher in Harlem. Day and other radical educators played a significant role in Mississippi where SNCC staffer Charles Cobb insisted that the movement's assault on 'the power structure' had to involve 'building up our own institutions to replace the old, unjust, decadent ones'.[28] A flexible curriculum for the freedom schools was drawn up during the spring of 1964 under the guidance of Spelman professor Staughton Lynd, a white historian sympathetic to the civil rights movement and the developing student-based New Left which was beginning to question many of the assumptions and institutions on which corporate capitalism subsisted in the United States.

COFO's determination to supply Mississippi blacks with the resources required to win their own freedom through their own efforts quickly ran into trouble. Al Lowenstein broke publicly with the organisation in the spring. A staunch anti-communist liberal, he criticised SNCC for its ties to two leftist civil rights groups, the National Lawyers Guild (which he flailed as 'a communist infiltrated organization') and SCEF.[29] Influenced in part by his connections to the NAACP, Lowenstein's blast did not prevent the recruitment of around 650 students – 90 per cent of them white, perhaps over a third of them women – for the Freedom Summer.[30] Two groups of volunteers attended training sessions in nonviolence

28. C. Cobb, 'Prospectus for a Freedom Summer School Programme', December 1963, reprinted in *Radical Teacher* 40 (1991), 36.
29. Chafe, *Never Stop*, p. 193.   30. Dittmer, *Local People*, p. 244.

sponsored by the National Council of Churches at the Western College for Women in Oxford, Ohio. There they were addressed by COFO staff, a small group of social scientists and psychologists from Columbia University, and several indigenous black leaders from Mississippi. The latter included Fannie Lou Hamer, who dominated proceedings with her powerful singing voice and exhortations against hatred, and the Rev. J.J. Russell who arrived in Oxford eager to explain the nature of the movement in Holmes County. A young female volunteer, Sally Belfrage, encountered Russell one lunch-time. She remembered him as 'a chamber of commerce for Holmes' who spoke passionately about the degree of economic power which black people in the area possessed. Tellingly, however, two other female volunteers present on the same occasion failed to understand the black preacher's Delta accent and a third questioned him further. 'He didn't understand her either', recalled Belfrage, whereupon '[e]veryone spoke very distinctly. . . .'[31] For these raw recruits to the movement, and indeed for the Rev. Russell himself, this small encounter was a foretaste of the cultural clashes which lay ahead.

Notwithstanding the minister's infectious optimism, none of the students were left in any doubt about the enormity of the task confronting them. For most of them 'Mississippi' was already a by-word for reaction – a potent symbol of the South's reputedly dysfunctional place in modern America. Comfortably well off yet idealistic and highly motivated, they were determined to play their part in exorcising racism from the national domain. The bulk of them were not subversive radicals (as most white and some black Mississippians believed them to be) but patriotic baby-boom liberals who, mobilised by the activities of the civil rights movement and the rhetoric of the late President Kennedy, wanted the Republic to live up to its fine ideals. If anyone was complacent about the dangers ahead, he or she was quickly disabused by Robert Kennedy's assistant, John Doar, who told them there was no possibility that civil rights workers could be completely protected from violence.[32] In fact by the time the second group of volunteers had been given this message, Andrew Goodman, a member of the first cohort, had already gone missing in Mississippi.

The 32 major projects set up in the sweltering heat of 1964 were primarily the work of SNCC and CORE. The latter had responsibility for affairs in Mississippi's Fourth Congressional District which

31. S. Belfrage, *Freedom Summer* (London, 1966), p. 6.   32. Ibid., p. 22.

covered the east-central portion of the state. SNCC had control of the other four districts which included not only the Delta region but also the Klan-infested southwest which embraced McComb, Natchez and Jackson. Each volunteer was assigned to a specific project and given a specific job to do on that project. The principal tasks involved were voter registration, teaching in the freedom schools, and work in a COFO community centre.

The Freedom Summer was the nearest the civil rights movement ever came to putting its concept of the beloved community into action, even though its ultimate effect was to exacerbate existing tensions within and between the cooperating organisations.[33] Critical to the success of many of the projects was the close bond which quickly developed between the movement workers and a large proportion of the indigenous African-American population. Generally speaking poor black Mississippians responded positively to the influx of white students or 'freedom riders' as they were commonly called. Cultural tensions certainly existed and the white students found the subservient manners of older blacks difficult to overcome. Sally Belfrage, for example, a volunteer librarian in Greenwood, was put up by a staunchly religious black family named the Amoses. Mr Amos, an illiterate odd-jobs man and gardener was too embarrassed to join the well-educated white woman at the dinner table until she told him to sit down.[34] White voter registration workers encountered similar problems when canvassing for the MFDP, particularly in the rural areas. Many black farm folk continued to play the subordinate roles expected of them by Jim Crow etiquette, their understandable suspicion of white outsiders increased by the knowledge that even speaking to a COFO worker could cost them their job. The majority of local blacks, however, appear to have been rather more appreciative of the students' efforts than many black SNCC and CORE staff members. The Freedom Summer gave the lie to the contention of white racists that blacks and whites could not cooperate on an equal basis. By journeying south and risking their lives to create a better America, the volunteers helped to undermine traditional mores and in so doing played a vital role in eroding the culture of deference which had done so much to bolster white supremacy in Mississippi. A quarter of a century later native blacks who had been active in the Freedom Summer were

33. For scholarly accounts of the Freedom Summer see Dittmer, *Local People*, pp. 242–71; N. Mills, *Like a Holy Crusade: Mississippi 1964 – The Turning of the Civil Rights Movement in America* (Chicago, 1992); Carson, *In Struggle*, pp. 111–23.

34. Belfrage, *Freedom Summer*, pp. 75–6.

convinced that this had been one of the volunteers' enduring achievements. '[They c]ome here and stay with us', recalled one Holmes County man interviewed in 1989, 'and prove to us that they wadn't no more than us, and it wasn't right for us saying no "Yes ma'am" or "No ma'am" or "Yes sir" to 'em. Say yes and no. They tol' us that. An' they done a good job with gettin' it across to us.'[35]

Although voter registration was regarded as the main weapon in the fight against deference, COFO's freedom schools also helped to promote black empowerment. John Dittmer estimates that roughly 2,500 local blacks attended movement schools where they were taught by volunteer teachers not only to read and write, but also to question existing institutions, to be aware of their own capabilities as black people and, most liberating of all, to think and act for themselves.[36] Students, old and young, most of them semi-literate at best, learned African-American history, found out about COFO and the objectives of the MFDP, and were encouraged to write and speak about their lives on the basis of their own experiences. The potential for personal intellectual development as well as broader social change was further augmented by the establishment of community centres in several towns. These provided foci for movement activity at the local level and contained small libraries stocked with books sent by northern well-wishers. The Freedom Summer may not have overturned the existing political system in Mississippi, but it continued the process of building black assertiveness. As one freedom school student wrote:

> *I've come this far to freedom*
> *And I won't turn back.*
> *I'm changing to the highway*
> *From my old dirt track.*
> *I'm coming and I'm going*
> *And I'm stretching and I'm growing*
> *And I'll reap what I've been sowing*
> *Or my skin's not black;*
> *I've prayed and slaved and waited*
> *And I've sung my song.*
> *You've slashed me and you've treed me*
> *And you've everything but freed me,*
> *But in time you'll know you need me*
> *And it won't be long.*[37]

35. Youth of the Rural Organizing and Cultural Center, *Minds Stayed on Freedom: The Civil Rights Struggle in the Rural South, an Oral History* (Boulder, San Francisco and Oxford, 1991), p. 127.

36. Dittmer, *Local People*, pp. 260–1.

37. Anonymous poem reprinted in *Radical Teacher* 40 (1991), p. 41.

There was, however, a less positive side to the Freedom Summer. Some of the white students proved to be insensitive to the position of black SNCC and CORE veterans who often resented what they regarded as arrogant attempts by rich, well-educated whites to impose their views on those they subconciously regarded as inferior. Interracial sex, particularly between white female students and black staff members, was also a source of friction. For some of the white women, the Freedom Summer was, their frequent assignment to teaching and secretarial jobs on the projects notwithstanding, an opportunity to escape the constraints of family and campus life at home. Liaisons with black males could be viewed as logical outgrowths of their deep commitment to an integrated society as well as the predictable fruit of an extraordinarily tension-laden climate in which highly motivated young people of both sexes were impelled to band together for security. Such coupling, however, was often regarded in a dim light by many of the black women on the projects who sensed, not entirely without justification, that the males were struck less by true love than the lure of the hitherto unattainable.[38]

By far the most serious strain on unity within the ranks of the civil rights movement was provided not by insensitive white volunteers or interracial sexual relationships, but by the ever-present threat of violence which affected all of those engaged in the Freedom Summer. For Mississippi racists responded to the movement with a new ferocity born of frustration at the changes taking place in their midst. A revived Ku Klux Klan was to blame for many of the attacks on movement personnel and headquarters as well as a spate of church burnings which took place over the summer. By the end of August 1964 four project workers had been murdered, four had been seriously wounded, 80 had been assaulted, hundreds had been arrested by local authorities, and over 60 black churches and homes had been bombed or burned.[39]

In one sense the violence played into the hands of the movement because its intensity combined with the presence of large numbers of white students to focus the attention of the national media on Mississippi. However, it took the disappearance in Neshoba County of two CORE workers and a white student volunteer to bring federal authorities into the state in force. Troops were ordered to help in the search for Michael Schwerner, a Jewish social worker from Manhattan's Lower East Side who had been working on a CORE project in southwestern Mississippi; James Chaney, a black Mississippian

38. D. McAdam, *Freedom Summer* (New York and Oxford, 1988), pp. 93–6.
39. Ibid., p. 96.

who had left his job as a plasterer's apprentice to assist Schwerner; and Andrew Goodman, a white anthropology major from Queens College who had been assigned to Schwerner's task force at the orientation session in Ohio. President Lyndon Johnson also dispatched the former head of the CIA, Allen Dulles, to Jackson where he (Dulles) discussed law enforcement problems with the state's Democratic governor and a number of influential private citizens. Dulles returned to brief the president on the urgent need for a greater federal presence in Mississippi. Johnson quickly pressed the long-serving FBI chief J. Edgar Hoover to send an additional 50 FBI agents to the state where they launched what eventually proved to be an effective campaign against the local Klan. The bodies of the three missing men were finally discovered outside the town of Philadelphia after a 44-day search. The FBI made a score of arrests later in the year. Among those seized were the Neshoba County sheriff's deputy Cecil Price who had conspired with local Klansmen in the deaths of the civil rights workers. Convictions were later obtained after the US Supreme Court had bolstered the protective capacity of the Fourteenth Amendment.[40]

The belated attempts of the federal government to provide adequate protection for Freedom Summer volunteers failed to convince most SNCC and CORE staff in the war zone that they had not been betrayed by the United States. Confronted daily with the possibility of death at the hands of white supremacists, stressed-out volunteers and field staff alike became increasingly disaffected with America's political leaders and institutions. For many, the bankruptcy of the movement's existing strategy was revealed most clearly at the national Democratic convention in Atlantic City, New Jersey. The convention was the scene of a bitter intra-party dispute occasioned by the request of MFDP delegates to be seated at the expense of Mississippi's lily-white regulars. Made up largely of semi-literate, black sharecroppers (a significant number of whom were women) the MFDP delegation posed a major problem for President Johnson who feared that its challenge might provoke a potentially disastrous secession of white southern Democrats from the convention. As Governor John Connolly of Texas put it: 'If those baboons walk onto the convention floor . . . we walk out.'[41]

The president's fear of a Dixiecrat exodus was heightened by the dramatic appearance of Mrs Fannie Lou Hamer before the credentials committee, empowered to determine the legitimacy of delegates

---

40. McAdam, *Freedom Summer*, pp. 128–82.
41. Quoted in Dittmer, *Local People*, p. 180.

seeking admission to the convention floor. Speaking on live television until media coverage was interrupted cynically by a hastily arranged presidential press conference, the MFDP activist provided graphic testimony about the conditions facing blacks in Mississippi and about her own beating in Winona. With tears of anger in her eyes, she concluded with a peroration of characteristic force:

> All of this on account we want to register, to become first-class citizens, and if the Freedom Democratic Party is not seated now, I question America, is this America, the land of the free and the home of the brave where we have to sleep with the telephones off the hooks because our lives be threatened daily because we want to live as decent human beings, in America?[42]

With several members of the credentials committee prepared to seat Mrs Hamer and the other MFDP delegates, Johnson co-opted his liberal allies, Senator Hubert Humphrey and labour leader Walter Reuther, into derailing the Freedom Democrats' challenge. Intense pressure was placed on black leaders to agree to a compromise solution in which the regulars would be seated, the MFDP would be allowed two at-large seats on the convention floor, and reforms were promised for the party's 1968 gathering. While the more conservative national civil rights leaders, Roy Wilkins and Whitney Young, supported calls for compromise, the MFDP's SNCC allies contended that a political deal would betray the thousands of ordinary men and women who had undergone enormous hardships to support the movement in Mississippi. Martin Luther King, ignoring advice from Bayard Rustin to shun the convention, voiced half-hearted support for the administration's position but confessed that had he been a member of the MFDP delegation he would have opposed compromise.[43] In the event the Mississippians chose to reject the views of the great and the good in order to make the point that moral principles could not be bartered away as lightly as Humphrey and his friends believed.

Although the events at Atlantic City ended whatever residual trust many SNCC members might have had in mainstream politics, the disappointed MFDP delegates declined to withdraw their support from Lyndon Johnson in his fight against Barry Goldwater. Like Roy Wilkins, Whitney Young and Martin Luther King, they retained sufficient faith in the political process to continue their struggle under the umbrella of the national Democratic Party. Such

---

42. Quoted in Mills, *This Little Light*, pp. 120–1.
43. Garrow, *Bearing the Cross*, p. 349.

faith did not prevent MFDP leaders from heightening their racial consciousness in the following months. Soon after her dramatic appearance in Atlantic City, Mrs Hamer was invited to join other SNCC personnel on a visit to Guinea hosted by President Sekou Touré. She was deeply affected by the experience. 'I had never in my life seen where black people were running banks', she later recalled. 'I had never seen nobody black running a government in my life. So it was quite a revelation to me. . . . Because then I could feel myself never, ever being ashamed of my ancestors or my background.'[44]

The concerted attempts by civil rights field workers to mobilise rural blacks in Mississippi and other Deep South states in the early 1960s were products of the faith which radical democrats like Ella Baker possessed in the power of grass-roots mobilising to effect fundamental social change in America. The stress on process over results, on nurturing rather than imposing leadership skills, and on self-reform as much as raising group consciousness proved remarkably effective in encouraging the growth of those talents which Baker, Moses and others believed to be essential to the success of the civil rights movement. There were, however, two major problems with the latter's stress on participatory democracy. Firstly, the organising tradition tended to emphasise the need for political change over the imperative demand for economic justice. Staff members present at SNCC meetings in Mississippi in 1964 certainly displayed an awareness of the structural problems confronting displaced black farm workers but generally speaking they appear to have believed that federal intervention and political participation would promote greater job security and increase wages. However, as Staughton Lynd observed, the movement had not even been able to provide adequate help for those Mississippi blacks made redundant because of their civil rights involvement, let alone stem the seemingly remorseless tide of rural depopulation caused by the rapid advance of agribusiness in the Delta.[45] 'Is what's intended a moral gesture only', he wrote pointedly in 1965, 'or a determined attempt to transform the American power structure?'[46]

Secondly, the technique of slow, steady organising on the basis of a tolerant and pragmatic awareness of the views of all sections

44. Quoted in Mills, *This Little Light*, p. 137.

45. S. Lynd, 'The New Radicals and "Participatory Democracy"', *Dissent* 12 (1965), 329.

46. Ibid., 333.

of the black community proved less and less appealing over time. Patience, in short, began to run out as movement workers in the field continued to be killed and harassed by white supremacists in the face of federal inaction. The very task of organising not only radicalised many southern blacks but it also embittered increasing numbers of SNCC and CORE staff members. Such men and women, passionately devoted as they were to the cause of civil rights, were inevitably influenced by the sight of individual blacks like Hartman Turnbow exercising the right of self-defence and by the perceived betrayal of the cause at Atlantic City. With around 85 white Freedom Summer volunteers swelling the ranks of SNCC staff in the wake of the project, black SNCC members began to reconsider their attitude to sacred cows of the movement like nonviolence, integration and coalition politics.[47] SNCC's journey from the organisational embodiment of the beloved community to a doctrinaire and racially chauvinistic clique had begun in earnest.

47. N.V. Bartley, *The New South 1945–1980* (Baton Rouge, 1995), p. 350.

CHAPTER 6

The Movement in Decline 1965–68

During the second half of the 1960s the civil rights movement became a victim of its own success and of powerful historical forces beyond its control. The destruction of the southern caste system, well advanced by late 1965 as a result of the coalition's multi-pronged strategy, did not lead to complacency. Serious urban riots in cities as far apart as Los Angeles, Chicago and Detroit made it clear that racism and poverty afflicted African Americans throughout the country and not just the South. The urgent need to redefine the movement in order to ensure that non-southern blacks, particularly urban black youth, did not fall prey to despair intensified the ongoing internal debate over goals and tactics. While the more conservative civil rights organisations maintained close ties to the high-spending administration of Lyndon Johnson and SNCC and CORE embraced black separatism, Martin Luther King endeavoured to shore up the centre by making nonviolent direct action relevant to the rapidly changing situation. Even though the SCLC's ambitious attempt to deploy the tactics of the southern movement against *de facto* segregation in Chicago ended in failure, King retained his faith in nonviolence until his tragic death in Memphis in April 1968. By this stage the intensification of US military intervention in southeast Asia had contributed further to the decline of the civil rights coalition as a cohesive national force. Significantly, however, neither the Vietnam War nor the growth of Black Power put a stop to civil rights activity at the local level. Aided by federal anti-poverty programmes, revivified NAACP branches, and grass-roots voters' leagues emboldened by passage of the Voting Rights Act, black and white activists worked to ensure that the movement left a rich legacy for the future.

Fissiparous tendencies

By August 1965 the civil rights movement was clearly in transition. Even though Washington proved frustratingly reluctant to dispatch federal registrars to the Deep South, the Voting Rights Act heralded the end of a political system which had largely excluded blacks from power. Renewed grass-roots voter registration activity (much of it carried out under the auspices of a second Voter Education Project) combined with limited federal action to produce a rapid increase in the number of southern black voters. By the end of the 1960s roughly 60 per cent of adult black southerners had registered to vote. Results in the rural areas of the lower South were the most impressive. Black enrolment in Alabama grew from 23 per cent in 1964 to 53 per cent in 1968. In Mississippi it leapt from 6.7 to 59.4 per cent during the same period.[1] For the first time since Reconstruction southern blacks could elect members of their own race to local and state offices or at least support white candidates perceived to be sympathetic to their needs. A genuine revolution took place in southern politics as the rapid increase in registered black voters led many one-time segregationist politicians down the path of racial moderation. Demographic realities (black voters remained a minority in most southern electoral districts) and a corresponding growth in white voter registration meant that there were distinct limits to the social and economic gains produced by the acquisition of the vote but, at the very least, participation in the political process presaged an end to racist demagogues and brought African Americans a sense of self-esteem and civic pride which many had never known during the days of the caste system.

Much, of course, remained to be done below the Mason–Dixon Line. Poverty was a major scourge, particularly in the countryside where mechanised agribusiness had vastly reduced the need for farm labour. Integrated schools were largely unknown outside parts of the peripheral South, notwithstanding a decade of litigation after the *Brown* decision. Employment discrimination and petty harassment continued to have a deleterious impact on black lives in spite of the passage of congressional civil rights legislation. For the most part, however, the substantial achievements of the movement meant that by August 1965 the South had begun to look a little less like the

1. J. Lawson, *Running for Freedom: Civil Rights and Black Politics in America Since 1941* (New York, 1991), p. 116.

nation's number one problem. Instead it was the North, specifically the urban North, which began to attract the attention of the nation's black leaders.

Five days after Lyndon Johnson signed the Voting Rights Act into law, rioting broke out in Watts, a black neighbourhood of Los Angeles in which community complaints over police brutality had failed to find a sympathetic hearing from the city's mayor, Sam Yorty. The routine arrest of a ghetto resident sparked off four days of mayhem in which at least 34 people (most of them black) were killed, 1,000 were injured and property valued at an estimated $200 million was destroyed.[2]

The most serious race riot since the Second World War signalled to all Americans that federal civil rights legislation had had little impact on the lives of northern blacks. The Great Migration had continued apace in the 1940s and 1950s with over three million blacks abandoning Dixie for the promised land. Although these migrants did find a more fluid society in the North, they, like the earlier arrivals, discovered city authorities ill-equipped to deal with their arrival and established white communities reluctant to pay anything more than lip service to the idea of racial integration. The vote brought them a measure of influence with big city machines but such meagre political power failed to reverse the corrosive effects of slum housing in the ghetto, poor quality education, high unemployment, unstable families and a pervasive sense of social alienation, particularly among the young. New York-based civil rights organisations like the NAACP and the National Urban League had long sought to overcome such problems by utilising the existing politico-legal system and enlisting the help of corporate capital. Watts, however, revealed the limited efficacy of conventional strategies and highlighted the need for more radical solutions to urban poverty and decay.

By this stage the federal government had already embarked on its own unprecedented effort to eradicate poverty from America.[3] In 1964 President Lyndon Johnson, determined to outshine his

2. G. Horne, *Fire this Time: The Watts Uprising and the 1960s* (Charlottesville and London, 1995), p. 3.

3. There is a substantial scholarly literature on the anti-poverty programmes of the 1960s. Particularly helpful are C. Brauer, 'Kennedy, Johnson, and the War on Poverty', *JAH* (1982), 98–119; A. Matusow, *The Unraveling of America: A History of Liberalism in the 1960s* (New York, 1984), pp. 97–127, 217–71; D. Chalmers, *And the Crooked Places Made Straight: The Struggle for Social Change in the 1960s* (Baltimore and London, 1991), pp. 55–67; M.I. Gelfand, 'The War on Poverty' in *The Johnson Years: vol. I – Foreign Policy, the Great Society and the White House*, ed. R. Divine (Lawrence, 1987), pp. 126–54; G. Davies, 'War on Dependency: Liberal Individualism and the Economic Opportunity Act of 1964', *JAS* 26 (1992), 205–31.

martyred predecessor, called for an 'unconditional war on poverty' and secured congressional support for his Economic Opportunity Act, the first of a series of anti-poverty statutes designed to promote 'the Great Society'. Programmes such as Medicare, Medicaid, VISTA, Job Corps, and Community Action were products of mid-1960s optimism. In the eyes of the nation's messianic liberal policymakers, modern government had the capacity to solve virtually any problem given both the will and the resources which the United States possessed in abundance. By 1964 the American economy was beginning to boom once again owing to a massive tax cut which greatly advantaged the better-off. Poverty, originally 'discovered' by the Kennedy administration, was not only an embarrassment to the United States in the Cold War, but it also sapped the nation's economic growth and furnished the conditions for social unrest. What better way to promote the welfare of the country, the Democratic Party and Lyndon Johnson himself than focus national energies on the task of bringing all Americans into the middle class through judicious application of federal largesse?

Although the service programmes of the Great Society were designed to benefit whites as well as blacks (and were certainly not sold politically as civil rights measures), the fact that over a third of African-American families lived below the official poverty line meant that the War on Poverty, like New Deal welfare policies before it, had a disproportionate impact on ordinary black people.[4] This was particularly true not only of welfare benefits such as Aid to Families with Dependent Children (AFDC), Food Stamps and Medicaid (basic federal health care for the poor of all races) but also pre-school education (Head Start) and the controversial Community Action Program (CAP) directed by a newcomer to the rapidly expanding federal bureaucracy, the Office of Economic Opportunity (OEO).

Placed under the control of Robert Kennedy's ambitious brother-in-law, Sargent Shriver, the OEO assumed overall command of the War on Poverty during the mid-1960s. In the face of stiff competition for resources from other federal agencies, notably the Department of Health, Education and Welfare (HEW) and the Bureau of Labor, the OEO sought to combine the traditional top-down approach to poverty with the contemporary radical emphasis on

4. In 1967 34 per cent of black families had incomes below the poverty line. Although this compared unfavourably with the figure for whites (9 per cent) it nonetheless marked a significant decrease from 1940 when 87 per cent of black families lived in poverty. US Bureau of the Census, *Poverty in the United States: 1992, Current Population Reports* P-60–175, Table 4.

participatory democracy. Crucial here were its attempts to channel federal funds into inner-city and rural areas by promoting the formation of community action agencies required by statute to encourage 'maximum feasible participation' from those who actually lived in these communities.

The War on Poverty had a mixed impact on the cause of civil rights. It certainly provided a source of jobs and patronage for black activists, many of whom were genuinely concerned to target the new-found resources on projects designed to promote a better life for the poor. Initially, the OEO proved to be sympathetic to their objectives. During the summer of 1965, for example, it provided a substantial Head Start grant to a new organisation, the Child Development Group of Mississippi (CDGM).[5] Although SNCC workers in the state believed the money was designed to sap the movement's energies by co-opting its most talented personnel, the CDGM was backed by some of Mississippi's most active black leaders. The CDGM used the funds to implement a successful programme of pre-school education and medical care for disadvantaged African Americans. Inevitably, however, the spectre of large amounts of federal funds falling into the hands of those they regarded as ignorant sharecroppers alarmed conservative white politicians. Powerful Mississippians in Washington like Senator John Stennis were soon complaining about the extent of corruption and radical involvement in the anti-poverty programme at home. As a result the OEO began to redirect Head Start money into the hands of a less controversial group, Mississippi Action for Progress, which was backed by the state's middle-class NAACP and leading white moderates like Hodding Carter. In spite of the fact that the CDGM received support from the Freedom Democrats, reduced funding after 1966 combined with administrative difficulties and divisions over Black Power to undermine the group's effectiveness by the time the OEO announced swingeing cuts in Head Start funding in 1968.

The War on Poverty had a similar impact elsewhere, energising civil rights efforts in some localities but in others feeding internal factionalism which could be exploited by entrenched elites such as southern planters or big-city mayors who resented the creation of alternative power loci and who quickly pressured the Johnson administration into reining in the OEO. Ultimately the radical potential

5. On the Great Society's impact on Mississippi see J. Dittmer, *Local People: The Struggle for Civil Rights in Mississippi* (Urbana and Chicago, 1994), pp. 363–88, and J.C. Cobb, ' "Somebody Done Nailed Us on the Cross": Federal Farm and Welfare Policy and the Civil Rights Movement in the Mississippi Delta', *JAH* 77 (1990), 912–36.

of the Great Society foundered on the harsh realities of American politics as well as the general public's opposition to the kind of radical income-transfer strategy which some political economists believed essential to eradicate poverty in America.

President Johnson's apparent determination to fulfil the promise of the New Deal, however, convinced many civil rights leaders after 1964 that their best option was to seek further gains in alliance with progressive elements in the national Democratic Party. This was the policy articulated most vigorously by one of the civil rights movement's premier strategists, Bayard Rustin, who rightly sensed that the freedom struggle had reached a crossroads. 'The civil rights movement', he wrote in 1964, 'is evolving from a protest movement into a full-fledged social movement – an evolution calling its very name into question. It is now concerned not merely with removing the barriers to full opportunity but with achieving the fact of equality.'[6] Rustin, still closely linked to King and Randolph, argued throughout the mid-1960s that coalition was the only sensible option for blacks as a minority race in a plural, majoritarian democracy.[7] After all, he reasoned, alignment with progressive whites had virtually destroyed the southern caste system; further cooperation with liberals, organised labour and the federal government would surely deliver the kind of social and economic gains which civil rights activists were now seeking. Rustin's views were shared by other movement leaders including Roy Wilkins, Whitney Young and Norman Hill, CORE's programme director, who sought in vain to transfer his own organisation's allegiance from direct action to electoral politics.

Mainstream coalition politics, however, seemed less attractive to black radicals in the wake of the traumatic Freedom Summer, Rustin's endorsement of compromise at Atlantic City, and Martin Luther King's perceived double-dealing at Selma. Events like these fed the growing sense among SNCC and CORE activists that a corrupt and racist liberal establishment (epitomised by a president prepared to commit large numbers of US troops to the ongoing civil war in Vietnam) was trying to divert the movement away from root-and-branch reform of American society. Once a hero to young black activists, Rustin was viewed increasingly as a dupe of the power elite. In mid-August 1964 his friend Norman Hill resigned from his

6. B. Rustin, 'From Protest to Politics: The Future of the Civil Rights Movement', in Rustin, *Down the Line: The Collected Writings of Bayard Rustin* (Chicago, 1971), p. 115.

7. Ibid., pp. 111–22.

post at CORE – a clear sign that pro-Rustin moderates were losing ground within the civil rights coalition.[8]

There was more to the developing split within the movement than events. Opposition to the integrationist strategy of Rustin and his allies was also a product of intra-organisational structural and intellectual change. Most deeply affected were SNCC and CORE, two very different organisations which were well on the way to endorsing black nationalism by the summer of 1965. CORE had become an integral member of the civil rights coalition owing to its wholehearted endorsement of militant nonviolent direct action and the resourceful leadership of James Farmer. As well as playing a prominent role in several southern organising campaigns, it had promoted the development of vibrant chapters in many northern cities. These chapters had spearheaded the urban struggle for equal rights, moving perceptibly from broadly integrationist causes such as fair housing and desegregated public facilities to ghetto-oriented concerns like unemployment, slums, police brutality and sub-standard schools.[9]

Targeting direct action tactics like demonstrations, picketing and extra-legal civil disobedience on neighbourhood improvement had two main consequences for CORE. Firstly, it attracted significant numbers of African-American students and working-class blacks to an organisation hitherto dominated by whites (a disproportionate number of whom were liberal Jews). By 1964 four-fifths of CORE's National Action Committee were black and the white majority in the organisation as a whole was being eroded rapidly.[10] Secondly, as contacts with ghetto residents increased, black CORE activists grew more receptive to the separatist teachings of groups like the Nation of Islam. The Nation's foremost spokesman, Minister Malcolm X, was a major influence on radical civil rights activists during the early 1960s. The son of a former Garveyite preacher, Malcolm had embraced the faith and discipline of the Black Muslims while serving a lengthy prison sentence for burglary in Massachusetts. He emerged to become the fieriest of all America's black radicals – not only a persistent and angry critic of white racism, liberal hypocrisy and black self-denigration, but also a constant thorn in the side of the civil rights movement. Radical activists and black youths were impressed by Malcolm's scathing attacks on the movement's pursuit of integration – a goal which he regarded as a mordant form

---

8. A. Meier and E. Rudwick, *CORE: A Study in the Civil Rights Movement 1942–1968* (New York, 1973), p. 325.
    9. Ibid., pp. 182–210.   10. Ibid., pp. 292, 304.

of political and cultural suicide – and his repeated insistence that
blacks had to close ranks (politically, economically and culturally)
if they were to progress in the United States. Heaping ridicule on
supposedly Uncle Tom leaders such as Wilkins and King and excori-
ating the white establishment in even harsher terms, Malcolm
provided frustrated northern blacks with an alternative to the movement's nonviolent philosophy which demonstrably had failed to
confront the needs and expectations of those trapped in the ghetto.
Although Rustin, Farmer and other moderate black leaders tried
to argue that Malcolm lacked any practical programme for black
advancement, their views cut little ice in inner-city America. As CORE
deepened its involvement in the ghetto, increasing numbers of black
chapter members began to question the assumption that the movement's strength lay in its insistence on interracial cooperation.

A primary feature of Malcolm X's strident critique of nonviolent direct action was his oft-repeated conviction that blacks should
exercise their right of self-defence when confronted by white supremacist violence. He and other like-minded radicals such as Robert
Williams mistakenly believed that the movement's central philosophy amounted to nothing more than passive resistance – a cringeing
response to virulent racism which was bound to play into the hands
of whites and ultimately exacerbate the black man's ingrained sense
of inferiority. Although CORE members in general did not renounce
their commitment to nonviolence immediately, many northern
activists welcomed Malcolm's rhetorical assault on established principles after Malcolm parted company with the Nation of Islam in
the winter of 1963. In April 1964 black CORE activist Lewis Robinson
responded to Malcolm's call for the formation of protective rifle
associations by announcing his intention to set up a gun club in
Cleveland, Ohio.[11] Robinson's action proved controversial within
his own chapter, but his move signalled CORE's declining attachment to the philosophy and strategy of nonviolent direct action
which had provided the organisation with its *raison d'être* since 1942.
Greater emphasis on civil disobedience and the ever-present threat
of Klan violence in the CORE stronghold of Louisiana merely served
to exacerbate the trend towards an acceptance of self-defence by
CORE chapters across the United States.[12]

As CORE's national office struggled to come to terms with the
erosion of organisational discipline, SNCC continued on its own

11. Ibid., pp. 301–2.
12. On CORE's activities in Louisiana see A. Fairclough, *Race and Democracy: The
Civil Rights Struggle in Louisiana, 1915–1972* (Athens, Ga, 1995), pp. 267–384, 395–401.

seemingly relentless path towards black separatism. Always the most intellectually vigorous of the mainstream civil rights organisations, it had become, by the time of the Watts riot, the property of a hardened band of staff members increasingly divided over such issues as the contribution of whites to the movement, the wisdom of greater internal centralisation, and the movement's relationship to politics. Most SNCC members, however, agreed that the Democratic Party was not a fit vehicle for civil rights activity and that Rustin's faith in the grand alliance of labour, liberals and blacks was badly misplaced. Factional strife was a major problem for SNCC throughout 1964 and 1965. Many black staffers resented the activities of whites in the organisation, particularly of those who had joined the group as a result of the Freedom Summer. There were also alarming signs of polarisation between so-called 'floaters' and 'hardliners'.[13] The former, representing the original anarchic side of SNCC, shunned organisational discipline and continued to display a marked reluctance to impose their values on the local blacks with whom they came into contact. The hardliners, often southern blacks themselves, criticised the ill-discipline of some staffers and contended that a greater degree of centralisation was necessary if SNCC were to achieve its objectives, increasingly defined as political power and social and economic justice for African Americans across the United States. Although neither of these loose factions had emerged triumphant by the summer of 1965, Bob Moses's characteristic reluctance to assume a leadership role in the wake of the Freedom Summer left a power vacuum for two northern blacks, James Forman and Stokely Carmichael, to fill. Together they made a major contribution to SNCC's growing affinity for black nationalism and secular radicalism.

Forman was older than most SNCC activists. Born in Chicago in 1928 and reared by his grandmother in rural Mississippi, he had returned north during the Second World War. After military service in the late 1940s, he completed a management degree at Chicago's mainly black Roosevelt University and, struck by the similarities between South African apartheid and Jim Crow, went on to undertake graduate work in African affairs at Boston University. In 1960 he joined a CORE affiliate while teaching in Chicago and the following year, having made contact with student leaders in Nashville,

    13. C. Carson, *In Struggle: SNCC and the Black Awakening of the 1960s* (Cambridge, Mass., and London, 1981), pp. 155–7, and C. Sellers with R. Terrell, *The River of No Return: The Autobiography of a Black Militant and the Life and Death of SNCC* (Jackson and London, 1990), pp. 130–46.

journeyed to Monroe, North Carolina, to aid civil rights forces in the area. Monroe at this date was a violent, segregated town, already headline news because of its maverick NAACP leader, Robert Williams, who had called on blacks 'to meet violence with violence' and been suspended by an embarrassed Roy Wilkins for his pains.[14] On 27 August Forman and other black demonstrators narrowly escaped death after being attacked by angry whites outside the county courthouse.[15] Forman spent a brief period in jail and then left town. Within two months he had given up a teaching job to become SNCC's executive secretary. A gifted administrator, Forman brought a measure of order to a chaotic organisation which regarded bureaucracy as a tool of the conservative establishment. Although he lacked Moses's spirituality, he provided a sharp cutting edge to SNCC, committed as he was to the pragmatic strategy of nonviolent direct action, a term he claimed to have learned from the Ghanaian nationalist, Kwame Nkrumah. 'What we needed in the United States, as black people', he later recalled in terms redolent of Ella Baker's influence, 'were committed souls to assist in the development of organizations that would survive the organizer. We did not need charismatic leadership, for this most often led to a disintegration once the charismatic leader was gone. My goal was to build structures that would perpetuate revolutionary ideas and programs, not personalities.'[16]

For all his suspicion of charismatic leaders, Forman rapidly emerged as a major figure in SNCC. His administrative training, particularly his awareness of the need for a sound organisational base, rendered him sympathetic to the views of hardliners like Cleveland Sellers, just as his inner fury at white oppression made him receptive to the growing calls for greater black participation in and leadership of in the civil rights movement.

Stokely Carmichael was ten years younger than Forman. A West Indian by birth, he possessed close links to New York leftists and was well read in contemporary political science. At Howard University he became immersed in civil rights activity as a member of the Nonviolent Action Group, one of the main student blocs represented at SNCC's inaugural meeting in Raleigh. As well as being charismatic and handsome (he attracted numerous female admirers

14. M.C. Barksdale, 'Robert F. Williams and the Indigenous Civil Rights Movement in Monroe, North Carolina, 1961', *Journal of Negro History*, 69 (1984), 73–89.

15. Forman's experiences in Monroe are related in J. Forman, *The Making of Black Revolutionaries*, (New York, 1972), pp. 174–211.

16. Ibid., pp. 105–6.

during the 1960s), Carmichael was an astute political organiser sensitive to shifts in grass-roots opinion. His socialist leanings, moreover, convinced him that a new emphasis on economic issues was an essential precondition for black progress in America. Occupying a strategic position mid-way between the two major factional groupings within SNCC, he was well-placed to capitalise on his organisation's continued drift from the mainstream.

Although Carmichael's organising talents were put to good use during SNCC's Mississippi campaigns, his chief contribution to the development of the civil rights movement was made in the immediate aftermath of Bloody Sunday in Selma. With media attention focused on the city as a result of the SCLC-sponsored marches, Carmichael headed a new SNCC organising drive in rural Lowndes County lying directly between Selma and Montgomery.

Lowndes typified the southern Black Belt in the mid-1960s. Notwithstanding the passage of landmark civil rights legislation in 1964, its black majority population continued to face severe political, economic and social discrimination. African Americans in Lowndes were disproportionately afflicted by poverty and largely bereft of power owing to the blatantly discriminatory efforts of white registrars. Whites owned most of the land and totally monopolised local government.[17]

Carmichael arrived in Lowndes County on 26 March, the day after Klansmen had murdered Viola Liuzzo, a northern white woman who was ferrying movement supporters along Interstate 80. There he made contact with the Lowndes County Christian Movement for Human Rights (LCCMHR), a group of local blacks recently mobilised after meetings with an SCLC team headed by James Bevel. The LCCMHR was led by several independent-minded individuals, notably John Hulett, whose institutional affiliations included the church, the NAACP and (as a foundryman in Birmingham during the 1950s) organised labour.[18] Carmichael, who was joined by other SNCC staffers in the spring and summer of 1965, found the task of organising difficult, for Jim Crow practices were entrenched in the area. Nonetheless, he was impressed by the militancy and

17. C.W. Eagles, 'From Shotgun to Umbrellas: The Civil Rights Movement in Lowndes County, Alabama' in *The Adaptable South: Essays in Honor of George Brown Tindall*, ed. E. Jacoway, D.T. Carter *et al.* (Baton Rouge, 1991), p. 218.
18. The best source on the indigenous black leadership in Lowndes is C.W. Eagles, *Outside Agitator: Jon Daniels and the Civil Rights Movement in Alabama* (Chapel Hill and London, 1993), pp. 122–6.

bravery of Hulett and his colleagues, particularly their determination to meet increasing white violence with armed resistance. When Carmichael attempted to convince Robert Strickland, a local leader employed as a construction worker in nearby Montgomery, of the virtues of nonviolence, Strickland reportedly told him, 'You turn the other cheek, and you'll get handed half of what you're sitting on.'[19] Close contact with militant rural blacks and the ever-present fear of white terror continued to erode SNCC's commitment to nonviolence – a commitment already diminished by the experience of the Freedom Summer and several contacts with Malcolm X before his assassination in Harlem in May 1965.[20] After the murder in August of Jonathan Daniels, a white Episcopalian priest assisting the SNCC registration drive in Lowndes, Carmichael vented the anger of movement activists in the community. 'We're going to tear this county up', he promised. 'Then we're going to build it back, brick by brick, until it's a fit place for human beings.'[21]

Stokely Carmichael's solution to the problems bedevilling local blacks represented an extension of his organising work in Mississippi. Convinced that efforts to work within the existing white-dominated Democratic Party organisation in Lowndes would bear meagre fruit, he persuaded Hulett and his colleagues to enter politics as an independent force. The result was the Lowndes County Freedom Organization (LCFO), an inevitably all-black party formally organised in April 1966. While the venture highlighted SNCC's growing dissatisfaction with mainstream politics, the new party's distinctive symbol of a snarling black panther confirmed the growth of a more aggressive black approach to racial injustice in America. In October 1966 Huey Newton and Bobby Seale, two community activists in Oakland, California, used the image as the basis for their Black Panther Party for Self-Defense dedicated to protection of the ghetto against white racist violence. Newton hit on the term 'panther' after reading about the LCFO in a pamphlet circulated by the Bay Area Friends of SNCC.[22]

SNCC and CORE were not the only mainstream political groups losing faith in the existing system by the time of the Watts riot. White radical adherents of the New Left, previously close allies of the civil rights movement, were also developing their opposition to

19. Quoted in C. Carson, *In Struggle*, p. 164.   20. Ibid., p. 135.
21. Quoted in ibid., p. 165.
22. H. Pearson, *The Shadow of the Panther: Huey Newton and the Rise of Black Power in America* (Reading, Mass., 1994), p. 108.

coalition with the national Democratic Party. Led mainly by student activists, many of them members of the campus-based Students for a Democratic Society (SDS), they spearheaded the rapidly evolving opposition to US foreign policy in southeast Asia. From their point of view coalition politics meant cooperation with a morally bankrupt administration bent on escalating American intervention in Vietnam. The white New Left historian Staughton Lynd contended in a caustic critique of Rustin's grand-alliance strategy that it undermined efforts to promote participatory democracy and threatened to rob the interracial movement for peace and brotherhood of its cutting edge. Lynd, a staunch friend of SNCC, attacked Rustin's controversial role at Atlantic City as well as his opposition to the nascent anti-war movement. He called for 'a new politics which forces the representative back to his people, and politics back to life' and insisted that nonviolent revolution was 'the only long-run alternative to coalition with the marines'.[23] Opposition to Johnson's Vietnam policy was widespread among SNCC and CORE activists. As early as April 1965 SNCC's executive committee announced its support for the Spring Mobilization in Washington, the first major anti-war demonstration of the decade which was addressed by, among others, Bob Moses.

Although representatives from the two most radical civil rights organisations continued to attend meetings of the Council of United Civil Rights Leadership during 1965, it was clear by August that the movement was in danger of collapsing as a national force. The NAACP and the Urban League not only endorsed coalition politics, but they also feared that SNCC and CORE were moving too far ahead of public opinion with their increasingly shrill criticism of the Johnson administration. Attacks on the president's civil rights and foreign policy, they argued, could only damage the movement's prospects at a time when the federal government was finally delivering on its promises. Several events confirmed the lack of empathy between the two wings of the black freedom movement, not least the withdrawal of state NAACP support for COFO in November 1964 and claims by Roy Wilkins (already concerned with the growth of black separatist tendencies) that SNCC had fallen prey to Chinese communist influence. When Watts erupted on 27 August the only man capable of forging a fragile unity between the major civil rights organisations was Martin Luther King.

23. S. Lynd, 'Coalition Politics or Nonviolent Revolution?' *Liberation* (June–July 1965), 18–21.

Strain at the centre: The SCLC's Chicago campaign

By the time Dr King visited riot-torn Los Angeles on 15 August 1965 he was under few illusions about the difficulties confronting him as the nation's most prominent civil rights leader. The moderate centre of the civil rights movement had to hold if further gains were to be achieved, yet the centrifugal pressures outlined above were placing huge strains upon the SCLC president. Vietnam was already a major problem for King. As a champion of militant non-violence, he was bound to be affected by Lyndon Johnson's escalation of the war. If nothing else, his Christian conscience told him to speak out, something he did as early as March 1965 when he called for the United States 'to move down a course of negotiated settlement' on the grounds that violence was unlikely to yield positive results.[24] His criticism, measured at first, grew stronger over the summer culminating in an outspoken statement in his address to the annual SCLC convention in Birmingham. There he urged President Johnson to announce his readiness to negotiate with the Vietcong whom he (King) regarded as Vietnamese nationalists rather than cyphers of communist China. To demonstrate its good faith, he said, the United States government should end its current bombing campaign and, along with the North Vietnamese, seek UN mediation for the conflict.

Realising that King's call for negotiations was bound to prove controversial, the SCLC convention took care to place some distance between itself and its outspoken leader. The delegates recognised King's right to criticise the war, but resolved that

> the primary function of our organization is to secure full citizenship rights for the Negro citizens of this country and that our major contribution to world peace and brotherhood is to create a truly democratic society here in America. Our resources are not sufficient to assume the burden of two major issues in our society[;] we would therefore urge that the efforts of SCLC in mass demonstrations and action movements be confined to the question of racial brotherhood.[25]

The resolution, drafted by Bayard Rustin and Andrew Young, failed to save King from a barrage of criticism, even though his call for

24. M.L. King, 'Statement on Vietnam War', 6 March 1965, Box 8, Series 3, Martin Luther King Papers, KC.

25. SCLC Resolution on Vietnam, August 1965, Box 26, Series 5, CORE Papers, WisHS.

negotiations fell short of his later attacks on the war.[26] None of the leading civil rights organisations had yet issued a formal statement on Vietnam, even though James Farmer was finding it hard to suppress anti-war sentiment within CORE and many SNCC activists were openly critical of the escalation. Most of King's fellow black civil rights leaders believed that forthright speaking on Vietnam would divide the grand alliance, alienate the Johnson administration and divert public attention from black demands for a more just social order. Their negative response, however, paled beside that of the White House which lost little time in disseminating the view that King was out of his depth when dealing with foreign policy. The president's close ally, Senator Thomas Dodd of Connecticut, insisted that King had 'absolutely no competence' in foreign affairs and confirmed the fears of the civil rights establishment by noting pointedly that he had 'alienated much of the support he previously enjoyed in Congress'.[27] Such reactions led King's advisers, particularly Rustin and Levison, to warn him against further pronouncements on Vietnam. For the moment the chastened SCLC leader, a committed advocate of coalition strategy, agreed to confine his attention to civil rights. It was a decision he would soon come to regret.

As the controversy surrounding King's early stance on the Vietnam War subsided, the SCLC leadership prepared to embark on a new and risky venture which would take the organisation away from its southern roots. King's visit to Watts, especially the hostile reception he received from many of the residents, brought home the desperate need for urban reform in the North and West if the growing trend towards cynicism, separatism and violence among American blacks were to be halted.

Watts did not introduce the SCLC to northern black poverty overnight. The previous summer had witnessed several outbreaks of civil disorder in the North. After rioting in the black ghetto of Rochester, New York, in July 1964, the National Council of Churches' Commission on Religion and Race had invited SCLC officials to visit the area. Andrew Young and James Bevel undertook a brief voter registration campaign but they found the younger residents of the ghetto disturbingly resistant to talk of nonviolence. The mobilisation drive was a flop and the SCLC team abandoned the city to secular organisers in less than a month.[28]

26. A. Fairclough, *To Redeem the Soul of America: The Southern Christian Leadership Conference and Martin Luther King, Jr* (Athens, Ga, 1987), pp. 271–2.
27. Quoted in ibid., p. 273.   28. Ibid., pp. 196–7.

Although its experience in Rochester highlighted the obstacles to a nonviolent approach to the ghetto's problems, the SCLC refused to rule out the possibility of moving north. Once the Selma campaign had borne fruit in the shape of the Voting Rights Act, King and his aides needed little prompting to refocus their attentions on the inner cities where CORE, the NAACP and the Urban League (not to mention the federal government) manifestly had failed to achieve equal justice for blacks. In his Montgomery address of 25 March, King had given a foretaste of the SCLC's northward shift, urging his followers to 'march on segregated housing, until every ghetto of social and economic deprivation dissolves and Negroes and whites live side by side in decent, safe and sanitary housing'.[29] The next month the SCLC executive board announced that the organisation would be extending its operations to the North. The financial coffers were relatively healthy in the wake of the favourable publicity wrought by Selma and hopes were high that a similarly well-planned campaign might procure even greater success above the Mason–Dixon Line.

Watts therefore speeded up a decision-making process already under way. On 1 September, just four days after the Los Angeles riot, Andrew Young announced a major new SCLC campaign focused on Chicago, Illinois. The decision was a brave one, for America's second city was a far larger and more complex target than anything the South had had to offer. As James Ralph has written, the city was 'gargantuan'.[30] Containing more than three million people, it dwarfed places like Albany, Selma and Birmingham. Seven hundred thousand blacks, many of them migrant southerners, were concentrated on the South and West Sides. Although a significant proportion of them were members of the city's prosperous black bourgeoisie or upwardly mobile working class, the bulk of them, particularly those on the poorer West Side, were fit targets for a movement whose activities appeared to have passed them by. The city itself possessed a broad economic base and in ethnic terms was extremely diverse. The two black ghettos were ringed by white working-class neighbourhoods populated by an array of white ethnic residents. Chicago politics were dominated by an entrenched urban Democratic machine headed by Mayor Richard J. Daley, a consummate pragmatist heavily reliant on the votes of blue-collar whites and

29. J.M. Washington, ed., *A Testament of Hope: The Essential Writings of Martin Luther King, Jr* (San Francisco, 1991), p. 229.

30. J.R. Ralph, Jr, *Northern Protest: Martin Luther King, Jr, Chicago, and the Civil Rights Movement* (Cambridge, Mass., 1993), p. 45.

blacks and on the support of the Roman Catholic Church. Daley's vice-like grip on the black vote was secured by client politicians, the most well known of whom was William Dawson, a Chicago congressman since 1928 who was frequently derided by black radicals for his subordinate function within the white-dominated power structure. Dawson and a coterie of ward-level politicians delivered a modicum of jobs and services to the black community in return for which Daley received consistent support from the vast majority of black voters.

The mayor's central importance to the national Democratic Party caused some of King's advisers, including Rustin, to warn him against launching a major campaign in Chicago. Direct action to promote a better quality of life for ghetto residents was bound to be interpreted as a threat by the machine with potentially serious consequences for the grand alliance. King, however, was determined to show northern blacks that southern tactics could produce results – that they did not have to fall prey to cynicism as a consequence of their situation. Chicago, moreover, its tremendous size and diversity notwithstanding, had several points in its favour. Firstly, King believed, perhaps naively, that Daley possessed sufficient power to alleviate the problems of the ghetto almost single-handed. Once pressed into action the mayor could ensure a major redistribution of resources within the city, if not with the stroke of a pen then by cajoling key interest groups such as business and labour into curbing discriminatory practices. A second point in Chicago's favour, one which it shared with Selma and Birmingham, was that local blacks seemed keen for the SCLC to come to town. The Coordinating Council of Community Organizations (CCCO), an umbrella civil rights group founded in 1963 to coordinate protests against conditions in the *de facto* segregated public schools, wanted King's presence to impart new energy to the faltering freedom struggle in the city. Even though the local NAACP remained aloof from the CCCO, the existence of a cooperative, relatively united and well-motivated civil rights movement at the local level proved attractive to King. He had already been rebuffed by several northern black leaders determined to protect their own turf from encroachment and knew from experience the potentially debilitating consequences of division within the movement. The third, and possibly most important, reason why the SCLC decided to target Chicago was the presence of James Bevel in the city. Bevel, the Baptist preacher who had helped to mastermind the victory in Birmingham, had been tempted to Chicago by an offer to participate in an outreach ministry on the West Side. His grass-roots work there presented the SCLC with a toehold in the community and made the West Side an obvious centre for the campaign.

Once the SCLC had announced its plans, Bevel began the job of organising West Side residents in preparation for the direct action phase scheduled to begin the following year.[31] Regular workshops and rallies were held not only to educate people in the philosophy and strategy of nonviolence but also to inject a greater sense of civic activism into the community. Bevel and his small team met with only limited success, for the urban poor proved difficult to mobilise, lacking as they did institutional allegiances and informal networks through which they could be reached. So strong was the opposition to the rhetoric of interracial brotherhood and nonviolence that the SCLC staffers were soon forced to emphasise the importance of racial solidarity in order to make headway. Bevel himself came up with the idea of forming tenant unions as the most effective way of challenging the dominance of the Chicago Real Estate Board (CREB) which, owing largely to the advice of William Moyer of the AFSC, he believed to be deeply implicated in the process of ghetto formation.

Not for the first time the charismatic presence of Martin Luther King kick-started a flagging campaign into action. The SCLC leader made several visits to Chicago early in 1966, one of these involving a well-publicised stay in a dilapidated tenement building in the Lawndale area. This personal witness had little impact on the way white Chicagoans viewed race relations, but King's appearance in the ghetto did something to alleviate the concerns felt by the CCCO leadership at Bevel's abrasive style. In January the two groups came together to form the Chicago Freedom Movement (CFM) in preparation for the forthcoming series of street demonstrations. While community organising continued to present major difficulties individual projects met with some success, particularly Operation Breadbasket. The latter, a recreation of a pilot project underway in Atlanta, brought consumer pressure to bear on local employers to make more jobs available to blacks. It was energetically promoted by one of the SCLC's latest recruits, Jesse Jackson, a veteran of the 1963 Greensboro sit-ins who had returned north to attend Chicago's

---

31. The following account of the Chicago campaign owes much to D.J. Garrow, *Bearing the Cross: Martin Luther King, Jr, and the Southern Christian Leadership Conference* (New York, 1986), pp. 431–525; Fairclough, *To Redeem*, pp. 279–307; A.B. Anderson and G.W. Pickering, *Confronting the Color Line: The Broken Promise of the Civil Rights Movement in Chicago* (Athens, Ga, and London, 1987); Ralph, *Northern Protest*.

Baptist Theological Seminary. As the direct action campaign began to pick up momentum, it won support from a number of sympathetic allies, both secular and religious. Organisations pledging their backing to the evolving struggle included the predominantly black United Packinghouse Workers (a stalwart of civil rights protest in Chicago since the 1930s), the United Auto Workers, and three liberal religious groups, the AFSC, the Catholic Interracial Council and the inter-denominational Chicago Conference on Religion and Race.

While the SCLC found a degree of support from white liberals in the metropolitan area, it was never able to count on the full backing of the black community. Significant numbers of blacks, particularly businessmen and those attached to the Daley machine, opposed the campaign as counter-productive. So too did the NAACP and King's long-time rival, the Rev. Joseph H. Jackson, who headed the influential National Baptist Convention. Separatist organisations such as the Nation of Islam remained aloof, but Chicago CORE, though wary of King's moderation, took up a position on the radical wing of the CFM. While black opposition and apathy disturbed King, his experiences in southern communities such as Birmingham taught him that racial solidarity was not an essential prerequisite for success. What was important was the carefully targeted application of pressure to force Daley to put his much-heralded support for racial equality into practice.

Efforts to build creative tension in the city were interrupted by the shooting of James Meredith in Mississippi on 6 June. Meredith, a black loner who had played a catalytic role in integrating the University of Mississippi in 1962, had undertaken a well-publicised walk across the Magnolia state to encourage local blacks to set aside fear and exercise their right to vote. Although Meredith survived the assassination attempt at the hands of a white racist, King was determined to protest the incident as vigorously as possible. The following day he flew to Memphis where the Mississippian was hospitalised. There he conferred not only with Meredith but also the CORE leader, Floyd McKissick, and Stokely Carmichael who had recently replaced the more moderate John Lewis as chairman of SNCC. Together they agreed that the movement should continue Meredith's project as a sign that southern blacks could no longer be intimidated by white violence. By the summer of 1966, however, agreement on tactics was unlikely given the growth of racial separatism within SNCC and CORE. This was made blindingly clear on the evening of 7 June when Roy Wilkins and Whitney Young joined their fellow civil rights leaders at the Lorraine Motel in Memphis. At this meeting Wilkins and Young insisted that the march should be used to express support for a new civil rights bill (directed principally against housing discrimination) then being debated in Congress. Carmichael, determined to isolate the two conservatives and pull King with him, attacked Johnson as 'a bigot' for refusing to enforce existing civil rights legislation and then accused Wilkins of selling out the black masses. Wilkins and Young left Memphis in disgust. King, torn between the coalition strategy of Bayard Rustin and the need to maintain links with the radicals, opted to stay. Along with Carmichael and McKissick he signed a manifesto calling on the White House to protect the civil rights of all Americans, to send federal voting registrars to every county in the Deep South, to increase federal spending on urban and rural poverty in America, and to strengthen the pending civil rights bill by accelerating integration of southern juries and police agencies.[32]

There followed what John Dittmer has called 'the last great march of the civil rights years'.[33] The mainly black demonstrators, led by Carmichael and King, set off for Jackson in reasonably good heart in spite of disagreements over the centrality of nonviolence to the march. Black Mississippians greeted them with enthusiasm along the route, particularly King whom they regarded as something of a messiah. Tensions increased, however, when the marchers entered the Delta. In Greenwood, Carmichael and two other SNCC workers were arrested by local police. After his release Carmichael asserted that justice would not come until every court-house in the state had been razed to the ground. The following night, 17 June, he and Willie Ricks skilfully worked a sympathetic audience with cries of 'Black Power'. King returned from a trip to Chicago to try to damp down the rhetoric of separatism and self-defence. Conferring with Carmichael and McKissick in Yazoo City, he urged them to adopt what he regarded as a more positive slogan such as 'black consciousness' or 'black equality'. Why, he asked pointedly, have a rallying cry 'that would confuse our allies, isolate the Negro community and give many prejudiced whites, who might otherwise be ashamed of their anti-Negro feeling, a ready excuse for self-justification?'[34] King's pleas led Carmichael to agree to tone down his rhetoric for the rest of the march, but Mississippi's law enforcement authorities merely contributed to the growth of radicalism within the movement.

32. Garrow, *Bearing the Cross*, pp. 478–9.   33. Dittmer, *Local People*, p. 392.
34. Quoted in J.A. Colaiaco, *Martin Luther King: Apostle of Militant Nonviolence* (Basingstoke, 1988), p. 164.

At Canton on 23 June, in what amounted to 'a police riot' rivalling the Selma outrage in ferocity, state troopers assaulted the marchers with clubs and tear-gas after they had refused an order to decamp from a local elementary school.[35] Crucially, however, the watching media were more interested in signs of division within the movement, particularly the Black Power slogan which they latched on to with alacrity. King appealed to the federal government to act but Attorney-General Nicholas Katzenbach, entirely out of sympathy with black radicals, failed to respond. The march ended in an empty display of movement unity at Jackson. King reiterated his dream of a more just society, but Carmichael and McKissick chose to elaborate further on the separatist theme. They also voted with representatives from the MFDP to exclude the maverick head of the state NAACP, Charles Evers, from speaking. In keeping with their mood throughout the march, it was a step calculated to widen the fissures within the movement, both in Mississippi and in the country at large.

King returned to Chicago desperate for a victory which would bolster his crumbling position at the centre. In late June he finally assented to a street campaign designed to bring about open (i.e. non-discriminatory) housing in the city. Although the housing issue was viewed by Bevel and others as central to the fight against black poverty, a number of civil rights activists considered it a singularly middle-class concern. Most ghetto residents, they reasoned, could not afford to move out of the inner city; therefore, what possible good could accrue from a campaign designed to free the suburbs for black settlement? King, however, was persuaded by William Moyer's contention that discriminatory real estate agents were to blame for the development of slums. The issue, moreover, appeared to be grounded solidly in the same meritocratic ethos which underpinned the Great Society and which had helped bring victory to the southern civil rights movement. With a municipal fair housing law already on the statute books and a federal open housing bill under consideration in Congress, the SCLC and its local allies seemed in little danger of moving too far ahead of public opinion.

The Chicago campaign began in earnest on 10 July with a rally at Soldier Field addressed by, among others, King and McKissick who did their best to create an appearance of unity. Within days, however, the city was rocked by serious outbreaks of black rioting on the Northwest Side. By the time it had ended two people were dead

---

35. Dittmer, *Local People*, p. 400.

and more than 80 had been injured. All agreed that the violence was a disaster, for it generated precisely the wrong kind of publicity. Mayor Daley lost no time in linking the unrest to the movement and called on the state governor to mobilise the National Guard to preserve order. But nervous though some of King's allies were after the riots, there was no suggestion that plans to march into white areas of the city should be abandoned, for the demonstrations were intended to provoke an angry response from lower-middle-class whites determined to preserve their ethnic neighbourhoods. Those who plotted strategy for the campaign knew from the southern experience that white violence was the best way not only to highlight racial hatred and discriminatory practices, but also to press the Daley administration into offering meaningful concessions.

The marches began with an all-night vigil on 29 July and continued on through most of August. As planned, they stirred up a veritable hornets' nest. White residents of areas like Gage Park, Marquette Park, Belmont-Cragin, and Chicago Lawn responded to the presence of interracial demonstrators in their midst with torrents of racist abuse and missiles. Fearful that an influx of black residents would result in increased crime, reduce the value of their homes, and undermine the cultural homogeneity of their neighbourhoods, they perceived themselves to be defending the community against unwarranted intrusion by outsiders – African Americans and their liberal white allies. To those in the movement, they were the northern counterparts of those southern whites who had resisted the black freedom struggle during the first half of the 1960s.

The marchers themselves remained well disciplined throughout August. Nearly half of them were whites, many of them liberal Roman Catholics recruited by the Interracial Council. Middle-class blacks were also well represented, indicating, as James Ralph has noted, that the campaign was not merely an extension of the original West Side organising effort. Black churches provided the facilities for morale-boosting evening rallies, but did not play a central role, partly because of the opposition of the National Baptist Convention.[36]

Direct action tactics had the desired effect of creating a crisis situation in Chicago. Mayor Daley was confronted by a major political dilemma. Heavily reliant on black and white votes, he discovered that the marches threatened to drive a wedge into the coalition which had brought him so much success since 1955. Particularly

36. Ralph, *Northern Protest*, pp. 135–7.

galling, since Daley had no desire to be labelled the Bull Connor
of the North, was the necessity to protect nonviolent civil rights
demonstrators against ethnic whites who provided vital support for
his administration. The deployment of large numbers of Chicago
police greatly angered Daley's erstwhile supporters among working-
class and lower-middle-class whites, causing the mayor to redouble
his efforts to find a quick solution to the crisis.

The marches had a similar impact on several groups belonging
to the city's establishment. The Catholic Church was particularly
torn, for, while Archbishop John Cody sympathised with the movement's goals, he feared that the direct action campaign was having
a divisive impact on his flock. Labour leaders had the same concerns,
some of which were voiced to King by his long-time ally, Walter
Reuther. The local print and electronic media also contributed to
a growing feeling that a solution had to be found before the violence got out of hand. On 9 August the city's Commission on Human
Relations began the search for that solution by urging the Chicago
Conference on Religion and Race to bring the interested parties to
the negotiating table. Eight days later a summit meeting convened.
Among those present were King, Bevel, Al Raby (head of the CCCO),
Daley, and representatives from the movement's bugbear, the CREB.
The mayor's own desire for an end to controversy was evinced by
the fact that the meeting was chaired by one of his closest political
allies in the business community, Ben Heineman, a top railway
executive.

Although the CREB delegates attempted to deny primary com-
plicity in *de facto* housing segregation, pressure from Daley and the
civil rights leaders was so intense that they agreed to withdraw their
opposition to fair housing legislation at the state level. Movement
representatives wanted more concrete results than this, but they
acquiesced in the formation of a sub-committee empowered to draw
up plans to end housing discrimination in the city and agreed to
reconvene the following week. What they did not do was call a halt
to the demonstrations – a decision which prompted Daley to secure
a local circuit court injunction limiting the size and time of marches
in Chicago. Those on the radical flank of the CCCO, including
Jesse Jackson and local CORE leaders, urged King to endorse extra-
legal civil disobedience. In spite of being angered by the injunction, King declined to support such a move. As well as being advised
by his legal counsel against breaking the law, he knew the movement possessed finite resources and that it could not continue to
press Daley indefinitely. The best he could offer the radicals was

an announcement that he would lead a march into Cicero, a notoriously racist, all-white town just outside the city limits (and therefore beyond the jurisdiction of the injunction) on 28 August. The threat of a violent confrontation between white residents, right-wing extremists, and an increasingly radical black freedom movement provided the backdrop for the reconvened summit on 29 August.

At that meeting at the downtown Palmer House Hotel King and his allies finally reached a settlement with the city authorities and the CREB. Included in the final text were an agreement by the CREB to withdraw its opposition to the 'philosophy' of open housing legislation at the state level (provided such legislation applied to owners as well as brokers), a commitment by various city departments to support integrated and decentralised public housing, and the setting up of a monitoring board under the auspices of the Chicago Conference on Religion and Race. As well as overseeing the shift to an open city, the new board was given the responsibility for undertaking 'a major effort in the pulpits, in the school systems, and in all other forums to educate citizens of the metropolitan area in the fundamental principle that freedom of choice in housing is the right of every citizen and in their obligations to abide by the law and recognize the rights of others, regardless of race, religion, or nationality'.[37] Presented with an agreement apparently committing elites and (indirectly) ordinary whites to a just future, King proclaimed victory and announced that the Cicero march had been 'deferred'.

Few of the SCLC leader's compromises proved as controversial as his decision to accept the terms offered to him at the Palmer House. Recognising, quite rightly, that the summit agreement lacked teeth – specifically a timetable for action, credible sanctions to enforce compliance, and a commitment from the CREB to drop its ongoing legal fight against the city's existing fair housing law – many of King's allies in the Chicago movement felt betrayed not only by his alleged surrender to Daley but also by his refusal to proceed with the Cicero march. Although some, including Bevel, Jackson and community leader Chester Robinson, reluctantly concurred with the decision, Robert Lucas, head of Chicago CORE, refused to give his blessing. On 4 September Lucas led a group of mainly black demonstrators, ghetto folk rather than movement

---

37. 'Agreement of the Subcommittee to the Conference on Fair Housing Convened by the Chicago Conference on Religion and Race' in *The Eyes on the Prize Civil Rights Reader*, ed. C. Carson *et al.* (New York, 1991), p. 309.

people, into Cicero to register their opposition to the summit deal.[38] There, flanked by Daley's police, they traded taunts and missiles with hostile whites.

Once King and the SCLC had left the city, the summit agreement was allowed to lapse. The monitoring board did try to secure compliance with the backing of the churches, but without strong support from the municipal authorities it had little chance of pressuring the CREB into undertaking meaningful reforms. Daley, though not entirely unsympathetic to the goals of the civil rights movement, was pre-eminently a political animal. His chief objective throughout the campaign had been to get King out of the city in order to limit the political damage to his administration. Once the summit agreement had accomplished this task, he had little incentive to provoke further white resistance to his rule by demanding action from powerful special interest groups. The extent to which Daley had outmanoeuvred the movement was revealed the following April when he was re-elected with a substantial majority. The patronage machine secured him more than 80 per cent of the black vote.

The Chicago campaign was not a total failure. The movement left a significant legacy of community activism in the city and the success of Operation Breadbasket subsequently resulted in its application in several other places. The summit agreement, moreover, was hardly less amorphous than the deal worked out between the SCLC and the city authorities in Birmingham in 1963 – a deal usually regarded as having capped one of King's most successful campaigns. The main difference between the two events was the response of the federal government. In Birmingham, Washington's intervention on the side of the movement not only brought whites to the negotiating table but also led directly to the introduction of what eventually became the 1964 Civil Rights Act. By contrast, the federal government made no attempt to influence developments in Chicago. As long as Daley's police maintained a fragile peace there was no political reason for President Johnson to step in and give King, already marked for his opposition to the Vietnam War, the victory he so desperately craved. The marches were embarrassing, certainly, but the efficient conduct of the Chicago police greatly reduced the chances of a dramatic publicity coup for the movement. Perhaps, as King later believed, a full extension of the campaign into Cicero might have helped. However, by mid-1966 his jeremiads against the problems of urban deprivation and *de facto* segregation

38. Linda Bryant Hall Interview in ibid., p. 315.

were finding a much less sympathetic hearing in the North than the movement's earlier attacks on southern segregation. Not only did these problems appear to be more complex and intractable but, in the view of many whites, the notion that blacks were hard done by was becoming counterbalanced by the apparent evidence of black unrest, black criminality and black welfare dependency. Politicians inside and outside Congress were already capitalising on this growing mood, evidence of which was gleefully received by white southerners tired of being singled out as un-American. Shortly after the signing of the Chicago summit agreement, southern Democratic senators filibustered to defeat a weakened open housing bill which had already confronted opposition from moderates in the lower house.[39] Commented a dispirited Dr King, 'I want somebody in Washington to know that when that bill died a lot of faith died in America.'[40]

Black Power

Two major factors led to the final collapse of the national civil rights coalition in the late 1960s. The first of these, the continuing growth of black nationalist sentiment, undermined the interracial complexion of the struggle and contributed hugely to the demise of inter-organisational cooperation during 1967 and 1968. The second principal reason for the movement's demise was the dramatic upsurge in anti-war protest activity as the body count in Vietnam increased and the draft began to hit middle-class America. As well as providing the *coup de grâce* to the ill-fated grand alliance (finally cutting off King from many of his liberal allies), the military escalation diverted valuable resources from the War on Poverty and soaked up energies which hitherto had been targeted on racial issues. Attempts were made to unite the peace movement and the black freedom struggle but, for a variety of reasons, these had come to nought by the time of the critical 1968 presidential election.

That Black Power took off after the Meredith March was hardly surprising. More slogan than concept it nevertheless proved appealing to many African Americans, educated by civil rights leaders and nationalist spokesmen alike to seize control of their lives, to take

39. H.D. Graham, *The Civil Rights Era: Origins and Development of National Policy 1960–1972* (New York and Oxford, 1990), pp. 260–2.
40. Quoted in Ralph, *Northern Protest*, p. 194.

pride in their colour, and to promote the political and cultural unity of the race in the face of entrenched white racism. Its very ambiguity proved to be its greatest strength, for each individual could interpret it as he or she wished. Stokely Carmichael and the political scientist Charles V. Hamilton came closest to providing a coherent intellectual framework for the emerging nationalist impulse with their influential tract, *Black Power: The Politics of Liberation in America.* Published in 1967, it attacked integration as a middle-class obsession and called on blacks, firstly, to abandon the supposedly discredited policy of seeking coalition with liberal whites and, secondly, to adopt the competitive interest-group strategy which had worked so well for white ethnic groups such as Irish Americans and Jewish Americans.[41] Significantly, while the two men urged blacks to understand their past, form their own community-level organisations, and set up independent political parties, their long-term goal was not a separatist one. 'The concept of Black Power rests on a fundamental premise:' they wrote, *'Before a group can enter the open society, it must first close ranks.'*[42] Heavily influenced by the rhetoric of Malcolm X and the dominant pluralist interpretation of American politics, Carmichael and Hamilton produced a moderate definition of Black Power grounded in the view that 'Negroes' should start to act as African Americans in order to achieve their rightful share of power.

Other blacks provided their own interpretation of Black Power. Some, such as Maulana Karenga and the poet, LeRoi Jones, rejected the politics of ethnicity in favour of a primary emphasis on cultural nationalism. Only by doing this, contended groups such as Karenga's US (United Slaves) on the West Coast, could blacks develop a strong sense of racial identity from which they could resist the violence and oppression of white America. Contemptuous of a philosophy which led blacks to stress their African roots, sport Afro hairstyles and wear dashikis, militant political groups like the Black Panthers demanded that self-defence be given top priority. Bringing the issue of police brutality centre stage, they urged blacks to regain control of their own neighbourhoods by carrying guns and developing self-help institutions. Significantly, their own leftist leanings prevented the Panthers from rejecting outright the notion of coalition with radical white allies.[43]

41. S. Carmichael and C.V. Hamilton, *Black Power: The Politics of Liberation in America* (Harmondsworth, 1969), pp. 49–70.

42. Ibid., p. 58.

43. G.M. Fredrickson, *Black Liberation: A Comparative History of Black Ideologies in the United States and South Africa* (New York and Oxford, 1995), pp. 296–7.

Confronted by a barrage of strident and often violent rhetoric, ordinary white Americans failed to discern the conservative roots of much nationalist thought during the late 1960s. For them Black Power carried the threat of black violence – a threat made explicit by polemics such as Julius Lester's *Look Out Whitey! Black Power's Gon' Get Your Mama!* and, perhaps more importantly, by the series of frightening race riots which swept the inner cities between 1964 and 1968.[44] Difficult though it is to establish a direct link between Black Power and the so-called white backlash ('so-called' because white resistance to black assertiveness clearly pre-dated the civil rights movement and the ghetto revolts), there can be little doubt that the backlash was fanned by fears engendered not only by sensationalist media coverage of the nationalist upsurge but also, and often quite consciously, by radical black nationalists.

While the civil rights movement had done much to spawn these developments, it proved unable to withstand the divisive forces unleashed by them. Predictably, separatist ideology strengthened its hold over SNCC and CORE. Although Carmichael and Forman continued to insist that whites still had an important role to play in the struggle for racial justice, internal pressures within SNCC for an end to white involvement in the organisation became too intense to resist by the close of 1966. Much of the demand for an expulsion of whites emanated from the Vine City Project in Atlanta. Headed by Bill Ware, a black Mississippian, the Project represented SNCC's first and most serious attempt to mobilise poor urban blacks in the South. Ware and his well-educated fellow staffers, roughly half of whom were northern blacks, worked to promote community control in one of Atlanta's most deprived neighbourhoods. As CORE had often found in the North, the most effective appeals to inner-city blacks were based on assertions of racial pride, identity and distinctiveness. By the spring of 1966 the Atlanta staff, radicalised by their experiences in the ghetto, began calling for an end to what remained of the white presence in SNCC. Debate rumbled on through the year culminating in a bitter staff meeting in December. At this gathering approximately 100 staff members heard Ware repeat his assertion that white participation in the movement was a major obstacle to black liberation. Whites who refused to leave SNCC voluntarily, he asserted, ought to be expelled. Although Forman, Carmichael and the veteran activist, Fannie Lou Hamer, argued against this proposal, the assembled staff finally voted 19 to 18 to terminate white participation in SNCC. When the increasingly

44. J. Lester, *Look Out Whitey! Black Power's Gon' Get Your Mama!* (New York, 1968).

insubordinate Atlanta Project staff were themselves expelled from
SNCC shortly afterwards, it was clear that the organisation's days as
an effective vehicle for civil rights reform were numbered.[45]

CORE's progress paralleled that of SNCC, though its drift towards
separatism was more drawn out.[46] Support for nationalist goals such
as community control and black leadership of the movement increased throughout the mid-1960s. It was particularly evident in the
urban North where CORE members had daily experience of ghetto
life. The resignation of the organisation's respected director, James
Farmer, in the winter of 1965–66 removed a potent force for moderation. Farmer was married to a white woman and, though sensitive
to the kind of nationalist urges which prompted a steady exodus of
whites from CORE, had never deviated from the notion of interracial cooperation. His successor, Floyd McKissick, proved more willing than Farmer to flirt with black nationalism but, like Carmichael,
his initial inclination was to define it in conventionally pluralist
terms. Other CORE activists, however, notably Roy Innis in New
York, continued to push the national leadership in a more overtly
chauvinistic direction. In 1967 the organisation finally deleted the
term 'multi-racial' from its constitution, having already discarded
its commitment to nonviolence. By the time whites were officially
expelled the following year, so few of them were left that the decision was little more than symbolic.

In practical terms the growth of black nationalism within SNCC
and CORE proved disastrous for both organisations. As Carmichael,
Forman, Farmer and McKissick were perfectly aware, the radical wing
of the civil rights movement was heavily reliant on white funding.
As late as August 1965, for example, 95 per cent of CORE monies
came from sympathetic whites, many of them liberal Jews.[47] Rhetorical excesses, some of them anti-Semitic in tone, on the part of
nationalist sympathisers within the movement had predictably deleterious consequences. Both SNCC and CORE were in serious financial straits by the end of 1966 much to the satisfaction of NAACP
and Urban League leaders who, by no means coincidentally, saw
their own funding increase significantly during the late 1960s.[48]

No matter how much conservatives and moderates in the civil
rights movement may have decried the growing appeal of Black

45. Carson, *In Struggle*, pp. 240–1.
46. On the decline of CORE see Meier and Rudwick, *CORE*, pp. 329–428.
47. Ibid., p. 336.
48. Herbert H. Haines, *Black Radicals and the Civil Rights Movement, 1954–1970*
(Knoxville, 1988), pp. 94, 97.

Power among ordinary African Americans, particularly the young, they had little choice but to seek some accommodation with the slogan. Whitney Young, head of the Urban League, had little in common with Black Power radicals who, taking their lead from Malcolm X, repeatedly attacked him as an Uncle Tom throughout the mid-1960s. Young's view, one which he continued to share with Randolph, Rustin and Wilkins, was that cooperation with the gov- ernment and white allies remained the only feasible way of delivering power to an essentially powerless people. 'Power', he announced pithily in January 1967, 'is not the result of . . . skin color . . . Power is the green of a one dollar bill; it is the brown of a textbook; it is the white of the ballot.'[49] Young's sense of realism, however, did not prevent him from being able to empathise with the African-American quest for identity, pride and dignity – a quality which made him well placed to convey the frustrations of black America to the white corporations which bankrolled the League. Pressure from the nationalist wing of the movement (as well as the urban riots) caused him to redirect his organisation's activities towards community organising and the attainment of economic and political self-sufficiency for blacks trapped in the ghetto. By July 1968 Young could attend a CORE convention in Columbus, Ohio, and announce to warm applause that his organisation was committed to 'that inter- pretation of black power which emphasizes self-determination – pride – self respect – participation and control of one's destiny and community affairs'.[50] Such rhetoric did little to convince militant blacks that Young was one of them, but his efforts to give Black Power a positive slant helped to ensure that the slogan never became the sole property of radical nationalists.

The NAACP leadership in New York was less inclined to see the positive side of Black Power, unsurprisingly perhaps, given its com- mitment to cooperating with the Democrats, its predominantly middle-class constituency and Roy Wilkins's acute sensitivity to criticism. That said, what was still the nation's largest civil rights organisation could hardly ignore the enormous political and cultural impact of black separatism. While the national office denounced what it regarded as reverse racism, it attempted to respond positively to radical criticism by pointing out the NAACP's longstanding sup- port for the right of self-defence and the study of black history. More indicative of the nationalist impact on the NAACP was the

49. Quoted in N.J. Weiss, *Whitney M. Young, Jr, and the Struggle for Civil Rights* (Princeton, 1989), p. 178.
50. Quoted in ibid., p. 183.

fact that a growing number of branches were prepared to endorse rhetoric and tactics at odds with the conservatism of the national office. Indeed, in many parts of the country local NAACP chapters stepped positively into the vacuum created by the demise of SNCC and CORE. In Louisiana, for example, where a mere five CORE staff members were active by the summer of 1966, assertive NAACP leaders, clearly influenced by the new mood in the country, formed new branches and revitalised old ones in order to pursue direct action campaigns against targets such as discriminatory employment. The city of Shreveport, largely quiet after the ruthless suppression of civil rights workers in the early 1960s, witnessed a remarkable renaissance of movement-style activity in late 1968 owing to the regeneration of the local NAACP by a young newspaperman, B.J. Mason.[51] In the final analysis, however, the NAACP proved unable to marshal its manifest grass-roots energies and institutional strength effectively. Efforts by 'Young Turk' reformers such as Eugene Reed and Chester Lewis to reorientate the Association's national office in a more radical direction were stifled by a labyrinthine election system which bolstered the leadership's attempts to maintain the status quo. Reed, a Brooklyn-born dentist and staunch Catholic, shared the conviction of many NAACP members that Roy Wilkins was out of touch with opinion in the ranks. In his view the critical issue was not, as the leadership depicted it, one of segregation versus integration, but one of the development

> of legitimate pride and self-respect among black people, versus teaching our people to imitate the immorality and stupidity of white culture. It is one of the development of black power versus depending upon white people to give us hand-outs. It is one of political independence versus being in the pocket of Lyndon Baines Johnson.[52]

The New York office's failure to move with the times increased the gulf between itself and the black masses who appeared to have lost all faith in the system. Whatever chance the organisation had of leading the movement into a new and more radical phase of its development, vanished with the demise of internal reform efforts.

The last months of Martin Luther King

America's most prominent civil rights leader emerged from the SCLC's first major foray into the North with a more realistic sense

---

51. Fairclough, *Race and Democracy*, pp. 381, 406–7.
52. Eugene T. Reed Interview (1968), CRDP.

of the enormous task ahead of him. Martin Luther King's sobering encounter with Mayor Daley made him aware of the depth of northern racism and combined with other factors to radicalise his thought during late 1966 and 1967. By the time of his death in April 1968 he was preparing to lead a poor people's campaign of civil disobedience in the nation's capital.

Although King never abandoned his personal faith in nonviolence and a messianic belief in a beloved community of all races, he was inevitably influenced by the tide of black nationalist sentiment sweeping across America. Rejecting violence as a solution to the problems confronting the black community, north and south, he nevertheless began to address a number of nationalist concerns in his public speeches. He praised Black Power's emphasis on self-esteem and lauded its commitment to 'instilling within the Negro a sense of belonging and appreciation of heritage, a racial pride'.[53] During the organising phase of the Poor People's Campaign in early 1968 he spoke of the need to educate blacks about their cultural heritage. 'We're going to let our young people know that Shakespeare, Euripides [*sic*], and Aristophanes are not the only poets that have lived in history', he told an audience in Clarksdale, Mississippi, only days before his death. 'We're going to let our children know about Countee Cullen and Langston Hughes.'[54] It was not only the cultural side of Black Power which King tentatively embraced. Gravely disappointed at the way many whites seemed to be abandoning the cause of equal justice, he perceived the virtues of plural politics as they had been articulated by Carmichael and Hamilton. Blacks, he said, must follow other ethnic groups and 'develop, from strength, a situation in which the government finds it wise and prudent to collaborate with us'. Like Jewish Americans, blacks had to develop strong community organisations, institutions and leaders and promote alliances on a basis of mutual self-interest. In one burst of apparent self-criticism, he attacked middle-class black leaders for their lack of genuine attachment to the grass-roots. 'The white establishment is skilled in flattering and cultivating emerging leaders', he wrote in 1967. 'It presses its own image on them and finally, from imitation of manners, dress and style of living, a deeper strain of corruption develops.'[55]

King's shift away from the mainstream was a product of many factors, not least his desire to preserve links with the radical wing

---

53. Quoted in J.H. Cone, *Martin & Malcolm & America* (pbk edn, London, 1993), p. 229.
54. Ibid., p. 230.   55. Washington, ed., *Testament of Hope*, p. 307.

of the movement and a growing disillusionment with American liberals. It was also part and parcel of his growing attachment to the New Left critique of the existing political and economic system. Capitalism, he began to believe, was the root cause of the black race's problems in the United States. The need for cheap labour confined blacks to squalid urban ghettos where they could be exploited at will. Increasing automation left the mass of unskilled blacks on the employment scrap-heap, contributing mightily to the acute social problems of the inner-city. Corporate capitalism's relentless search for overseas markets and raw materials was to blame for the Vietnam War which was diverting precious national resources from the Great Society.

In early 1967 King decided to end his near public silence on the Vietnam War. It was a bold decision, for he knew that in speaking out he was bound to further alienate the Johnson administration. The president had committed himself totally to the war and, as always, had no tolerance for the concept of a loyal opposition. Black and white allies in the movement were deeply divided over the conflict in southeast Asia and many were unlikely to look favourably on an anti-war statement from King. The latter, however, recognised that the peace movement had grown in strength since 1965 (when he had first tested the waters on this topic) and that consequently he would no longer be a voice crying out in the wilderness. More importantly, he had begun to develop a more global approach to nonviolence in the wake of his receipt of the Nobel Peace Prize. A citizen of the world and a devout exponent of universal Christian love, he was deeply troubled by a war which was killing thousands of innocent men and women. Faith and reason told him that he could stay silent no longer.

Although the SCLC leader renewed his assault on Johnson's foreign policy in Los Angeles in March 1967, he reserved his principal speech for New York's Riverside Church, spiritual home of liberal Protestantism in the United States, on 4 April. In that searing address, he called his country 'the greatest purveyor of violence in the world today' and urged the government to halt its campaign of aggression against the communist forces in Vietnam.[56] A fundamental revolution of values was necessary, he insisted, if the people and governments of the materialistic West were to defeat Communism and enter the beloved community. Shortly after his Riverside sermon, King participated in the Spring Mobilization (or 'Mobe'),

56. Washington, ed. *Testament of Hope*, p. 233.

the largest demonstration in American history. Standing on a platform at the United Nations Plaza in New York with the SCLC's James Bevel (who had been appointed to direct the Mobilization Committee) and Stokely Carmichael, he repeated his calls for an end to the war and his support for conscientious objection. No vital interests were involved in the struggle, he insisted: 'The security we profess to seek in foreign adventures we will lose in our decaying cities.'[57]

King's decision to declare his backing for the burgeoning peace movement won him few friends among conservatives, black or white, but for radical peace campaigners it appeared to open up the enticing prospect of a merger between opponents of the Vietnam War and supporters of black rights.[58] The white leftists behind the Spring Mobilization were delighted to have King's support. Their appointment of James Bevel at the head of the organising team had been designed to attract the SCLC president who, they believed, would help broaden the peace movement's popular base and build a multi-issue coalition for domestic change. Efforts to unite the two most powerful social movements of the 1960s, however, were frustrated by King's reluctance to subordinate the struggle for civil rights to the left-liberal search for an end to the Vietnam War. Desperate to retain his position in 'the vital centre' of what remained of the civil rights movement and aware of damaging fissures within both reform coalitions, he told listeners at the UN Plaza that he did not favour 'a mechanical fusion' of the two groupings. What was needed, he said, was a radical peace movement imbued with the moral fervour of the black freedom struggle.[59]

King's reluctance to see his people's cause subsumed by the anti-war crusade was paralleled by his announcement at the end of April 1967 that he would not be available as a candidate for the following year's presidential election. White radicals like the veteran socialist, Norman Thomas, and the anti-war campaigner, Benjamin Spock, had perceived King as the only national figure who commanded sufficient respect to lead an interracial peace coalition to victory in

57. M.L. King, 'Address at UN Plaza', 15 April 1967, Box 12, Series 3, Martin Luther King Papers, KC, pp. 5–6, 19–20.
58. For some federal officials (who lost no time in informing the president of their suspicions) King's Riverside Address was positive proof that he was a communist stooge. FBI chief J. Edgar Hoover told Johnson: 'Based on King's recent activities and public utterances, it is clear that he is an instrument in the hands of subversive forces seeking to undermine our nation.' T. Wells, *The War Within: America's Battle over Vietnam* (Berkeley and London, 1994), p. 131.
59. M.L. King, 'Address at UN Plaza', pp. 23–4.

1968. Stanley Levison, however, continued to advise the SCLC leader against too close an involvement with fringe elements in the peace movement and King feared that a decision to enter politics might further alienate those blacks who believed his real objective to be personal advancement.[60] Any lingering hopes that King might be the linchpin for a radical attack on the Johnson regime were finally dispelled by the chaotic events at the National Conference for a New Politics (NCNP) gathering in Chicago in August 1967.

The NCNP was designed to spearhead the New Left's assault on what was seen as a profoundly corrupt political and socio-economic order. Involving several prominent civil rights activists, including Julian Bond, formerly of SNCC, the effort to forge a grass-roots national political bloc to challenge the hegemony of the Democrats and Republicans culminated in a call for delegates to attend the organising conference in Chicago. Responding to the call, King addressed a motley collection of liberals, radicals and Black Power activists on 31 August. He attacked the Vietnam War for diverting funds from the War on Poverty and testified to his own disillusionment with the system after the SCLC's Chicago campaign. The SCLC, he announced, was taking steps to end its affiliation with the Democratic Party. Capitalism, he went on, was not benign. It had been built on slavery and was now leaving the poor to rot in 'domestic colonies' (the then fashionable term for the ghettos). The only way forward was for right-thinking people to demand full employment and secure a transfer of power and money into the hands of inner-city residents. The West, he added, should support, not oppose, third-world revolutions across the globe.[61]

King's efforts to galvanise the convention failed completely. Many of the 3,500 delegates regarded him as a tool of the establishment and either heckled him or walked out. The conference itself subsequently ended in chaos as black radicals demanded an equal share of the vote in spite of their minority position within the convention.[62] The fiasco revealed the extent of splits in the New Left and indicated the problems confronting anyone seeking to promote interracial amity in the era of Black Power. It also confirmed the wisdom of Stanley Levison's view that an alliance with faction-prone radicals on the margins of politics could never deliver results.

60. Garrow, *Bearing the Cross*, p. 556; Fairclough, *To Redeem*, p. 342.

61. M.L. King, 'The Three Evils of Society', Speech at New Politics Convention, Chicago, 31 August 1967, Box 13, Series 4, Martin Luther King Papers, KC.

62. R. Weisbrot, *Freedom Bound: A History of America's Civil Rights Movement* (New York, 1991), pp. 254–6.

Notwithstanding his failure in Chicago and the demise of his flirtation with the New Left, Martin Luther King remained the only black leader in America capable of carrying the civil rights movement forward. His task was a daunting one, for the entire country seemed mired in decay, despair and disarray. Serious urban riots left over 90 people dead in the summer of 1967. Nearly half of them died in July's Detroit uprising which was finally quashed by trigger-happy National Guardsmen. Increasing numbers of white Americans concluded that the government's main priorities should be the suppression of rampant crime and social disorder not the extermination of poverty or the attainment of full employment. The Johnson administration did set up a committee to investigate the riots but its progressive report (which called for massive federal spending on the inner cities) found little favour with Congress.[63] The Vietnam War, meanwhile, continued to sap spending on Great Society programmes, many of which had already been hijacked by political elites, north and south.

King was also confronted by the reality that the civil rights coalition had ceased to exist. The national NAACP and the Urban League, backed by Bayard Rustin, remained wedded to cooperation with the labour-dominated liberal wing of the Democratic Party in spite of the fact that the latter was deeply riven over Vietnam. CORE and SNCC had abandoned nonviolence and mainstream coalition politics, preserving what some saw as their integrity at the expense of funding. SNCC itself was divided over the high-profile leadership role of Stokely Carmichael (or Stokely Starmichael as he was known to some of his critics) who led the organisation into an ill-fated merger with the Black Panthers at the beginning of 1968.[64] The Council of United Civil Rights Leadership had ceased to exist as a viable forum for discussion among the various civil rights organisations and was wound up in early 1967.[65]

Determined to inject a new sense of hope and mission into the crumbling centre, King embarked on what would be his – and the national movement's – last campaign.[66] Marian Wright, a black lawyer

---

63. *Report of the National Advisory Commission on Civil Disorders* (pbk edn, New York, 1968), pp. 410–82.

64. C.M. Payne, *I've Got the Light of Freedom: The Organizing Tradition and the Mississippi Freedom Struggle* (Berkeley, Los Angeles and London, 1995), p. 378.

65. N.J. Weiss, 'Creative Tensions in the Leadership of the Civil Rights Movement' in *The Civil Rights Movement in America*, ed. C.W. Eagles (Jackson and London, 1986), p. 45.

66. On Memphis and the Poor People's Campaign see Garrow, *Bearing the Cross*, pp. 575–624, and Fairclough, *To Redeem*, pp. 357–83.

working for the Inc Fund, suggested that a group of dispossessed people should go to Washington to protest at the appalling poverty in Mississippi. Encouraged by Stanley Levison, King and his SCLC advisers formulated plans for a poor people's campaign. These envisaged dispatching impoverished urban and rural people of all races to Washington, DC in 1968. There, representatives of the nation's underclasses would set up camp on the Mall and, if necessary, utilise the tactics of nonviolent civil disobedience to secure concessions from the nation's political elite. The campaign evinced continuity with the movement's past, seeking as it did to combine grass-roots organising with a spectacular interracial direct action protest designed to exert pressure on the federal government. Economic deprivation, King told a BBC interviewer, was 'probably the most critical and crucial problem of the Negro community . . . [W]e're going to escalate nonviolence and seek to make it as dramatic, as attention-getting, as anything we did in Birmingham or Selma, without destroying life or property in the process.'[67]

Although the Poor People's Campaign was hampered by covert FBI operations, the SCLC's limited resources, and internal divisions over the wisdom of the project, the initial organising drive was well under way by March 1968. Fears were rife that the campaign might provoke counter-productive violence in the capital, but King continued to insist that direct action could secure his ultimate goal of an integrated society, now redefined as power-sharing with whites. His plans, however, were interrupted by a fateful decision to participate in a labour dispute in Memphis, Tennessee. Black sanitation workers there had struck for recognition of their union and a pay rise and in so doing had won the support of local black ministers and the city's NAACP chapter. As King had long believed that labour support was an essential precondition for the development of a powerful rainbow coalition, he journeyed to Memphis at the behest of his old friend, the Rev. James Lawson, to voice his backing for the strikers. Ten days later, on 28 March, he headed a downtown rally to further publicise the cause. The demonstration was poorly organised. Violence erupted at the back of the march as gang leaders and angry black youths peeled off to smash shop windows and indulge in indiscriminate looting. Appalled, King rejected the safe option of abandoning Memphis and chose instead to get the local movement back on the rails. On the night of 3 April

67. M.L. King, BBC Interview, 4 April 1968, Box 14, Series 3, Martin Luther King Papers, LC.

he delivered a typically rousing speech. Speaking at a mass rally at the pentecostal Mason Temple – one which recalled the halcyon days of the movement earlier in the decade – he urged Memphis blacks to unite peacefully in the face of injustice. Then, having reviewed some of the great civil rights campaigns of the 1960s, he concluded by saying that he did not care about the many death threats he had received in Tennessee:

> Well, I don't know what will happen now. We've got some difficult days ahead. But it doesn't matter with me now. Because I've been to the mountaintop. And I don't mind. Like anybody, I would like to live a long life. Longevity has its place. But I'm not concerned about that now. I just want to do God's will. And he's allowed me to go up to the mountain. And I've looked over. And I've seen the promised land. I may not get there with you. But I want you to know tonight, that we, as a people will get to the promised land. And I'm happy, tonight. I'm not worried about anything. I'm not fearing any man. Mine eyes have seen the glory of the coming of the Lord.[68]

The next day the modern Moses of his race was shot dead by an assassin as he stood on the balcony of the Lorraine Motel in Memphis. He was just 39 years old.

King's death, apparently at the hands of a lone southern white gunman, set the ghettos ablaze once again and occasioned a massive outpouring of grief in the country at large. His funeral at the Ebenezer Church in Atlanta on 9 April was attended by friends and numerous dignitaries. After a brief, moving service, the slain civil rights leader's casket was loaded onto a mule-driven farm wagon for transportation to the memorial service at nearby Morehouse College. 'We chose the mule train to transport Martin's body through the streets of Atlanta', recalled his widow, Coretta, 'because it was symbolic of the Poor People's Campaign and of the conditions among the poor of this nation with whom he wanted to be identified . . .'[69] At Morehouse, President Benjamin F. Mays lauded his former pupil as a prophet sent by God to expound the doctrine of nonviolence. King, he intoned, transcended the petty barriers of ordinary human experience. 'He was supra race, supra nation, supra denomination, supra class, and supra culture. He belonged to the world and to mankind. Now he belongs to posterity!'[70]

68. Washington, ed., *Testament*, p. 286.
69. C.S. King, *My Life With Martin Luther King, Jr* (London, 1970), p. 342.
70. Ibid., p. 368.

Congress responded to the shock of King's death by passing a
new civil rights act on 10 April.[71] Backed by the Johnson administration it aimed to provide belated statutory protection for southern
civil rights workers and contained a fair housing section which
hitherto had proved too controversial to pass. Also included (and
indicative of the divided public reaction to inner-city violence) was
an anti-riot provision designed to assuage white fears about rising
black lawlessness. The act had little impact. It came too late to
mollify the few civil rights workers left in the field and lacked the
necessary enforcement mechanism to end *de facto* housing segregation. Essentially, the direct action phase of the civil rights struggle
– at least on the national level – was over. Any hopes that King's successor, Ralph Abernathy, could re-energise the crusade were ended
with the demise of the Poor People's Campaign in June 1968. Badly
planned and organised, the campaign petered out when the authorities finally demolished the SCLC's mud-caked shantytown, Resur-
rection City, on the Mall. Without King to hold them together, his
egocentric lieutenants fell out among themselves.[72] Like SNCC and
CORE, the one remaining direct-action organisation imploded under
the weight of internal and external pressures.

The only leader left in America capable of forging a progressive
interracial and cross-class alliance in the build-up to the 1968 presidential election was Robert F. Kennedy. Apparently possessing a
deeper social conscience than his brother, the youthful New York
senator had been moved by his experience of black poverty in
rural Mississippi in 1966 and sought constructive ways to reduce its
effects not only there but also in the inner-city ghettos of his adopted
state.[73] When Lyndon Johnson, worn down by the opposition to his
war in Vietnam, announced his decision not to seek re-election,
Kennedy, a genuine hero to many blacks and Hispanics as well as
whites, began to emerge as a strong contender for the Democratic
presidential nomination. His assassination on 4 June, the night of
his stunning victory over Eugene McCarthy in the California primary, threw American liberals into despair. The only winner, as the
Democratic Party fractured over Vietnam and the presidential nomination, was likely to be the Republican nominee, Richard Nixon.

71. For an insightful account of the act's history and passage see Graham, *Civil
Rights Era*, pp. 255–77.
72. Fairclough, *To Redeem*, pp. 385–94.
73. A.M. Schlesinger, Jr, *Robert Kennedy and His Times* (London, 1978), pp. 785–90,
796–8.

The national Democratic convention in Chicago in August 1968 was notable primarily for the zeal with which Mayor Daley's police waded into peace protesters demonstrating against the Vietnam War. The same gathering, however, also witnessed the admission of an interracial delegation from Mississippi made up of radical MFDP supporters and moderates belonging to, or aligned with, Charles Evers's state NAACP. Although the admission of black Mississippians represented an advance on events at Atlantic City four years previously, the failure of the MFDP to control the delegation was symptomatic of the movement's faltering progress in the interim. Unable to win the backing of Mississippi's urban black middle class (or, indeed, of many rural blacks) the MFDP lost most of its political contests in the mid-1960s – the main exception being the election in 1967 of Holmes County's Robert Clark to the state legislature. Such evident weakness, which impelled compromise with the NAACP-led faction, was in part a product of the general decline of the patient organising tradition in the distinctly impatient climate which prevailed after 1965. The numerous ghetto uprisings which took place during this period, the Johnson administration's controversial commitment to the war in Vietnam and the growing strength of black nationalism were clearly central to the growth of a less tolerant milieu within the movement itself and in the country at large. Each of these developments helped to polarise American public opinion, thereby reducing the chances that a dynamic centrist strategy such as that envisaged by Martin Luther King in 1967–68 could transform the civil rights struggle into a broad-based movement for radical change, not only in the United States but in the West as a whole. But while a good case can be made for regarding the riots, the war, and Black Power as primary factors in the eventual collapse of the grand alliance, it would be wrong to suggest that the civil rights movement would automatically have gone on to greater things without these obstacles. As we have seen, the inter-organisational coalition was in deep trouble before the worst of the inner-city violence occurred or, indeed, before the marines arrived at Da Nang in the spring of 1965 or before racial chauvinism had taken a grip on SNCC and CORE. The real problem was that increasing numbers of civil rights activists, influenced in no small measure by their experience of urban black poverty, southern white violence and the temporising activities of the federal government, had begun to reject orthodox politics *and* nonviolent direct action as tools of social change. As a result, at a critical historical juncture when the structural reform of

American society might – just might – have been possible, internal divisions within the civil rights coalition prevented the movement from pressurising America's pragmatic power elites into making further concessions to the forces of racial justice. Richard Nixon's election in 1968 confirmed what most people already knew – that the politics of morality, of nonviolent direct action, of creative tension had lost out to normalcy. Black Power itself was in part a reflection of that awareness. For better or for worse the black freedom struggle was about to enter a new phase of its development – one which would prove disorientatingly deficient in the moral certainties of the early 1960s.

CHAPTER 7

The Roots of Success

The civil rights movement's destruction of the southern caste system was a towering achievement and one that is too easily dismissed today as the memories of segregation begin to fade. The foundations of this triumph were many and varied but the effectiveness of the movement's leadership, organisation and strategy at all levels was clearly a critical factor in sustaining the black freedom struggle during the first half of the 1960s. Although it is impossible to discount the moral and political influence of Martin Luther King, much of the spadework was undertaken by field workers and citizenship school teachers whose task was to develop a broader seam of indigenous leaders along the lines laid out by Ella Baker and others. Without the resources provided by the core civil rights groups such personnel, King included, would have lacked the wherewithal necessary to promote equal justice on a regional and national scale. The ethos of nonviolence which underpinned their activities at least until 1964–65 not only enabled many black communities to overcome the divisions of class and gender to a remarkable degree but also made it easier for whites to recognise the movement as a legitimate historical force. This recognition allowed several white-dominated groups to provide important aid to the freedom struggle at critical junctures in its progress. The interracial character of the movement became increasingly controversial in black nationalist circles as time wore on, but support from sections of the majority community did much during the early 1960s to confirm that integration was a viable objective for African Americans in the United States.

217

Leadership and organisation

While the civil rights movement was grounded solidly in the resource base provided by southern black institutions developed under
Jim Crow, it was heavily reliant on the activities of mainstream civil
rights organisations operating at both the national and local levels.
Leadership, a controversial topic in movement circles during the
1960s, was vital to success at both these levels, for without it grass-
roots mobilisation would have been difficult to achieve (certainly
to sustain) and the cause would have lacked direction. Leaders
provided their followers with persuasive diagnoses of the problems
confronting the race at all levels, constructive solutions to those
problems, and effective strategies designed to achieve the central
goal of racial equality in the present.[1]

For most blacks and whites in the 1960s Martin Luther King was
the movement's chief figurehead. Instantly recognisable by dint of
his frequent media appearances, the SCLC president symbolised
more than any other leader the ongoing search for integration. He
did so by speaking to blacks and whites alike in language which
both races could understand and by articulating what was for many
Americans a compelling vision of an inclusive national community tolerant of diversity and intolerant of prejudice and poverty.
Evangelical religion lay at the heart of his appeal, unsurprisingly
so since he remained first and foremost a minister of God and a
devotee of the Social Gospel throughout his twelve years of service
as an active participant in the civil rights movement. As he told an
interviewer shortly before his death, 'All that I do in civil rights, I
consider a part of my ministry, because I think the Gospel in its
essence ministers to the whole man . . .'[2]

King's father and maternal grandfather were preachers at the
Ebenezer Baptist Church in Atlanta. Both patriarchs, Mike King
and the Rev. A.D. Williams, were self-made men from humble back-
grounds who built up a thriving church on Auburn Avenue, just
east of downtown Atlanta. Ebenezer attracted a socially diverse mix
of people attracted to the fiery call-and-response preaching of the
incumbent minister. Young 'M.L.' absorbed his father's sermons
on the potent themes of suffering, struggle and deliverance – the
traditional staples of evangelical black Protestantism – as well as his

1. On the several functions of leadership see R.C. Tucker, *Politics as Leadership*
(Columbia, Mo, and London, 1981), pp. 18–19.
2. M.L. King, BBC Interview, 4 April 1968, Box 14, Series 3, Martin Luther King
Papers, KC.

conviction that African Americans should participate actively in community affairs. King's world view also owed much to the loving nurturance of his mother and grandmother and the relative security of the middle-class district in which the family resided. His rebellion (if such it can be called) against the firm discipline of his father manifested itself primarily during his student years at Benjamin Mays's Morehouse College (Atlanta's premier secondary school for young black males), and two liberal white schools: Crozer Theological Seminary in Pennsylvania (from which he graduated in 1951), and Boston University where he completed his doctorate four years later. Contemporaries remembered him as a charismatic figure, serious in intent but with a pronounced liking for fine clothes and good-looking women.[3] Even though prolonged immersion in western philosophy and theology took him away from his black church roots, it did not lead him to abandon them altogether. A familiarity with the works of Hegel and Barth certainly helped the ambitious preacher's son to secure the vacant ministerial post at Montgomery's well-to-do Dexter Avenue Church, but it did not prevent him from developing a synthetic sermonic mode which blended dramatic elements of black folk Christianity with white homiletics and reasoned argument in the western liberal tradition. Notwithstanding his elite education, King was steeped in a theology which, as Albert Raboteau has written, regarded God 'not just as the creator and ruler of the cosmos, but as the lord of history, a God whose sovereign will was directing all things toward an ultimate end, drawing good out of evil'.[4] Until the final years of his life when he finally began to despair of liberalism, this legacy enabled King to superimpose a catastrophic Old Testament view of social change on the optimistic and gradualist liberal variant which he inherited from writers like the Social Gospel exponent, Walter Rauschenbusch.[5]

King's ability to operate at the interface of black and white culture contributed to his effectiveness as a communicator of black objectives to white Americans.[6] Along with his powerful rhetorical style and profound commitment to a more just society, it was a central element of the charismatic personality which produced such

3. 'Conversation between Cornish Rogers and David Thelen', *JAH* 78 (1991), 45.

4. A.J. Raboteau, 'Exodus, Ethiopia, and Racial Messianism: Texts and Contexts of African American Chosenness' in *Many Are Chosen: Divine Election and Western Nationalism*, ed. W.R. Hutchison and H. Lehmann (Minneapolis, 1994), p. 176.

5. R. Lischer, *The Preacher King: Martin Luther King, Jr and the Word That Moved America* (New York and Oxford, 1995), p. 57.

6. D. Thelen, 'Becoming Martin Luther King', *JAH* 78 (1991), 11–22.

unyielding devotion in so many of his contemporaries. These traits also helped to make him the linchpin of the civil rights movement, located as he was in creative tension between the conservative wing of the movement represented by the NAACP and the Urban League and the more radical activists in SNCC and CORE. No other civil rights leader functioned so successfully or consistently as an inter-group and intra-group mediator, though all the civil rights organisations possessed capable leaders who did, at various stages, offer plausible explanations for black ills and who could excite their own followers and build bridges to the white majority. What the others lacked, and what King possessed, was a broad constituency – a constituency which was, in part, the creation of a white-dominated media which found King a much more interesting and popular figure than, say, the staid and overly bureaucratic Roy Wilkins. Until he started to oppose the Vietnam War and endorse social demo-cracy towards the end of his life, King was generally depicted in a positive light by the nation's television networks – so much so that white southerners were known to refer derogatorily to CBS as 'the Colored Broadcasting System'. The SCLC president was not simply a creation of the white liberal establishment as black radicals like Malcolm X sometimes suggested, but the attention lavished upon him by sections of the media clearly contributed to the public's belief that he was *the* leader of the civil rights movement.

King's contribution to the cause was, without doubt, substantial. Not only did he play a major role in holding together a fractious coalition (at least until 1966), but he also injected a vital sense of historical urgency and mission into the campaign for equal rights. Quite simply he elevated the movement into a great moral cam-paign which seemed to many Americans to be consonant with the very meaning of the Republic. He did so not only through frequent use of his rich, impassioned voice but also by consciously manip-ulating the nation's civil religion for his own ends. No other civil rights leader was as adept as King at deploying patriotic canons such as the Declaration of Independence and the Battle Hymn of the Republic to legitimise and promote the drive for immediate black emancipation. Malcolm X was also convinced that whites had to understand the urgency of black demands, but his rhetoric, though powerful, was too angry for most whites and many blacks, and during his lifetime his constituency remained limited, by and large, to the urban North. King knew America had to change, and change quickly, but in the early 1960s he possessed sufficient faith in his compatriots to consider this objective attainable. Although his rhetoric could be strident, it was, until 1967–68, seldom negative. Surprisingly large numbers of whites were simultaneously moved, inspired and cajoled by a leader who told them that the nation must live up to its lofty ideals. Malcolm regarded those ideals as hot air and at times seemed to have little to offer whites beyond excoriation. In short, then, King must be accorded pride of place in any discussion of the civil rights movement. It was he who best articulated southern black hopes and desires to white America and his organisation, the SCLC, which took the lead in creating a climate of public opinion favourable to the passage of seminal civil rights legislation during the 1960s.

Yet while his high-profile, visionary leadership proved invaluable to the black freedom struggle, the movement itself was far from dependent on the top-down leadership of King or any other organisational head. Also important were secondary and local level leaders who provided the impetus for those day-to-day civil rights activities which frequently failed to interest the national press and TV. Strong-minded, able and intelligent staff members provided the backbone for all the mainstream organisations in their headquarters and on the ground in the southern states and the urban North.

The SCLC relied heavily on King for fund-raising and publicity, but the organisation's president owed much to his advisers and those who directed SCLC field operations. The SCLC's local affiliates were dominated by energetic black Baptist preachers like Fred Shuttlesworth in Birmingham, Hosea Williams in Savannah, and, until he became the SCLC's executive director in July 1960, Wyatt Walker in Petersburg, Virginia. These men were skilled at mobilising church-based resources in black communities across the South and much of the SCLC's political agenda was set by the clergy-headed affiliates in the context of their own localities. Broader strategy was the work of staff discussions in which King generally had the last word after hearing views from principal staff members. At these meetings King typically played the role of arbitrator and synthesiser, often using the more cautious views of Andrew Young as a foil for impulsive aides like James Bevel and Hosea Williams.[7] Although King was clearly *primus inter pares* his lieutenants, more black male preachers like himself, were policymakers in their own

·7. A. Fairclough, *To Redeem the Soul of America: The Southern Christian Leadership Conference and Martin Luther King, Jr* (Athens, Ga, 1987), p. 169.

right. It was Wyatt Walker, for example, who played a major role in the SCLC's shift to coercive nonviolence, and Bevel who devised the masterstroke of using schoolchildren in the Birmingham campaign of 1963. Although the SCLC was pre-eminently a clerical organisation, King was also indebted to lay advisers like the black college teacher, Lawrence Reddick, and northern leftists, including Bayard Rustin and Stanley Levison. Each of these men contributed to King's published works and speeches and proffered important advice on strategy and tactics. The Levison connection was one of the reasons why King attracted the interest of the FBI during the late 1950s and 1960s, but without the Jewish socialist King would have found it more difficult to keep his eyes on the larger picture.

The NAACP was the most bureaucratic of all the civil rights organisations, but it would be wrong to see Roy Wilkins as the man who pulled all the strings. As executive director Wilkins certainly played a major role in administering Association policy which was set by the national board, an unwieldy group derided by one critic as 'a group of old men . . . walking toward the tombs'.[8] Local branches, however, did not have to clear everything they did with New York and remained largely undisturbed as long as their efforts were 'within the framework' of national policy.[9]

Once the direct action phase of the civil rights movement was under way in earnest, Wilkins and his assistants found it increasingly difficult to control grass-roots protest efforts. High-school and student members of NAACP youth councils proved to be a constant headache, frequently straining at the leash to match the radicalism of SNCC and CORE. The New York office did its best to curtail demonstrations likely to damage the organisation's moderate and staunchly patriotic image. In November 1963, for example, the national staff were confronted by the Oakland youth chapter's appeal to local black schoolchildren to boycott the daily pledge of allegiance.[10] An adult witness reported that many of the NAACP's California units 'were not wholesome' and upbraided the New York office for failing to spot the danger.[11] Laplois Ashford, the NAACP's national youth secretary, responded by calling for the release of a

8. C. King Interview (1969), CRDP.   9. H.L. Moon Interview (1967), CRDP.
10. H. Petty to Oakland Public Schools, 28 October 1963, Youth File, General Department File, Oakland, Cal., Refusal to Salute the Flag, Group 3, NAACP Papers, LC.
11. L. Ashford to G. Current, 12 November, 2 December 1963, Youth File, General Department File, Oakland, Cal., Refusal to Salute the Flag, 1963, Group 3, NAACP Papers, LC.

general memorandum urging youth members to eschew 'extreme measures' which could be 'misconstrued as being unpatriotic'. 'We can ill afford', added Ashford, 'bad public relations which result from unfortunate acts which have a good purpose but which will be reviewed by the majority group in an adverse light.'[12]

Roy Wilkins's problem when faced with incidents like this was that he had to find a balance between moderation and radicalism – one which would satisfy the board of directors and the majority of middle-class NAACP members, yet one which would also prevent the Association from losing the support of black youth. Physically predisposed towards caution (a colostomy operation in 1946 made it difficult for him to aspire to the same level of activity as Martin Luther King), Wilkins shunned political radicalism as counterproductive and preferred to maintain his good relations with the Johnson White House.[13] However, his power was not so great that he could prevent individual branches, especially those in large northern and western cities, from engaging in protest activities far more controversial than those decried by Ashford in 1963. A number of NAACP branches and youth councils in the North were radicalised by the events and intellectual currents of the mid-1960s. These included chapters in Milwaukee (where the youth members participated in stormy fair-housing demonstrations led by a Roman Catholic priest, Father James Groppi) and Philadelphia where the civil rights movement was dominated by the city's NAACP branch headed by Cecil B. Moore.[14] Moore, a former Marine Corps veteran and long-time NAACP member whose views were not dissimilar to those of Robert Williams, was openly contemptuous of Martin Luther King and, owing to his outspoken advocacy of black nationalism and the right of self-defence, a constant thorn in the side of his organisation's national office. Sporadic power struggles occurred between Moore and his superiors but the former exhibited few signs of deferring to the 'hard core, plantation darkies' who, he believed, were responsible for the NAACP's declining membership figures during the 1960s.[15] Southern NAACP leaders and branches tended to be a little more pliant but the New York office found it hard to rein

---

12. Ibid.
13. R. Wilkins with T. Mathews, *Standing Fast: The Autobiography of Roy Wilkins* (New York, 1982), p. 191.
14. For a first-hand account of the unrest in Milwaukee, see S. Finley to G. Current, 15 September 1967, Branch File, Milwaukee, Wis., 1966–67, Box C33, Group 4, NAACP Papers, LC.
15. C.B. Moore Interview (1967), CRDP.

in several of its representatives below the Mason–Dixon Line – not least Charles Evers, a small-time Chicago crook who succeeded his brother, Medgar, as head of the Mississippi state NAACP in 1963.[16]

CORE and SNCC were very different entities from the other mainstream organisations, but they were no less dependent for success on traditional leadership qualities. Although Ella Baker may have been convinced that strong people did not have to be dependent on charismatic individuals, she was fully aware of the importance of leadership, particularly at the grass-roots level. As we have seen, her own contacts with established southern black leaders like Amzie Moore in Mississippi were crucial to the evolution of SNCC as a successful civil rights organisation and SNCC itself concentrated much of its own energies on fostering the growth of indigenous leadership in the Black Belt. Brave, flexible and intelligent individuals like Sam Block and Fannie Lou Hamer were essential recruits for the southern movement if ordinary black folk in the region were to be mobilised effectively. Like those at the national level these local leaders needed not only to demonstrate their ability, bravery and integrity but also to avoid tangential concerns and keep their eyes on the ultimate prize.

Although SNCC was often condemned by its critics for being un-American and even communistic, its initial emphasis on participatory democracy and self-transformation was well within the nation's synthetic Christian, capitalist and republican ideological tradition. This tradition stigmatised dependence as unhealthy and held open the possibility of personal conversion – the kind of self-reforming experience which many civil rights leaders believed to be an essential precondition for the destruction of the caste system. It was also consistent with the view of the contemporary political thinker, Hannah Arendt, who contended that active involvement by private citizens in politics was an essential bulwark against the development of totalitarianism.[17]

Predictably, in the light of its staunch opposition to dependency and the influence of Miss Baker, SNCC operated as an organisation around the concept of collective leadership. Real power was exercised increasingly by the full-time field staff whose numbers grew steadily from 40 in the summer of 1962 to 130 at the start

16. J. Dittmer, *Local People: The Struggle for Civil Rights in Mississippi* (Urbana and Chicago, 1994), pp. 177–8.
17. R. King, *Civil Rights and the Idea of Freedom* (New York and Oxford, 1992), pp. 25–6.

of the Freedom Summer and a maximum of 230 in the spring of 1965.[18] The staff met irregularly on projects and en bloc during the early 1960s to evaluate not only tactics and strategy but also the very meaning of civil rights activity in the light of changing experiences and historical circumstances. Individual staff members (the bulk of whom during the early years were relatively well-educated southern black college dropouts) possessed genuine decision-making authority and were expected to use their own initiative while working on the organisation's main projects. All of them possessed integral leadership qualities such as intelligence, moral fervour, a high degree of bravery and self-discipline and, in some cases, a fair amount of charisma and administrative capability.

SNCC had a deserved reputation as the most anarchic and unstructured of all the civil rights organisations. The young field staff reveled in their lack of dependence on authority and believed, quite rightly, that this contributed to the organisation's appeal to young blacks and northern white students in a decade in which all established sources of power in America came to be suspect. SNCC, however, could not have functioned as effectively as it did without some form of centralised administration. This was provided by the organisation's cramped headquarters on Atlanta's Raymond Street, home to the important communications section headed by Julian Bond. Bond typified the middle-ranking leadership which was so important to the strength of the civil rights movement. The product of a well-to-do Georgia family (his father was a prominent black educator who had helped to prepare the NAACP's brief in *Brown v. Board of Education*), Bond abandoned his studies at Morehouse when the student sit-ins broke out in North Carolina. He became a leading figure in the Atlanta movement and was present at SNCC's formation in Raleigh. Along with his assistant, Mary King, Bond directed SNCC's relations with allied civil rights organisations and the media. King, a white southerner and daughter of a Methodist minister, recalled how the SNCC press office cultivated good relations with sympathetic journalists and barraged the media with factual information (partly to stimulate federal intervention in the South, but also to furnish a greater measure of security for SNCC field operatives). Bond, it was clear, was ideally suited for the job. Urbane, witty and 'maddeningly self-contained', he possessed an agile mind largely unencumbered with hostility towards whites. Mary

18. N.V. Bartley, *The New South 1945–1980* (Baton Rouge, 1995), pp. 315–16.

King admired him greatly. 'He was talented and articulate', she later observed, and 'also managed to stand above the fray of daily conflict.'[19]

Other SNCC leaders like James Forman, John Lewis, Bob Moses and Stokely Carmichael possessed similar qualities. While they were all wary of 'the preacher syndrome', each of these men had the ability to attract loyalty from those outside the ranks of their own organisation. None of them, however, came close to rivalling Martin Luther King as a favourite among southern blacks, partly because they had little desire to set themselves up as messiahs and partly because the white media tended to regard SNCC as a junior player in the civil rights movement. Until Carmichael rose to fame on the wave of Black Power, their influence remained fairly localised. Bob Moses, for example, was extremely popular among rural blacks but he feared the power of his own charisma and consciously limited his input into staff discussions where the bulk of SNCC policy was formulated in the early 1960s. James Forman provided much of the administrative expertise which enabled SNCC to function, but he too made little attempt to impose his will upon the organisation. Had he wanted to do so he would have found it difficult, for SNCC simply did not operate in that way. Moses and SNCC's other black leaders were influential figures but their ability to mould policy stemmed from the respect with which they were held by staff members, not their position within the organisation's loose structure. Other staffers, white as well as black, listened to their ideas in meetings but were not afraid to advance their own points of view. Ultimately, most SNCC staff discussions resulted in a fragile consensus which then became the basis for future operations. If individuals did choose to strike out on their own, there were, at least in the early days, no sanctions against them.

CORE provided the movement with another batch of able young civil rights workers. Somewhat larger, more centralised and more tightly structured than SNCC, CORE was headed by a New York-based National Action Council which oversaw the activities of the national secretary, his subordinate programme director, and the various chapters dotted around the country. CORE, however, resembled SNCC in devoting far greater resources to its field staff than the NAACP. The difference in emphasis gave CORE the edge over the latter in terms of flexibility of response and grass-roots appeal to

19. M. King, *Freedom Song: A Personal Story of the 1960s Civil Rights Movement* (New York, 1987), p. 236.

the young. After the sit-ins and Freedom Rides of 1960–61 the organisation attracted the attention of scores of black and white college students who went on to make CORE one of the most potent vehicles for direct action in the country. Prominent among the early recruits were young men like Dave Dennis, formerly a student at Dillard University in New Orleans, who helped form a CORE chapter in Shreveport and then signed on as one of the organisation's full-time field secretaries. Described by one historian as 'a person of extraordinary ability who combined passionate dedication to the cause with superior organisational skills and a vision that extended beyond the ongoing programmes of voter registration', Dennis became one of the movement's most effective organisers in Mississippi.[20] A powerful and moving speaker when angry (as he showed at the funeral of James Chaney in August 1964), he was as capable as Moses and Carmichael at communicating with the illiterate or semi-literate black folk of the Deep South. Along with other CORE organisers – blacks like Marvin Robinson, Robbie Moore, Oretha Castle and Weldon Rougeau; whites like Mike Lesser, Miriam Feingold, Steve Miller and William Yates – Dennis mobilised numerous southern blacks like Chaney, helping to empower that crop of indigenous leaders whose efforts were critical to the long-term success of the movement.

The effectiveness of the civil rights movement in the early 1960s was due in no small measure to the interaction of national organisations, often represented by their salaried field staff, with local black communities. Success was dependent on the effective mobilisation of various segments of the indigenous community. In some of the more remote areas of the Deep South this task had to be undertaken from scratch. In others, like the towns and counties of the Mississippi Delta, field staff were aided by the presence of existing civil rights leaders and organisations. The ensuing campaign might take the form of a voter registration drive (a powerful mobilising tool in itself) and a series of direct action protests (sit-ins, jail-ins, picketing, marches and so forth) designed to publicise black dissatisfaction with the status quo. While such street activity appealed heavily to younger blacks, adults tended to favour the consumer boycott as a complementary (and indirect) form of protest. Aimed at the same downtown merchants as the sit-ins, the boycott was favoured in part because it could be supported anonymously and therefore did not carry with it the threat of a humiliating jail

20. Dittmer, *Local People*, p. 186.

sentence (or worse). Morale was sustained by regular mass meetings like the one which launched the Montgomery bus boycott in
December 1955. These meetings, an often joyous fusion of the
sacred and the secular, enabled those involved in the local movement to gather news from civil rights workers and to foster a sense
of common purpose through song.

Music, in fact, was one of the distinguishing features of the movement in its early years. Contributing heavily to the maintenance of
morale (in jail as well as at meetings and on marches), haunting freedom songs such as 'Freedom Is a Constant Dying' and 'Hallelujah
I'm A-Travelling' drew on a wide range of musical traditions. Blending folk songs (black and white), labour anthems, spirituals and
hymns, civil rights activists like Guy and Candie Carawan, Bernice
Johnson Reagon and Sam Block generated a rich corpus of music
which could be adapted continuously by those involved in the
movement's various campaigns. In spite of their diversity, the early
freedom songs invariably stressed the determination of the singers
to endure and ultimately to triumph over the forces of oppression.
'We Shall Overcome' typified the genre not only in its optimism
and emphasis on the struggle for an integrated community but also
in its synthetic origins. Beginning life as a gospel hymn sung in
black churches across the South, it was taken up by striking black
tobacco workers in Charleston, South Carolina, in 1945. Zilphia
Horton, music director of the Highlander Folk School, learned it
from them and taught it to several prominent singer-activists including Pete Seeger and Guy Carawan. Carawan, a young white organiser
particularly interested in preserving the traditional music of the
Carolina Sea Islands, sang it at a series of Highlander workshops in
the spring of 1960 and then joined some of those who had attended
the workshops in a repeat performance at the inaugural SNCC
meeting in Raleigh. Updating the song by adding a contemporary
soul beat, the students quickly made it into the unofficial anthem
of the civil rights movement.[21] Significantly, however, as the movement became more radical in the mid-1960s, so too did the words
of the freedom songs. 'We Shall Overcome', for example, was eventually transformed into 'We Shall Overrun'. By the time the civil
rights coalition had collapsed in 1967 most of the singing had
stopped altogether – the freedom songs derided by black radicals
as 'a sellout to false harmony and religious sentimentalism'.[22]

21. P. Seeger and B. Reiser, *Everybody Says Freedom: A History of the Civil Rights Movement in Songs and Pictures* (New York and London, 1989), pp. 8–9.
22. Lischer, *Preacher King*, p. 250.

Every campaign was unique, evolving in the context of particular local circumstances and heavily dependent on historical contingencies. In the more remote rural areas of Mississippi, the Arkansas Delta, southwestern Georgia and northern Louisiana, the activities of CORE and SNCC field secretaries often played a critical role in mobilising local people whose only extant civil rights vehicles were a dormant branch of the NAACP or a voter registration club which delivered black ballots into the hands of populist white Democrats. This was also the case in small towns on the fringe of the Black Belt – places like Danville, Virginia, and Cambridge, Maryland. The latter, a caste- and class-ridden community on the Eastern Shore, was the site of a vigorous direct action campaign in the early 1960s led by the Cambridge Nonviolent Action Committee (CNAC). The CNAC was founded in 1961 in the wake of demonstrations organised by SNCC field officers Reginald Robinson and Bill Hansen and representatives from the Civic Interest Group, a student-based organisation in nearby Baltimore.[23] Confronted with a conservative and largely inactive branch of the NAACP, a group of local blacks had sought to maintain the momentum generated by the demonstrations by establishing an organisation to coordinate future direct action protests. Under the militant leadership of Gloria Richardson, the CNAC became an affiliate of SNCC and drew on the help of several other outside groups in its efforts to win concessions on desegregation, jobs, and housing from an intransigent city government through the instigation of street demonstrations and voter registration activities during 1962 and 1963.[24] SNCC field workers did not initiate demonstrations in Danville, a segregated textile town in southern Virginia in May 1963, but they provided essential support for the clergy-headed Danville Christian Progressive Association which was set up in the wake of the SCLC's Birmingham campaign. Backing here was also forthcoming from the SCLC which preferred to channel the campaign into voter registration after encountering fierce resistance from the local city council.[25]

Large cities outside the Black Belt, especially those containing clusters of colleges and politically active churches, were most likely to be what Aldon Morris has termed 'movement centres'.[26] Nashville

23. On the CIG see A. Meier, *A White Scholar and the Black Community 1945–1965: Essays and Reflections* (Amherst, 1992), pp. 24–7, 120–5, 137–47.

24. Summer Staff, Cambridge Non-Violent Action Committee, 'The Negro Ward of Cambridge, Maryland: A Study in Social Change', mss. report [1963], WisHS.

25. On the Danville campaign see King, *Freedom Song*, pp. 79–119; Fairclough, *To Redeem*, pp. 145–7, 160–1.

26. A.D. Morris, *The Origins of the Civil Rights Movement: Black Communities Organizing for Change* (New York and London, 1984), pp. 40–76.

was the leading movement centre in the upper South owing to the presence in the city of Fisk, Vanderbilt, Meharry Medical College, the American Baptist Theological Seminary and Tennessee Agricultural and Industrial State University. New Orleans became a power-base for CORE which recruited students from several local universities including Roman Catholic Loyola, black Dillard, and elite Tulane. Atlanta was the regional headquarters for SNCC and the SCLC not only because it was the most important commercial centre in the region but also because it was home to a number of tertiary sector institutions including Morehouse, Spelman, Georgia Tech, Atlanta University and Emory.

Unstable community-level coalitions of indigenous leaders, ordinary working people, middle-class professionals, students and civil rights field workers were forged throughout the South in the early 1960s, but moderate and radical factions often developed, the latter being student-based groupings affiliated to SNCC, CORE, or the youth wing of the NAACP; the former generally favoured by the local adult branch of the NAACP which tended to favour negotiation and litigation rather than direct action. The generational fault-line within the civil rights movement was discernible in most areas of civil rights activity in the 1960s. Older blacks who had been brought up in the heyday of the caste system displayed an understandable reluctance to challenge Jim Crow on the streets. They had more to lose than younger blacks and, having grown up at a time when lynching was still relatively common in the South, had greater reason to fear the consequences of demonstrations and picketing. Because they tended to have lesser expectations and a more gradualist mentality than the young, adults were also less likely to be disappointed with government attempts to promote racial justice.

Most southern communities witnessed tensions between an older generation of civil rights activists and a more impatient younger one. In Alabama, for example, Charles Gomillion campaigned for equal rights as soon as he arrived to teach at Tuskegee Institute in the late 1920s.[27] The leading light in the Tuskegee Civic Association (TCA), he battled for improved public services, independent credit facilities and a much greater political role for blacks. When white elites failed to grant more than token justice to blacks after the Second World War, he stepped up the campaign by organising a boycott of white stores in June 1957 and by taking legal action to

27. The following account of the generational conflict in Tuskegee is based on R.J. Norrell, *Reaping the Whirlwind: The Civil Rights Movement in Tuskegee* (New York, 1985), pp. 164–90.

quash the state's attempt to contain black votes through the passage of gerrymandering legislation. Although some white liberals and businessmen displayed a willingness to share a greater measure of power with the black majority in their county, younger blacks believed that whites were not moving fast enough. Unfairly, perhaps, they blamed Gomillion, by this time in his mid-sixties, for what they regarded as the slow pace of progress on school desegregation and other issues. Matters came to a head in the autumn of 1964 when the TCA backed the town's relatively liberal white sheriff for probate judge. A group of younger blacks led by Howard Puryear, a 28-year-old political scientist at Tuskegee Institute, supported a black candidate, Detroit Young, for the post. After Young was defeated, a number of Tuskegee students proved receptive to the radicalising activities of SNCC organisers who were seeking recruits for the voter registration campaign which would eventually result in the drama at Selma. The recruits rejected what they saw as the accommodationist, middle-class values of Gomillion and his generation and ignored mainstream coalition politics in favour of picketing downtown stores and, even more controversially, demonstrating to end segregation in local churches. Gomillion attacked the use of direct action as irresponsible but his leadership came under increasing threat as the students grew more impatient and aggressive, and as integrationist fervour gave way to demands for an all-black party. In 1966 a black candidate was finally elected as county sheriff, much to the discomfort of Gomillion who persisted in his belief that events were moving too quickly.

Although generational friction was a divisive factor within the civil rights movement, it would be wrong to suppose that older blacks were always more conservative than student insurgents. The NAACP's 'Young Turks' who tried in vain to reform their organisation from within during the second half of the 1960s were mature adults. So were influential leftists in the movement like Ella Baker. It would also be unwise to suggest that all young blacks were radicals. Most black high-school and college students certainly sympathised with the goals of the southern civil rights movement and a relatively high proportion of them participated in the movement at some stage of their college career. In Tallahassee, for example, nearly two-thirds of Florida A & M students appear to have engaged in protest activities between 1960 and 1963.[28] Black students, however,

---

28. J.M. Fendrich, *Ideal Citizens: The Legacy of the Civil Rights Movement* (Albany, NY, 1993), pp. 2–3.

were no less concerned about their future careers than their white counterparts (a majority of whom did not participate in the campus protests of the 1960s), nor were they subject to fewer parental pressures to stay out of trouble – particularly to stay out of jail. A willingness to picket or to march, moreover, was not necessarily a badge of political radicalism. The vast majority of student demonstrators in the South were not members of CORE and SNCC or even the NAACP, and few regarded themselves as anything less than patriotic Americans fighting for their constitutional and God-given rights.

Unity and nonviolence

Although the civil rights movement was riven with fault-lines, the extent of internal divisions should not be exaggerated. The mainstream organisations were perfectly capable of cooperating with each other (witness the March on Washington and numerous instances of successful coalition building at the local level) even though they were engaged in often fierce competition for resources. Many of the organisations possessed overlapping memberships (at the top and at the grass-roots) and the Council of United Civil Rights Leadership functioned reasonably successfully between 1963 and 1966 as a means of defusing the inevitable internal tensions. To some extent the differing specialisms of the mainstream organisations proved to be complementary. The Inc Fund provided legal backing for groups like CORE and SNCC who (sometimes literally) were organising in the field. The national NAACP continued to fight for precedent-setting court decisions and congressional legislation while the SCLC attempted to develop citizenship education and spotlight the denial of constitutional rights in the southern states by stirring up creative tensions. Competition, when it did occur, was not necessarily destructive. The battle for financial resources encouraged the several organisations to develop a variety of funding strategies designed to appeal to a range of donors including philanthropic foundations, labour unions, churches, allied civil rights groups and the general public.[29] The search for publicity by all the mainstream civil rights organisations (a search which was closely linked to the need for money) helped to focus media attention on

29. H.H. Haines, *Black Radicals and the Civil Rights Movement, 1954–1970* (Knoxville, 1978), pp. 77–128.

what was happening in the remoter parts of the Deep South. This, in turn, stimulated greater public awareness of the oppressive nature of segregation and contributed significantly to the successful pursuit of federal intervention. Even the developing split between moderates and radicals could be turned to positive use. Leaders like Martin Luther King and Whitney Young were skilled at using the spectre of black militancy to win concessions from white elites. Malcolm X came to recognise that his notoriety had value for mainstream civil rights leaders, once complaining to the actor, Ossie Davis, 'I don't know why they [Malcolm's black critics] hate me. I raise hell in the backyard and they run out front and The Man puts money in their hands.'[30] An impressive degree of unity was also achieved by the willingness of many activists to place the welfare of the cause above organisational loyalty. Civil rights leaders like Dave Dennis and Bob Moses frequently frustrated SNCC and CORE headquarters because of their unselfish willingness to act with, and give credit to, other civil rights groups.

At no stage, of course, did the civil rights movement achieve 100 per cent unity among African Americans. Such cohesion would have been impossible given the diversity of the black population and the intensity of the debate over civil rights strategy. This said, it is clear that the movement would not have achieved the downfall of the southern caste system without a significant degree of internal cohesion. The capacity of protest activity to transcend class barriers within many southern black communities during the 1950s and 1960s astonished many people. Yancey Martin, for example, a college student at the time of the Montgomery bus boycott, marvelled at the unified response of local blacks to the MIA's call for action. 'I had never seen that happen in Montgomery', he recalled, 'and I must admit that I have never seen that happen anywhere among black people.'[31] The sense of fighting against a common enemy generated a solidarity of its own, but equally important so far as unity of purpose was concerned was the movement's own philosophy-cum-strategy of nonviolence and the knowledge that the cause was a just one. Feelings of comradeship and kinship, of shared suffering inside and outside jail, of righteous indignation – all of which contributed towards internal cohesion – were most intense among SNCC and CORE field workers who laboured in the emotional

30. Quoted in N.J. Weiss, *Whitney M. Young, Jr, and the Struggle for Civil Rights* (Princeton, 1989), p. 123.

31. Quoted in H. Raines, *My Soul Is Rested: Movement Days in the Deep South Remembered* (New York, 1983), p. 59.

pressure-cooker of the rural South. For SNCC veteran Casey Hayden, the movement 'was everything: home and family, food and work, love and a reason to live'.[32] For Jerome Smith, a founder member of New Orleans CORE, the greatest memory was 'the absence of loneliness . . . the magic of every moment being wrapped in love – that kind of spiritual thing was, to this day, the greatest thing'.[33]

The relative unity of purpose and the deep sense of comradeship and community which were such distinctive features of the civil rights movement in the 1960s were rooted in the movement's core philosophy of nonviolence. In part, nonviolence was a natural product of the profoundly patriotic impulse which drove so many people in the early 1960s to join the black freedom struggle. Participants in the early civil rights movement generally saw themselves as staunch American nationalists who wanted to strengthen their country's claims to global supremacy by closing the domestic gap between ideals and reality. They were not communist subversives as southern segregationists and J. Edgar Hoover believed, even though a small number of committed leftists like Ella Baker and Bayard Rustin were active behind the scenes. On the whole, the McCarthyite response to the Cold War, Stalinist excesses and the Soviet invasion of Hungary had served to discredit Marxism-Leninism as a viable ideology on which to build a successful social movement in the United States. Suggestions that the movement was cooperating with the nation's enemies were therefore strongly denied by black leaders throughout the 1950s and early 1960s, not only because taints of Communism would have undermined the efficacy of protest activity but also because Communism was generally perceived, inside and outside the movement, as an alien creed. Even SNCC, which outraged Roy Wilkins by accepting aid from the left-wing National Lawyers Guild during the Freedom Summer, was, during its early years, a fundamentally patriotic organisation. 'We didn't need a foreign ideology', recalled Mary King. 'Our movement was affirming in a naked and tangible way the promise of the Constitution. Not only was this not revolutionary, it was, in a pure sense, conservative.'[34] The failure of the federal government to protect field workers, to respond more swiftly and decisively to black demands, and to cease engagement in the Vietnam War wrought significant changes in the way activists thought about their country in the

32. C. Hayden, 'Preface' to King, *Freedom Song*, p. 8.
33. Quoted in K.L. Rogers, *Righteous Lives: Narratives of the New Orleans Civil Rights Movement* (New York and London, 1993), p. 135.
34. King, *Freedom Song*, pp. 276, 284.

mid-1960s. But when the civil rights movement was at its zenith, it was, unquestionably, a peaceable movement of national renewal and rejuvenation, not one of violent revolution, sedition and disloyalty.

This desire to improve the Republic by ridding it of segregation, racism and poverty manifested itself in numerous ways – not least the ongoing attempt to revitalise the nation's political system by destroying the power of segregationist Democrats. It was also an extension of the movement's distinctive, almost therapeutic, focus on self-reform – the attempt to rid ordinary southern blacks of the mental chains imposed by decades of slavery and segregation. Nonviolence was central to this struggle to make better people, better communities and a better nation. A synthetic credo, it combined neo-Gandhian tactics and methodology with the intense religious commitment of many southern blacks. Mahatma Gandhi had many admirers in the United States. Several prominent black educators including Benjamin F. Mays, Howard Thurman and Mordecai Johnson visited India in the 1930s and 1940s and sought to communicate their enthusiasm for nonviolence to African Americans back home.[35] During the Second World War A. Philip Randolph launched the March on Washington Movement in what became an increasingly conscious attempt to replicate Gandhian tactics in America. CORE, in its early years the most Gandhian of all the civil rights organisations, was founded in 1942 by, among others, the black Methodist James Farmer who had been a student of Thurman at Howard University. The young Martin Luther King first became aware of Gandhianism after hearing a lecture at Crozer Theological Seminary delivered by Mordecai Johnson in 1950.[36] In truth, however, Gandhianism impinged little on the lives of most African Americans and many of those who explicitly endorsed it as a viable strategy for American blacks did so as a way of legitimising what seemed to them common-sense tactics. Randolph was certainly no Gandhian and drew primarily on the labour activism of the 1930s for his March on Washington in 1941. For him Gandhian-style civil disobedience was largely a means to an end – one strategy among many with more indigenous roots than foreign ones. King himself did arrive at an understanding of Gandhian thought and tactics after the Montgomery bus boycott, mainly owing to the efforts of American Gandhians like Bayard Rustin, Glenn Smiley, Harris

---

35. S. Kapur, *Raising Up a Prophet: The African-American Encounter with Gandhi* (Boston, 1992), pp. 72–100, 144–9.
36. Ibid., pp. 146–7.

Wofford and James Lawson. Mordecai Johnson's 1950 lecture, however, did little in itself to convince the young King that Gandhi had found an answer to the massive problems confronting the post-war world. Commenting in a short college essay on the possibility of applying pacifist doctrines to the nuclear arms race, King insisted that absolute pacifism, A.J. Muste's 'so-called non-violence', could 'become more violent than war. That Gandhi was successful against the British is no reason that the Russians would react in the same way.'[37]

More important than Gandhianism as a source of, as opposed to a technical blueprint for, nonviolent direct action, were the deep-rooted folkways of African-American Christianity which militated against a violent campaign of emancipation.

Nonviolence was not, as some of its radical critics asserted, a passive strategy. It was developed as an effective (and broadly patriotic) means of undermining an entrenched racial caste system. Far from requiring blacks to throw themselves cravenly at the feet of their oppressors in pursuit of justice and equality, the intent was to transform oppressors and oppressed alike by the step-by-step application of direct and indirect pressure to various points of weakness in the white power structure. As a tactic it demanded substantial reservoirs of self-discipline, patience, bravery, morale, and even love (if not of the oppressor, then of oneself) on the part of its practitioners. Such qualities were widely evident among civil rights activists at mid-century and were rooted chiefly in New Testament concepts of Christian love and forgiveness.

At this point it is vital to distinguish between Christianity as a religion – as a basis for personal and group action – and the Christian church as an institution. The leading representatives of the mainstream Protestant denominations in the southern states played a secondary role in the civil rights movement. This was true not only of white church leaders who, at best, supported a gradual reform of the caste system, but also, to some extent, of the black church which has been depicted by some observers as the bedrock of the movement.[38]

The southern black church was certainly not the only indigenous black institution to provide aid for the civil rights movement. Indeed, so minimal was the involvement of many clergymen in the black freedom struggle that the churches came under strong attack

37. C. Carson, ed., *The Papers of Martin Luther King, Jr: Vol. I – Called to Serve January 1929–June 1951* (Berkeley, Los Angeles and London, 1992), p. 435.
38. Morris, *Origins*, p. 4.

from critics in the 1960s. Modern scholars such as John Dittmer and Adam Fairclough have confirmed that secular organisers and grass-roots community institutions such as labour unions, women's civic clubs, teachers' associations, voter registration organisations, and fraternal societies like the Prince Hall Masons all played a critical role in the movement at the local level. In contrast, black ministers in Mississippi were often conspicuous by their absence from the front ranks of the movement, partly because local whites used religion as a form of social control and partly as a consequence of the state's rural character which worked against the formation of inter-denominational ministerial alliances.[39] According to Fairclough, black preachers in Louisiana seldom initiated protest activity and when they did they proved to be poor organisers and unhelpfully authoritarian. Other black professionals – lawyers, dentists, doctors, teachers and businessmen – played a much more positive role in civil rights activities in the Pelican state.[40] Many of the major southern campaigns, including the Montgomery and Tallahassee bus boycotts, the student sit-ins, the Freedom Rides, and the Mississippi Freedom Summer were initiated by individuals without formal ties to the black church, while several local movements (Cambridge, Maryland, is a good example) lacked significant input from the black clergy.

But while one can agree that the role of the black church in the civil rights movement has been exaggerated (partly because of too narrow a focus on Martin Luther King), it would be wrong to suggest that the institution (and still less the evangelical world-view of so many southern blacks) played a minor part in the events of the mid-twentieth century. The black church was an extremely diverse institution. The dominant Baptist and Methodist churches embraced a wide variety of opinion on the wisdom and necessity of civil rights involvement. A minority of activist clergy did exist during the early and later phases of the civil rights movement. These included outspoken preachers like William Holmes Borders, an Atlanta minister who used local black radio to encourage opposition to racial segregation and political disfranchisement in the 1940s, and his contemporary, the Rev. Ralph M. Gilbert of Savannah who, with his wife, established at least 50 NAACP chapters in Georgia.[41] King's

39. Dittmer, *Local People*, pp. 75–6.
40. A. Fairclough, *Race and Democracy: The Civil Rights Struggle in Louisiana, 1915–1972* (Athens, Ga, 1995), pp. 71–2.
41. Lischer, *Preacher King*, pp. 48–50; P. Sullivan, *Days of Hope: Race and Democracy in the New Deal Era* (Chapel Hill and London, 1996), pp. 141–2.

predecessor at Dexter, Vernon Johns, sought in vain to initiate public protests against segregation in Montgomery during the same decade.[42] Even Adam Fairclough has found that individual black preachers in Louisiana took the lead in opposing Jim Crow. In New Orleans, for example, the Rev. L.L. Haynes persuaded over 90 per cent of his congregation to join the NAACP in the 1940s and roughly a third of the state's NAACP branches were headed by black ministers before the onset of massive resistance.[43]

The majority of socially aware southern black clergymen, cognisant of the church's historic role in spreading the gospel of deliverance but wary of stirring up white opposition and internal dissent, advocated a composite form of social action which combined self-help with moderate protest in varying proportions. The young Martin Luther King occupied a mid-road position prior to becoming president of the MIA. Convinced, as he told his Dexter Avenue flock on his arrival in Montgomery, that '[l]eadership never ascends from the pew to the pulpit, but . . . invariably descends from the pulpit to the pew', King quickly appointed a number of new committees to promote better church organisation.[44] He also encouraged members to join the NAACP and become registered voters. For all this, however, he took a secondary role in the negotiations between the city council and secular black leaders in 1954 and 1955. Only when the black union representative, E.D. Nixon, consciously solicited clerical involvement did King enter the fray as a leading figure in the bus boycott. The same was true of other moderate black ministers in Montgomery.

The important point is not that King and others like him were initially secondary actors in the movement, but that their involvement in the struggle was deemed critical by secular leaders. As communist organisers had discovered in the 1930s, evangelical Protestantism was so integral a part of southern culture that no attack on Jim Crow segregation could take place in a religious vacuum.[45] Even though the civil rights struggle moved into the churches more often than the churches initiated direct assaults on Jim Crow, it was heavily dependent on religious values and institutions for success. A large proportion of the leaders and staff members of all the mainstream

42. T. Branch, *Parting the Waters: America in the King Years 1954–1963* (New York, 1988), pp. 14–15.

43. Fairclough, *Race and Democracy*, pp. 71–2.

44. Quoted in D.J. Garrow, *Bearing the Cross: Martin Luther King, Jr., and the Southern Christian Leadership Conference* (New York, 1986), p. 50.

45. R.D.G. Kelley, *Hammer and Hoe: Alabama Communists During the Great Depression* (Chapel Hill and London, 1990), pp. 107–8.

civil rights organisations operating in the South possessed religious roots. Equally significantly, Christianity provided not only the principal intellectual well-spring for nonviolent direct action but also large numbers of rank-and-file supporters of the movement.

Nonviolence worked in the South because it tapped the spirituality of so many ordinary black people. Black evangelical Protestants had been taught for decades by their preachers that although their condition was unjust and impermanent, they should shun bitterness and hatred and, at the very least, practise the golden rule in their daily lives. This did not mean that most southern blacks loved white people. Even Martin Luther King confessed to hating whites for their efforts to degrade the 'coloured' race.[46] However, a conviction that God would inevitably reward a suffering people combined with the gospel accounts of Christ's life in the world and a heavy dose of common sense to predispose large numbers of southern blacks towards a nonviolent approach to civil rights struggle.

A crucial factor in the development of this tendency and the emergence of a genuinely mass movement was the recruitment of thousands of black female churchgoers into the civil rights movement. Although the mainstream organisations did something to encourage women's involvement in civil rights, female activism was chiefly a product of the strong links which existed between the black church and black women.

Historically, the latter played a leading role in black society – a much more prominent one than their peers in white culture where male economic dominance was only slowly coming under threat after the Second World War. Under slavery black women served as inter-generational transmitters of African-American culture through their role as mothers, yet also performed back-breaking work on the cotton plantations of the Deep South. After emancipation they withdrew some of their labour from the fields but continued to act as breadwinners and family organisers. Regular attendance at church services enabled them to escape the pressures of everyday life under Jim Crow and engage in a spiritually satisfying form of communal worship. While it is true that the Christ-centred black church was based on a patriarchal mode of organisation (male preachers led predominantly female congregations), sufficient space existed for women to duplicate the activist function which they usually performed in the home. On Sundays, and indeed throughout the week, women served in a variety of positions which rendered their

46. Garrow, *Bearing the Cross*, p. 35.

contribution to church life as crucial as their role in the civil rights movement. As well as being Sunday School teachers, custodians, caterers, secretaries, choir members and organists, they often formed civic clubs designed to promote community uplift. Such clubs grew out of female involvement in the church and gave some black women, particularly urban middle-class women, the opportunity to expand their organisational talents and to engage in proto-political activity. As we have seen, the existence of established female networks in many southern communities enabled movement field workers to 'co-opt' large numbers of women when they began their organising drives in the early 1960s.[47]

Because religion was so central to it, the civil rights movement relied heavily on grass-roots female support and expertise. Individual women did occupy positions in the top echelons of the movement, but for the most part the internal task system which developed re-plicated that in the wider society: men tended to lead, while women preferred to organise.[48]

The reluctance of most black women to assume positions of leadership frustrated young liberal whites like Casey Hayden and Mary King who sought to raise women's consciousness within SNCC in the wake of the Freedom Summer.[49] Convinced that their organ-isation's male staffers had yet to acknowledge the need for women's liberation as well as black freedom, Hayden and King compiled an anonymous position paper for discussion at SNCC's retreat at Waveland, Mississippi, in November 1964. In it they cited evid-ence of sexist behaviour within the organisation and asserted that '[a]ssumptions of male superiority are as widespread and deep-rooted and every much as crippling to the woman as the assump-tions of white supremacy are to the Negro.'[50] The paper elicited a lukewarm response from female staffers and, Bob Moses and Charles Cobb aside, an even more negative one from the men. The debate led indirectly to Stokely Carmichael's notorious remark that the proper position for women in the movement was prone, although Mary King herself later asserted that the comment was actually intended to ridicule male chauvinism.[51] Black female staffers failed to react more positively to the paper for the same reason that black

---

47. See above, pp. 160, 163.
48. C. Payne, 'Men Led But Women Organized: Movement Participation of Women in the Mississippi Delta' in *Women in the Civil Rights Movement: Trailblazers and Torch-bearers, 1941–1965*, ed. V.L. Crawford *et al.* (New York, 1990), pp. 1–11.
49. The influence of the civil rights struggle on the emerging women's movement in America is explored in S. Evans, *The Roots of Women's Liberation in the Civil Rights Movement and the New Left* (pbk edn, New York, 1980), pp. 24–101.
50. King, *Freedom Song*, p. 568.   51. Ibid., p. 452.

women in general subsequently failed to respond to the women's liberation movement in America. That is to say, they were wary of endorsing white criticism of African-American males at a time when they were engaged in a struggle for racial emancipation – one which necessarily required raising the self-confidence of black men. Black women, moreover, may have been less concerned with the consequences of patriarchy because they themselves played a more significant role in both community life and the movement than many of their white peers. Influential black female SNCC workers manifestly had less reason to complain about their treatment from men inside the movement.[52]

Sexism certainly abounded in the civil rights movement. Ella Baker witnessed it in the SCLC where women were relegated to a much more subordinate position than those in SNCC or CORE.[53] So too did the citizenship school organiser, Septima Clark, who experienced the patronising attitude of Martin Luther King's male lieutenants towards herself. 'I had a great feeling', she remembered, 'that Dr King didn't think much of women either.'[54] While other civil rights organisations were similarly riddled with male chauvinism this is hardly to be wondered at given the extent of patriarchal values in society at large. Such sexism did not, moreover, prevent women, particularly church women, from stamping their authority on the grass-roots movement.

God-fearing black women made a massive contribution to the southern civil rights movement – singing freedom songs, initiating direct action protests, mobilising resources, taking a visible role in consumer boycotts and voter registration efforts, and providing informal support for numerous campaigns. Their efforts required enormous reserves of bravery and self-motivation, qualities provided in no small measure by their profound Christian faith. 'I asked the Lord to take care o' me' and just went on out there', recalled Viola Williams, one of hundreds of black women mobilised by the civil rights movement's activities in the Mississippi Delta.[55] For most black women a nonviolent approach to the problems confronting the race was the only option. If their own Christian faith did not rule

52. C.G. Fleming, 'Black Women Activists and the Student Nonviolent Coordinating Committee', *Journal of Women's History* 4 (1993), 72; R. Gatlin, *American Women Since 1945* (Jackson and London, 1987), pp. 86–7.

53. Fairclough, *To Redeem*, pp. 49–50.

54. C.S. Brown, ed., *Ready from Within: Septima Clark and the Civil Rights Movement* (Trenton, NJ, 1990), p. 77.

55. Youth of the Rural Organizing and Cultural Center, *Minds Stayed on Freedom: The Civil Rights Struggle in the Rural South, an Oral History* (Boulder, San Francisco, and Oxford, 1991), p. 84.

out more militant options, then their own gendered experiences certainly did. 'Who better than women,' mused one female activist, 'should know that battles can be won without resort to physical strength? Who better than we should know all the power that resides in noncooperation?'[56]

Although their high visibility in the movement was often a function of their church involvement, women may also have featured prominently in civil rights protests because they consciously recognised the perils of black male activism in the Deep South. A number of prominent female activists testified that women often took the lead in initiating protests against Jim Crow because southern white males were less likely to commit murderous acts of violence against black women than black men. Fannie Lou Hamer, for example, explained that the MFDP offered three female candidates for election in 1965 because it would have been 'too dangerous to put men up as candidates'.[57] Although women were often assigned stereotypical roles on the Freedom Summer projects, the presence of a female on a picket line or registration team could reduce the chances of violence against male activists. According to one chronicler of the summer project, Mary Aikin Rothschild, 'Women in general were less likely than men in general to experience violence for their civil rights work.'[58] None of these points, however, should obscure the fact that direct action carried with it huge risks for women as well as men. Reprisals, as Charles Payne observes, affected whole families, not just individuals, and Rothschild herself notes that black women were more likely than white female students to be attacked or arrested by white Mississippians.[59] Fannie Lou Hamer, badly beaten in a Winona jail and dismissed from her plantation job, was just one of many southern black women who suffered grievous personal violence for enlisting in the civil rights movement.

While fear of death was a very real psychological barrier for all protagonists in the black freedom struggle, it is evident that the crusade against the southern caste system was won without the appalling loss of life incurred in many contemporary liberation struggles. (At least 26 black and white civil rights workers died in movement-related killings between early 1960 and the spring of

56. Quoted in B. Linden-Ward and C.H. Green, *American Women in the 1960s: Changing the Future* (New York, 1993), p. 50.

57. Ibid., p. 38.

58. M.A. Rothschild, *A Case of Black and White: Northern Student Volunteers and the Southern Freedom Summer, 1964–1965* (Westport, Conn., 1982), p. 135.

59. Ibid., p. 135; C. Payne, *'I've Got the Light of Freedom': The Organizing Tradition and the Mississippi Freedom Struggle* (Berkeley, Los Angeles, and London, 1995), p. 270.

1965.[60] By contrast in South Africa in March 1960, 67 people were shot dead in the Sharpeville massacre alone.)[61] There were several reasons for this, not least the growing threat of federal intervention and the reluctance of business elites and a majority of ordinary southern whites to see their communities torn apart by a race war. However, the infusion of large numbers of black, Christian women into the movement may also have contributed to the relatively low level of fatalities in the southern states in the 1960s. White racists existed in large numbers throughout the South, but public shows of violence against women contravened the region's patriarchal honour code, not to mention its admittedly over-hyped culture of civility.

More conjectural is the possibility that the feminisation of the black freedom struggle in the early 1960s (both in terms of rank-and-file membership and ideology) may have been instrumental in garnering crucial white support for the movement's objectives. Black radicals like Malcolm X had little compunction in depicting non-violence as an unmanly strategy – one which served only to perpetuate the emasculation of black men by white supremacists. Civil rights activists certainly did not perceive direct action in this light, but it is not impossible that, subconsciously at least, many white people were persuaded to view the movement sympathetically in part because it contained large numbers of women who espoused the non-threatening tenets of nonviolence. As the struggle became more militant, more assertively and self-consciously masculine, with the advent of Black Power in the mid-1960s, a majority of white Americans withdrew their support from a crusade which appeared to have abandoned feminine, Christian values for more macho, secular ones.[62]

Although religious-based nonviolence lay at the heart of movement culture, it would be wrong to suggest that the relationship between the freedom struggle and violence was entirely clear cut. As the Albany, Birmingham and Selma campaigns revealed, nonviolence was an evolving strategy – one which shifted perceptibly in the early 1960s from a determined attempt to shame the oppressor into changing his ways to a blatantly coercive bid to secure federal intervention by demonstrating the repressive powers of southern

60. M.R. Belknap, *Federal Law and Southern Order: Racial Violence and Constitutional Conflict in the Post*-Brown *South* (Athens, Ga, and London, 1987), p. 124.

61. L. Thompson, *A History of South Africa* (New Haven and London, 1990), p. 210.

62. On the impact of Black Power on African-American women see J. Jones, *Labor of Love, Labor of Sorrow: Black Women, Work, and the Family from Slavery to the Present* (pbk edn, New York, 1986), p. 312.

segregationists to the outside world. Frustration with the slow pace of change, moreover, severely diminished the amount of support for nonviolent direct action within the movement. SNCC and CORE field workers soon began to doubt its utility when confronted with racist attacks in the South – their growing opposition legitimised in intellectual terms by the rhetoric of Malcolm X and the work of the black francophone radical, Frantz Fanon. Fanon, whose *Wretched of the Earth* was required reading for disenchanted SNCC activists after its appearance in translation in 1965, contended that an oppressed people could only win true freedom – psychological as well as physical liberation – by undertaking to fight the oppressor. 'At the level of individuals', wrote Fanon, 'violence is a cleansing force. It frees the native from his inferiority complex and from his despair and inaction; it makes him fearless and restores his self-respect.'[63] Such notions controverted the mainstream view, propounded by Martin Luther King and others, that violence was a negative force – destructive of society and community, rather than a vehicle for inter-group solidarity – but they struck the likes of James Forman and Stokely Carmichael as eminently persuasive in the light of the slow progress being made towards freedom in the southern states during 1963–64.

While such views helped to destroy the nonviolent consensus of 1960, there was no linear transition from peaceable resistance to self-defence, media-driven white perceptions to the contrary. Even during the early years of the movement pent-up black anger at the grass-roots often threatened to undermine the discipline of non-violent protests in the South. Ugly clashes between black youths and segregationists threatened to split the movement along racial, generational and class lines, but those which occurred in Birmingham in May 1963 helped to persuade government officials that positive action on civil rights was imperative. On the other hand, when black frustration nationally did spill over into full-blown riots and separatist rhetoric, most African Americans shunned the idea of armed struggle. This is not to say that the minority of rioters who set the ghettos aflame in the 1960s did not reflect in part the feelings of the nonviolent majority. The rioters' actions may well have contributed to the growth of federal anti-poverty programmes, but whether they did more in the long-term to build than destroy is a moot point well beyond the range of this particular study.

63. Quoted in R.H. King, *Civil Rights*, p. 182.

Allies

The civil rights movement was organised and led primarily by African Americans themselves. Inevitably, however, given the minority position of blacks in the United States and the historic injustices to which the race had been subjected, the movement devoted much of its energies to the search for allies in the wider society. The aid of numerous individuals, private organisations and state institutions inside and outside the confines of the civil rights coalition was an important factor in the downfall of the southern caste system.

Prominent among the support groups belonging to the civil rights coalition were white-led bodies labelled 'movement halfway houses' by Aldon Morris.[64] These included organisations like the Fellowship of Reconciliation (FOR), the Southern Conference Education Fund (SCEF) and the Highlander Folk School which contributed direct aid to civil rights activities at critical periods during the black freedom struggle. While the pacifist FOR gave birth to CORE in the early 1940s, Highlander furnished the expertise for political education after the Second World War, first in an informal capacity and later as an adjunct of the SCLC. SCEF, headed in the early 1960s by two white Louisville radicals, Anne and Carl Braden, served as a southern-based support agency for the mainstream civil rights groups. In spite of being red-baited during the McCarthy era and suffering the indignity of having its New Orleans headquarters raided by the police in October 1963, SCEF undertook a number of important projects. Particularly valuable was its decision to fund a full-time southern field worker on the SNCC staff – specifically to develop support for civil rights in the white community. Two white Methodist preachers' sons, Bob Zellner and Sam Shirah, served in this capacity during the early 1960s, their efforts to tap youthful idealism bearing a modicum of fruit with the formation of the Southern Students Organizing Committee in Nashville in April 1964.[65] Although SCEF's activities were inevitably circumscribed by its reputation as a communist-front organisation (the national NAACP avoided all contact as a result), its very existence indicated that some southern whites – admittedly a tiny minority – were prepared to devote themselves to the black freedom struggle. Such signals were essential if Martin Luther King and other mainstream leaders were to persuade the bulk of southern blacks that integration was a viable objective.

64. Morris, *Origins*, pp. 139–73.
65. C. Carson, *In Struggle: SNCC and the Black Awakening of the 1960s* (Cambridge, Mass., and London, 1981), pp. 101–2.

Although the movement benefited from the information-gathering services of the reformist Southern Regional Council based in Atlanta, white southern institutions, particularly the mainline Baptist, Methodist, and Presbyterian churches, provided minimal support. Evidence does exist to suggest that some state- and regional-level white church officials attempted to accommodate their institutions to the changing times, but they faced strong opposition from the laity in the southern Black Belt.[66] The movement secured much greater support from national religious bodies such as the National Council of Churches (NCC), the Catholic Interracial Council, the American Friends Service Committee (AFSC), and the Episcopal Society for Cultural and Racial Unity (ESCRU). These liberal organisations provided vital aid at critical junctures in the movement. The NCC, for example, threw its weight behind the campaign for a national civil rights act to outlaw *de jure* segregation, financed the training sessions which preceded the Freedom Summer, and supported a ministerial project, the Delta Ministry, designed to enhance the quality of life for blacks in rural Mississippi.[67] The Quaker-run AFSC was active in many parts of the South during the 1960s, as evidenced by its attempts to find alternative education for local blacks after the closure of public schools in Prince Edward County, Virginia, in 1960, and the determination of its members to promote dialogue between civic leaders and protest organisers in various cities across the region, including Baton Rouge.[68] ESCRU, founded in Raleigh in 1959 by a group of 100 Episcopalians, mostly clergy and over half of them southerners, was the first national religious body to support the student sit-ins and participated in most of the classic movement campaigns of the 1960s.[69]

If liberal Protestant and Catholic activists helped the civil rights movement to capitalise on the tensions produced by direct action, Jewish Americans furnished equally valuable support. Broadly sympathetic to black civil rights because of their own experiences with racial prejudice and their political ties to the black community through the Democratic Party, many left-leaning and liberal northern Jews were integral players in the movement proper, either

66. M. Newman, 'Southern Baptists and the Civil Rights Movement in Recent Historical Literature', *Over Here* 14 (1994), 61–9.

67. J.F. Findlay, Jr, *Church People in the Struggle: The National Council of Churches and the Black Freedom Movement, 1950–1970* (New York and Oxford, 1993), pp. 48–139.

68. B. Smith, *They Closed Their Schools: Prince Edward County, Virginia, 1951–1964* (Chapel Hill, 1965), p. 196; Fairclough, *Race and Democracy*, pp. 332–5.

69. C.W. Eagles, *Outside Agitator: Jon Daniels and the Civil Rights Movement in Alabama* (Chapel Hill, 1993), pp. 39–40.

through their membership of, or financial support for, the NAACP and CORE. Others indicated their opposition to Jim Crow through their work with the labour movement, by participating directly in southern civil rights campaigns, or as a bi-product of their membership of either the American Jewish Congress or the American Jewish Committee, both important members of the Leadership Conference on Civil Rights. Notwithstanding the importance of this aid (which was gratefully acknowledged by mainstream black leaders), the extent of Jewish support for the civil rights movement should not be exaggerated. Southern Jews provided little formal backing, their assimilation into regional society having been accomplished at the expense of considerable compromise with the caste system.[70] Northern Jews were increasingly alienated by the anti-Semitic tone of some black nationalist rhetoric and by the end of the decade relations between Jewish Americans and African Americans had deteriorated greatly.[71]

Predominantly secular forces in white society were also at work on the side of civil rights, although their importance should not be overestimated any more than that of the white religious bodies. Some of these had roots in the developing New Left which contributed so much to the anti-authoritarian strain of 1960s radicalism. The civil rights movement's chief ally among northern white students was Students for a Democratic Society (SDS). Heavily influenced by the black freedom struggle (particularly SNCC's drive towards participatory democracy), SDS had aligned itself closely with the radical wing of the civil rights coalition by the time of the Freedom Summer. As well as providing a number of volunteers for southern field work, the organisation initiated some of the movement's early forays into the northern ghettos with its ill-starred Economic Research and Action Project in 1964.[72] Like the movement's other campus-based allies in the New Left, such as the Northern Student Movement, SDS lost much of its influence as young white Americans began to channel the bulk of their energies into opposing the Vietnam War. Increasingly doctrinaire and isolated, the organisation was torn apart by the vicious in-fighting which afflicted the American Left in the second half of the decade.[73]

70. C. Webb, 'Southern Jews and the Civil Rights Movement' in *Southern Landscapes*, ed. T. Badger, W. Edgar, and J.N. Gretlund (Tübingen, 1996), pp. 157–64.

71. R. Weisbrot, *Freedom Bound: A History of America's Civil Rights Movement* (pbk edn, New York, 1991), pp. 242–3.

72. Evans, *Personal Politics*, pp. 127–55.

73. J.P. Diggins, *The Rise and Fall of the American Left* (New York and London, 1973), pp. 218–76.

Although SDS functioned as a loyal ally of SNCC in the early 1960s, most of the other civil rights organisations preferred to look to organised labour for support. This was understandable, given the extent of trade union backing for equal rights during the New Deal and the Second World War, labour's prominent role in the Democratic Party, and the substantial number of organised black workers in the North. Several factors, however, prevented the AFL–CIO from occupying a place in the forefront of the civil rights movement during the 1960s.

Labour was by no means a marginal force in the black freedom struggle. Individual unions such as the Packinghouse Workers, the United Auto Workers and Jimmy Hoffa's controversial Teamsters Union did provide funding for some of the mainstream civil rights organisations. The AFL–CIO hierarchy was broadly sympathetic to the goals of the civil rights movement – witness the many public expressions of support from national leaders like Walter Reuther and the activities of labour officials within the Leadership Conference. Some state-level labour councils bravely tried to implement official policy in the Deep South with a view to democratising politics in the region and some faltering steps were taken to reduce the extent of racism among white workers.[74] Unfortunately the persistence of such racism, particularly among blue-collar workers in large parts of the Deep South, acted as a brake on biracial unionism in the region during the 1960s.[75] The eclipse of left-wing union activity in the early phase of the Cold War, moreover, had deprived the southern labour movement of its most ardent grass-roots civil rights campaigners and even the most progressive of state council leaders, men like Claude Ramsay in Mississippi, found it hard to overcome the prejudices of their members. Equally problematic was the fact that the AFL–CIO's accommodation with corporate capitalism and mainstream Democratic Party politics in the 1950s prevented its leaders at all levels from empathising with the more radical goals of the civil rights movement. Reuther, for example, was far too close to Lyndon Johnson to understand the MFDP's position at the Democratic convention in 1964. Claude Ramsay was equally unsympathetic to the black challenge at Atlantic City and rejected partnership with

---

74. A. Draper, *Conflict of Interests: Organized Labor and the Civil Rights Movement in the South, 1954–1968* (Ithaca, 1994).

75. On the extent of white working-class racism in the South during the 1950s and 1960s see R.J. Norrell, 'Labor Trouble: George Wallace and Union Politics in Alabama' in *Organized Labor in the Twentieth-Century South*, ed. R.H. Zieger (Knoxville, 1991), pp. 250–72.

the Freedom Democrats (or 'anarchists' as he referred to them) in favour of participation in a moderate coalition with the state NAACP.[76] While national civil rights leaders like King, Wilkins and Rustin continued to lay great stress on the need to consolidate the movement's links with organised labour, prospects for an interracial, working-class alliance were undermined by the stalling of trade union membership outside the South (a product, largely, of technological change), by labour's failure to organise and protect southern black farmworkers, and by constant friction caused by white working-class racism, the growth of black nationalism and the escalation of the Vietnam War. Although cooperation between the AFL–CIO and the NAACP survived the collapse of the civil rights movement, SNCC activists, like their New Left allies, regarded organised labour as part of the problem rather than a solution. As Casey Hayden put it in November 1964: 'We know more than the labor unions, that don't deal with the people they should.'[77]

In some ways the civil rights movement relied more heavily on help from outside the immediate confines of the coalition. Many southern businessmen played an important role in desegregation at the local level, if only because they were so sensitive to the impact which direct action had on investor confidence in their own communities. Various branches and agencies of the federal government, particularly the Justice Department, also played a secondary role in the demise of Jim Crow, although it must be emphasised that most of them would not have acted as effectively as they did without pressure from the movement. Individual circuit court and district court judges, some of them southern-born whites like John Minor Wisdom, J. Waties Waring and Frank M. Johnson, were broadly sympathetic to the goals of the black freedom struggle and frequently frustrated the efforts of segregationists to thwart protest activity. The US Civil Rights Commission joined the courts and several executive departments in institutionalising civil rights policy in the second half of the 1960s and beyond. Federal aid may have been slow in coming but without it the movement could not have brought about the destruction of southern segregation as quickly as it did.

Perhaps the most effective 'allies' of all were those white racists whose brutal treatment of peaceful black demonstrators enabled civil rights activists, via the press and the electronic media, to dramatise

76. Dittmer, *Local People*, pp. 346–7, 351.
77. Waveland Retreat Minutes, 9 November 1964, Workshop on Labor and Employment, Box 26, Series 5, SNCC Papers, KC.

the inherent evils of the southern caste system. Jim Crow might well have enjoyed a longer career had not Bull Connor, Jim Clark, Al Lingo and other unreconstructed whites taken it upon themselves to defend their privileges through the application of brute force. To grant most of the credit for the demolition of segregation to such men, however, would be grossly unjust. African Americans were the principal architects of their own success – a fact of great importance in terms of self-esteem and community uplift. In seeking to solve the enormous problems still confronting the race in the last third of the twentieth century, this central lesson would not be forgotten.

CHAPTER 8

The Struggle Continues

With SNCC and CORE moribund and the SCLC rendered largely ineffective by the death of Martin Luther King, the direct action phase of the civil rights movement had ground to a halt by the middle of 1968. Street protests in the United States continued – the bulk of them involving young whites mobilised by continuing American intervention in southeast Asia. Black unrest did not cease either, particularly on college campuses where students demanded greater control over curricula. But what had been lost was the sense of a national movement – a relatively cohesive, focused, and inter-organisational struggle for equal rights which effectively harnessed popular, community energies in the fight against racial discrimination. In spite of the destruction of Jim Crow, major problems such as inner-city deprivation, drug abuse, rural poverty, job discrimination, unstable families and segregated schools persisted. It was hardly surprising, therefore, that the waning of direct action did not signal the end of the black freedom struggle. In the last three decades of the twentieth century the fight to promote better social and economic conditions for African Americans took several forms, all of them grounded firmly in the achievements of the 1960s.

Violent revolutionary activity was not one of the roads taken. After the federal government launched its counter-intelligence (COINTELPRO) operations against black radical groups in 1967, it became clear to even the most starry-eyed nationalist that the American state was not going to yield to what most whites regarded as criminal violence. The Black Panthers, the most notorious of the black 'terrorist' groups, were effectively crushed by the FBI. Several Panthers were killed (27 in 1969 alone) in shoot-outs with police, the group was heavily infiltrated by informers, and its leading members were either jailed or, in the case of Eldridge Cleaver, forced

into exile by 1970.[1] State repression rendered the group popular
with young urban blacks and antiwar leftists, but the Black Panther
Party rapidly dissolved into gangsterism and internal feuding. Huey
Newton, hailed as a revolutionary hero by white radicals like the
actress Jane Fonda, was released from jail in August 1970 but soon
eschewed black liberation for the apparently headier sustenance of
cocaine.[2] By that stage the Panthers had been abandoned by their
flailing SNCC allies who, having considered a merger between the
two organisations, found that the Panthers had rather less to offer
in terms of cognitive help and grass-roots support than they had
hitherto supposed. COINTELPRO operations exacerbated existing
divisions between the SNCC and Panther leaders which resulted in
a final, acrimonious split in July 1968.[3]

If the major forms of civil rights endeavour in the late twentieth
century were less spectacular than the media-conscious activities of
the Panthers, they not only served to block efforts by conservatives
to undermine the movement's achievements but also brought further
gains in terms of social policy and black self-respect. Foremost among
these spheres of activity were ongoing attempts by elements in the
federal government to institutionalise and expand the rights revolution of the 1960s, lobbying work at Washington by the Leadership
Conference on Civil Rights, and greater involvement by African
Americans in mainstream electoral politics.

By the late 1960s and early 1970s the American public had
become aware of the dramatic policy changes wrought by the civil
rights movement. Developments deep in the heart of the modern
administrative state helped sustain some of the momentum of the
1960s. Not only did they help to thrust highly contentious issues
such as busing and affirmative action to the forefront of the political
agenda, but they also helped to constrain attempts by unsympathetic
politicians to obstruct or delay civil rights reform. Richard Nixon
was the first of these politicians to discover how strong some of
these constraints could be.

The Nixon years

According to the socialist historian, Manning Marable, 'the forces
of racial inequality . . . won a major victory with the election of

---

1. M. Marable, *Race, Reform, and Rebellion: The Second Reconstruction in Black America,
1945–1990* (Basingstoke, 1991), p. 111.
2. H. Pearson, *The Shadow of the Panther: Huey Newton and the Price of Black Power
in America* (Reading, Mass., 1994).
3. C. Carson, *In Struggle: SNCC and the Black Awakening of the 1960s* (Cambridge,
Mass., and London, 1981), pp. 284–5.

Richard Nixon.'[4] At first sight the evidence marshalled in support of this case is powerful. As Marable rightly asserts, the new president cracked down hard on black radicals like the Black Panthers and made little secret of his opposition to forced desegregation. His chosen second in command, Governor Spiro T. Agnew of Maryland, was an outspoken critic of black rioters and Nixon himself appears to have had a fairly dim view of black capabilities. White House Chief of Staff H.R. Haldeman noted the president's belief, articulated at a staff meeting in April 1969, that the country's burgeoning welfare problem was essentially a racial one but that it was no longer possible to state this in public. Nixon, noted Haldeman, '[p]ointed out that there has never in history been an adequate black nation, and they are the only race of which this is true'.[5] Take into account the president's fall from grace in the Watergate affair and it is hardly surprising that Marable's charge seems to carry so much conviction.

The reality is rather more complicated than Marable suggests. Richard Nixon was elected in November 1968 on a platform which eschewed controversy. His main strategy was to avoid the mistake made by the Republican contender, Barry Goldwater, in the previous presidential contest. The conservative Arizona senator had gone to the country in 1964 as an advocate of state sovereignty and burdened with a hawkish foreign policy. Against a backdrop of economic prosperity, solid popular support for civil rights, and deep-rooted fears of nuclear war, Goldwater appeared as an irresponsible right-wing extremist alongside the liberal candidate, Lyndon Johnson. Once the Democrats had torn themselves apart over Vietnam, Nixon went to great pains in the 1968 campaign to depict himself as the moderate candidate most likely to appeal to the silent majority of Americans who wanted peace with honour in Vietnam and an end to domestic unrest. With Governor George Wallace of Alabama running as an independent and Hubert Humphrey failing to unite the Democrats after their shambolic convention in Chicago, Nixon had to do little more than run a restrained campaign to defeat his rivals. He did just that. Although his share of the popular vote was only 43.4 per cent compared to Humphrey's 42.7 and Wallace's 13.5, he won a comfortable majority of the electoral college vote. Wallace capitalised on the white reaction to federal policies by carrying Arkansas, Louisiana, Mississippi, Alabama and Georgia. By fighting as a responsible conservative Nixon swept the remaining

4. Marable, *Race*, p. 113.
5. H.R. Haldeman, *The Haldeman Diaries: Inside the Nixon White House* (New York, 1995), p. 66.

states in the South, a region clearly in the process of abandoning its previous attachment to the national Democratic Party.

In common with his immediate predecessors Richard Nixon's chief priority on entering the White House was foreign policy. The Vietnam War had replaced civil rights as the public's number one concern and he was determined to heal the internal divisions which had torpedoed Lyndon Johnson's political career. His preoccupation with the goal of a negotiated peace settlement in southeast Asia, therefore, rendered domestic policy a secondary sphere of interest for the incoming administration. If the new president did have a consistent objective in the domestic field it was summed up by his advocacy of the 'New Federalism'. According to the revisionist historian, Joan Hoff, this represented less a design to reduce federal spending than a wish to circumvent the power of the federal bureaucracy by centralising policy-making in the White House and devolving greater powers to the localities and the individual states.[6]

Richard Nixon was a complex man. A pragmatic politician without a keen moral sense to guide him, he possessed a siege mentality grounded in the conviction that liberal elites, their power entrenched in the universities and the media, were out to ruin him and the ordinary, decent folk he represented. This 'disturbed personality' was counterbalanced by a shrewd understanding of the American political system and the mind-set of the average voter.[7] An active player in national politics for nearly three decades, he understood the power of race in American life. His own record on civil rights was a relatively progressive one. Having established a reasonably sound rapport with black leaders as Eisenhower's vice-president, he had supported the major legislation of the 1960s and cautioned against Republican attempts to manipulate the white backlash for cynical political gain. In spite of condemning urban rioters, Nixon recognised the need to show that he did not intend to take up an extreme position on racial matters in the presidential campaign. Eight years previously he had watched John F. Kennedy steal black votes with his famous phone call to Coretta King. He determined not to make the same mistake again and attended Martin Luther King's funeral in April 1968.

The results of the 1968 election confirmed that blacks were unlikely to vote for Nixon because of their close affiliation to the Democrats and that large numbers of southern whites would support him on the basis of his conservatism. Convinced that Wallace

---

6. J. Hoff, *Nixon Reconsidered* (New York, 1994), p. 66.
7. J.M. Blum, *Years of Discord: American Politics and Society, 1961–1974* (New York and London, 1991), p. 319.

voters could be enticed into his camp in 1972, the new president embarked on a controversial bid for southern white votes – the first step towards the creation of what one aide presciently called 'the emerging Republican majority': a conservative majority based on southern whites, the booming western sunbelt, blue-collar ethnic voters in the North, and the suburban middle class.[8]

Nixon's southern strategy (or, more accurately, border-state strategy) rejected any attempt to reverse the major legislative gains of the civil rights movement but sought to hold the line against what whites in this region perceived as further assaults on their society and honour. Not only that, but it required turning a deaf ear to assertive civil rights leaders, particularly men like Ralph Abernathy of the SCLC who followed Martin Luther King in endorsing social democracy. When Abernathy led a coloured people's delegation to the White House in May 1969, his demands for greater federal aid in the struggle against social and economic inequality led the president to counsel against future such meetings.[9] The failure of black leaders to gain the ear of the president contrasted sharply with their often warm treatment at the Johnson White House. No starker evidence could have been provided that the cause of equal rights had been relegated to the second rank of political concerns.

Nixon's decision to befriend the white South against vindictive liberals took several forms during his first administration. He attempted, for example, to place a conservative southerner on the Supreme Court; to render the Voting Rights Act less offensive to southern sensibilities; and to slow the pace of school integration by assailing the controversial practice of busing (which involved the mandatory transportation of children to break down *de facto* segregation). Ironically, his bid for southern support was initially undermined by the administration's backing for affirmative action. The outcome of these sometimes contradictory efforts highlights the extent to which political, judicial and administrative developments helped to maintain some of the momentum built up by the civil rights movement.

One of the chief political obstacles to a diminution of federal activity in the civil rights sphere was continued Democratic control of both chambers of Congress. Responsive to the demands of the Leadership Conference on Civil Rights – well established as one of the most effective lobbying organisations in Washington – liberal Democrats in the Senate led a successful fight to block the

---

8. Ibid., p. 332. Kevin Phillips's *The Emerging Republican Majority* was published in 1969.
9. Haldeman, *Diaries*, pp. 69–70.

administration's attempts to replace the disgraced liberal judge, Abe Fortas, with a southern conservative. Angered, the president denounced the Senate's rejection of G. Harrold Carswell in April 1970 as 'regional discrimination' against the South.[10] Carswell had publicly supported Jim Crow when running for a seat in the Georgia legislature and was poorly qualified to serve on the nation's highest legal tribunal. His defeat (along with that of the Mississippian, Clement Haynsworth the previous year) indicated that in alliance with the Democratic Party the mainstream civil rights establishment had not entirely lost its ability to influence events.

The Leadership Conference's major accomplishment in the Nixon years was renewal of the 1965 Voting Rights Act. The president did not actually wish to terminate the statute. Public opinion outside the Deep South was strongly supportive of a measure which had proved so effective a purveyor of political rights for American blacks. What he did want to do was place a national ban on the use of literacy tests and eliminate the preclearance section of the act. The latter (section five which provided for the monitoring of state electoral legislation) was being interpreted broadly by the Supreme Court to allow extensive federal judicial review of new southern voting laws. Many of these statutes evinced a shift to at-large voting in several states of the Deep South – a covert attempt on the part of white political elites to dilute the impact of majority-black constituencies. As its reaction to the Carswell débâcle had revealed, the administration was particularly keen to ensure that the South ceased to be stigmatised for its dismal civil rights record. It was also determined to limit federal intervention in state affairs.

Once again the president's strategy foundered on the rock of a Democratic-controlled Senate. Aided by moderate northern Republicans, who themselves opposed any suggestion of roll-back on voting rights legislation, liberal Democrats worked successfully to retain preclearance as a central feature of the Voting Rights Act, the provisions of which were extended for five years. Nixon, however, did get his way on nationalising the statute. A new trigger formula was applied to cover states outside the South and literacy tests were banned throughout the country until August 1975.[11]

10. S.E. Ambrose, *Nixon: The Triumph of a Politician 1962–1972* (New York, 1989), p. 338.

11. H.D. Graham, *The Civil Rights Era: Origins and Development of National Policy 1960–1972* (New York and Oxford, 1990), pp. 346–65; A.M. Thernstrom, *Whose Votes Count? Affirmative Action and Minority Voting Rights* (Cambridge, Mass., and London, 1987), pp. 31–42.

The administration's rather belated attempts to revise the Voting Rights Act in a direction acceptable to the white South paled beside its opposition to busing. More than a decade after the *Brown* decision, the bulk of southern schools remained segregated owing to the creative avoidance strategies of southern whites and the readiness of federal district courts to accept gradual plans for integration. By 1966 the Department of Health, Education and Welfare, empowered by Title VI of the Civil Rights Act to withhold federal funds from recalcitrant school districts, had grown impatient with the slow pace of progress on school integration and issued guidelines to increase the pace of change. These guidelines were upheld in December of that year in a critical decision of the Fifth Circuit Court in New Orleans (*US v. Jefferson County Board of Education*).[12] Only when HEW threatened to withhold federal funds to promote school desegregation in Chicago did President Johnson, fearful of political fallout, display signs of cold feet. Sensing that it at last possessed the backing of the executive branch, the Supreme Court had finally demanded an end to delay in *Green v. New Kent County* in 1968. The following year, in *Alexander v. Holmes County*, it had ordered that all school districts had to abandon segregated school systems 'at once'.[13] Two years later, in *Swann v. Charlotte-Mecklenburg Board of Education*, the Supreme Court went one stage further by upholding the use of busing to achieve speedy and effective integration. Interpreting their powers widely (for busing appeared to have been barred by the 1964 Civil Rights Act) the judges built on the notion propounded in *Green* that positive action was necessary to remedy the injustices of the past. Nixon was less than pleased with the decision and, in spite of publicly stating his determination to uphold the law, privately urged Justice Department chiefs 'to keep their left wingers in step with my express policy – Do what the law requires and not one bit more.'[14]

Nixon's opposition to busing reflected both his own personal opposition to the practice and an astute awareness of its unpopularity with many whites throughout the country. The idea of liberal judges forcing white children to attend school with blacks was anathema to many people, northerners included, who cherished the concept of the neighbourhood school and who frequently held

---

12. On the most important public school desegregation decisions of the late 1960s and early 1970s see D.G. Nieman, *Promises to Keep: African-Americans and the Constitutional Order, 1776 to the Present* (New York and Oxford, 1991), pp. 176–9, 191–200.

13. Ibid., p. 193.   14. Quoted in Ambrose, *Nixon*, p. 460.

stereotypical views of African Americans as criminally inclined, ignorant, and lazy. Even though the Supreme Court's decision in *Milliken v. Bradley* (1974) stymied court-ordered busing between white suburbs and largely black metropolitan areas, the practice proved to be a powerful tool for social change.[15] By the autumn of 1972 southern schools were the most integrated in the nation – a dramatic turnaround since the mid-1960s.

Ultimately, Richard Nixon was able to come to terms with busing for the simple reason that it paid substantial political dividends. As long as the administration made plain its own dim view of the practice he could continue to sell himself to southern whites and beleaguered working-class and lower-middle-class voters in the North as the silent majority's best friend in high places. In March 1972, shortly before his re-election campaign began, he appeared on national television to urge Congress to impose a moratorium on busing. Privately he welcomed the fact that his proposal remained buried in the House Rules Committee over the summer, for the issue played a significant role in his impressive election win over George McGovern in November.[16]

If Congress and the federal courts were important agents in continuing the civil rights revolution after the demise of the movement, the same was true of certain elements in the federal bureaucracy. Particularly active in this capacity were those governmental agencies set up as a direct response to America's racial crisis in the late 1950s and 1960s. Foremost among them were the Civil Rights Commission (originally a creation of the 1957 Civil Rights Act) and two outgrowths of the Great Society: the Equal Employment Opportunity Commission (EEOC) and the Office of Federal Contract Compliance (OFCC). As the policy historian, Hugh Davis Graham, has suggested, these Washington agencies rapidly became integral points of what political scientists have termed 'iron triangles'. These triangles involved not only the government departments which administered policy, but also the congressional committees which funded the agencies, and the latter's principal client group: the civil rights lobby. By the late 1960s, argues Graham, these triangles had been extended to iron quadrilaterals by the onset of additional support from an activist federal judiciary.[17] Locked together these elements constituted a formidable force for policy development in

---

15. Nieman, *Promises*, pp. 198–200.   16. Ambrose, *Nixon*, pp. 523–4, 587.
17. Graham, *Civil Rights Era*, pp. 38, 362–5, 470.

the realm of civil rights. The most dramatic of all the initiatives which ensued was the drift towards affirmative action in the second half of the 1960s.

The notion that blacks were entitled to compensatory treatment to make up for past injustices was a controversial one in the 1960s and proved increasingly so as the century wore on. Although the civil rights movement convinced the majority of whites that African Americans had been deprived of their constitutional rights under Jim Crow, it was much less successful in persuading them that blacks were held back by historic and current patterns of social and economic discrimination in all parts of the country. However, as technological change began to reduce the number of unskilled jobs available to blacks in the United States after 1945, the need to push more energetically for better and greater work opportunities increased. The NAACP and the National Urban League were the initial spearheads for reform. Herbert Hill, the NAACP's white labour secretary, was an outspoken opponent of racism in the labour movement – particularly in the building trades where racism and closed apprenticeship systems kept black employment to a minimum. Calls for affirmative action, however, were few and far between in the early 1960s. Not only did the concept jar uneasily with the basic meritocratic values of the wider society (values which most civil rights leaders had been reluctant to question), but it also threatened to promote divisions between black organisations and their allies in the labour movement. When National CORE and the Urban League's Whitney Young did begin to endorse the idea of 'preferential treatment' during 1962 and 1963, many blacks rejected the policy on strategic grounds.[18]

Lawrence Reddick, a close associate of Martin Luther King, articulated the problem in a letter written in November 1963. Advising the SCLC president on possible topics for a forthcoming speech in Baltimore, Reddick told him to talk of 'maximum' rather than 'preferential' treatment for blacks. Since blacks had received such poor educational and training opportunities in the past, noted Reddick:

> we could well demand the best now. But this is not the same as saying that wh[i]te boys who have struggled hard to prepare themselves for jobs should be asked to step back for Negroes. We can never get

18. A. Meier and E. Rudwick, *CORE: A Study in the Civil Rights Movement 1942–1968* (New York, 1973), pp. 187, 191–2; N.J. Weiss, *Whitney M. Young, Jr, and the Struggle for Civil Rights* (Princeton, 1989), pp. 151–2.

away with this. It violates our principle of equality. And it is so contrary
to the American spirit that our opponents would fasten upon it as
our main objective and mobilize opposition against it.[19]

For the most part mainstream civil rights leaders followed Reddick's
advice and avoided any suggestion that they wanted to take jobs
away from whites in order to make up for the sins of the past.

As the movement's focus shifted from the regional problem of
Jim Crow to the deep-rooted national woes highlighted by growing evidence of urban black unrest, the wisdom of some form of
affirmative action took a stronger hold. Although President Kennedy
did include the phrase 'affirmative action' in an executive order of
1961, Lyndon Johnson was the first incumbent of the White House
to embrace the concept in public.[20] On 4 June 1965, in a com-
mencement address at Howard University drafted primarily by White
House aide Richard Goodwin, Johnson expressed his support for
the idea of compensatory treatment for blacks:

> You do not take a person who, for years, has been hobbled by chains
> and liberate him . . . and then say, 'you are free to compete with all
> the others,' and still justly believe that you have been completely fair.
>
> Thus it is not enough just to open the gates of opportunity. All our
> citizens must have the ability to walk through those gates.
>
> This is the next and the more profound stage of the battle for civil
> rights. We seek not just legal equity but human ability, not just equality
> as a right and a theory but equality as a fact and equality as a result.[21]

The president's comments were not simply designed to impress the
predominantly black audience at Howard. On 24 September Johnson
issued Executive Order 11246. This authorised the creation of the
OFCC by the Secretary of Labor, gave the new sub-agency the power
to withhold federal funds from discriminatory contractors, and
authorised it to use 'affirmative action' (the phrase was lifted directly
from Kennedy's 1961 order) to promote its chief goal of opening
up skilled jobs to blacks.[22] There was no suggestion at this stage that
government departments had been given the green light to use racial
quotas to boost black employment. The very notion of 'reverse discrimination' (as the policy was called by its critics) was anathema to
many Americans, not least to Jews who had suffered adversely from

19. L.D. Reddick to M.L. King, 27 November 1963, Box 20, Series 1, Martin Luther
King Papers, KC.

20. Graham, *Civil Rights Era*, p. 28.

21. *Public Papers of the Presidents: Lyndon B. Johnson 1965* (Washington, DC, 1966),
p. 636.

22. Graham, *Civil Rights Era*, p. 188.

quotas in the past – hence the language of the 1964 Civil Rights Act which appeared to outlaw quotas. By the end of the decade, however, affirmative action was recognised as a legitimate weapon of government policy notwithstanding the fact that it seemed to many Americans to represent a perversion of meritocratic values. How did this situation come about?

Hugh Davis Graham suggests that a number of political and structural factors were responsible for the dramatic shift in federal policy over affirmative action. The NAACP, he argues, was partly responsible because it led an effective national drive to flood the EEOC with protests concerning employment discrimination. Swamped by the number of complaints and charged with the task of ending employment discrimination, the agency was impelled to develop new strategies to deal with the massive problems confronting it. As well as computerising its records and introducing racial classifications into the process of data collection, the EEOC searched for ways to obviate the irksome need to prove discriminatory intent on the part of employers. Most of these focused on the agency's capacity to act in the same way as other regulatory agencies: that is, firstly, to make and enforce rules and, secondly, to show general patterns of racial discrimination rather than furnish evidence of intent to discriminate in individual cases.[23]

In May 1966 Sonia Pressman, a Jewish staff lawyer working for the EEOC, suggested that employment statistics could be used to show the existence of such broad patterns and that the agency should attempt to apply the legal doctrine of the prima facie case in order to substitute an effects-based policy for one grounded in proof of intent.[24] That is, if blacks could be shown statistically to be excluded from certain occupations, judges might be persuaded to infer the existence of racial discrimination in the hiring procedures of federal contractors.

Although moves were made to put Pressman's ideas into practice during 1967 and 1968 it was the incoming Nixon administration which really threw its weight behind affirmative action by supporting implementation of the Philadelphia Plan in 1969.[25] The latter, an affirmative action scheme devised by the OFCC to end the high incidence of racial discrimination in the construction industry, had been blocked originally on technical grounds by the US Solicitor-General. Nixon, however, recognised that the Plan provided him

23. Ibid., pp. 234–44.   24. Ibid., pp. 244–7.
25. For a full account of the origins of the Philadelphia Plan see ibid., pp. 278–97.

with an ideal opportunity to drive a stake into the heart of the Democratic coalition. Specifically it would enable him to divide the civil rights establishment from organised labour by stirring up opposition to affirmative action in the building trades.[26] Consequently, he allowed the liberal secretary of labor, George Schultz, to implement a plan which did indeed provoke trouble within the civil rights camp but also produced rules designed to ensure a representative enrolment of minorities in the construction industry. Even though the OFCC lacked the necessary enforcement machinery to produce radical changes in this and other sectors of the economy, its senior partner in the fight against employment discrimination, the EEOC, was given greater teeth by the 1972 Equal Employment Opportunity Act. Backed by strong support from an expanding rights lobby in Washington which included women's groups as well as the Leadership Conference, Congress granted the EEOC enhanced powers to enforce its rulings in the courts. It also extended the agency's coverage to include state and federal government employees. Although the Nixon administration did succeed in preventing the EEOC from gaining cease-and-desist authority, the act nonetheless represented an important victory for the cause of black rights in America. Employment discrimination against blacks, other minorities, and women did not end but the threat of litigation induced increasing numbers of business companies to adopt affirmative action programmes which complied with federal guidelines.

Crucial to the institutionalisation of affirmative action in the late 1960s and early 1970s was the backing which the doctrine received from the courts. By the time the Third Circuit Court of Appeals had upheld the legality of the Philadelphia Plan in April 1971 the notion that historic wrongs could be remedied in the present seemed to be well established in the federal courts. The critical decision, so far as employment discrimination was concerned, was *Griggs v. Duke Power Co.* handed down by the US Supreme Court on 8 March 1971.[27] Speaking for a unanimous court Chief Justice Warren Burger, a moderate conservative who proved rather more progressive on civil rights than many observers expected, struck down a lower court decision upholding an aptitude test instituted by Duke Power at its plant in Draper, North Carolina. Prior to passage of the 1964 Civil Rights Act the company's labour force had been segregated in line with Jim Crow practices elsewhere in the Deep South. Blacks, therefore, were confined to the lowest paid jobs in the plant and, because

26. Graham, *Civil Rights Era*, p. 325.   27. Ibid., pp. 383–90.

seniority lines were racially segregated, were deprived of the chance to earn the same salaries as whites. When Title VII of the Civil Rights Act became effective in July 1964, the company introduced an aptitude test for employees of all races seeking promotion to the higher grades. Although the Supreme Court accepted that the test itself was racially neutral, Burger declared it unlawful on the grounds that it contravened Title VII. Specifically he ruled that Section 702(a)(2) was designed to prohibit practices that had a 'disparate impact' on groups protected by the act. In this particular case the existence of systemic employment discrimination in the past ensured that historic injustices would remain entrenched, the existence of an apparently neutral test notwithstanding.

Significantly, Burger also accepted the EEOC's view that results were more important than intent. Even though affirmative action clearly conflicted with some of the most basic tenets of American liberalism (not least its emphasis on group rather than individual rights) and appeared to many to be unlawful under the congressional legislation of 1964, the highest court in the land had labelled it right and proper.[28] What had once been a marginal opinion even within the civil rights movement itself was now confirmed as mainstream federal policy.

Clearly, Richard Nixon was not, as he claimed privately, 'ultraliberal' on matters of race.[29] Nor, equally patently, was he a reforming president in the same mould as Lyndon Johnson. However, to condemn him as a counter-revolutionary on the civil rights front is to miss the point. The direct action phase of the black freedom struggle had largely come to an end by 1968 but manifestly the cause retained sufficient impetus in the courts, the federal bureaucracy, and Congress to promote further progress in the controversial spheres of school desegregation and employment discrimination (both areas in which the civil rights movement had had limited impact) and to launch new initiatives in the realm of voting rights. Richard Nixon did not like all of these developments. His increasingly outspoken opposition to busing was one reason why Bishop Stephen G. Spottswood, national chairman of the NAACP, told the Association's annual conference in 1972 that 'the NAACP considers itself in a state of war against President Nixon and his Constitution wreckers'.[30] Nixon, moreover, never gave civil rights top priority as

28. H.D. Graham, 'Race, History, and Policy: African Americans and Civil Rights Since 1964', *Journal of Policy History* 6 (1994), 23.
29. R.M. Nixon, *The Memoirs of Richard Nixon* (pbk edn, London, 1979), p. 444.
30. Quoted in Graham, *Civil Rights Era*, p. 446.

his predecessor had done and was, as James Farmer quite correctly observed, far more interested in power politics than acting as a moral exemplar for the rest of the nation.[31] However, given the extent of black support for the Democratic Party and the rapid unravelling of the civil rights consensus in the mid-1960s, it was perhaps more surprising that the administration, preoccupied as it was with foreign relations, developed as many civil rights initiatives as it did. As well as endorsing the Philadelphia Plan, Nixon set up the Office of Minority Business Enterprise to signal his support for black capitalism and backed the Family Assistance Plan, a radical, but ill-fated proposal to provide the indigent and working poor with a government-supplied income.[32] Although the administration did attempt, with some success, to undermine the bureaucratic structures of the Great Society (particularly the OEO and the CAP), it embraced the notion that poverty was a legitimate concern of American government. As a result, federal expenditure on poverty programmes increased dramatically under Nixon. By the time he left office in disgrace in August 1974, Social Security and welfare payments had doubled since he became president. Federal spending on food stamps, for example, a vital weapon in the war against malnutrition in the rural South and the inner cities, was $5 billion in 1975 compared with $36 million at the dawn of the Great Society in the mid-1960s. Coverage had been extended from 633,000 people to 20 million.[33] Spending on departmental resources in the fight against racial discrimination also grew. In 1968 the EEOC possessed a staff of just 359 and a budget of $13.2 million. Four years later 1,640 persons worked for the agency and its budget had more than doubled.[34] In no small measure did the War on Poverty outlast both Lyndon Johnson and the civil rights movement itself.

Statistics indicate that the growth of federal anti-poverty efforts did have a meliorative impact on social conditions in the black community – at least in combination with domestic economic prosperity. The median income gap between blacks and whites decreased significantly during the Johnson and Nixon years as increasing numbers of blacks were brought into the middle class by greater job opportunities – many of them provided by affirmative action

31. J. Farmer, *Lay Bare the Heart: An Autobiography of the Civil Rights Movement* (New York and Scarborough, Ont., 1985), p. 334.

32. Ambrose, *Nixon*, pp. 293–4, 314–15, 328, 366–7, 391, 404–6.

33. D. Chalmers, *And the Crooked Places Made Straight: The Struggle for Social Change in the 1960s* (Baltimore and London, 1991), p. 63.

34. Graham, *Civil Rights Era*, p. 448.

programmes in the public and private sectors of the economy. By 1974 just under a third of black families had incomes below the poverty line compared with nearly half in 1960 (and 87 per cent in 1940).[35]

The gains wrought by the civil rights movement's central strategy of seeking greater federal intervention in American life are clearly apparent in these figures. However, further progress (as distinct from simple protection of the status quo) on civil rights was dependent on two factors. The first was continued economic prosperity in the United States. The second was maintenance of a political consensus on the importance of government action to end racial discrimination in fields like housing, employment and education. By the mid-1970s the country had been hit hard by 'stagflation' – a debilitating mix of economic recession and inflation which greatly reduced the public's enthusiasm not only for high government spending but also 'zero sum' policies like affirmative action which appeared to reward minorities at the expense of the white majority. What Donald Nieman has called 'the Indian Summer of the civil rights movement' had faded to winter by the end of the decade.[36]

Litigation and lobbying in the 1970s and 1980s

Although the direct-action wing of the national civil rights coalition had virtually expired by the late 1960s, the conservative wing of the movement, led principally by the NAACP and the National Urban League, survived intact. Under Nixon, the latter functioned almost as a quasi-public agency of the federal government, favoured as it was by an administration which regarded black radicals with the utmost suspicion.[37] The NAACP remained the nation's largest civil rights group. Roy Wilkins's determination to pursue a moderate course had helped to preserve the organisation intact, even if survival had been achieved at the expense of intellectual dynamism

---

35. Figures provided by S. Thernstrom, 'The Quest for Equality: Race and Racism in America and Britain', unpublished paper delivered at the Institute of United States Studies Fulbright Colloquium, Senate House, University of London, 27 March 1995.

36. Nieman, *Promises*, p. 191.

37. H.H. Haines, *Black Radicals and the Civil Rights Movement, 1954–1970* (Knoxville, 1988), p. 125.

and much grass-roots appeal. In conjunction with the Inc Fund, the Association persisted in its historic effort to reduce racial discrimination through litigation and lobbying. When the Supreme Court gave the green light to busing, the NAACP played a major role in launching school desegregation suits and publicly backing integration orders in the lower courts. The strategy proved controversial in the black community. While conservatives feared it would contribute further to the growth of a white backlash, many blacks, by no means all of them radicals, demanded that resources be channelled into improving the quality of education in black schools rather than into complicated busing plans. Fears of an adverse reaction on the part of lower-class whites, one resembling the response to the *Brown* decision, were certainly justified. The most vigorous response, however, occurred not in the South but in Boston, the scene of black school protests since the early 1960s.

When Federal District Judge W. Arthur Garrity called for immediate implementation of a school integration plan in June 1974, the new leader of the city's NAACP branch, Thomas Atkins, came out strongly in favour of the court order, thereby inflaming passions in the mostly Irish-American, working-class district of South Boston.[38] Viewing the court order as a premeditated plan on the part of the liberal establishment and its black clients to destroy their community, the inhabitants formed a well-organised anti-busing movement to defend neighbourhood institutions from what they regarded as outside attack. Representative of the 'silent majority' to whom Nixon had sought to appeal throughout his term of office, South Bostonians used the civil rights protests of the previous decade as a model for their own campaign. As well as setting up their own alternative schools along the lines of the parallel structures developed in Mississippi, they also sought to galvanise support through the use of such familiar tactics as prayer marches and sit-ins. In the spring of 1975 they even organised their own March on Washington.[39] Although the anti-busing movement in Boston had lost momentum by the late 1970s, it contributed significantly to the general trend towards private education and white flight from the cities which undermined desegregation efforts throughout the country. Along with affirmative action, the busing controversy made race one of the most salient factors in late-twentieth-century American politics.

38. R.P. Formisano, *Boston Against Busing: Race, Class, and Ethnicity in the 1960s and 1970s* (Chapel Hill and London, 1991), p. 72.
39. Ibid., pp. 140–2.

Although the NAACP's continuing efforts to promote integration through litigation proved counter-productive at times, its lobbying activities in Washington did much to prevent the achievements of the civil rights revolution from being undermined. This was true throughout the conservative 1970s and 1980s when the NAACP, in its capacity as the most important black organisation in the Leadership Conference on Civil Rights, helped not only to stymie conservative forces in Congress but also to promote actively the welfare of blacks and other minorities. Arguably its greatest triumph behind the scenes in Washington was secured in 1981–82 when the Leadership Conference won a 25-year extension to the Voting Rights Act.

The victory was a remarkable one because it came at a time when the forces of American conservatism appeared to be massing for a full-scale assault on the faltering liberal notion that federal power could be deployed to reduce the incidence of racial discrimination and poverty in the United States.[40] The immediate cause for concern was the election of Ronald Reagan in November 1980. As Republican governor of California between 1966 and 1975 the former Hollywood actor had won plaudits for facing down black radicals, anti-war protesters and hippies. At the end of the 1970s he capitalised on a growing sense of national decline and entered the White House promising to restore America's hegemony on the world stage and to revitalise the country domestically by cutting taxes and reducing the amount of federal government intrusion in everyday life. Although Reagan did not run for president as a white supremacist, he appeared to represent a much greater threat to the gains of the civil rights era than Richard Nixon. Certainly a states' rights campaign speech at Philadelphia, Mississippi, the scene of one of the worst atrocities of the 1960s, seemed poorly calculated to discourage the rise of racist sentiment in the South. Accordingly, the NAACP and its allies in the Leadership Conference mobilised to confront the new president and other right-wing Republicans elected to national office in 1980.

By 1981 the Leadership Conference had become one of the largest umbrella groups in Washington, incorporating 165 separate organisations representing a variety of constituencies including blacks, Hispanics, women, the disabled and the elderly.[41] Elephantine though it had grown since its foundation in 1950, internal power still rested with the long-established axis between the NAACP and

---

40. The following account of the 1981–82 campaign to extend the Voting Rights Act owes much to Thernstrom, *Whose Votes Count?*, pp. 79–136.

41. Ibid., p. 110.

the organised labour movement. Even though the latter's influence was on the wane in America, it remained an important player alongside blacks in the national Democratic Party. Together the two blocs hoped to utilise their connections with the Democratic leadership in Congress to forestall an expected assault on the Voting Rights Act, due to expire in August 1982. In so doing they also sought to overturn a recent decision of the US Supreme Court (*City of Mobile v. Bolden*) placing the burden of proof in preclearance cases on plaintiffs – not the first indication that the court was beginning to move in a more conservative direction on matters pertaining to civil rights.

Leading the fight to prevent right-wingers like Strom Thurmond of South Carolina and Orrin Hatch of Utah from gutting the bill to renew the Voting Rights Act was Ralph Neas, the Leadership Conference's new executive director. Encouraged by the NAACP's Washington lobbyist, Althea Simmons, Neas set up a steering committee in the spring of 1981 to formulate strategy during the coming months. Essentially the aim was to marshal overwhelming support in the House of Representatives in order to reduce the chance of opposition in the conservative Senate (where Hatch and Thurmond occupied important committee posts) or the possibility of an executive veto.

By working closely with influential liberal Democrats on the House Judiciary Committee, Neas succeeded in his first objective: the holding of congressional hearings likely to increase public awareness of the potential threat to minority voting rights. In pursuit of the same objective he also initiated a well-orchestrated campaign to bring constituency pressure to bear on members of Congress. The campaign, underwritten financially by some of the same philanthropic foundations which had been active in support of the civil rights movement, represented a more sophisticated variant of the one which had preceded passage of the 1964 Civil Rights Act. As well as benefiting from substantial media exposure, it also made effective use of the grass-roots memberships of the NAACP and the National Organization of Women.

Neas's second step was to attempt to win the backing of Chicago's Republican congressman, Henry Hyde. Hyde, who represented the white voters of Cicero as well as black and Hispanic voters on the West Side, was the ranking Republican on the Civil Rights Subcommittee of the House Judiciary Committee and a staunch foe of preclearance. (In common with many conservatives he believed that preclearance was not only a recipe for proportional representation but also an insult to the South. 'For sovereign states to go through that procedure', he contended 'was demeaning, like sitting in the back of the bus.')[42] If Hyde could be induced to support a compromise bill acceptable to the Leadership Conference's steering committee, then it was highly unlikely that conservatives would oppose it.

Although Neas failed to win Hyde's backing for such a bill, he won the House battle by getting two moderate Republicans to co-sponsor a more radical proposal acceptable to the steering committee which itself had been deeply divided over the compromise strategy. The Republican support was crucial, for the measure received almost unanimous backing from the House sub-committee and was then passed by the full House by 389 votes to 24. In the Senate the moderate Kansas Republican Robert Dole took control of the bill which passed the Senate 85–5 on 18 June. The civil rights forces were elated. Even though they had not won a permanent extension to the Voting Rights Act, they had secured a 25-year extension and reversed the damage done by the Supreme Court in the *Mobile* case. (The statute made clear that the existence of a pattern of discrimination was sufficient to prove that an electoral district had unlawfully discriminated against certain groups of voters.) Particularly impressive was the size of support for the bill. Even conservative Republicans like Strom Thurmond had been persuaded that the American public would countenance no counter-revolution on voting rights.

The primacy of politics

The very fact that a former arch-segregationist like Thurmond could be induced to support an extension to what, initially, had been a blatantly sectional statute was clear evidence of the transformation which had taken place in southern politics since the mid-1960s. The main reason why Thurmond supported passage of the 1982 legislation was that one-third of his constituents were blacks – people empowered by the original Voting Rights Act.[43] As the elderly Republican (and former Dixiecrat) explained on the floor of the Senate, 'I must take into account the common perception that a vote against the bill indicates opposition to the right to vote and, indeed, opposition to the group of citizens who are protected under the Voting Rights Act.'[44]

42. Quoted in M. Pertschuk, *Giant Killers* (New York and London, 1986), p. 158.
43. Thernstrom, *Whose Votes Count?*, p. 109.
44. Quoted in N. Cohodas, *Strom Thurmond and the Politics of Southern Change* (New York, 1993), p. 480.

Politics, broadly defined to include community building efforts as well as mainstream electoral participation, was the sphere into which the bulk of black protest energies were channelled after the waning of the civil rights movement. Signs that the latter had instilled into African Americans a much stronger sense that they possessed the capacity to influence the world around them could be found throughout the United States in the last third of the twentieth century. Frequently their efforts to nurture healthier communities testified to the existence of a growing sense among black people that integration was not the panacea which some civil rights leaders had once (and in some cases, still) believed it to be. They also indicated that direct action tactics remained weapons in the arsenal of grass-roots organisations, the relative lack of national co-ordination for such protest activities notwithstanding.

A plethora of campus and community groups, not a few of them spawned by the civil rights movement and energised by the corresponding growth in black consciousness, targeted a wide range of salient issues, some of them grouped around the search for greater black control over education. Among the most important objectives was community control of neighbourhood schools – an objective threatened, ironically, by the advent of court-ordered school desegregation. Northern urban radicals had long viewed integration as an obstacle to black cultural and political unity. Campaigns to secure more jobs for black teachers and greater emphasis on black-oriented studies were a feature of protest activity in several cities in the mid-1960s and had a predictably baleful impact on relations between black community leaders and white-dominated teachers' unions.

Southern blacks were largely unaffected by public school desegregation until the Supreme Court ordered its immediate implementation in the late 1960s. Once the integration process was under way they frequently discovered that it was taking place on white terms – that black teachers were suffering disproportionately from job losses and that black children were being bused into white schools rather than vice versa. Although this made sense in material terms (the white schools were invariably better equipped than their black equivalents), it also had a devastating impact on community education in black areas. As a result African Americans in some parts of the South united to oppose the developing trend. Among them were the inhabitants of rural Hyde County in North Carolina, a remote area hitherto untouched by the civil rights movement. When the local school board found itself threatened

with the loss of HEW funding in 1968 if it did not commence desegregation, it decided, without consultation, to open up the county's
white schools to black children and shut down the two black schools
in the area. Instead of accepting this development, Hyde County
blacks perceived a central pillar of their community to be under
attack and, with the help of the SCLC, inaugurated a year-long
movement-style campaign involving demonstrations, sit-ins and a
pupil strike. In November 1969 white voters refused to grant higher
taxes to expand the county's white schools to accommodate black
students. As a result the education board was forced to maintain the
black schools under its jurisdiction, allowing the African-American
community to claim a famous victory.[45]

Protests such as this revealed the determination of black people
to mobilise in defence of their communities. Dependent for success
on a range of grass-roots institutions as well as outside help, such
campaigns were clearly contests for power even though they were
not necessarily pursued through the medium of a political party.
The 1965 Voting Rights Act, however, did present southern blacks
with the opportunity to participate actively in mainstream electoral
politics and it was into that realm that much of the energy deriving
from the civil rights movement was directed. The results were
impressive and, to some degree, justified Bayard Rustin's belief
that the civil rights cause could only succeed through involvement
in coalition politics.[46]

Although abortive attempts were made to set up a national black
political organisation during the early 1970s, most prospective black
office-holders perceived the Democratic Party as the most effective
vehicle for securing power.[47] Sloughing off increasing numbers of
southern whites as a consequence of its support for civil rights, the
national Democratic organisation became the principal vehicle for
black political aspirations in the late twentieth century while the
Republicans shifted simultaneously to the right. The resulting transformation in the South meant that what had once been the main
organ of white supremacy was, in many areas, heavily dependent on
black votes. Just as southern Republican parties had been liberalised by their black voting constituencies during Reconstruction,

---

45. D.S. Cecelski, *Along Freedom Road: Hyde County, North Carolina, and the Fate of Black Schools in the South* (Chapel Hill, 1994).

46. B. Rustin, 'From Protest to Politics: The Future of the Civil Rights Movement', in Rustin, *Down The Line: The Collected Writings of Bayard Rustin* (Chicago, 1971), pp. 111–21.

47. For an account of the ill-fated National Black Political Assembly see Marable, *Race*, pp. 122–3, 133–4, 137.

their Democratic counterparts in the 1970s and 1980s emerged as the main proponents of positive state action in opposition to the conservative, anti-tax Republicans who drew strong support from the suburban middle-classes and white voters in the old plantation districts.

The Voting Rights Act and its subsequent extensions transformed southern politics by empowering the region's once disfranchised minority. In the districts where blacks formed a significant majority (roughly 60 per cent or over) of the total population, they often won control of their own localities. This meant that in some parts of the Deep South they elected black city councillors, state legislators and members of Congress for the first time since Reconstruction. For example, Lowndes County, Alabama, a centre of civil rights activity in the mid-1960s, began to fall under black political control in 1970 when John Hulett was elected sheriff.[48] Other former Jim Crow strongholds in rural areas of the Deep South took longer to capture, but ultimately many of them proved unable to withstand the influx of blacks into the local polity. Plaquemines Parish, the stronghold of the racist Perez dynasty in Louisiana, elected an African American to the local council in 1979. Bogalusa, scene of some of Louisiana's worst racial violence in the 1960s, chose an NAACP leader as president of the city council in the same year.[49]

Continuing white migration from city centres to the region's growing suburbs enabled southern blacks to exercise political power in urban areas as well. By 1970 blacks constituted 51 per cent of the total population of metropolitan Atlanta. In 1972 they played an important role in electing one of Martin Luther King's lieutenants, Andrew Young, to Congress. The following year they were the critical factor in the election of Morehouse graduate, Maynard Jackson, as mayor. Although other urban victories followed, perhaps the most impressive southern black triumph occurred in 1979 when Richard Arrington was elected mayor of Birmingham, Alabama, with overwhelming support from local blacks and the backing of a small minority of liberal whites and business leaders.[50] The process begun in that notoriously violent city by the election of a white moderate, Albert Boutwell, and the ensuing SCLC campaign in 1963 appeared to have reached its logical conclusion.

48. C.W. Eagles, *Outside Agitator: Jon Daniels and the Civil Rights Movement in Alabama* (Chapel Hill and London, 1993).
49. A. Fairclough, *Race and Democracy: The Civil Rights Struggle in Louisiana, 1915–1972* (Athens, Ga, 1995), pp. 465–6.
50. H.L. Perry, 'The Evolution and Impact of Biracial Coalitions and Black Mayors in Birmingham and New Orleans' in *Racial Politics in American Cities*, ed. R.P. Downing, D.R. Marshall and D.H. Tabb (New York and London, 1990), pp. 142–3.

Northern blacks also chalked up spectacular political gains during the same period as they tried to break free from the urban machines which had helped to limit their progress in the first two-thirds of the twentieth century. Harold Washington's stunning seizure of power in the Windy City in 1983 provided clear evidence that the energies dissipated by the collapse of the civil rights movement had not vanished completely.[51] Washington, the son of a black minister, had occupied a variety of positions in municipal government under the administration of Mayor Richard J. Daley, Martin Luther King's nemesis during the SCLC's abortive open-housing campaign in 1966. When Daley died of a heart attack in 1976 his powerful machine began to surrender its grip on the city. The first major sign of this was the election of Jane Byrne as mayor in April 1979. Byrne, an Irish-American Democrat, had campaigned as a reform candidate and appealed directly to black voters (roughly 40 per cent of the city's voting-age population) who had become soured with the crumbling machine. Once Byrne was in office, however, she failed to implement campaign promises to the black community and attempted to undermine the latter's political influence by reducing the number of black wards in the city. Chicago blacks were galvanised into action by the mayor's efforts to ride roughshod over them and Harold Washington, by this time a congressman, emerged as the man most likely to unite them.

Washington's route to city hall was a tortuous one. Crucial to his success was the mobilisation of Chicago's disparate black community by a loose coalition of civil rights groups reminiscent of the heady days of the 1960s. Prominent among these groups were the local branches of the NAACP and the National Urban League, the Rev. Jesse Jackson's People United to Save Humanity (PUSH), and Lu Palmer's Chicago Black United Committees, an umbrella organisation representing numerous civic groups active at the grass-roots level. During 1982–83 100,000 new voters were added to the electoral roll owing to financial aid from the wealthy black businessman, Edward Gardner, and the efforts of more than 200 indigenous black organisations, many of them legacies of the civil rights movement.[52] The coalition also organised a successful boycott of the city's annual lakefront summer festival in order to dramatise what rapidly came to resemble an old-style civil rights crusade. Buoyed

---

51. The following account of the 1983 mayoral election in Chicago is based largely on P. Kleppner, *Chicago Divided: The Making of a Black Mayor* (De Kalb, Ill., 1985), and R.T. Starks and M.B. Preston, 'Harold Washington and the Politics of Reform in Chicago: 1983–1987' in *Racial Politics*, ed. Downing *et al.*, pp. 88–107.

52. Kleppner, *Chicago Divided*, p. 146.

by the many manifestations of community solidarity, Washington
finally announced his decision to challenge Mayor Byrne in the
Democratic primary.

Washington won the ensuing contest for two reasons. Firstly,
Chicago blacks, successfully mobilised by the racially polarised atmosphere and the many exhortations to vote, turned out in record
numbers to support their candidate. As a local journalist put it,
they had, for the first time, been made to see voting as 'the advancement of the civil rights movement' with the result that registering
at the polls became 'as much in vogue . . . as marching was in the
1960s'.[53] Secondly, the opposition was divided between Byrne and
Richard M. Daley, son of the late mayor. The two white candidates
split the white vote allowing Washington to secure the Democratic
nomination with almost unanimous black support and a smattering
of votes from Latinos and wealthy lakeside liberals. In the general
election he defeated the Republican candidate, Bernard Epton,
who fought a racist campaign, aided and abetted by the disaffected
chairman of the Cook County Democratic Party. An estimated 98.9
per cent of voters in the city's black wards supported Washington.
He picked up over 40 per cent of the lakefront vote and ran well
among Hispanics, but his average vote in the white wards was a
paltry 5.4 per cent.[54]

One of the most significant features of Harold Washington's
triumph was the high level of turnout among poor inner-city blacks
– over 80 per cent (roughly equivalent to the registration rates in
working-class and middle-class areas). This was the section of the
nation's black population which even the civil rights movement
had struggled to mobilise and which was renowned for its political
cynicism. The events in Chicago indicated that poor people could be
galvanised into acting politically by appeals to racial solidarity and
the prospect of tangible material rewards. As such they appeared to
indicate that Jesse Jackson's dream of the Democratic presidential
nomination were far from fanciful.

Jesse Jackson was the most important black politician of the
1980s. A South Carolinian by birth (his father was an illiterate sharecropper) and a graduate of North Carolina A & T in Greensboro,
he had enrolled at the Chicago Theological Seminary and risen to
a position of influence within the SCLC as head of its successful
Operation Breadbasket in the second half of the 1960s. After King's

---

53. Quoted in Kleppner, *Chicago Divided*, p. 146.
54. Electoral statistics are contained in ibid., p. 98.

assassination, Jackson's forceful personality and endorsement of black capitalism caused some white commentators to herald him as King's natural heir. Jackson himself did little to dispel such notions, indicating as he did that he had cradled the dying King in his arms. Viewed as an inveterate self-publicist by some SCLC staff members, Jackson was disciplined by Ralph Abernathy in December 1971 after revelations of financial improprieties in the running of the Black Expo, an arts, crafts and business forum, in Chicago.[55] He immediately left the SCLC and founded his own Chicago-based organisation, PUSH. Essentially an outgrowth of Operation Breadbasket, PUSH not only developed as a nationwide pressure group to open up more jobs for blacks in private industry but also constituted a solid launching pad for Jackson's political ambitions. In 1984 and 1988 the Chicago minister campaigned strongly for the Democratic presidential nomination as head of a newly formed organisation, the Rainbow Coalition. Jackson failed to secure the nomination on either occasion but his efforts helped to keep black concerns at the forefront of the political agenda in a decade when most white Americans seemed bent on ignoring them. The two campaigns not only enhanced Jesse Jackson's reputation as the legitimate heir of the civil rights movement, but also highlighted the strengths and limitations of mainstream political action.

Jackson's 1984 bid received much of its initial momentum from the strong opposition to President Ronald Reagan which existed among most African Americans. Although the administration had failed in its attempt to dilute the preclearance provisions in the Voting Rights Act, it found many other ways to assault black civil rights. Responsive mainly to recession-soured white voters who wanted an end to welfare handouts (generally, though wrongly, held to benefit blacks alone) and the introduction of tax cuts, Reagan had entered the White House strongly committed to the idea that government was the source of, not the solution to, America's ills. Blacks stood to suffer disproportionately from major cuts in welfare spending because of their prevalence among the country's poor: in 1980 they constituted 11.7 per cent of the country's population but furnished 43 per cent of those receiving Aid to Families with Dependent Children, 34.4 per cent of subsidised housing recipients, and 35.1 per cent of persons on food stamps.[56] Reagan's appointment of the

55. A. Fairclough, *To Redeem the Soul of America: The Southern Christian Leadership Conference and Martin Luther King, Jr* (Athens, Ga, 1987), pp. 392–4.

56. I. Morgan, *Beyond the Liberal Consensus: A Political History of the United States Since 1965* (London, 1994), p. 168.

conservative Arizona judge, Sandra Day O'Connor, to the Supreme
Court in 1981, the Justice Department's public opposition to affirmative action, and an ill-advised attempt in 1982 to allow segregated
southern colleges to benefit from federal tax breaks all added to
the sense that the president was a dangerous right-winger in the
mould of Barry Goldwater rather than Richard Nixon. Little wonder,
therefore, that blacks rallied behind one of their own when Jesse
Jackson first offered himself as a candidate for the presidency.

Jackson's principal strategy was to forge an alliance of the dispossessed in America.[57] This meant garnering support from the same
kind of minority ethnic and occupational groups to whom the SCLC
and Robert Kennedy had sought to appeal in 1968 and who had
failed to turn out to vote in the ensuing decade. The all-time low
turnout in the 1980 presidential election – 53 per cent – revealed
not only that the American political system was losing legitimacy
but also the existence of a vast pool of untapped support. Jackson,
therefore, hoped to unite poor whites, Hispanics, Native Americans,
Arab Americans, Asian Americans and sympathetic white liberals
with his core support in the black community under a broadly
populist banner. The vision was less that of a truly integrated society
or a social democratic utopia (King's dreams of 1963 and 1968
respectively) than of a just, plural and capitalist republic in which
different ethnic groups lived and worked together in harmony.
Practically, this meant a deeper understanding of racial differences,
a fairer distribution of the national wealth and an end to the hawkish
imperialism of the Reagan administration.

Jesse Jackson's 1984 bid for the Democratic presidential nomination was modelled solidly on the civil rights movement and in some
senses can be seen as an extension of the Poor People's Campaign.
This was particularly true of his effort to mobilise local communities behind an explicitly national agenda using the substantial
resources of the black church. By casting himself as a charismatic
leader in the same mould as Martin Luther King, he fashioned less
a regular political campaign than a moral crusade to end injustice
in the United States. Jackson meetings were invariably emotional
affairs in which community religion and protest politics were blended

57. On Jackson's presidential campaigns in the 1980s see A.L. Reed, Jr, *The Jesse
Jackson Phenomenon: The Crisis of Purpose in Afro-American Politics* (New Haven and London, 1986); A. Fairclough, 'What Makes Jesse Run?' *JAS* 22 (1988), 77–86; K. Tate,
From Protest to Politics: The New Black Voters in American Elections (Cambridge, Mass.
and London, 1993); J. White, *Black Leadership in America: From Booker T. Washington
to Jesse Jackson* (London and New York, 1990), pp. 173–89.

expertly in the long-established tradition of the black church. Struggle and deliverance were prominent themes in Jackson's political sermons, just as they had been in those of his late mentor. Even though the candidate placed less stress on love than King, his frequent biblical allusions, visions of a better America and calls for greater toleration of racial and cultural differences in the United States tapped the same rich vein of black spirituality and patriotism as the SCLC in its heyday. Jackson's campaign was also dependent for money and support on a broad network of black ministers and churches. According to one estimate it had received the backing of over 90 per cent of the black clergy within two months of its inauguration.[58] It was also endorsed by the powerful National Baptist Convention headed by the Rev. Theodore Jemison, the man who had masterminded the Baton Rouge bus boycott in 1953, and was run by staffers including the veteran SCLC activist, the Rev. C.T. Vivian.[59]

Although Jackson received strong backing from the church in 1984, he failed to win wholehearted support from other black leaders, particularly those like Andrew Young, the mayor of Atlanta, who possessed closer ties to the national Democratic Party. As well as disliking what they saw as his self-seeking efforts to don the robe of Martin Luther King, they also resented Jackson's claims to speak for the black community in America and believed that the only politician who stood any chance of defeating Reagan in the general election was Walter Mondale, the preferred candidate of the liberal-labour wing of the Democratic Party and formerly Humphrey's go-between at the 1964 Atlantic City convention. Lacking the support of established black leaders, Jackson also damaged his appeal to sympathetic whites by forging an alliance with the controversial black nationalist, Louis Farrakhan, by calling for the creation of a Palestinian state, and by referring to New York City as 'Hymietown'.

Whatever it may have lacked in terms of political nous and organisation, Jackson's campaign was remarkably successful. Overall he finished third out of seven candidates in the Democratic primary race, winning over 3.5 million votes and finishing first in Louisiana and the District of Columbia. His support for policies such as affirmative action ensured that he ran particularly well among middle-class and aspiring middle-class black voters. Whites made up roughly a fifth of his total support. At the Democratic convention in San

---

58. White, *Black Leadership*, p. 185.
59. S.F. Lawson, *Running for Freedom: Civil Rights and Black Politics in America Since 1941* (New York, 1991).

Francisco on 17 July he failed to secure significant concessions from the victorious Mondale but stole the show with a vigorous speech in which he urged Americans to build on the achievements of the civil rights movement. 'Our time has come', he insisted. 'We must leave the racial battleground and find the economic common ground and moral higher ground.'[60]

Although Mondale's candidacy did little to fire the imagination of ordinary blacks (turnout in November 1984 was no higher than it had been four years earlier and Mondale suffered one of the worst defeats in American political history), Jackson had at least demonstrated his ability to mobilise and unify significant numbers of African Americans – roughly a third of blacks eligible to vote – with his distinctive brand of protest politics.[61] In 1988 he made an even stronger bid to become the Democratic presidential nominee. Attempting to broaden his support base beyond its black core, he avoided alienating Jewish Americans, employed experienced white campaign advisers, and laid greater stress on issues likely to appeal to disaffected liberals. By tying himself more closely to the Democratic Party, he also won the support of the vast majority of black leaders who hitherto had viewed him as a maverick independent. The tactics paid off. Jackson doubled his vote, winning the key southern primaries as well as the important Michigan caucus. In most states he won more than 90 per cent of the black primary vote. Whites made up 40 per cent of his coalition – an impressive figure which helped him to claim second spot to the Massachusetts senator, Michael Dukakis, who defeated him in the critical New York contest. Jackson's improved showing gave him greater leverage at the national convention, but Dukakis's determination to avoid the stigma of liberalism led him to appoint a conservative Texan, Lloyd Bentsen, as his running mate. This decision ended Jackson's hopes of becoming the first black man to receive the vice-presidential nomination of a major party. Once again he was left with the consolation prize of a major convention speech. After emphasising continuities with the civil rights movement by introducing Mrs Rosa Parks to the floor, he held up the vision of an America which 'keeps hope alive' by targeting the multiplicity of problems confronting America's poor. Jackson's pledge of support for Dukakis indicated the Chicagoan's reluctance to step out of the political mainstream once he had secured his place within it. However, it did nothing to embolden

60. Quoted in C. Carson *et al.*, eds, *The Eyes on the Prize Civil Rights Reader* (New York, 1991), p. 709.
61. Tate, *From Protest*, p. 165.

Dukakis who fought a defensive, lacklustre campaign which offered precious little hope to Jackson's constituency. His opponent, George Bush, depicted himself as a kinder, gentler Reagan but also capital-ised successfully on the racially charged law-and-order theme which had garnered so many white votes for Nixon and Reagan. Under the command of Lee Atwater, a combative white southerner and former Thurmond aide experienced in the art of 'hardball race-coded campaigning', Bush's election team lambasted Dukakis as an irresponsible and outmoded liberal.[62] Contributing to this image was a controversial Republican advertisement depicting a black killer, Willie Horton, who had raped a white woman while on furlough in April 1987. As governor of Massachusetts eleven years previously, Dukakis had vetoed a bill prohibiting furloughs for first-degree murderers. This action enabled Atwater and his colleagues to link the Democratic candidate closely to the widespread public sense that liberals were soft on crime and overly eager to expend (white) tax dollars on (black) welfare recipients. Bush triumphed easily in the election, carrying every state in the South and Southwest. Blacks voted overwhelmingly for the Democratic candidate as usual but significantly their turnout declined by about 5 per cent.[63]

Conclusion: unfinished business

Jesse Jackson's two attempts to capture the Democratic presidential nomination in the 1980s indicated the distance that blacks had come since the passage of the Voting Rights Act. Involvement in party politics had brought major gains. Twenty years after the assassination of Martin Luther King a black man was able to make a serious bid for the presidency. Black mayors could be elected in virtually every major city in the United States and parts of the rural South were also under black political control. Affirmative action, an outgrowth of black influence within the Democratic Party and government fears of ghetto unrest, had played a major role in creating a black middle class constituting roughly a third of the country's entire African-American population. The South itself had been modernised – brought into the political and economic mainstream – and key

62. T.B. Edsall and M.D. Edsall, *Chain Reaction: The Impact of Race, Rights, and Taxes on American Politics* (New York and London, 1992), p. 221.
63. Lawson, *Running For Freedom*, p. 258.

American institutions, including the army, were integrated and open to blacks on the same terms as whites.[64]

One of the best indications of progress was the substantial increase in the number of elected black office-holders in the United States during the 1970s and 1980s – a direct consequence of the Voting Rights Act and the subsequent growth of black involvement in mainstream politics. By 1987 over 6,600 blacks held elected office at all levels of government. Most significant, in terms of wielding power at the national level, was a steady increase in the size of the Congressional Black Caucus in Washington. Founded in 1971 to increase black legislative solidarity, the Caucus numbered 38 after the 1992 elections. Embracing a new generation of black political leaders including Carol Moseley Braun, the first black woman to be elected to the United States Senate, and the Maryland Congressman (and later NAACP head), Kweisi Mfume, it exercised an important, if not perhaps decisive, influence on federal policy-making in the late twentieth century. As well as supporting a broadly liberal agenda on domestic issues such as health care and welfare, the Caucus also stood firm against an aggressive, right-wing foreign policy during the period of Republican governance between 1981 and 1993. Insisting, as had SNCC, CORE and Martin Luther King, that military adventures abroad took away valuable resources from domestic reform, black congressional leaders provided some of the most caustic internal criticism of the Gulf War in 1992.[65] Earlier they had won a major victory in 1986 when Congress voted to apply economic sanctions against the apartheid regime in South Africa, long a target for black civil rights activists in the United States.[66] If, overall, these gains did not add up to King's beloved community or SNCC's participatory democracy, they represented in many respects an enormous advance on the situation pertaining at the end of the Second World War.

What these achievements did not prove was that political involvement alone had the capacity to deliver a dignified and fulfilling life to most African Americans. Black poverty actually increased during the second half of the 1970s and the 1980s as a consequence of economic downturns, government policies, de-industrialisation, and a disturbing growth in the number of one-parent black families

64. On the integration of the US army see C. Moskos, 'How Do They Do It?', *New Republic*, 5 August 1991, 16–20.

65. A. Puddington, 'Black Leaders vs. Desert Storm', *Commentary*, May 1991, 28–34.

66. Marable, *Race*, pp. 214–15.

headed by women. In 1990 one-third of blacks and half of all black children lived below the poverty line, either in rural areas of the South or, more commonly, in the country's inner cities. Another third could be categorised as working class or lower middle class living on incomes derived from low-status, low-skilled jobs in the low-wage, non-unionised service sector of the economy. Blacks earned on average 56 per cent of the earnings of whites – a significant drop of seven percentage points on the corresponding figure for 1975.[67]

The high incidence of poverty resulted in an often brutish social existence for those urban blacks hit by the disadvantages of race, class and, for women, gender discrimination. Although drug abuse, violent crime and ill health characterised urban black life throughout the twentieth century, such afflictions ravaged the so-called black 'underclass' with even greater ferocity as the millennium approached. Blacks constituted roughly 12 per cent of the total population in 1990 but they furnished 43.2 per cent of arrested rapists, 54.7 per cent of those accused of murder, and 69.3 per cent of those arrested for robbery.[68] Such statistics explained not only why many blacks had lost faith in the American justice system, but also why wealthy whites had become so fearful of black crime that they began to protect their suburbs with security guards, barriers, and fences in the manner of their peers living in crime-ridden Rio de Janeiro or Johannesburg. The black poor, however, suffered most from crime in the 1990s. Homicide was the leading cause of death for blacks aged between 18 and 34, and African Americans in general were six times as likely as whites to be victims of violent crime. Whites grew similarly anxious over the spiralling costs of medical insurance in the 1990s, but again it was impoverished blacks who suffered most from America's troubled health-care system. Harvard Sitkoff has observed that the 1990 infant black mortality rate of 18.6 per 1,000 births was higher than that of Bulgaria or Costa Rica.[69]

Political involvement, then, proved no more successful than the civil rights movement in solving the complex problem of black poverty. There were several reasons for this. The imperative to forge coalitions with potentially sympathetic allies often diluted the radicalism of black appeals to the public. Big city mayors like Tom Bradley in Los Angeles, Harold Washington in Chicago and David Dinkins in New York not only had to ensure that they did not

67. Morgan, *Liberal Consensus*, p. 256.
68. H. Sitkoff, *The Struggle for Black Equality 1954–1992* (New York, 1993), p. 227.
69. Ibid., p. 227.

alienate white liberals by displaying too much favouritism to blacks, but they also found it necessary to cooperate with the mainly white corporate elites who dominated the local economy. White allies and big business did accept that black political control meant African Americans would gain a greater share of government and private sector jobs – hence their support for affirmative action programmes which largely benefited blacks with skills and education. The power of the purse, however, enabled whites to place strict limits on the kind of radical policies which might have lifted greater numbers of black people out of the poverty trap or produced a more sensitive approach to urban renewal. In the South, this meant that even in areas where blacks had seized control of their communities as a consequence of the Voting Rights Act, blacks were prevented from gaining a significantly larger share of the economic pie. Lowndes County, Alabama, for example, one of the great political success stories of the post-movement era, was the fifth poorest county in the United States in 1980.[70]

To some extent black political power was also limited by the growth of political conservatism among African Americans. In one sense this development was a sign of black political maturity. As one prominent Chicago committeeman answered in response to a question concerning the future of black politics in the city:

> When you say black politics, I am not really certain what that means. There is implicit in the phrase a feeling of homogeneity, that all blacks are going to be responsive to the same stimuli, and that all blacks are going to do a certain thing and vote a certain way. What people don't realize is that as this country has grown and developed, and as more and more blacks have moved into the main stream of life, that there are as many stratifications of thought and as many approaches to what is the quality of life among black people as there are among white people. We probably will not have a unanimous kind of thought process as to what is best for our group.[71]

Although the amount of black support for Jesse Jackson and the Democratic Party in the 1980s suggested the persistence of a good deal of group voting on the basis of racial allegiance, a small but growing number of prominent African Americans such as the economists Walter Williams of George Mason University and Thomas

---

70. C.W. Eagles, 'From Shotgun to Umbrellas: The Civil Rights Movement in Lowndes County, Alabama' in *The Adaptable South: Essays in Honor of George Brown Tindall*, ed. E. Jacoway, D.T. Carter, *et al.* (Baton Rouge and London, 1991), p. 234.

71. Interview with Cecil Partee in M.L. Rakove, ed., *We Don't Want Nobody Sent: An Oral History of the Daley Years* (Bloomington and London, 1979), p. 160.

Sowell of Stanford and President Reagan's choice to head the EEOC, Clarence Thomas, emerged as outspoken critics of the established civil rights orthodoxy.[72] Attacking liberal policies for fostering dependency and poverty, they embraced Ronald Reagan's rhetorical emphasis on the free market, self-reliance, thrift, and hard work with an enthusiasm reminiscent of Booker T. Washington. While their fondness for self-help occasionally spilled over into black nationalism (Thomas was known to speak approvingly of Louis Farrakhan), black conservative thought in the 1980s was essentially a product of the growth of the black middle class; it was a worldview grounded in the latter's desire to be included in the American mainstream and one which, according to its critics, was overly dismissive of past struggles and the historic importance of government assistance to the black freedom struggle.[73] Its growth was not immediately translated into Republican votes (no more than a fifth of blacks voting in 1988 supported George Bush) but an awareness of the phenomenon's potential impelled President Bush to appoint Clarence Thomas to the Supreme Court in 1991. Thomas, the son of a Georgia sharecropper, controversially succeeded the veteran civil rights protagonist Thurgood Marshall as the only black representative on the Court. As Bush had hoped, he soon joined the nascent conservative majority on the supreme bench which continued to chip away at affirmative action in the wake of the Court's 1978 decision in *Regents of the University of California v. Bakke* – a ruling which declared the use of rigid quotas to be an infringement of the equal protection clause of the Fourteenth Amendment and the 1964 Civil Rights Act.[74]

The emergence of a conservative Republican majority on the Rehnquist Court in the late 1980s and 1990s indicated that the longstanding alliance with the Democratic Party was no guarantee against roll-back on the civil rights front. The coalition did play a major part in the passage of the 1991 Civil Rights Act which overturned a US Supreme Court decision shifting the onus in job discrimination cases onto the plaintiffs. However, even when it enjoyed executive as well as legislative power, the national Democratic Party failed to promote policies tailored to address the enormous social

72. *NYT*, 13 July 1991, pp. 1, 7.
73. See e.g. A.L. Higginbotham, Jr, 'An Open Letter to Justice Clarence Thomas from a Federal Judicial Colleague' in *Race-ing Justice, En-gendering Power: Essays on Anita Hill, Clarence Thomas, and the Construction of Social Reality*, ed. T. Morrison (London, 1993), pp. 3–39.
74. Nieman, *Promises*, pp. 209–11.

problems confronting the black poor. This was true both of the Carter and Clinton administrations. President Jimmy Carter, a homely, enlightened product of the New South shaped in part by the civil rights movement, appointed blacks to a number of high-profile positions in the mid-1970s, not least Andrew Young as American ambassador to the United Nations. He also supported affirmative action, presided over the EEOC's most active period in its short history and made human rights the touchstone of United States foreign policy.[75] Black hopes that the Great Society would be revived under the new Democratic administration, however, were frustrated by the president's conviction, born of recession-era constraints, that citizens should not expect too much from government. The latter, he insisted in his 1978 State of the Union Address, could not 'eliminate poverty', 'provide energy' or 'mandate goodness'.[76] What John Dumbrell has called Carter's 'post-liberalism' seriously disillusioned the country's established black leadership. Confronted by a black unemployment rate more than twice as high as the white variant, Bayard Rustin and Jesse Jackson joined the NAACP's Benjamin Hooks and Vernon Jordan of the National Urban League in accusing the administration of 'callous neglect' of African Americans.[77]

By the time Bill Clinton, a more pragmatic son of the New South, was elected president in November 1992 social conditions in the inner cities had deteriorated even further. Seven months previously young blacks in South Central Los Angeles went on the rampage after a suburban jury delivered a not-guilty verdict on four white policemen accused of using unnecessary force to arrest a black man, Rodney King, in March 1991. A white observer had videotaped the officers administering a severe beating to King who, the defence counsel alleged, was high on drugs at the time of his arrest. Residents of South Central, an impoverished neighbourhood seriously neglected by the moderate, pro-business administration of Democratic Mayor Tom Bradley, were accustomed to police brutality. In 1979 two officers from the Los Angeles Police Department had shot a 39-year-old black widow twelve times after she tried to stop a utility man from switching off her gas.[78] The failure to convict the four officers in the Rodney King case epitomised the lack of equal justice

---

75. For a judicious survey of Carter's civil rights policy see J. Dumbrell, *The Carter Presidency: A Re-evaluation* (Manchester and New York, 1993), pp. 86–109.

76. Ibid., p. 3.   77. Ibid., pp. 98–9.

78. R.D.G. Kelley, *Race Rebels: Culture, Politics, and the Black Working Class* (New York, 1994), p. 184.

in Los Angeles and brought festering anger and frustration to the surface. Some of it was directed against Korean shopkeepers accused, like Jews in the 1960s, of exploiting the poor in their midst. After four days of rioting 47 people lay dead, 2,100 had been injured and 9,000 were under arrest. The rioting was the worst incident of civil disorder in America since the Detroit riot of 1967 and appeared to signal the need for immediate action.

While the Republican administration of George Bush reacted predictably by placing the blame for the disorder on the rioters, civil rights leaders expected more positive action from President Bill Clinton. Even though the former Arkansas governor had sought to distance himself from radical blacks during the 1992 campaign, his winning coalition was made up of large numbers of African-American voters. Like Jimmy Carter before him, however, Clinton was wary of being targeted as a big-spending liberal in the mould of Lyndon Johnson and, even more than Carter, recognised that the undercurrent of racism in American life and the deepening opposition to cultural pluralism ('multiculturalism') made him vulnerable on issues like affirmative action. There was certainly no possibility that the new president would support enactment of a domestic Marshall Plan – Jesse Jackson's proffered solution to the problems highlighted by the Los Angeles riot. Instead, Clinton preferred to focus on issues likely to appeal to the supposedly forgotten middle-class voters who had supported him in the election. His administration's efforts to produce meaningful reforms in the critical areas of welfare and health care, however, were seriously endangered by Republican successes in the 1994 congressional elections. A Democrat in the White House, even one who was capable of winning a second term in 1996, was manifestly no guarantee that the fundamental problems of black life in America could be adequately targeted by those in power.

Politics, in short, was unlikely to prove a panacea for black ills because of the persistence of widespread racism and class prejudice among American whites. It is true that a majority of whites had come to accept the idea that blacks were entitled to equal treatment under the law, seemed prepared to acknowledge the substantial black cultural contribution to American life in many spheres (especially music, sports, television and film), and were generally intolerant of overt manifestations of racial hatred. The bulk of them, however, displayed few signs of empathy for the 'underclass'. Evidence of this was not difficult to find at the end of the twentieth century. Except in a few integrated middle-class areas such as Mount

Airy in Philadelphia, blacks and whites continued to live apart from one another.[79] White flight from the public schools in the South combined with the Supreme Court's opposition to busing across district lines and *de facto* housing segregation in the North to limit the extent of school desegregation. Opposition to higher taxes and income transfer on a broad scale – perhaps the only viable solutions to poverty in America – remained deeply rooted.

In August 1994 the extent of the problems still facing black America were brutally symbolised by the mugging of Rosa Parks in Detroit. Eighty-one years old at the time, Mrs Parks was attacked in the sanctuary of her own home by a young, black male in search of money for drugs. Although she survived the incident, it was a fitting metaphor for the times: the woman whose name was legendary in civil rights folklore beaten and robbed by a man who had failed to benefit from the reforms of the 1960s.[80] Other events re-emphasised the fact that race remained one of the most divisive features of American life in the late twentieth century. For over eight months in 1994 the sensational trial of the black movie actor and former football star O.J. Simpson for the first-degree murder of his estranged white wife and her lover gripped the nation in the manner of a real-life soap opera. The racially polarised reaction to the court's not-guilty verdict – blacks largely joyful, whites generally disbelieving – spoke volumes for the fractured state of race relations in the United States.[81] So too did a rash of arson attacks on black churches in the southern states during 1995 and Louis Farrakhan's Million Man March in October of the same year when black males flooded into Washington, DC to signal, peacefully, their concern for prevailing social conditions and their pride in the race. A less sensational but no less telling event was an unseemly dispute between the National Park Service and the family of Martin Luther King over the construction of a visitors' centre at the King National Historic Site in Atlanta. The principal issue at stake appeared to be concerns on the family's part that the Park Service might attempt to sanitise King's later career in its various multi-media depictions of the former civil rights leader.[82] At a time when some form of consensus was an

79. *US News and World Report*, 22 July 1991, pp. 22–8.

80. *The Times* (London), 1 September 1994.

81. In February 1997 a civil court found Simpson liable for the deaths of Nicole Brown Simpson and Ronald Goldman. He was ordered to pay a total of $33.5 million in punitive and compensatory damages. *The Times* (London), 11 February 1997.

82. *NYT*, 16 January 1995.

essential precondition for racial progress, even the historic legacy of the movement was in doubt.

Of course, major historical events and figures will always be contested and the civil rights movement is no exception. Whatever the rights and wrongs of the debate over the King site, it is clear that the Second Reconstruction was an unfinished revolution. Aided in part by the modernisation of the old plantation economy after the Second World War and the onset of a liberal political climate in the 1960s, the movement succeeded in its paramount objective: the demolition of Jim Crow segregation below the Mason–Dixon Line. In destroying the caste system which had endured since the end of the nineteenth century, it gave southern blacks the fundamental rights of citizenship which most people take for granted in a modern democracy. The result was a major enhancement of individual and group self-esteem, most clearly evidenced by a substantial increase in the number of blacks registered to vote. Equally significantly, by democratising regional politics, the movement played a critical role in ending the South's dysfunctional place in the American polity. Although the Confederate flag remains a potent symbol for many whites, particularly those left behind by the rapid economic changes which have swept the region over the last half century, the business progressives who dominate the political and economic life of the prosperous New South look to the future, not the past.[83] While this, on balance, can only be good news for southern blacks, the civil rights movement patently failed in its later attempts to remove the burden of poverty from African Americans in all parts of the country. It is not impossible, of course, that a Third Reconstruction – a combination, possibly, of self-help, grass-roots organising, issue-oriented coalition politics, carefully calibrated street protest and decisive federal action – could end this scourge for good. The prospect of such an event taking place in the conservative, cynical 1990s may seem unlikely, but social revolutions are more easily detected in hindsight than predicted by historians. One thing, however, is certain: on the evidence of their past conduct, African Americans will not rest until the day of deliverance. For the one indisputable lesson of the civil rights movement – indeed, of the entire black experience in the United States – is that freedom will not come without a struggle.

83. T. Horwitz, 'A Death for Dixie', *The New Yorker*, 18 March 1996, 64–70, 72–7.

Select Bibliography

A. Manuscript sources

Congress of Racial Equality Papers, WisHS.
Martin Luther King, Jr Papers, KC.
Staughton Lynd Papers, WisHS.
National Association for the Advancement of Colored People Papers, LC.
National Conference for New Politics Papers, WisHS.
President's Committee on Civil Rights, Records Relating to Meetings, Hearings, and Staff Interviews of the Committee (UPA microfilm, 1984).
Roy Wilkins Papers, LC.
Sam Shirah Papers, WisHS.
Southern Christian Leadership Conference Papers, KC.
Student Nonviolent Coordinating Committee Papers, KC.
Student Nonviolent Coordinating Committee Papers, CRDP.
Students for a Democratic Society Papers, WisHS.

B. Interviews (all CRDP)

SAUL ALINSKY, 1967
ELLA BAKER, 1968
GLOSTER CURRENT, 1968
JAMES MCBRIDE DABBS, 1968
GLORIA RICHARDSON DANDRIDGE, 1967
VIRGINIA DURR, 1968
MILTON GALAMISON, 1970
RUBY HURLEY, 1968
ANNIE MAE KING, 1968
CELES KING, 1969
STANLEY LEVISON, 1970
RUFUS LEWIS, 1968
FLOYD MCKISSICK, 1968

HENRY MILTON, 1970
HENRY LEE MOON, 1967
CECIL B. MOORE, 1967
JOSEPH RAUH, 1967.
EUGENE T. REED, 1968
SCOTT SMITH, 1968

C. Printed primary sources

BLAUSTEIN, ALBERT P. AND ZANGRANDO, ROBERT L., *Civil Rights and the American Negro* (New York: Trident Press, 1968).

CARSON, CLAYBORNE, GARROW, DAVID J. *et al.*, *The Eyes on the Prize Civil Rights Reader: Documents, Speeches, and Firsthand Accounts from the Black Freedom Struggle, 1954–1990* (New York: Penguin, 1991).

HAMPTON, HENRY AND FAYER, STEVE, *Voices of Freedom: An Oral History of the Civil Rights Movement from the 1950s through the 1980s* (New York: Bantam, 1990).

HILL, RUTH EDMONDS, *The Black Women Oral History Project* (10 vols, Westport and London: Meckler, 1991).

IANNIELLO, LYNNE, ED., *Milestones Along the March: Twelve Historic Civil Rights Documents – From World War II to Selma* (London: Pall Mall Press, 1965).

LOGAN, RAYFORD W., ED., *What the Negro Wants* (Chapel Hill: University of North Carolina Press, 1944).

President's Committee on Civil Rights, *To Secure These Rights* (Washington, DC: US Government Printing Office, 1947).

RAINES, HOWELL, *My Soul Is Rested: Movement Days in the Deep South Remembered* (New York: Penguin edn, 1983).

RUSTIN, BAYARD, *Down the Line: The Collected Writings of Bayard Rustin* (Chicago: Quadrangle, 1971).

WASHINGTON, JAMES M., ED., *A Testament of Hope: The Essential Writings and Speeches of Martin Luther King, Jr* (San Francisco: HarperCollins, 1986).

D. Secondary works

I BOOKS AND PAMPHLETS

ABERNATHY, RALPH D., *And the Walls Came Tumbling Down* (New York: Harper Perennial, 1990).

AMBROSE, STEPHEN E., *Eisenhower: The President, 1952–1969* (London and Sydney: Allen and Unwin, 1984).

AYERS, EDWARD, *The Promise of the New South: Life After Reconstruction* (New York and Oxford: Oxford University Press, 1992).

BADGER, TONY, *The New Deal: The Depression Years, 1933–1940* (Basingstoke: Macmillan, 1989).

BADGER, TONY, EDGAR, WALTER AND GRETLUND, JAN NORBY, *Southern Landscapes* (Stauffenburg Verlag: Tübingen, 1996).

BARNARD, WILLIAM D., *Dixiecrats and Democrats: Alabama Politics 1942–1950* (Tuscaloosa: University of Alabama Press, 1974).

BARNES, CATHERINE A., *Journey from Jim Crow: The Desegregation of Southern Transit* (New York: Columbia University Press, 1983).

BARTLEY, NUMAN V., *The Rise of Massive Resistance: Race and Politics in the South during the 1950's* (Baton Rouge: Louisiana State University Press, 1969).

BARTLEY, NUMAN V., *The New South 1945–1980* (Baton Rouge: Louisiana State University Press/The Littlefield Fund for Southern History of the University of Texas, 1995).

BELFRAGE, SALLY, *Freedom Summer* (London: André Deutsch, 1966).

BELKNAP, MICHAEL R., *Federal Law and Southern Order: Racial Violence and Constitutional Conflict in the Post-Brown South* (Athens, Ga, and London: University of Georgia Press, 1987).

BERNSTEIN, BARTON J., ED., *Politics and Policies of the Truman Administration* (London: Quadrangle, 1970).

BERNSTEIN, IRVING, *Promises Kept: John F. Kennedy's New Frontier* (New York and Oxford: Oxford University Press, 1991).

BILES, ROGER, *The South and the New Deal* (Lexington, Ky: University of Kentucky Press, 1994).

BLACK, EARL AND BLACK, MERLE, *Politics and Society in the South* (Cambridge, Mass., and London: Harvard University Press, 1987).

BLOOM, JACK T., *Class, Race and the Civil Rights Movement* (Bloomington and Indianapolis: Indiana University Press, 1987).

BLUM, JOHN M., *V Was for Victory: Politics and American Culture During World War II* (New York and London: Harcourt Brace Jovanovich, 1976).

BLUM, JOHN M., *The Progressive Presidents: Roosevelt, Wilson, Roosevelt, Johnson* (New York and London, 1980).

BLUM, JOHN M., *Years of Discord: American Politics and Society, 1961–1974* (pbk edn, W.W. Norton: New York and London, 1992).

BRANCH, TAYLOR, *Parting the Waters: America in the King Years 1954–1963* (New York: Touchstone, 1989).

BRAUER, CARL, *John F. Kennedy and the Second Reconstruction* (New York: Columbia University Press, 1977).

BROWN, CYNTHIA STOKES, ED., *Ready from Within: Septima Clark and the Civil Rights Movement* (Trenton, NJ: Africa World Press, 1990).

BROWNELL, HERBERT WITH JOHN BURKE, *Advising Ike: The Memoirs of Attorney General Herbert Brownell* (Lawrence, Ka: University of Kansas Press, 1993).

BROWNING, RUFUS P., MARSHALL, DALE ROGERS AND TABB, DAVID H., EDS, *Racial Politics in American Cities* (New York and London: Longman, 1990).

BUHLE, MARI JO, BUHLE, PAUL AND KAYE, HARVEY J., EDS, *The American Radical* (New York and London: Routledge, 1974).

BURNER, ERIC, *And Gently Shall He Lead Them: Robert Parris Moses and Civil Rights in Mississippi* (New York and London: New York University Press, 1994).

BYRNES, JAMES F., *All In One Lifetime* (New York: Harper and Bros., 1958).

CARMICHAEL, STOKELY AND HAMILTON, CHARLES V., *Black Power: The Politics of Black Liberation in America* (Harmondsworth: Penguin, 1969).

CARSON, CLAYBORNE, *In Struggle: SNCC and the Black Awakening of the 1960s* (Cambridge, Mass., and London: Harvard University Press, 1981).

CARTER, DALE, ED., *Cracking the Ike Age: Aspects of Fifties America* (Aarhus: Aarhus University Press, 1992).

CARTER, DAN T., *Scottsboro: A Tragedy of the American South* (rev. edn, Baton Rouge and London: Louisiana State University Press, 1979).

CECELSKI, DAVID S., *Along Freedom Road: Hyde County, North Carolina, and the Fate of Black Schools in the South* (Chapel Hill and London: University of North Carolina Press, 1994).

CHAFE, WILLIAM H., *Civilities and Civil Rights: Greensboro, North Carolina, and the Black Struggle for Freedom* (New York and Oxford: Oxford University Press, 1980).

CHAFE, WILLIAM H., *Never Stop Running: Allard Lowenstein and the Struggle to Save American Liberalism* (New York: Basic Books, 1993).

CHAPPELL, DAVID L., *Inside Agitators: White Southerners in the Civil Rights Movement* (Baltimore and London: Johns Hopkins University Press, 1994).

CLEAVER, ELDRIDGE, *Soul On Ice* (London: Jonathan Cape, 1969).

COBB, JAMES C., *The Most Southern Place on Earth: The Mississippi Delta and the Roots of Regional Identity* (Oxford: Oxford University Press, 1992).

COLBURN, DAVID R., *Racial Change and Community Crisis: St. Augustine, Florida, 1877–1980* (Gainesville: University of Florida Press, 1991).

CONE, JAMES H., *Martin & Malcolm & America: A Dream or a Nightmare* (Maryknoll, NY: Orbis, 1991).

CRAWFORD, VICKI L., ROUSE, JACQUELINE A. AND WOODS, BARBARA, EDS, *Women in the Civil Rights Movement: Trailblazers and Torchbearers, 1941–1965* (Brooklyn: Carlson, 1990).

DALFIUME, RICHARD M., *Desegregation of the US Armed Forces: Fighting on Two Fronts 1939–1953* (Columbia, Mo: University of Missouri Press, 1969).

DANIEL, PETE, *Standing at the Crossroads: Southern Life Since 1900* (New York: Hill and Wang, 1986).

DAVIDSON, CHANDLER AND GROFMAN, BERNARD, EDS, *Quiet Revolution in the South: The Impact of the Voting Rights Act, 1965–1990* (Princeton: Princeton University Press, 1994).

DIGGINS, JOHN PATRICK, *The Rise and Fall of the American Left* (New York and London: W.W. Norton, 1973).

DITTMER, JOHN, *Local People: The Struggle for Civil Rights in Mississippi* (Urbana and Chicago: University of Illinois Press, 1994).

DIVINE, ROBERT, ED., *The Johnson Years: Vol. I, Foreign Policy, the Great Society and the White House* (Lawrence, Ka: University of Kansas Press, 1987).

DRAPER, ALAN, *Conflict of Interests: Organized Labor and the Civil Rights Movement in the South, 1954–1968* (Ithaca: ILR Press, 1994).

DUMBRELL, JOHN, *The Carter Presidency: A Re-evaluation* (Manchester and New York: Manchester University Press, 1993).

DUNBAR, ANTHONY P., *Against the Grain: Southern Radicals and Prophets 1929–1959* (Charlottesville, Va: University of Virginia Press, 1981).

EAGLES, CHARLES W., ED., *The Civil Rights Movement in America* (Jackson and London: University of Mississippi Press, 1986).

EAGLES, CHARLES W., *Outside Agitator: Jon Daniels and the Civil Rights Movement in Alabama* (Chapel Hill and London: University of North Carolina Press, 1993).

EDSALL, THOMAS BYRNE AND EDSALL, MARY D., *Chain Reaction: The Impact of Race, Rights, and Taxes on American Politics* (New York and London: W.W. Norton, 1992).

EGERTON, JOHN, *Speak Now Against the Day: The Generation Before the Civil Rights Movement in the South* (New York: Alfred A. Knopf, 1994).

ELY, JAMES W., JR, *The Crisis of Conservative Virginia: The Byrd Organization and the Politics of Massive Resistance* (Knoxville: University of Tennessee Press, 1976).

ESCOTT, PAUL D., ED., *W.J. Cash and the Minds of the South* (Baton Rouge and London: Louisiana State University Press, 1992).

EVANS, SARA, *Personal Politics: The Roots of Women's Liberation in the Civil Rights Movement and the New Left* (pbk edn, New York: Vintage, 1980).

EYERMAN, RON AND JAMISON, ANDREW, *Social Movements: A Cognitive Approach* (Cambridge, Polity Press, 1991).

FAIRCLOUGH, ADAM, *To Redeem the Soul of America: The Southern Christian Leadership Conference and Martin Luther King, Jr.* (Athens, Ga, and London: University of Georgia Press, 1987).

FAIRCLOUGH, ADAM, *Martin Luther King* (London: Cardinal, 1990).

FAIRCLOUGH, ADAM, *Race and Democracy: The Civil Rights Struggle in Louisiana, 1915–1972* (Athens, Ga, and London: University of Georgia Press, 1995).

FARMER, JAMES, *Lay Bare the Heart: An Autobiography of the Civil Rights Movement* (New York and Scarborough, Ont: Plume, 1985).

FENDRICH, JAMES M., *Ideal Citizens: The Legacy of the Civil Rights Movement* (Albany: SUNY Press, 1993).

FINDLAY, JAMES F., JR, *Church People in the Struggle: The National Council of Churches and the Black Freedom Movement, 1950–1970* (New York and Oxford: Oxford University Press, 1993).

FONER, ERIC, *Reconstruction: America's Unfinished Revolution 1863–1877* (New York: Harper and Row, 1988).

FOREMAN, JAMES, *The Making of Black Revolutionaries* (New York: Macmillan, 1972).

FORMISANO, RONALD P., *Boston Against Busing: Race, Class, and Ethnicity in the 1960s and 1970s* (Chapel Hill: University of North Carolina Press, 1991).

FOX, RICHARD W., *Reinhold Niebuhr: A Biography* (New York: Pantheon, 1985).

FRANKLIN, JOHN HOPE AND MEIER, AUGUST, EDS, *Black Leaders of the Twentieth Century* (Urbana and Chicago: University of Illinois Press, 1982).

FREDRICKSON, GEORGE M., *Black Liberation: A Comparative History of Black Ideologies in the United States and South Africa* (New York and Oxford: Oxford University Press, 1995).

FREEMAN, JO, ED., *Social Movements of the Sixties and Seventies* (New York: Longman, 1983).

GAINES, KEVIN K., *Uplifting the Race: Black Leadership, Politics, and Culture in the Twentieth Century* (Chapel Hill and London: University of North Carolina Press, 1996).

GARFINKEL, HERBERT, *When Negroes March: The March on Washington Movement in the Organizational Movement for FEPC* (New York: Atheneum, 1969).

GARROW, DAVID J., *Protest at Selma: Martin Luther King, Jr, and the Voting Rights Act of 1965* (New Haven: Yale University Press, 1978).

GARROW, DAVID J., *Bearing the Cross: Martin Luther King, Jr., and the Southern Christian Leadership Conference* (New York: William Morrow, 1986).

GARROW, DAVID J., ED., *Martin Luther King, Jr.: Civil Rights Leader, Theologian, Orator* (3 vols, Brooklyn: Carlson, 1989).

GARROW, DAVID J., ED., *Martin Luther King, Jr. and the Civil Rights Movement* (3 vols, Brooklyn: Carlson, 1989).

GATLIN, ROCHELLE, *American Women Since 1945* (Jackson and London: University of Mississippi Press, 1987).

GILLON, STEVEN M., *Politics and Vision: The ADA and American Liberalism* (New York and Oxford: Oxford University Press, 1987).

GOINGS, KENNETH W., *'The NAACP Comes of Age': The Defeat of Judge John J. Parker* (Bloomington and Indianapolis: Indiana University Press, 1990).

GOLDFIELD, DAVID R., *Black, White, and Southern: Race Relations and Southern Culture 1940 to Present* (Baton Rouge and London: Louisiana State University Press, 1990).

GRAHAM, HUGH DAVIS, *The Civil Rights Era: Origins and Development of National Policy 1960–1972* (New York and Oxford: Oxford University Press, 1990).

GRANTHAM, DEWEY, *The Life and Death of the Solid South: A Political History* (Lexington, Ky: University of Kentucky Press, 1988).

GRAY, FRED D., *Bus Ride to Justice: Changing the System by the System; the Life and Works of Fred D. Gray* (Montgomery, Ala: Black Belt Press, 1995).

GREENBERG, JACK, *Crusaders in the Courts: How a Dedicated Band of Lawyers Fought for the Civil Rights Revolution* (New York: Basic Books, 1994).

GREENBERG, STANLEY B., *Race and State in Capitalist Development: Comparative Perspectives* (New Haven and London: Yale University Press, 1980).

HAINES, HERBERT H., *Black Radicals and the Civil Rights Movement, 1954–1970* (Knoxville: University of Tennessee Press, 1988).

HAMILTON, CHARLES V., *The Bench and the Ballot: Southern Federal Judges and Black Voters* (New York: Oxford University Press, 1973).

HENRY, CHARLES P., *Culture and African American Politics* (Bloomington and Indianapolis: Indiana University Press, 1990).

HINE, DARLENE CLARK, *Black Victory: The Rise and Fall of the White Primary in Texas* (Millwood, NY: KTO Press, 1979).

HOFF, JOAN, *Nixon Reconsidered* (New York: Basic Books, 1994).

HONEY, MICHAEL K., *Southern Labor and Black Civil Rights: Organizing Memphis Workers* (Urbana and Chicago: University of Illinois Press, 1993).

HORNE, GERALD, *Communist Front? The Civil Rights Congress, 1946–1956* (Rutherford, Madison, Teaneck, London and Toronto: Associated University Presses, 1988).

HORNE, GERALD, *Fire this Time: The Watts Uprising and the 1960s* (Charlottesville and London: University of Virginia Press, 1995).

HUTCHISON, WILLIAM R. AND LEHMANN, HARTMUT, EDS, *Many Are Chosen: Divine Election and Western Nationalism* (Minneapolis: Fortress Press, 1994).

JACOBSON, JULIUS, ED., *The Negro and the American Labor Movement* (Garden City, NY: Anchor, 1968).

JACOWAY, ELIZABETH, CARTER, DAN T., LAMON, LESTER C. AND MCMATH, ROBERT C., EDS, *The Adaptable South: Essays in Honor of George Brown Tindall* (Baton Rouge and London: Louisiana State University Press, 1991).

JEFFREY-JONES, RHODRI AND COLLINS, BRUCE, EDS, *The Growth of Federal Power in American History* (Edinburgh: Scottish Academic Press, 1983).

JONES, JACQUELINE, *Labor of Love, Labor of Sorrow: Black Women, Work, and the Family from Slavery to the Present* (New York: Vintage, 1986).

KAPUR, SUDARSHAN, *Raising Up a Prophet: The African American Encounter with Gandhi* (Boston: Beacon Press, 1992).

KELLEY, ROBIN D.G., *Hammer and Hoe: Alabama Communists During the Great Depression* (Chapel Hill and London: University of North Carolina Press, 1990).

KELLEY, ROBIN D.G., *Race Rebels: Culture, Politics, and the Black Working Class* (New York: The Free Press, 1994).

KING, CORETTA S., *My Life With Martin Luther King, Jr* (London: Hodder and Stoughton, 1970).

KING, MARY, *Freedom Song: A Personal Story of the 1960s Civil Rights Movement* (New York: William Morrow, 1987).

KING, RICHARD H., *Civil Rights and the Idea of Freedom* (New York and Oxford: Oxford University Press, 1992).

KLEPPNER, PAUL, *Chicago Divided: The Making of a Black Mayor* (De Kalb, Ill.: Northern Illinois University Press, 1985).

KLUGER, RICHARD, *Simple Justice: The History of Brown v. Board of Education and Black America's Struggle for Equality* (London: André Deutsch, 1977).

LACEY, MICHAEL J., ED., *The Truman Presidency* (Cambridge: University of Cambridge Press, 1989).

LAWSON, STEVEN F., *In Pursuit of Power: Southern Blacks and Electoral Politics, 1965–1982* (New York: Columbia University Press, 1985).

LAWSON, STEVEN F., *Running for Freedom: Civil Rights and Black Politics in America Since 1941* (New York: McGraw-Hill, 1991).

LEMANN, NICHOLAS, *The Promised Land: The Great Black Migration and How It Changed America* (London: Macmillan, 1991).

LEWIS, DAVID L., *King: A Biography* (2nd edn, Urbana: University of Illinois Press, 1978).

LEWIS, DAVID L., *W.E.B. Du Bois: Biography of a Race 1868–1919* (New York: Henry Holt, 1993).

LEWIS, EARL, *In Their Own Interests: Race, Class and Power in Twentieth-Century Norfolk, Virginia* (Berkeley, Los Angeles, and Oxford: University of California Press, 1991).

LINCOLN, C. ERIC, ED., *Martin Luther King, Jr: A Profile* (New York: Noonday Press, 1984).

LINCOLN, C. ERIC AND MAMIYA, LAWRENCE H., *The Black Church in the African American Experience* (Durham, NC, and London: Duke University Press, 1990).

LINDEN-WARD, BLANCHE AND GREEN, CAROLE HURD, *American Women in the 1960s: Changing the Future* (New York: Twayne, 1993).

LINK, WILLIAM A., *The Paradox of Southern Progressivism, 1880–1930* (Chapel Hill and London: University of North Carolina Press, 1992).

LISCHER, RICHARD, *The Preacher King: Martin Luther King, Jr and the Word That Moved America* (New York and Oxford: Oxford University Press, 1995).

MARABLE, MANNING, *Race, Reform, and Rebellion: The Second Reconstruction in Black America, 1945–1990* (Basingstoke: Macmillan, 1991).

MARSHALL, RAY, *The Negro and Organized Labor* (New York, London and Sydney: John Wiley, 1965).

MATUSOW, ALLEN J., *The Unraveling of America: A History of Liberalism in the 1960s* (New York: Harper and Row, 1984).

MAYS, BENJAMIN, *Born to Rebel: An Autobiography* (Athens, Ga, and London: University of Georgia Press, 1987).

MCADAM, DOUG, *Political Process and the Development of Black Insurgency 1930–1970* (Chicago and London: University of Chicago Press, 1982).

MCADAM, DOUG, *Freedom Summer* (New York and Oxford: Oxford University Press, 1988).

McKiven, Henry, Jr, *Iron and Steel: Class, Race, and Community in Birmingham, Alabama, 1875–1920* (Chapel Hill and London: University of North Carolina Press, 1995).

McMillen, Neil R., *The Citizens' Council: Organized Resistance to the Second Reconstruction, 1954–64* (Urbana, Chicago, and London: University of Illinois Press, 1971).

McMillen, Neil R., *Dark Journey: Black Mississippians in the Age of Jim Crow* (Urbana and Chicago: University of Illinois Press, 1989).

McNeil, Genna Rae, *Groundwork: Charles Hamilton Houston and the Struggle for Civil Rights* (Philadelphia: University of Pennsylvania Press, 1983).

Meier, August, *A White Scholar in the Black Community 1945–1965: Essays and Reflections* (Amherst: University of Massachusetts Press, 1992).

Meier, August and Rudwick, Elliott, *CORE: A Study in the Civil Rights Movement 1942–1968* (New York: Oxford University Press, 1973).

Meier, August and Rudwick, Elliott, *Black Detroit and the Rise of the UAW* (New York and Oxford: Oxford University Press, 1979).

Miller, Keith D., *Voice of Deliverance: The Language of Martin Luther King, Jr. and Its Sources* (New York: The Free Press, 1992).

Mills, Kay, *This Little Light of Mine: The Life of Fannie Lou Hamer* (New York: Dutton, 1993).

Mills, Nicolaus, *Like a Holy Crusade: Mississippi 1964 – The Turning of the Civil Rights Movement in America* (Chicago: Ivan R. Dee, 1992).

Morgan, Iwan, *Beyond the Liberal Consensus: A Political History of the United States Since 1965* (London: C. Hurst & Co., 1994).

Morris, Aldon D., *The Origins of the Civil Rights Movement: Black Communities Organizing for Change* (New York and London: Free Press/Collier Macmillan, 1984).

Morrison, Toni, ed., *Race-ing Justice, En-gendering Power: Essays on Anita Hill, Clarence Thomas, and the Construction of Social Reality* (London: Chatto & Windus, 1993).

Nieman, Donald, *Promises to Keep: African-Americans and the Constitutional Order, 1776 to the Present* (New York and Oxford: Oxford University Press, 1991).

Nixon, Richard M., *The Memoirs of Richard Nixon* (pbk edn, London: Arrow, 1979).

Norrell, Robert J., *Reaping the Whirlwind: The Civil Rights Movement in Tuskegee* (New York: Alfred A. Knopf, 1985).

Oates, Stephen B., *Let the Trumpet Sound: The Life of Martin Luther King, Jr* (London and Tunbridge Wells: Search Press, 1982).

O'BRIEN, MICHAEL, *The Idea of the American South 1920–1941* (Baltimore and London: Johns Hopkins University Press, 1979).

PEARSON, HUGH, *The Shadow of the Panther: Huey Newton and the Rise of Black Power in America* (Reading, Mass: Addison-Wesley, 1994).

PECK, JAMES, *Freedom Ride* (New York: Simon and Schuster, 1962).

PELTASON, J.W., *58 Lonely Men: Southern Federal Judges and School Desegregation* (Urbana, Chicago, and London: University of Illinois Press, 1971).

PERMAN, MICHAEL, *The Road to Redemption: Southern Politics, 1869–1879* (Chapel Hill: University of North Carolina Press, 1984).

PERRY, BRUCE, *Malcolm: The Life of a Man Who Changed Black America* (New York: Station Hill, 1991).

PERTSCHUK, MICHAEL, *Giant Killers* (New York and London: W.W. Norton, 1986).

PFEFFER, PAULA, *A. Philip Randolph: Pioneer of the Civil Rights Movement* (Baton Rouge and London: Louisiana State University Press, 1990).

PINKNEY, ALPHONSO, *The Myth of Black Progress* (Cambridge: Cambridge University Press, 1990).

PIVEN, FRANCIS FOX AND CLOWARD, RICHARD A., *Poor People's Movements: Why They Succeed, How They Fail* (New York: Pantheon, 1977).

RABINOWITZ, HOWARD N., *The First New South 1865–1920* (Arlington Heights, Ill.: Harlan Davidson, 1992).

RALPH, JAMES R., JR, *Northern Protest: Martin Luther King, Jr, Chicago, and the Civil Rights Movement* (Cambridge, Mass., and London: Harvard University Press, 1993).

REED, ADOLPH L., JR, *The Jesse Jackson Phenomenon: The Crisis of Purpose in Afro-American Politics* (New Haven and London: Yale University Press, 1986).

RICHARDSON, ELMO, *The Presidency of Dwight D. Eisenhower* (Lawrence, Ka: University of Kansas Press, 1979).

ROBINSON, ARMSTEAD L. AND SULLIVAN, PATRICIA, EDS, *New Directions in Civil Rights Studies* (Charlottesville and London: University of Virginia Press, 1991).

ROBINSON, JO ANN GIBSON, *The Montgomery Bus Boycott and the Women Who Started It: The Memoir of Jo Ann Gibson Robinson*, ed. David J. Garrow (Knoxville: University of Tennessee Press, 1987).

ROGERS, KIM LACEY, *Righteous Lives: Narratives of the New Orleans Civil Rights Movement* (New York and London: New York University Press, 1993).

ROSENGARTEN, THEODORE, *All God's Dangers: The Life of Nate Shaw* (New York: Vintage, 1974).

ROSSWURM, STEVE, ED., *The CIO's Left-Led Unions* (New Brunswick: Rutgers University Press, 1992).

ROTHSCHILD, MARY A., *A Case of Black and White: Northern Volunteers and the Southern Freedom Summers, 1964–1965* (Westport, Conn: Greenwood Press, 1982).

SALMOND, JOHN, *A Southern Rebel, The Life and Times of Aubrey Williams 1890–1965* (Chapel Hill: University of North Carolina Press, 1983).

SCHER, RICHARD K., *Politics in the New South: Republicanism, Race, and Leadership in the Twentieth Century* (New York: Paragon House, 1992).

SCHLESINGER, ARTHUR M., JR, *Robert Kennedy and His Times* (London: André Deutsch, 1978).

SEEGER, PETE AND REISER, BOB, *Everybody Says Freedom: A History of the Civil Rights Movement in Songs and Pictures* (New York and London: W.W. Norton, 1989).

SELLERS, CLEVELAND WITH RICHARD TERRELL, *The River of No Return: The Autobiography of a Black Militant and the Life and Death of SNCC* (Jackson and London: University of Mississippi Press, 1990).

SILBERMAN, CHARLES, *Crisis in Black and White* (London: Jonathan Cape, 1965).

SITKOFF, HARVARD, *A New Deal for Blacks – The Emergence of Civil Rights as a National Issue: Vol. I, The Depression Decade* (New York: Oxford University Press, 1978).

SITKOFF, HARVARD, *The Struggle for Black Equality 1954–1992* (New York: Hill and Wang, 1993).

SMITH, BOB, *They Closed Their Schools: Prince Edward County, Virginia, 1951–1964* (Chapel Hill: University of North Carolina Press, 1965).

SMITH, CHARLES U. AND KILLIAN, LEWIS M., *The Tallahassee Bus Protest* (New York: Anti-Defamation League of B'nai B'rith, 1958).

SOSNA, MORTON, *In Search of the Silent South: Southern Liberals and the Race Issue* (New York: Columbia University Press, 1977).

STERN, MARK, *Calculating Visions: Kennedy, Johnson and Civil Rights* (New Brunswick: Rutgers University Press, 1992).

STOKES, MELVYN AND HALPERN, RICK, EDS, *Race and Class in the American South Since 1890* (Oxford and Providence: Berg, 1994).

SULLIVAN, PATRICIA, *Days of Hope: Race and Democracy in the New Deal Era* (Chapel Hill: University of North Carolina Press, 1996).

TATE, KATHERINE, *From Protest to Politics: The New Black Voters in American Elections* (Cambridge, Mass., and London: Harvard University Press, 1993).

TAYLOR, QUINTARD, *The Forging of a Black Community: Seattle's Central District from 1870 through the Civil Rights Era* (Seattle and London: University of Washington Press, 1994).

THERNSTROM, ABIGAIL, *Whose Votes Count?: Affirmative Action and Minority Voting Rights* (Cambridge, Mass., and London: Harvard University Press, 1987).

THOMAS, RICHARD W., *Life for Us Is What We Make It: Building Black Community in Detroit, 1915–1945* (Bloomington and Indianapolis: Indiana University Press, 1992).

TUSHNET, MARK V., *The NAACP's Legal Strategy against Segregated Education, 1925–1950* (Chapel Hill and London: University of North Carolina Press, 1987).

VAN DEBURG, WILLIAM L., *New Day in Babylon: The Black Power Movement and American Culture, 1965–1975* (Chicago and London: University of Chicago Press, 1992).

WAGY, TOM, *Governor LeRoy Collins of Florida: Spokesman of the New South* (Tuscaloosa: University of Alabama Press, 1985).

WALTON, HANS, JR, *The Political Philosophy of Martin Luther King, Jr* (Westport: Greenwood Press, 1971).

WARD, BRIAN AND BADGER, TONY, EDS, *The Making of Martin Luther King and the Civil Rights Movement* (Basingstoke: Macmillan, 1996).

WATSON, DENTON L., *Lion in the Lobby: Clarence Mitchell, Jr's Struggle for the Passage of Civil Rights Laws* (New York: William Morrow, 1990).

WEISS, NANCY J., *Whitney M. Young, Jr, and the Struggle for Civil Rights* (Princeton: Princeton University Press, 1989).

WELLS, TOM, *The War Within: America's Battle over Vietnam* (Berkeley, Los Angeles, and London: University of California Press, 1994).

WHITE, JOHN, *Black Leadership in America 1895–1968* (London and New York: Longman, 1985).

WHITE, JOHN, *Martin Luther King, Jr, and the Civil Rights Movement in America* (British Association for American Studies pamphlet, 1991).

WHITE, WALTER, *A Man Called White: The Autobiography of Walter White* (London: Victor Gollancz, 1949).

WILKINS, ROY WITH MATHEWS, TOM, *Standing Fast: The Autobiography of Roy Wilkins* (New York: Viking, 1982).

WILKINSON, J. HARVIE, III, *From Brown to Bakke: The Supreme Court and School Integration: 1954–1978* (New York and Oxford: Oxford University Press, 1979).

WOLTERS, RAYMOND G., *Negroes and the Great Depression: The Problem of Economic Recovery* (Westport: Greenwood Press, 1970).

WOODWARD, C. VANN, *The Strange Career of Jim Crow* (2nd rev. edn, New York: Oxford University Press, 1966).

WRIGHT, GAVIN, *Old South, New South: Revolutions in the Southern Economy Since the Civil War* (New York: Basic Books, 1986).

Youth of the Rural Organizing and Cultural Center, *Minds Stayed on Freedom: The Civil Rights Struggle in the Rural South, An Oral History* (Boulder, San Francisco, and Oxford: Westview Press, 1991).

ZANGRANDO, ROBERT L., *The NAACP Crusade Against Lynching, 1909–1950* (Philadelphia: Temple University Press, 1970).

ZIEGER, ROBERT H., ED., *Organized Labor in the Twentieth-Century South* (Knoxville: University of Tennessee Press, 1991).

II ARTICLES AND PAMPHLETS

ARSENAULT, RAYMOND, 'The End of the Long Hot Summer: The Air Conditioner and Southern Culture', *JSH* 50 (1984), 597–628.

BARKSDALE, MARCELLUS C., 'Robert F. Williams and the Indigenous Civil Rights Movement in Monroe, North Carolina, 1961', *Journal of Negro History* 69 (1984), 73–89.

BARNETT, BERNICE M., 'Invisible Southern Black Women Leaders in the Civil Rights Movement: The Triple Constraints of Gender, Race, and Class', *Gender and Society* 7 (1993), 162–82.

BILLINGTON, MONROE, 'Lyndon B. Johnson and Blacks: The Early Years', *Journal of Negro History* 62 (1977), 26–42.

BRACEY, JOHN H. AND MEIER, AUGUST, 'Allies or Adversaries? The NAACP, A. Philip Randolph and the 1941 March on Washington', *Georgia Historical Quarterly* 75 (1991), 1–17.

BRAUER, CARL M., 'Kennedy, Johnson, and the War on Poverty', *JAH* 69 (1982), 98–119.

CAMPBELL, SUSAN, ' "Black Bolsheviks" and Recognition of African-America's Rights to Self-Determination by the Communist Party USA', *Science and Society* 58 (1994–95), 440–70.

CAPECI, DOMINIC J., JR, 'The Lynching of Cleo Wright: Federal Protection of Constitutional Rights during World War II', *JAH* 72 (1986), 859–87.

CARTER, ROBERT L. AND MARSHALL, THURGOOD, 'The Meaning and Significance of the Supreme Court Decree', *Journal of Negro Education* 24 (1955), 397–404.

COBB, JAMES C., ' "Somebody Done Nailed Us on the Cross": Federal Farm and Welfare Policy and the Civil Rights Movement in the Mississippi Delta', *JAH* 77 (1990), 912–36.

DANIEL, PETE, 'The Metamorphosis of Slavery, 1865–1900', *JAH* 66 (1979), 88–99.

DANIEL, PETE, 'The Transformation of the Rural South 1930 to the Present', *Agricultural History* 55 (1981), 231–48.

DANIEL, PETE, 'Going Among Strangers: Southern Reactions to World War II', *JAH* 77 (1990), 886–911.

DAVIES, GARETH, 'War on Dependency: Liberal Individualism and the Economic Opportunity Act of 1964', *JAS* 26 (1992), 205–31.

FAIRCLOUGH, ADAM, 'What Makes Jesse Run?', *JAS* 22 (1988), 77–86.

FAIRCLOUGH, ADAM, 'Historians and the Civil Rights Movement', *JAS* 24 (1990), 387–98.

FINKLE, LEE, 'The Conservative Aims of Militant Rhetoric: Black Protest during World War II', *JAH* 60 (1973), 692–713.

GENOVESE, EUGENE D., 'Blacks in the United States: From Slavery to the Present Crisis', *The New Review* 4 (1977), 3–11.

GLENNON, R.J., 'The Role of Law in the Civil Rights Movement: The Montgomery Bus Boycott, 1955–1957', *Law and History Review* 9 (1991), 59–112.

GOLDBERG, ROBERT A., 'Racial Change on the Southern Periphery: The Case of San Antonio, Texas, 1960–1965', *JSH* 49 (1983), 349–74.

GOLDFIELD, MICHAEL, 'Race and the CIO: The Possibilities for Racial Egalitarianism During the 1930s and 1940s', *International Labor and Working-Class History* 44 (1993), 1–32.

GRAHAM, HUGH DAVIS, 'Race, History, and Policy: African Americans and Civil Rights Since 1964', *Journal of Policy History* 6 (1994), 12–39.

HART, JOHN, 'Kennedy, Congress and Civil Rights', *JAS* 13 (1979), 165–78.

HONEY, MICHAEL K., 'Operation Dixie: Labor and Civil Rights in the Postwar South', *Mississippi Quarterly* 45 (1992), 439–52.

HOROWITZ, DAVID ALAN, 'White Southerners' Alienation and Civil Rights: The Response to Corporate Liberalism, 1956–1965', *JSH* 54 (1988), 173–200.

KELLEY, ROBIN D.G., ' "We Are Not What We Seem": Rethinking Black Working-Class Opposition in the Jim Crow South', *JAH* 80 (1993), 75–112.

KING, RICHARD H., 'Citizenship and Self-Respect: The Experience of Politics in the Civil Rights Movement', *JAS* 22 (1988), 7–24.

KLARMAN, MICHAEL J., 'How *Brown* Changed Race Relations: The Backlash Thesis', *JAH* 81 (1994), 81–118.

KLIBANER, IRWIN, 'The Travail of Southern Radicals: The Southern Conference Educational Fund, 1946–1976', *JSH* 49 (1983), 179–202.

KORSTAD, ROBERT AND LICHTENSTEIN, NELSON, 'Opportunities Found and Lost: Labor, Radicals, and the Early Civil Rights Movement', *JAH* 75 (1988), 786–811.

LAWSON, STEVEN F., 'Freedom Then, Freedom Now: The Historiography of the Civil Rights Movement', *AHR* 96 (1991), 456–71.

LERNER, GERDA, 'Early Community Work of Black Club Women', *Journal of Negro History* 59 (1974), 158–67.

LING, PETER, 'Local Leadership in the Early Civil Rights Movement: The South Carolina Citizenship Education Program of the Highlander Folk School', *JAS* 29 (1995), 399–422.

MAYER, MICHAEL S., 'With Much Deliberation and Some Speed: Eisenhower and the *Brown* Decision', *JSH* 52 (1986), 43–76.

MCMILLEN, NEIL R., 'Black Enfranchisement in Mississippi: Federal Enforcement and Black Protest in the 1960s', *JSH* 43 (1977), 351–72.

MEIER, AUGUST AND BRACEY, JOHN H., JR, 'The NAACP as a Reform Movement, 1909–1965: "To Reach the Soul of America"', *JSH* 59 (1993), 3–30.

MODELL, JOHN, GOULDEN, MARC AND MAGNUSSON, SIGURDUR, 'World War II in the Lives of Black Americans: Some Findings and an Interpretation', *JAH* 76 (1989), 838–48.

NELSON, BRUCE, 'Organized Labor and the Struggle for Black Equality in Mobile during World War II', *JAH* 80 (1993), 952–88.

NORRELL, ROBERT J., 'Caste in Steel: Jim Crow Careers in Birmingham, Alabama', *JAH* 73 (1986), 669–94.

PAYNE, CHARLES, 'Ella Baker and Models of Social Change', *Signs* 14 (1989), 885–99.

PERLSTEIN, DANIEL, 'Teaching Freedom: SNCC and the Creation of the Mississippi Freedom Schools', *History of Education Quarterly* 30 (1990), 297–324.

RABINOWITZ, HOWARD N., 'More than the Woodward Thesis: Assessing the Strange Career of Jim Crow', *JAH* 75 (1988), 842–56.

ROBINSON, ARMSTEAD L., 'Beyond the Realm of Social Consensus: New Meanings of Reconstruction for American History', *JAH* 68 (1981), 276–97.

RUNCIE, JOHN, 'The Black Culture Movement and the Black Community', *JAS* 10 (1976), 185–214.

SINSHEIMER, JOSEPH A., 'The Freedom Vote of 1963: New Strategies of Racial Protest in Mississippi', *JSH* 55 (1989), 217–44.

SITKOFF, HARVARD, 'Racial Militancy and Interracial Violence in the Second World War', *JAH* 58 (1970), 661–81.

SITKOFF, HARVARD, 'Harry Truman and the Election of 1948: The Coming of Age of Civil Rights in American Politics', *JSH* 37 (1971), 597–616.

ULMER, S. SIDNEY, 'Earl Warren and the *Brown* Decision', *Journal of Politics* 33 (1971), 689–702.

WATSON, DENTON L., 'Assessing the Role of the NAACP in the Civil Rights Movement', *The Historian* 55 (1993), 453–68.

WIENER, JONATHAN M., 'Class Structure and Economic Development in the American South, 1865–1955', *AHR* 84 (1979), 970–92.

WOODMAN, HAROLD D., 'Sequel to Slavery: The New History Views the Postbellum South', *JSH* 43 (1977), 523–44.

WOODRUFF, NAN ELIZABETH, 'Mississippi Delta Planters and Debates over Mechanization, Labor, and Civil Rights in the 1940s', *JSH* 60 (1994), 263–84.

WYNN, LINDA T., 'The Dawning of a New Day: The Nashville Sit-Ins, February 13–May 10, 1960', *Tennessee Historical Quarterly* 50 (1991), 42–54.

YOUNG, JEFFREY R., 'Eisenhower's Federal Judges and Civil Rights Policy: A Republican "Southern Strategy" for the 1950s', *Georgia Historical Society Quarterly* 77 (1994), 536–65.

Maps

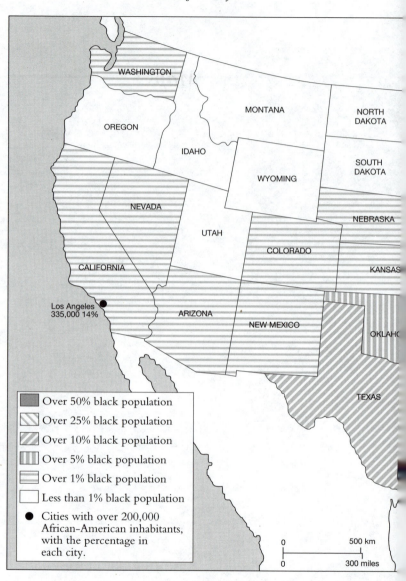

Map 1. USA: African-American population, 1965. After Martin Gilbert *American History Atlas* (London, 1968) p. 107.

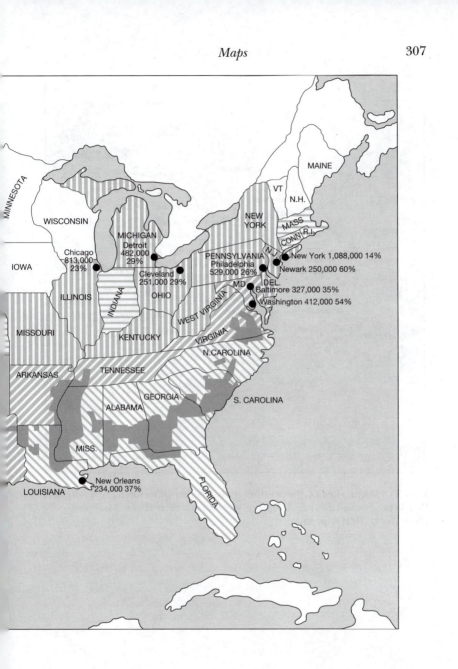

Map 2.   Major sites of the southern civil rights movement. After Robert
Weisbrot, *Freedom Bound: A History of America's Civil Rights Movement*
(New York, 1991), p. xi.

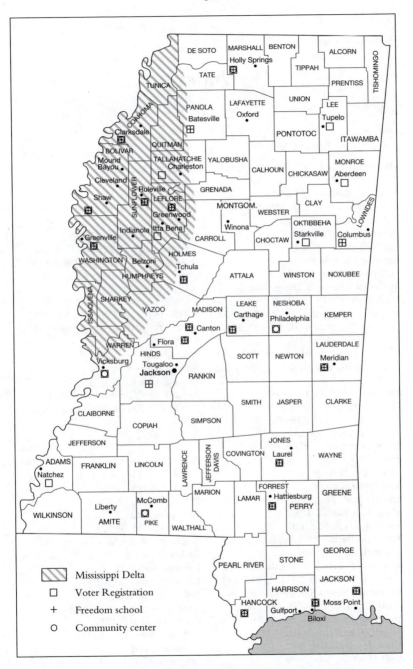

Map 3. Mississippi: principal centres of civil rights activity, 1961–4.
After Charles M. Payne, *I've Got the Light of Freedom: The Organising
Tradition and the Mississippi: Freedom Struggle* (Berkeley, Los Angeles and
London, 1995), p. viii, and Len Holt, *The Summer that Didn't End*
(London, 1966), p. 195.

Index